Beyond Uneconomic Growth

ADVANCES IN ECOLOGICAL ECONOMICS

Series Editors: Jeroen C.J.M. van den Bergh, *ICREA Professor, Universitat Autònoma de Barcelona, Spain and Professor of Environmental and Resource Economics, Vrije Universiteit, Amsterdam, The Netherlands* and Matthias Ruth, *Northeastern University, USA*

Founding Editor: Robert Costanza, *Professor and Chair in Public Policy, Crawford School of Public Policy, Australian National University, Canberra, Australia*

This important series makes a significant contribution to the development of the principles and practices of ecological economics, a field which has expanded dramatically in recent years. The series provides an invaluable forum for the publication of high quality work and shows how ecological economic analysis can make a contribution to understanding and resolving important problems.

The main emphasis of the series is on the development and application of new original ideas in ecological economics. International in its approach, it includes some of the best theoretical and empirical work in the field with contributions to fundamental principles, rigorous evaluations of existing concepts, historical surveys and future visions. It seeks to address some of the most important theoretical questions and gives policy solutions for the ecological problems confronting the global village as we move into the twenty-first century.

Titles in the series include:

Ecological Economics and Sustainable Development
Selected Essays of Herman Daly
Herman E. Daly

Sustainable Welfare in the Asia-Pacific
Studies Using the Genuine Progress Indicator
Edited by Philip Lawn and Matthew Clarke

Managing without Growth
Slower by Design, Not Disaster
Peter A. Victor

Carbon Sinks and Climate Change
Forests in the Fight Against Global Warming
Colin A.G. Hunt

Macroeconomics and the Environment
Essays on Green Accounting
Salah El Serafy

Innovations in Sustainable Consumption
New Economics, Socio-technical Transitions and Social Practices
Maurie J. Cohen, Halina Szejnwald Brown and Philip J. Vergragt

From Uneconomic Growth to a Steady-State Economy
Herman E. Daly

Beyond Uneconomic Growth
Economics, Equity and the Ecological Predicament
Edited by Joshua Farley and Deepak Malghan

Beyond Uneconomic Growth

Economics, Equity and the Ecological Predicament

Edited by

Joshua Farley

Professor, University of Vermont, USA

Deepak Malghan

Assistant Professor, Indian Institute of Management Bangalore, India

ADVANCES IN ECOLOGICAL ECONOMICS

EE Edward Elgar
PUBLISHING

Cheltenham, UK • Northampton, MA, USA

Published by
Edward Elgar Publishing Limited
The Lypiatts
15 Lansdown Road
Cheltenham
Glos GL50 2JA
UK

Edward Elgar Publishing, Inc.
William Pratt House
9 Dewey Court
Northampton
Massachusetts 01060
USA

A catalogue record for this book
is available from the British Library

Library of Congress Control Number: 2015957866

This book is available electronically in the **Elgar**online
Economics subject collection
DOI 10.4337/9781783472499

ISBN 978 1 78347 248 2 (cased)
ISBN 978 1 78347 249 9 (eBook)

Typeset by Servis Filmsetting Ltd, Stockport, Cheshire
Printed and bound by CPI Group (UK) Ltd, Croydon, CR0 4YY

Contents

Contributors

Peter G. Brown, Professor, McGill University, Montreal, QC, Canada

Clifford Cobb, Editor, *American Journal of Economics and Sociology*, Sacramento, CA, USA

John B. Cobb, Jr, Professor Emeritus, Claremont School of Theology and Co-director of the Center for Process Studies in Claremont, Claremont, CA, USA

Robert Costanza, Professor and Chair in Public Policy, Crawford School of Public Policy, Australian National University, Canberra, Australia

Brian Czech, Interdisciplinary Bilogist, US Fish and Wildlife Service, National Wildlife Refuge System Headquarters; President, Center for the Advancement of the Steady State Economy, Arlington, VA; Visiting Professor of Natural Resource Economics, Virginia Polytechnic Institute and State University, National Capitol Region, USA

Salah El Serafy, International Economic Consultant; Formerly Senior Economist and Adviser at the World Bank

Joshua Farley, Professor, Community Development and Applied Economics, University of Vermont, VT, USA

The late **Robert Goodland**, formerly Social and Environmental Assessment Specialist, Sustainable Development and former Head Environmental Adviser to the World Bank Group

John Gowdy, Professor of Science and Technology Studies and Professor of Economics, Department of Economics, Rensselaer Polytechnic Institute, Troy, New York, USA

Jonathan M. Harris, Senior Research Associate and Director of the Theory and Education Program, Global Development and Environment Institute, Tufts University, Medford, MA, USA

Philip Lawn, Professor of Ecological Economics, Flinders Business School, Flinders University, Adelaide, Australia

Deepak Malghan, Assistant Professor, Centre for Public Policy, Indian Institute of Management Bangalore, India

Joan Martinez-Alier, Professor, ICTA, Autonomous University of Barcelona, Spain

William E. Rees, Professor Emeritus of City and Regional Planning, School of Community and Regional Planning, University of British Columbia, Vancouver, BC, Canada

Arild Vatn, Professor in Environmental Sciences, Department of International Environment and Development Studies, Norwegian University of Life Sciences, Norway

Peter A. Victor, Professor in Environmental Studies, York University, Toronto, Ontario, Canada

Preface

This volume originated as a Festschrift for Herman Daly, the central figure in modern ecological economics. While we had discussed the project through 2005–06, it took concrete shape only after Herman's friend and colleague, Robert Goodland, threw his weight behind the project and also joined the team as an editor. We formally launched the project in 2007 at the biennial conference of the United States Society for Ecological Economics. We had hoped to complete the project by the time of the 2009 conference. Robert's home in northern Virginia had for several years served as the site where ecological economists and kindred spirits were at their convivial best. Robert had graciously agreed to host the launch party for the Festschrift volume at his home. However, numerous unexpected delays kept us from wrapping up this book as quickly as we would have like. When we finally started to edit the volume and work through the publication process, we were enveloped with a sense of great sadness at Robert's passing away. We have greatly missed Robert's wisdom and comradeship during the last two years.

Robert's oeuvre is best reflected in the many ways in which he tried reforming the World Bank and making the institution sensitive if not always responsive to its ecological and human rights record around the world. At the Bank, Robert worked closely with Herman Daly whom he had helped recruit. We are grateful to Herman for graciously agreeing to allow us to reprint his Goodland obituary essay that was first published in the journal, *Ecological Economics*, **100**, 208–9 in 2014. The honoree of a Festschrift volume writing an obituary essay for one of its editors is a predicament no project should have to deal with. However, we believe that in Robert's case there can be no better way to acknowledge and celebrate his many contributions. We also thank *Ecological Economics* for the permission to reprint the essay.

Burlington and Bangalore
October 2015

Remembering Robert Goodland by Herman Daly

Robert Goodland was the first ecologist hired by the World Bank and worked hard for 30 years to improve that institution's environmental and human rights practices. He was the first winner of the IUCN's Harold Jefferson Coolidge medal for lifetime achievement in the conservation of nature.

Robert was initially assigned to the task of screening every single proposed World Bank project, and selecting for scrutiny those with the largest potential impacts, for which Robert would draft recommendations. But project designers resisted implementing his recommendations. As a remedy, Robert took a lead role in drafting overall environmental and social standards for the World Bank Group, notably covering Environmental Assessment, Indigenous Peoples, Natural Habitats, and Physical Cultural Resources. Robert did much to open the World Bank to dialog with the NGO community.

Robert Goodland (1939–2013)

Robert's work on indigenous peoples led the institution to hire a cadre of anthropologists. A key issue was to prevent forced resettlement, and to mitigate its adverse impacts when it did occur. Robert also worked to complete the "Environmental Assessment Sourcebook," which became a key worldwide reference on various aspects of environmental assessment. As a capstone to Robert's work on the principles of environmental and social assessment, he served a term as president of the International Association of Impact Assessment in 1994–1995.

Earlier Robert taught tropical ecology and environmental assessment at the University of Brasilia and the National Amazonian Research Institute in Manaus. His time in Brazil led him to co-author with Howard Irwin the

book "Amazon Jungle: Green Hell to Red Desert." It became a seminal work in the birth of the international environmental movement.

Robert developed ways to stop the World Bank Group from financing projects involving tobacco and asbestos, as well as avoiding the most destructive types of agricultural and forestry projects. Later, after Robert had analyzed the impacts of some of the world's largest hydro-electricity projects, he played a key role in the establishment of the World Commission on Dams in 1997.

Robert cooperated with Salah El Serafy, Herman Daly and Roefie Hueting to develop a series of conferences throughout the 1980s on Greening the UN System of National Accounts. They also collaborated, under Robert's leadership, on a critique of the 1992 "World Development Report" (the first on the theme of development and the environment), entitled "Environmentally Sustainable Economic Development: Building on Brundtland," published by UNESCO.

Robert co-authored with Jeff Anhang a 2009 article entitled "Livestock and Climate Change," which assessed how replacing some livestock products – and reforesting land thereby freed from livestock and feed production – could be a pragmatic way to stop climate change. Robert was invited by the UN Food and Agriculture Organization to speak about this work in Rome and Berlin, and also invited to deliver a keynote speech to the Chinese Academy of Social Sciences in Beijing.

After Robert's official retirement from the World Bank in 2001, Emil Salim recruited him to play a key role in the independent Extractive Industries Review. In retirement Robert worked all over the world as a consultant, often *pro bono*, in protection of the environment and of indigenous peoples. He once remarked that in retirement he was doing much the same things as when in the World Bank, but the difference was that now the people he worked for were more cooperative.

Throughout his career Robert encouraged many people who benefitted greatly from his kindness. Robert's life and career is an example of how with quiet courage, unfailing courtesy, and hard work, one can accomplish much even in a politically adversarial environment.

Herman Daly

PART I

Introduction

1. The foundations for an ecological economy: an overview

Joshua Farley

1.1 INTRODUCTION

This book began as a single-volume Festschrift to honor the work of Herman Daly, one of the pioneers of ecological economics. Unfortunately, the destiny of too many Festschrifts is to sit on the shelf unread, and we believe that among all economists, Daly's ideas are the most important to disseminate and apply. Furthermore, given the significance of Daly's contributions and the numerous scholars he has influenced, a single volume would be inadequate. We have therefore chosen to publish two volumes in different formats: one volume available in print or as an ebook with Edward Elgar Publishing and the other an online, open-access ebook downloadable at http://www.uvm.edu/~jfarley/BUG.

Daly came of age as an economist during the 1960s, a time of increasing alarm over the ecological impacts of economic growth, population growth and global inequality. Mainstream economists as a whole were largely complacent about these issues, trusting in technology and substitution to address resource limits (Barnett and Morse, 1963; Simpson et al., 2005) and in markets to distribute wealth in proportion to an individual's role in creating it (Clark, 1908). Continuous economic growth would provide the resources to protect the environment and eliminate poverty and incentives to have fewer children, stabilizing the global population (see Daly, 1977 for a detailed discussion).

Daly, in contrast, had the crucial insight that the human economy is a subsystem sustained and contained by a delicately balanced global ecosphere, which in turn is fueled by finite flows of solar energy. As the economy expands, it transforms more ecosystem structure into economic products and generates greater flows of waste, both of which reduce the capacity of ecosystems to generate life sustaining ecosystem services and other amenities. He realized that ever-increasing material consumption must have devastating impacts on natural systems and the non-market benefits they generate and was therefore neither socially desirable nor biophysically possible. Economic analysis must begin with the recognition that the economy is wholly dependent on the finite global ecosystem. Furthermore, given finite resources, their just distribution within and between generations is an unavoidable focus of economic analysis. As early as the late 1960s, he began calling for a steady-state, no-growth economy with a more equal distribution of wealth and income (Daly, 1968, 1973). For a brief period in the 1960s and 1970s, it almost seemed that Daly's view might win out on the policy level. The United States and other developing nations passed major legislation to protect the environment and to improve the distribution of wealth.

Unfortunately, since then global environmental problems have grown significantly worse, income inequality has skyrocketed and the global population pushes toward ten billion. In the world's richest country, the United States, the poverty rate has actually increased. Paradoxically, despite a doubling in per capita income since the 1960s, there seems to be a growing belief that we can no longer afford to tackle environmental problems and inequality.

Herman has nonetheless continued to dedicate his professional life to creating the transdisciplinary field of ecological economics that seeks to balance what is biophysically possible with what is socially, ethically and psychologically desirable. We believe that the best tribute to Herman is to help advance this agenda before it is too late. The goal of these books is therefore to build on Herman's work to propose sustainable, just and efficient solutions to society's most pressing ecological and economic problems. The goal of this chapter is to briefly describe the problems we face, explain why the current economic system is failing to address them and suggest how Daly's work is capable of transforming our complex ecological economic system. The chapter concludes with a brief introduction to the remaining chapters in this book and its companion volume, all contributed by scholars and activists working toward the creation of a sustainable and desirable economy.

1.2   ENVIRONMENTAL PROBLEMS AND THE ANTHROPOCENE

Geologists divide geologic time into epochs, which correspond to dramatic changes in biophysical events on our planet. Our current official epoch, the Holocene, has been characterized by an unusually stable climate that has provided conditions conducive to the development of agriculture. Agriculture in turn allowed the population density, accumulation of surplus production and division of labor that were essential to developing civilization.

Human society is profoundly influenced by environmental conditions. *Homo sapiens* first appeared about 200 000 years ago during a period of dramatic climate instability that persisted for the first 95 percent of human history. In spite of climate instability, small bands of humans character- ized by remarkably similar stone-age technologies and highly egalitarian political and economic systems nonetheless managed to spread across the planet. When the Holocene arrived around 11 700 years ago, many of these spatially-separated groups responded to a newly stable climate in remark- ably similar ways. For example, although the North American popula- tions were completely isolated from the old world, when the Europeans 'discovered' the major American civilizations in the sixteenth century, they found large cities, agricultural systems and hierarchical political, economic and religious institutions that were instantly recognizable, though none of these institutions had evolved in the many millennia preceding the Holocene (Richerson et al., 2001).

Humanity is again facing dramatic environmental changes, but this time as a result of our own actions. Though climate change is the most widely discussed, biodiversity loss, nitrogen and phosphorous cycles, ocean acidification, land use change, freshwater use, ozone depletion, chemical pollution and atmospheric aerosol loading also threaten unacceptable environmental change that may be incompatible with continued human development or even survival (Rockstrom et al., 2009). In fact, the human influence on the environment is now so profound that many scientists argue that we have entered a new geologic epoch, the Anthropocene: human impacts on the environment are now on the scale of geological forces (Crutzen, 2002). There is considerable debate over when the Anthropocene actually began, but one powerful contender is the start of the Industrial Revolution, when the vast power of fossil fuels (and their immense waste emissions) was first unleashed. Not coincidentally, the origins of both the modern market economy and the theory describing it both date to this same era. There is little debate that a Great Acceleration in human activi- ties and their environmental impacts began around 1950. Among other radical changes, the human population and species extinctions doubled in only 50 years, fossil fuel use and water use more than tripled, fertilizer use increased five fold and the size of the economy (as measured by gross domestic product (GDP)) increased 15 fold (Steffen et al., 2011).

The impacts of the Anthropocene on human development may be at least as profound as those of the Holocene, but with potentially devastat- ing consequences. Humans, like all species, depend on well-functioning ecosystems for their survival, and human civilization almost certainly depends on agriculture. Unfortunately, agriculture may be the greatest single threat to global ecosystems (Brown, 2012; Godfray et al., 2010;

Tilman et al., 2011). Our global economy also depends on fossil fuels, which provide 86 percent of our energy supply, and fossil fuel emissions vie with agriculture as the dominant threat to global ecosystems. Critical economic and ecological thresholds are in direct conflict. Society must thread a narrow path between ecological and economic collapse.

Growing inequality only exacerbates the problems of ecological degradation. The Great Acceleration initially coincided with the Great Compression: a period during which wages, incomes and the distribution of wealth became dramatically more equal, largely as a result of government policies influenced by the Great Depression and Keynesian economics. Economic inequality in the United States reached a minimum during the early 1970s, but has since increased nationally and globally to record levels in what is known as the Great Divergence (Alvaredo et al., 2013; Piketty and Saez, 2006).

A brief look at our most important economic sector – agriculture – can help illustrate the severity of the challenges we currently face. Most economists would agree that there are rising marginal costs to economic production, and diminishing marginal benefits. The goal of economists is generally to maximize net benefits, which occur when marginal costs (which translate into a supply curve in market economics) are equal to marginal benefits (the demand curve).

The supply curve should include not only the marginal costs of labor, capital and material inputs, but also those of ecological degradation. Recent studies suggest that agricultural impacts already threaten or exceed ecological thresholds (Foley et al., 2011; IPCC, 2013; Millennium Ecosystem Assessment, 2005; Reid et al., 2010; Rockstrom et al., 2009; Steffen et al., 2011) beyond which the marginal costs of continued activity become immeasurably high. Thresholds represent the limits of marginal analysis: a marginal change in supply leads to non-marginal change in costs. To paraphrase Herman Daly, at a threshold, one marginal step takes us over the precipice (Daly, 1977). It's reasonable to assume that the supply curve for conventional agriculture becomes increasingly vertical as it approaches one of these thresholds.[1]

The demand curve is determined by marginal benefits. Humans confront a physiological threshold when they fail to consume enough food to survive, at which point the physiological demand curve for food becomes vertical. Once we have met our basic survival needs, the marginal benefits from food fall dramatically. Arguably, for the one billion malnourished people on the planet who may suffer retarded development, high mortality rates and so on, the marginal benefits from additional nutrition are immeasurably high already.

The demand curve described here is quite different from market

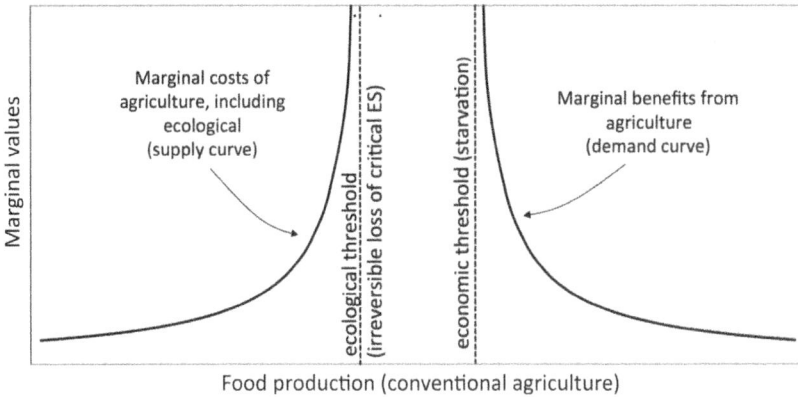

Figure 1.1   *Conceptual supply and demand curves for food production that account for ecological costs and the preferences of the poor, assuming current technologies and economic institutions*

demand, which weights preferences by purchasing power. Global agriculture produces enough to feed the world, but an unequal distribution of purchasing power results in a highly unequal distribution of food. During the food crisis of 2007–08, when drought, increased ethanol production and speculation led the price of staple grains to double, the richest countries with the highest levels of per capita food consumption saw negligible change in demand or in the percentage of food being thrown away. Poor countries, in contrast, saw a significant increase in malnutrition, social disruption and political turmoil. When income is highly unequal, markets may allocate essential resources to those who gain the least marginal benefit (Farley et al., 2015).

Figure 1.1 depicts supply and demand curves based on these assumptions concerning marginal costs and benefits. With current production practices, economic institutions and human populations, the supply and demand curves do not intersect, and we are forced to choose between unacceptably high ecological or social costs. Ecological catastrophe of course will also lead to unacceptable social costs. We require agricultural systems that reduce ecological impacts while producing adequate food, as well as a much better distribution of the food we do produce. We require economic institutions that incentivize those agricultural systems and distribute food more equitably.

This economic (but non-market) analysis of supply and demand for food systems applies to the supply and demand of other essential resources and to the economy as a whole. For example, greenhouse gas emissions currently exceed absorption capacity, threatening runaway climate change in the future. If we immediately reduce emissions to sustainable levels, the resulting economic disruption could prove catastrophic. Aggregate economic activity already exceeds ecological thresholds, while in our current system failure to keep growing leads to unemployment, poverty and misery. We need a new economic system capable of addressing these ecological and physiological thresholds before the former become irreversible and catastrophic, and the latter result in social or economic collapse. Herman Daly's economic theories can help create this system.

1.3 THE RESPONSE OF MAINSTREAM ECONOMICS[2]

While some mainstream economists are responding to the dual challenges of the Great Acceleration and the Great Divergence, the evolution of the discipline as a whole has likely exacerbated these trends. The Great Acceleration began around the time that mainstream economics became obsessed with economic growth. Prior to 1947, the phrase 'economic growth' appeared just once in all the economic journal articles indexed in Econlit, while in the decade of the 1950s it appeared 178 times, and has shown exponential increase since then.

Concerns over biophysical constraints to growth surfaced in the 1940s and 1950s (The President's Materials Policy Commission, 1952), but among economists and policy makers, largely gave way in the 1960s to faith in technological progress and endless substitutability (Barnett and Morse, 1963; Milliman, 1962; Spengler, 1961). The advent of Earth Day, petroleum price shocks and the publication of numerous environmental critiques of growth in the early 1970s reignited concerns over biophysical constraints. Economists initially reacted to these concerns with condescension and hostility, referring, for example, to *Limits to Growth* (Meadows et al., 1972) as 'such a brazen, impudent piece of nonsense that nobody could possibly take it seriously' (Beckerman, 1972, p. 327); one of the 'doomsday models' that are 'bad science and therefore bad guides to public policy' (Solow, 1973, p. 43); 'an empty and misleading work . . . less than pseudoscience and little more than polemic fiction' (Passell et al., 1972, p. 1); and an example of crying wolf (Kaysen, 1972; all cited in Yissar, 2013). In spite of these vicious criticisms, economists began responding to concerns over resource depletion in sufficient numbers to form the sub-discipline of natural resource economics, which focused on the optimal use of raw materials and fossil fuels, considered obligations to future generations and integrated natural resources into economic growth models. Nonetheless, most economists continued to assume that capital, labor and technology were near perfect substitutes for natural resources (Dasgupta and Heal, 1979; Hartwick, 1977; Nordhaus et al., 1973; Solow, 1974a, 1974b, 1997; Stiglitz, 1974, 1997), rather than complements to resources, as Daly and others argued (Daly, 1997). Resource scarcity would not limit growth.

Economists also began to consider environmental amenities (aka ecosystem services) and pollution (Ayres and Kneese, 1969; Krutilla, 1967; Smith and Krutilla, 1979) – common property whose values are often ignored by market decisions – giving rise to the sub-discipline of environmental economics. Environmental economists generally accepted limitless substitution for natural resources, though not necessarily for benefits provided by unique ecosystems. However, the general conclusion is that if appropriate policies such as environmental taxes, cap and trade systems and economic incentives for providing or protecting ecosystem services internalize these failures into market prices, growth can continue unabated (Simpson et al., 2005).

The emergence of natural resource and environmental economics is certainly promising, and these sub-disciplines favor some of the same policies as ecological economics. Nonetheless, the reaction of mainstream economics to the Great Acceleration falls short for two reasons. One problem lies within these sub-disciplines, which continue to view the planetary ecosystem as the part and the economy as the whole, as epitomized by the definition of environmental problems as externalities that can be internalized into economic decisions. Efficient allocation is assumed to generate sustainable outcomes, and just distribution is rarely addressed. Endless economic growth remains the goal. Ecological economists, in contrast, believe that the nature of the economy as a physical subsystem of a finite planet makes continuous exponential growth impossible. Irreducible uncertainty concerning ecological impacts means that future costs are unknowable. Ecological sustainability and just distribution must take precedence over efficient allocation. Other important differences between these neoclassical sub-disciplines and ecological economics are nicely summarized elsewhere (Daly, 2007; van den Bergh, 2001), and therefore need not be reviewed here.

The second major problem is that natural resource and environmental economics have had little impact on mainstream economics as a whole. One prominent economist states that '[n]ature did not appear much in twentieth century economics, and it doesn't do so in current economic modelling. When asked, economists acknowledge nature's existence, but most deny that she is worth much' (Dasgupta, 2008, p. 1). Another argues that while 'there is a branch of growth theory that includes environmental and resource variables . . . this has not affected the core of growth theory and associated policy debate. Moreover, most growth models with resources exclude realistic constraints on the substitution possibilities between energy and capital' (Ayres et al., 2013, p. 80). In short, natural resource, environmental and ecological economics all 'remain somewhat isolated from the main body of contemporary economics, especially as the discipline is presented in textbooks and journals' (Dasgupta, 2008, p. 2).

The Great Divergence in turn coincides with the period during which standard economics largely abandoned any concern over the distribution of wealth. Previously, many economists recognized that diminishing marginal utility implied that a more equal distribution of wealth increased total utility, all else equal (for example, Marshall, 1890). In the 1970s, however, mainstream economics solidified its position that since it was impossible to compare utility between individuals, economists should focus on the supposedly value-neutral goal of satisfying subjective preferences (for example, Stigler and Becker, 1977), typically failing to explicitly acknowledge that markets weight preferences by purchasing power. Essential needs were treated the same as 'tastes.' The result was the use of 'wealth rather than happiness as the criterion for an efficient allocation of resources' (Posner, 1985, p. 88). Redistribution may reduce incentives to accumulate wealth, and equality and efficiency are in conflict (Okun, 1975). It is not unusual for conventional economists to acknowledge that '[w]e live in a world of staggering and unprecedented income inequality' but to then assert that '[o]f the tendencies that are harmful to sound economics, the most seductive and . . . the most poisonous, is to focus on questions of distribution' (Lucas, 2004). From this perspective, it was perfectly efficient and utility-maximizing for those consuming the least amount of food to reduce consumption by the most during the 2007–08 food crisis, since they were 'unwilling' to pay as much for food as the rich.

In recent years it has become increasingly common for influential economists to acknowledge that growing inequality is a serious problem (for example, Piketty, 2014; Piketty and Saez, 2006; Stiglitz, 2014, see also Paul Krugman's weekly column in the *New York Times*). However, within the mainstream, the importance of distribution is obscured by the economist's obsession with efficiency, as economists define it. Few, if any, mainstream economists question the efficiency of market allocation, regardless of income distribution or the essential nature of a particular resource. Few, if any, challenge the assumption that allocating resources according to preferences weighted by purchasing is optimal, or ask if the world's poor would offer a different definition of optimality.

Mainstream economists therefore have an entirely different interpretation of supply and demand than was presented in Figure 1.1. If belief in technological progress and the capacity for substitution is virtually unlimited, marginal costs will never become immeasurably large. For example, the influential *Stern Review* on the economics of climate change (Stern, 2006) assumes that even if we do nothing to mitigate climate change, continued economic growth ensures that future generations will be better off than the present. Marginal benefits for food cannot become immeasurably high because the destitute essentially drop off the demand curve when the price of staple grains exceeds their capacity to pay.

In distinct contrast, Herman Daly and his supporters argue that economic theory must acknowledge that the economy is entirely dependent on the raw materials, energy flows and ecosystem services that nature provides. Furthermore, we cannot solve ecological problems without simultaneously pursuing a just distribution of wealth and resources: in a world of pronounced income inequality, addressing the conflict between food production and ecosystem services by internalizing the costs of ecological degradation into market prices would result in severe hardships for the poor, and, at most, mild inconvenience for the rich. The decision to prioritize the preferences of the rich and the current generation is purely normative. We urgently require an economic system that prioritizes ecological sustainability, just distribution and obligations to future generations while acknowledging the profound uncertainty inherent to complex systems. Herman Daly and the scientists in these volumes are actively working to develop economic theories that support this transition. They recognize that climate change, resource depletion, population growth, the unjust distribution of resources and the current financial crisis are all interrelated components of a single complex system. We turn now to the challenge of changing complex systems.

1.4   EFFECTING CHANGE IN COMPLEX SYSTEMS

After decades of study using computer models and empirical evidence, Donella Meadows came up with a series of leverage points that are particularly effective at changing complex systems (Meadows, 2009). By conscious design or intuition, Daly's work concentrates on three of the most powerful of these levers: changing the paradigm; changing the goals; and changing the rules.

A paradigm is the worldview underlying the theory and methods of a field or discipline. Herman has changed the conventional economic paradigms concerning biophysical possibility and human behavior. In regards to biophysical possibility, Daly rejects analysis of the economic system as the whole, capable of expansion without limit, and the ecosystem as a part that supplies useful raw materials and services. Instead, Daly argues that economic analysis must begin with the recognition that the economic system is sustained and contained by the finite global ecosystem, which supplies all raw materials required for economic production, absorbs all resulting waste flows and provides irreplaceable ecosystem services essential to our survival (Daly, 1973, 1991). Energy is an essential input into all economic production. We have finite stocks of terrestrial energy sources, finite flows of solar energy and useful energy is always lost in the economic process. The raw materials that the economy transforms into economic goods and services alternatively serve as the structural building blocks of ecosystems. Arranged in particular configurations, these materials create ecosystem funds capable of transforming solar energy into a flux of ecosystem services essential to the survival of humans and all other species (Malghan, 2011). Resource extraction and waste emissions significantly alter these configurations, threatening the essential and non-substitutable services they generate, including the reproduction of renewable resources. Continuous *physical* growth of the economy is therefore impossible within a larger, non-growing, biophysical system (Daly, 1996).

Daly has also challenged the ruling paradigm concerning human behavior. Conventional economists model people as perfectly rational, self-interested and insatiable individuals who gain utility only from consumption, not from interaction with others, except as that contributes to consumption. Daly, in contrast, rightfully insists that we are persons-in-community who define ourselves more by our relationships and associations with other individuals and groups than by the stuff we own. If you take away these relationships, there is little left of the individual (Daly and Cobb, 1994). Within mainstream economics, the sub-discipline of behavioral economics also challenges conventional assumptions of human behavior, but so far has had little impact on the discipline's core assumptions as presented in introductory textbooks. In fact, simply studying economics makes people more likely to conform to conventional assumptions (Cipriani et al., 2009; Kirchgässner, 2005).

Daly argues that acknowledgement of biophysical limits and our nature as persons in community forces us to change the goals of economic activity. Conventional economists prioritize efficient allocation, defined as any allocation in which it is impossible to make one person better off without making someone else worse off, and claim that free markets achieve this goal. Efficient allocation boils down to the maximization of monetary value subject to the initial distribution of wealth and resources, hence economists pursue the dynamic goal of ever-increasing GDP.[3] Daly offers instead three alternative economic goals: ecological sustainability; just distribution; and efficient allocation (Daly, 1992). Humanity depends for its survival on the life support functions of the planetary ecosystem. If we show any moral concern for future generations, and the current generation as a whole is not destitute, ecological sustainability is essential. The goal of sustainability limits the total amount of resources any single generation can consume, in which case we must ensure that available resources are justly distributed. Daly redefines efficiency as attaining the greatest level of human welfare from a sustainable flow of throughput (Daly, 1996). Markets can contribute to the efficient allocation of resources, but fail to address sustainability or justice, which take priority over efficiency. GDP fails to accurately measure human welfare, and must be replaced with an indicator that accounts for the costs as well as the benefits of economic activity. Along with John and Clifford Cobb, Daly pioneered the Index of Sustainable Economic Welfare (ISEW), which does exactly this (Daly and Cobb, 1994). While GDP continues to grow, in most countries the ISEW peaked decades ago (Lawn, 2003).

Finally, Daly calls for new rules for the economy. Conventional economists prioritize rules that promote the functioning of competitive free markets and the price mechanism. Daly, in contrast, argues that 'ecological and ethical decisions are price determining, not price determined' (Daly, 1986, p. 321). We must have rules that ensure sustainable scale and just distribution before we can trust in market allocation via the price mechanism. For example, one possible rule for achieving sustainable scale would be to set quantitative limits on throughput from outside the market economy, and let these limits determine prices. One possible rule for achieving just distribution would be to allot everyone an equal share of resources created by society or nature as a whole. Market allocation will only be efficient once these first two rules are satisfied (Daly, 2007).

It's certainly worth noting that conventional economists are often supportive of cap and trade systems, which are one application of Daly's rules. Daly also shares with conventional economists support for policies such as green taxes. The major difference is that conventional economists focus on the Pareto efficiency of these rules in maximizing monetary value, which they generally treat as necessary and sufficient. Daly, in contrast, focuses on the rules' effectiveness in achieving a just, steady-state economy, defined as an economy in which flows of throughput are non-increasing, equitably distributed and within the biophysical carrying capacity of the planet (Daly, 1973, 1991).

We must either achieve a steady-state economy through conscious choice or nature's feedback loops will force it upon us, perhaps catastrophically. Until we change the economic paradigm concerning what is biophysically possible, society will not recognize the need for a steady-state economy. Until we change our goals concerning what is socially, psychologically and morally desirable, society will view a steady state as an unacceptable sacrifice. Until we make our economic institutions more just, sustainable and efficient, a steady-state economy is not possible. Daly has laid the groundwork. It is the task of Daly's intellectual and moral heirs to move us forward.

1.5   ORGANIZATION OF THE BOOK

The remaining chapters in these volumes provide not only an overview of Herman's foundational work in ecological economics, but also showcase continuing efforts to build a new economic system that is value driven, science based and solutions oriented. The volumes are divided into six parts, including an introduction and conclusions. The middle sections parallel the leverage points for changing complex systems described above: 'Changing the paradigm,' 'Changing the goals' and 'Changing the rules,' with an additional section on the 'Steady-state economy.' There is some overlap between the parts. In the remainder of this overview, we will use *chapter* to refer to the Edward Elgar edition and *article* to the online volume.

The second chapter in the Introduction section is by Daly's long-time collaborator and World Bank colleague, Robert Goodland (see the eulogy in the Preface). Goodland provides a superb overview of Herman's lifetime contribution to economics, divided between a brief but excellent synthesis of his theoretical contributions and specific solutions to global problems ranging from ecological degradation to financial instability. The chapter concludes with a reference list with particular emphasis on Daly's earlier works. A chapter by Daly's long-time collaborator, Robert Costanza, describes their efforts over the past 35 years to build a sustainable and desirable future. The online companion volume adds to this an interview with Herman Daly edited by Deepak Malghan.

Part II on 'Changing the paradigm: what is biophysically possible, and how do humans behave?' begins with an online article in by David Batker, one of Daly's former students and the Executive Director of Earth Economics, a non-governmental organization (NGO) dedicated to developing ecological economic solutions to pressing societal problems. Batker's article places Daly's theoretical work in the context of previous revolutions in economics, explaining how new paradigms generate new goals, new institutions to achieve them and new ways to measure their success. The article also explains how Earth Economics has applied this theory to help solve real-life problems. Chapter 4 by Jonathan Harris, a Senior Research Associate and Director of the Theory and Education Program at Tufts University's Global Development and Environment Institute, presents the biophysical evidence supporting the paradigm that the economic system is sustained and contained by our finite global ecosystem. He concludes that market forces will not solve the challenges this presents, and calls for an activist macroeconomics that simultaneously achieves both justice and sustainability. Chapter 5 is by Arild Vatn, an institutional economist at the Norwegian University of Life Sciences and former President of the European Society for Ecological Economics. His chapter addresses limits, both those imposed by the biological and physical constraints of our finite planet and those imposed by society. He also addresses social constructions of no-limits, essentially the beliefs that finite resources place no limits on consumption, and that there is no limit to the human desire to consume. This provides a nice segue to Chapters 6 and 7, which focus on human behavior. Conventional economists have traditionally assumed that people are rational and primarily motivated by self-interest. Chapter 6 is by John Gowdy, an ecological economist at Rensselaer Polytechnic Institute and former President of the International Society for Ecological Economics. Gowdy's chapter explores how behavioral economics, evolutionary psychology and neuroscience have changed our understanding of human behavior, with profound implications for conventional economic models and public policy. He concludes that different economic institutions can stimulate or inhibit humanity's innate propensity for the cooperative behavior required to manage biophysical constraints, and that markets may inhibit such behavior. The concluding chapter in Part II (reprinted as an article in the online edition) is by William Rees, Professor Emeritus of City and Regional Planning at the University of British Columbia, developer of ecological footprint analysis and winner of the Blue Planet Prize. Rees applies insights from the evolutionary biology of human cognition to understand why conventional economists and policy makers have largely rejected Daly's worldview of the economy as sustained and contained by a finite global ecosystem. He concludes that new information and rational argument rarely undermine deeply held convictions. Getting people to accept the dramatic changes needed to confront ecological overshoot will require 'a world program of social re-engineering. . .to assert humanity's collective intelligence and reason over people's predisposition to defend the status quo.'

Part III on 'Changing the goals: what is socially, psychologically and ethically desirable?' explores the goals of sustainable scale, just distribution and efficient allocation. Chapter 8 by Philip Lawn, Professor of Ecological Economics at Flinders University, Australia, explains the importance of these goals and the order in which they should be addressed. Arguing that distribution becomes increasingly important on a full planet and has too often been neglected in theory and practice, he proposes several policies for achieving an equitable distribution of resources within and between nations. An article by Gary Flomenhoft, former lecturer and research associate at the University of Vermont now doing his doctoral work at the University of Queenland, Australia, also focuses on just distribution. Gary explains how the adoption of Pareto efficiency as the central goal of conventional economics led the discipline to largely ignore problems with distribution, and documents how inequality has exploded in recent years. He then suggests a number of policies for addressing both inequality and poverty. Chapter 9 by Salah El Serafy, a former senior economist and colleague of Herman Daly and Robert Goodland at the World Bank, focuses on measuring real income, defined as the maximum amount one can consume over some time period and still be as well off at the end as at the beginning. He explores the implications of this definition for national income accounts, capital stocks (including natural capital), the steady-state economy and the purpose of economic activity. An article by Mathis Wackernagel, co-developer with Rees of the ecological footprint, co-recipient of the Blue Planet Prize and Director of the Global Ecological Footprint Network, provides a brief overview of the organization's annual report, which was dedicated to Herman Daly. The report adopts sustainability and justice as fundamental goals: the global footprint currently exceeds global productive capacity, which is unsustainable, and many nations currently exceed their national productive capacity, imposing ecological costs on others, which is unjust.

Part IV turns to 'Changing the rules: institutions for a sustainable and desirable future.' Chapter 10 by Clifford Cobb, co-developer of the Index of Sustainable Economic Welfare and the Genuine Progress Indicator, focuses on shifting taxes from earned to unearned income, particularly that generated by land and other natural resources, as a policy that simultaneously promotes a more just, efficient and sustainable allocation of resources. An article by Lester Brown, founder of World Watch, founder and President of the Earth Policy Insitute and world-renowned environmental analyst, focuses on shifting subsidies from taxes onto activities that harm the environment. The bumper sticker summaries of these two chapters are 'tax what we take, not what we make' and 'tax bads, not goods.' Chapter 11 by John Cobb, co-author with Herman Daly of *For the Common Good*, global authority on Whiteheadian Process Thought and theologian at Claremont University, focuses on the monetary system. Specifically, Cobb shows that modern monetary systems based on interest bearing debt demand never-ending economic growth to avoid financial collapse, which is impossible on a finite planet. He proposes instead a 100 percent fractional reserve system and decentralization of the monetary system, both fundamental changes in one of the economy's most important institutions. An article by Sabine O'Hara, current President of the

International Society for Ecological Economics and Dean of the College of Agriculture, Urban Sustainability and Environmental Sciences at the University of the District of Columbia, concludes the section with an article on production in the context of the biophysical and social processes required to sustain it. She explains why a theory of economic production must expand its boundaries to account for these contextual processes, and offers a policy agenda for ensuring their maintenance.

Part V turns to one specific institution that is a prerequisite for avoiding ecological collapse: 'The steady-state economy.' This section is similar in both the online and Edward Elgar editions, but the chapters in the latter have been significantly updated. Peter Victor, Professor at York University and recent recipient of the Boulding Award, initiates Part V with a detailed history of the steady-state economy in economic thought, followed by a brief overview of his simulation models that show how such an economy could plausibly be achieved in both the United States and Canada. Joan Martinez-Alier, Professor at the Autonomous University of Barcelona and founding member and former President of the ISEE addresses the need for degrowth en route to a steady-state economy. For degrowth to be socially sustainable, the richest economies will have to shrink enough that the poorest countries can still expand without exceeding environmental constraints. After discussing degrowth in the context of the financial crisis, oil prices, carbon dioxide (CO_2) emissions and social and political movements from the south, he concludes that we can only transition to a steady-state economy if we change our economic goals to emphasize a good life (buen vivir) rather than materialistic consumption as measured by GDP. The online version was written shortly after the ongoing 2007–08 financial crisis, while the book chapter updates this to 2014. Brian Czech, founder and President of the Center for the Advancement of a Steady State Economy (www.Steadystate.org), Professor of Ecological Economics at Virginia Tech and wildlife biologist, concludes this section by tackling the politics of a steady-state economy. He describes several problems that impede political support for the steady state, and argues that one important step to overcoming the obstacles is to document widespread support for such an economy by leading academic societies. He describes his own increasingly successful efforts to generate and document such support.

After identifying the leverage points for changing complex systems, Meadows adds that the most powerful lever is to transcend the paradigm, never allowing ourselves to become too bound to a particular preanalytic vision. It is therefore fitting that both volumes conclude with a chapter by Peter Brown, Professor at McGill University, that presents ecological economics as only a partial step on the path to a sustainable and desirable future. To complete its journey, ecological economics must adopt a new system of ethics that extends moral standing to life as a whole, explicitly recognizing that humans are simply one subset of citizens in the grander ecological community.

Together, these volumes explain the origins of some of the most serious threats currently faced by human society, and offer concrete suggestions for solving them. We hope the economic theory presented here can help transform the economic system.

NOTES

1. It is important to note that both flow thresholds and stock thresholds exist. Using the example of greenhouse gases (GHGs), we exceed a threshold when the stock of GHGs results in an unacceptable degree of climate change, for example, one that causes positive feedback loops of rising methane emissions or falling albedo. We exceed a flow threshold when the emission of GHGs exceeds the capacity of ecosystems to absorb them and they accumulate into an ever-growing stock. Unfortunately, it may be impossible to accurately predict precisely where a threshold lies. Furthermore, given the frequent time lags between cause and effect in complex ecosystems, we may not suffer the impacts of crossing a threshold until decades into the future.
2. Conventional or mainstream economics in this chapter refers to neoclassical economics, or more specifically to the belief that the goal of economic activity at any point in time is the satisfaction of subjective individual preferences, which in a market economy leads to an equilibrium that balances supply with demand across all goods and services in an economy and maximizes economic surplus, typically measured in monetary terms. People are generally considered insatiable, so the goal over time is continuous economic growth. However, the worldview that the economy is the whole and the ecosystem the part permeates many heterodox schools of economic thought as well.
3. A growing number of economists recognize that GDP is a poor measure of economic welfare (Stiglitz et al., 2009; van den Bergh, 2009), which only makes mainstream economics' continued obsession with the metric more puzzling.

REFERENCES

Alvaredo, F., A.B. Atkinson, T. Piketty and E. Saez (2013). The top 1 percent in international and historical perspective. *Journal of Economic Perspectives* **27**, 3–20.

Ayres, R.U. and A.V. Kneese (1969). Production, consumption, and externalities. *American Economic Review* **59** (3), 282–97.

Ayres, R.U., J.C.J.M. van den Bergh, D. Lindenberger and B. Warr (2013). The underestimated contribution of energy to economic growth. *Structural Change and Economic Dynamics* **27**, 79–88.

Barnett, H. and C. Morse (1963). *Scarcity and Growth: The Economics of Natural Resource Availability*. Baltimore, MD: Johns Hopkins University Press.

Beckerman, W. (1972). Economists, scientists, and environmental catastrophe. *Oxford Economic Papers* **24**, 327–44.

Brown, L. (2012). *Full Planet, Empty Plate: The New Geopolitics of Food Scarcity*. Washington, DC: Earth Policy Institute.

Cipriani, G.P., D. Lubian and A. Zago (2009). Natural born economists? *Journal of Economic Psychology* **30**, 455–68.

Clark, J.B. (1908). *The Distribution of Wealth: A Theory of Wages, Interest and Profits*. New York: The Macmillan Company.

Crutzen, P. (2002). Geology of mankind. *Nature* **415**, 23.

Daly, H.E. (1968). On economics as a life science. *Journal of Political Economy* **76**, 392–406.

Daly, H.E. (1973). *Toward a Steady-state Economy*. San Francisco, CA: W.H. Freeman and Co.

Daly, H.E. (1977). *Steady-state Economics: The Political Economy of Bio-physical Equilibrium and Moral Growth*. San Francisco, CA: W.H. Freeman and Co.

Daly, H.E. (1986). Thermodynamic and economic concepts as related to resource-use policies: comment. *Land Economics* **62**, 319–22.

Daly, H.E. (1991). *Steady State Economics: 2nd Edition with New Essays*. Washington, DC: Island Press.

Daly, H.E. (1992). Allocation, distribution, and scale: towards an economics that is efficient, just, and sustainable. *Ecological Economics* **6**, 185–93.

Daly, H.E. (1996). *Beyond Growth: The Economics of Sustainable Development*. Boston, MA: Beacon Press.

Daly, H.E. (1997). Georgescu-Roegen versus Solow/Stiglitz. *Ecological Economics* **22**, 261–6.

Daly, H.E. (2007). *Ecological Economics and Sustainable Development, Selected Essays of Herman Daly*. Cheltenham, UK and Northampton, MA, USA: Edward Elgar Publishing.

Daly, H.E. and J.B. Cobb, Jr (1994). *For the Common Good: Redirecting the Economy Toward Community, the Environment, and a Sustainable Future* (2nd edn). Boston, MA: Beacon Press.

Dasgupta, P. (2008). Nature in economics. *Environmental and Resource Economics* **39**, 1–7.

Dasgupta, P.S. and G.M. Heal (1979). *Economic Theory and Exhaustible Resources*. Cambridge: Cambridge University Press.

Farley, J., A. Schmitt Filho, M. Burke and M. Farr (2015). Extending market allocation to ecosystem services: moral and practical implications on a full and unequal planet. *Ecological Economics* **117**, 244–52.

Foley, J.A., N. Ramankutty, K.A. Brauman et al. (2011). Solutions for a cultivated planet. *Nature* **478**, 337–42.

Godfray, H.C.J., J.R. Beddington, I.R. Crute et al. (2010). Food security: the challenge of feeding 9 billion people. *Science* **327**, 812–18.

Hartwick, J.M. (1977). Intergenerational equity and the investment of rents from exhaustible resources. *American Economic Review* **67** (5), 972–4.

IPCC (2013). *Climate Change 2013. The Physical Science Basis Summary for Policymakers*. United Nations, available at http://www.ipcc.ch/ (accessed 16 December 2015).

Kaysen, C. (1972). The computer that printed out W*O*L*F*. *Foreign Affairs* **50**, 660–68.

Kirchgässner, G. (2005). (Why) are economists different? *European Journal of Political Economy* **21**, 543–62.

Krutilla, J. (1967). Conservation reconsidered. *American Economic Review* **57**, 777–86.

Lawn, P.A. (2003). A theoretical foundation to support the Index of Sustainable

Economic Welfare (ISEW), Genuine Progress Indicator (GPI), and other related indexes. *Ecological Economics* **44**, 105–18.

Lucas, R.E., Jr (2004). *The Industrial Revolution: Past and Future. 2003 Annual Report Essay*. The Region, Federal Reserve Bank of Minneapolis, https://www.minneapolisfed.org/publications/the-region/the-industrial-revolution-past-and-future (accessed 16 December 2015).

Malghan, D. (2011). A dimensionally consistent aggregation framework for biophysical metrics. *Ecological Economics* **70**, 900–909.

Marshall, A. (1890). *Principles of Economics*. New York: The Macmillan Company.

Meadows, D. (2009). Leverage points: places to intervene in a system. *Solutions* **1**, 41–9.

Meadows, D.H., D.L. Meadows, J. Randers and W. Behrens (1972). *The Limits to Growth: A Report for the Club of Rome's Project on the Predicament of Mankind*. New York: Universe Books.

Millennium Ecosystem Assessment (2005). *Ecosystems and Human Well-being: Synthesis*. Washington, DC: Island Press.

Milliman, J.W. (1962). Can people be trusted with natural resources? *Land Economics* **38**, 199–218.

Nordhaus, W.D., H. Houthakker and R. Solow (1973). The allocation of energy resources. *Brookings Papers on Economic Activity*, 529–76.

Okun, A.M. (1975). *Equality and Efficiency: The Big Tradeoff*. Washington, DC: Brookings Institution Press.

Passell, P., M. Roberts and L. Ross (1972). Review of 'The Limits to Growth'. *New York Times Book Review*, 2 April, Section 7, 1, 10, 12–13.

Piketty, T. (2014). *Capital in the 21st Century*. Cambridge, MA: Harvard University Press.

Piketty, T. and E. Saez (2006). The evolution of top incomes: a historical and international perspective. *American Economic Review* **96**, 200–205.

Posner, R.A. (1985). Wealth maximization revisited. *Notre Dame Journal of Law, Ethics and Public Policy* **2**, 85–105.

Reid, W.V., D. Chen, L. Goldfarb et al. (2010). Earth system science for global sustainability: grand challenges. *Science* **330**, 916–17.

Richerson, P.J., R. Boyd and R.L. Bettinger (2001). Was agriculture impossible during the Pleistocene but mandatory during the Holocene? A climate change hypothesis. *American Antiquity* **66**, 387–411.

Rockstrom, J., W. Steffen, K. Noone et al. (2009). A safe operating space for humanity. *Nature* **461**, 472–5.

Simpson, R.D., M.A. Toman and R.U. Ayres (2005). *Scarcity and Growth Revisited: Natural Resources and the Environment in the New Millenium*. Washington, DC: Resources for the Future.

Smith, K.V. and J. Krutilla (1979). *Scarcity and Growth Reconsidered*. Baltimore, MD: Johns Hopkins University Press.

Solow, R.M. (1973). Is the end of the world at hand? *Challenge* **16**, 39–50.

Solow, R.M. (1974a). Intergenerational equity and exhaustible resources. *Review of Economic Studies* **41**, 29–45.

Solow, R.M. (1974b). What do we owe to the future? *Nebraska Journal of Economics and Business* **13**, 3–16.

Solow, R.M. (1997). Georgescu-Roegen versus Solow-Stiglitz. *Ecological Economics* **22**, 267–8.

Spengler, J. (1961). *Natural Resources and Economic Growth*. Washington, DC: Resources for the Future.

Steffen, W., J. Grinevald, P. Crutzen and J. McNeill (2011). The Anthropocene: conceptual and historical perspectives. *Philosophical Transactions of the Royal Society A: Mathematical, Physical and Engineering Sciences* **369**, 842–67.

Stern, N. (2006). *Stern Review: The Economics of Climate Change*. Cambridge: Cambridge University Press.

Stigler, G.J. and G.S. Becker (1977). De Gustibus Non Est Disputandum. *American Economic Review* **67**, 76–90.

Stiglitz, J.E. (1974). Growth with exhaustible natural resources: efficient and optimal growth paths. *Review of Economic Studies* **41**, 123–37.

Stiglitz, J.E. (1997). Georgescu-Roegen versus Solow/Stiglitz. *Ecological Economics* **22**, 269–70.

Stiglitz, J.E. (2014). Inequality is not inevitable. *New York Times*, 27 June.

Stiglitz, J.E., A. Sen, J.-P. Fitoussi et al. (2009). *Report by the Commission on the Measurement of Economic Performance and Social Progress*, available at http://www.stiglitz-sen-fitoussi.fr/en/documents.htm (accessed 16 December 2015).

The President's Materials Policy Commission (1952). *Resources for Freedom: A Report to the President. Volume I: Foundations for Growth and Security*. Washington, DC: United States Government Printing Office.

Tilman, D., C. Balzer, J. Hill and B.L. Befort (2011). Global food demand and the sustainable intensification of agriculture. *Proceedings of the National Academy of Sciences* **108**, 20260–64.

van den Bergh, J. (2001). Ecological economics: themes, approaches, and differences with environmental economics. *Regional Environmental Change* **2**, 13–23.

van den Bergh, J.C.J.M. (2009). The GDP paradox. *Journal of Economic Psychology* **30**, 117–35.

Yissar, R. (2013). Neoclassical economic theory and the question of environmental limits to growth, 1950–1975. Master's thesis, Porter School of Environmental Studies, Tel Aviv University.

2. 'The world in over-shoot': a celebration of Herman Daly's contributions to ecological economics – the science of sustainability

Robert Goodland

2.1 INTRODUCTION

This chapter is a celebration of Herman Daly's lifework. The chapter does this mainly by quoting Herman directly. He writes so pellucidly that he cannot be edited for clarity, so direct quotation is preferable. Of course, reading his works directly is far better than reading any compilation. But I have distilled a tiny fraction of his prodigious and brilliant output through the mind of an ecologist and repeated a few of Herman's major advances that I feel are important to fellow ecologists. Other contributors to this book have empha-sized Herman's economic contributions, although it is not clear what is eco-nomic and what is ecologic as he is the most effective bridge-builder between the two disciplines. So, let me be clear: this chapter is entirely Herman's work. I am merely a compiler. I have restricted myself to condensing four decades of Herman's publications into ten pages of synthesis and seven pages toward solutions. Most generously, Herman has revised and approved the result.

One of Herman's most influential achievements was the creation of the discipline of ecological economics, from the early 1970s with his friends Robert Costanza, Joan Martinez-Alier, AnnMari Jansson, Roefie Hueting and others. While Herman was in the World Bank (1988–94), they created the International Society for Ecological Economics (ISEE), then the ISEE journal, then the major textbooks on ecological economics.

This chapter highlights Herman's thinking behind steady-state econom-ics, sustainability and the risks of seeing growth as a panacea. Ironically, development economists (for example, Commission on Growth and Development, 2008) reaffirmed growth as the main solution for economic development at precisely the same time as the first international congress focused on 'degrowth.'[1] It took Herman and others nearly four decades of persuasion until the first 'degrowth' publication appeared in 2009, further undermining faith in GDP and growth (Costanza, 2009; Hueting, 2010; Jackson, 2009; Porritt, 2009; Victor, 2008). As of 2009, the neoclassicals' over-reliance on growth starkly contrasts the ecological economists' goals of environmental sustainability and degrowth. Given the 2008–09 economic meltdown, which pole looks more prudent?

2.2   WHAT IS THE PROBLEM?

What problem do ecological economists have with the neoclassical panacea of continuous growth? The crackpot dogma of salvation by growth constitutes the abyss between mainstream and ecological economists. The prescription of continued economic growth as a solution to problems originating in underdevelopment and misdistribution of wealth is harming the world. Mainstream (also known as neoclassical) economists consider sustainability to be a fad and are overwhelmingly committed to growth. Most economists disparage both the depletion of natural resources and the damage to sink capacities. Development economics has a misguided and unrealistic vision of development as the generalization of Northern over-consumption to the rapidly multiplying masses of the South. Mainstream economists downplay natural capital and have moved toward globalization. The critical flaw in current economics is that it fails to take into account how economic processes consume resources and generate waste, and reduce assimilative capacities of the environment to detoxify and recycle wastes. The classical economists (Adam Smith, Ricardo, Malthus and Mill) paid much more attention to 'nature' (environment) than do most contemporary economists; consequently ecological economics is more rooted in classical than neoclassical economics.

2.2.1   Growth

Growth is widely thought to be the panacea for all the major economic ills of the modern world. Our traditional economic problems (poverty, overpopulation, unemployment, unjust distribution) have all been thought to have a common solution, namely, an increase in wealth.[2] All problems are easier if we are richer. The way to get richer has been thought to be economic growth, usually as measured by GDP. Herman doesn't question the first proposition that richer is better than poorer, other things being equal. But he questions whether what we persuasively label 'economic growth' is any longer making us richer. Physical throughput growth is at the present margin and in the aggregate increasing illth[3] faster than wealth, thus making us poorer rather than richer. Consequently, our traditional economic problems become more difficult with further growth. The correlation between throughput growth and GDP growth is sufficiently strong historically so that in the absence of countervailing policies even GDP growth frequently increases illth faster than wealth.[4]

The facts are plain and incontestable: the biosphere is finite, non-growing and closed (except for the constant input of solar energy). Any subsystem, such as the economy, must cease growing at some point and adapt itself to a dynamic equilibrium, something like a steady state. To achieve this equilibrium, birth rates must equal death rates, and production rates of commodities must equal depreciation rates. Economists have not recognized the new pattern of scarcity, which has become natural capital, no longer artificial capital. Ecological limits are rapidly converting 'economic growth' into 'uneconomic growth' – that is, throughput growth that increases costs by more than it increases benefits, thus making us poorer, not richer.

Promoting the concept of environmental sustainability to dogmatic growth-economists has failed to persuade them. Mainstream economists disparage both the depletion of natural resources and the damage to sink capacities. They label them externalities.[5] They are not externalities but they overlook them, or forget them and move on to more important – to them – topics. Neoclassical economists promote growth as the topmost priority of economic policy. Because growth means faster extraction and depletion of natural resources and ever more waste to be assimilated by overstressed sinks, the panacea or goal of growth (Box 2.1) has led the human economy into a perilous trap.[6]

BOX 2.1   THE IRONY OF GROWTH AS THE PANACEA

Poverty? Just grow the economy (that is, increase the production of goods and services and spur consumer spending) and watch wealth trickle down. Don't try to redistribute wealth from rich to poor because that slows growth.

Unemployment? Increase demand for goods and services by lowering interest rates on loans and stimulating investment, which leads to more jobs as well as growth.

Overpopulation? Just push economic growth and rely on the resulting demographic transition to reduce birth rates, as it did in the industrial nations during the twentieth century.

Environmental degradation? Trust in the so-called environmental Kuznets curve, an empirical relation purporting to show that with ongoing growth in gross domestic product (GDP), pollution at first increases, but then reaches a maximum and declines.

2.2.2 Sustained Growth

Mainstream economists still adhere to the goal of yet more growth. In 2008, for example, the prestigious Commission on Growth and Development released its final 180-page report, *The Growth Report*, which 'looks at how developing countries can achieve fast sustained and equitable growth' (Commission on Growth and Development, 2008).

If 'sustained growth' means that the global economy might grow at 7 percent for 25 years (duplicating the experience of the 13 star performing non-typical and largely small countries whose economic expansion has since ceased), that means the world economy will increase by a factor of 5.4. At the end of 25 years will that be enough, or might we need a 25-year encore? We are not told, but inasmuch as the concept of 'enough' is absent from the analysis, one expects a series of encores. Recent estimates of an environmentally sustainable production level for the world arrive at 50 percent of the current level. A 'mere' quintupling of the scale of the economic subsystem relative to the scale of the non-growing and containing ecosystem should by itself trigger a few questions. Are the remaining environmental sources and sinks sufficient to regenerate the resources and absorb the wastes of the larger metabolic flow or through-put of resources necessary to sustain the quintupled global economy? Did the rapidly growing 13 states use more than their share of the world's remaining sources and sinks, including the most accessible ones, effectively precluding the generalized repetition of their accomplishment? Indeed, even at the present scale, what makes this blue-ribbon Commission believe that the extra ecological and social costs of growth are not already larger than the extra production benefits?

Is growth a short-term process necessary to arrive at some desired, sufficient state, which thereafter is maintained, like the stationary state of J.S. Mill and James Meade? Or is it the process of growth itself that is permanently desirable and presumably limitless? This question gets no consideration at all. The assumption seems to be that growth will continue forever. Since the report's subtitle refers to both growth and development, one would expect some useful distinction, such as ecological economists have introduced – namely, that growth is quantitative physical increase, while development is mainly qualitative improvement.

2.2.3 Sustainable Development

One could define sustainable development as development without growth beyond biophysical carrying capacity. In other words, sustainable development is qualitative improvement in lifestyles, design, technology, efficiency, ordering of priorities and the like, without quantitative increase in the throughput from environmental sources to sinks. *The Growth Report*, however, follows its north star of GDP and lumps together these different processes.

The report does not call growth 'sustainable' (thankfully), but even more incongruously refers to it as 'sustained,' meaning that for 13 countries in the past it once lasted for 25 years and therefore might do so for the whole world for the next 25 years, the Commission hopes. More growth must be good because that is what makes us richer.

No: growth in net wealth makes us richer, but GDP, as currently estimated, does not measure additions to net wealth or income – even the units are different. Growth in GDP will make us better off and ultimately richer only if at the current margin it increases beneficial activities more than costly activities. GDP does not even distinguish between costs and benefits.

What kind of growth – in throughput, GDP or welfare? Continual growth in physical throughput in a finite, non-growing and entropic world is impossible. Beyond some point, throughput growth becomes the main reason for environmental unsustainability by overwhelming environmental source and sink capacities. At or before that point throughput growth becomes uneconomic growth, which increases social and environmental costs faster than it increases production benefits. Even Resources for the Future has agreed that some ecosystem services have been impaired by overexploitation, and some renewable resources have been exploited faster than regeneration rates.

Sustainability is not a new idea in economics (for example, Malthus, Mill, Meade, Marshall), it is also embedded in the very concept of income. As defined by Sir John Hicks, income is the maximum that can be consumed in a given year without reducing the capacity to produce and consume the same amount next year. By definition, income is sustainable consumption. Whatever part of consumption is unsustainable is by definition not income, but capital consumption. If income is by definition sustainable, then so is its growth. Then why all the fuss about sustainability? Because contrary to the theoretical definition of income, we are in fact consuming productive capacity and counting it as income in our national accounts. Natural capital lies outside the accounting domain and is being used beyond the natural capacities of the environment to regenerate raw materials and to absorb wastes. Depletion of natural capital and consequent reduction of its life-sustaining services is the meaning of unsustainability.

While intoning the term 'sustainable development' at every opportunity, the World Trade Organization, the World Bank (Box 2.2) and the

---

BOX 2.2   THE WORLD BANK ON SUSTAINABILITY

Curiously, in the 2003 World Development Report, *Sustainable Development in a Dynamic World*, the World Bank adopted the ecological economists' vocabulary of 'sources' and 'sinks' but did not tie them together with the concept of throughput – the entropic flow from source to sink (World Bank, 2002). Even less do they consider the scale of the throughput or its entropic directionality. In dismissing the idea of overconsumption they say: 'But the overall level of consumption is not the source of the problem. It is the combination of the specific consumption mix and the production processes that generates the externality. And for these there are well-established policy prescriptions from public finance' (p. 196). So much for scale – it is not important – allocative efficiency via right prices is everything! Changing consumption and production in the direction of environmental sustainability would clearly lead to lower production, consequently to a lower GDP.

International Monetary Fund (IMF) continue to support the goal of infinite growth for the world, especially the high-consumption societies. They cannot imagine poor countries doing much more than selling their products to rich countries. How else can they earn the foreign exchange to pay back World Bank and IMF loans? Therefore, they think it is vital for rich countries to become ever richer, so they can buy more from the poor. Global trickle-down remains their solution to poverty.

Of course sustainability cannot be our only goal. If it were, then we could easily attain it by returning to a hunter-gatherer economy with a low population density and low per capita consumption. The economic goal is to attain sufficient per capita resource consumption for a good life for all the world's people for a long time. If the product of current per capita resource use and population is so large that it cannot be attained without consuming the earth's capacity to support future life in conditions of sufficiency, then we must reduce per capita resource use, or population, or both. This will be easier to do if we can also improve resource productivity.

But improved resource productivity will be slow to happen in a regime of cheap resources. The best way to improve resource efficiency is to make it more necessary by restricting the resource throughput (lowering per capita resource use). This means higher resource prices. That is a hardship for the poor, making serious reduction in income inequality even more necessary. However, continuing a subsidized price for petroleum, and other natural resources, means a greater subsidy to the biggest user, which is itself a regressive shift in real income distribution.

2.3   ENVIRONMENTAL SUSTAINABILITY

Environmental sustainability (ES) refers to the world's biophysical carrying capacity. Achieving ES demands that biophysical carrying capacity cannot be exceeded. Therefore, ES means not impairing the two aspects of carrying capacity – the source capacities of the global ecosystem to supply raw materials and the sink capacities to absorb our wastes. Pithily put, ES is defined as 'maintenance of source and sink capacities.' Some eco-economists call this 'non-declining source and sink capacities.'[7]

Sustainability is an objective concept. As a fundamental objective value, not a subjective individual preference, one would expect general agreement on it among informed people. There isn't. The Brundtland Commission's standard inspired utilitarian definition of sustainability cannot be operationalized. It can serve at best as a (not so useful) heuristic.

2.3.1   The Time Period of Sustainability

The time period of sustainability aims to maximize the cumulative number of lives over time lived at a level of per capita resource consumption sufficient for a good life. We seem to have chosen instead to maximize the present per capita resource consumption, seeking a luxurious life for a 'sufficient number' of people, usually taken as the elite of the present generation and possibly the next. This is an ethical choice, a balancing of many good lives versus fewer luxurious lives. The biblical answer is 'neither poverty nor riches,' but sufficiency. Neither alternative lasts forever.

Sufficiency for all should take precedence over luxury for some and insufficiency for others. No one has a right to luxuries while others lack necessities. The position can be stated in utilitarian-efficiency terms if one accepts the law of diminishing marginal utility of income, and the democratic principle that everyone's utility counts equally. On these premises the sum of utility is a maximum when, *ceteris paribus*, income is equally distributed. (Assuming uniformity of needs and inter-personal comparability – two big assumptions; El Serafy, personal communication 2009.) Thus, 'frugality first'[8] gives us 'efficiency second' as a consequence, but efficiency first simply makes frugality less necessary. This is the Jevons Paradox or rebound effect (Polimeni et al., 2008). Frugality and sufficiency may not be the same thing, but they are closely related.

In the past 'doing the best we can' seems to have meant a larger and larger population consuming more and more stuff. Now we see that too many people alive at one time and consuming a lot per capita reduce or overburden the carrying capacity of the earth, leading to fewer people or lower consumption per capita in the future, and a lower cumulative total of people to live at a level sufficient for a good life. If our ethical understanding of the value of longevity (sustainability) is to maximize cumulative lives lived at a per capita consumption level sufficient for a good life, then we must limit the load we place on the earth. This means fewer people, lower per capita resource consumption and more equitable distribution. None of this is what the world wants to hear.

It is more operational to internalize sustainability by setting sustainable quantity limits, and then let the market calculate the proper rationing price. If we try to calculate the price first on the basis of willingness to pay or accept, or even replacement costs, we are saying implicitly, 'You can have as much as you want as long as you pay this price.' We can always have more by growing more is the message, and limits fade away. A higher price for the good in question slows its rate of use, but the income from the higher price can be used to increase consumption. The price internalization approach is good for efficient allocation, but insufficient for limiting scale.

2.3.2 Why did Sustainability, Steady-state and Ecological Economics become so Important?

The global economy is now so large that society can no longer safely pretend it operates within a limitless ecosystem. Developing an economy that can be sustained within the finite biosphere requires new ways of thinking. The world has changed from being a relatively empty world to being a relatively full world, from a world of unemployed biophysical carrying capacity to a world of fully employed carrying capacity. When the world was relatively empty of people and their artifacts, throughput could be considered a flow from an infinite source to an infinite sink. The services of Nature were free, hence not regarded as a cost because they were not scarce. Environmental sink services, such as assimilation of greenhouse gas in the atmosphere, oceans and forests have often been treated as open-access free goods, and therefore outside the purview of economics.

In an empty world it made sense to focus on human artifacts because they were in short supply and were the limiting factor for economic activity. Production of human artifacts was maximized: saws to produce timber from forests, fishing boats and nets to catch fish, buildings to house people. The sources of trees and fish, for example, were abundant, so the sources were not conserved. This situation has changed drastically. Natural resources are finite and have recently become scarce. Deforestation and overfishing are two of the biggest problems of our age. Too many boats are chasing too few fish.

The other huge change in carrying capacity is related to the new scarcity of natural resources. Sink capacity, infinite for all of human existence, suddenly became damaged. Our wastes and pollution no longer were assimilated free and fast by environmental sink capacities. In fact, the accumulation of carbon dioxide in the atmosphere now is leading to climatic disruption. The vast oceans, mildly alkaline for eternity and extraordinarily buffered, have started to acidify. Economics has great difficulty in acting on the new scarcity and limits to growth. This is the critical flaw in economic theory: it fails to take into account how economic processes consume resources and generate wastes, deplete resources and reduce assimilative capacities.

The huge change in carrying capacity from infinite sources and sinks, to finite sources and sinks – and even to depleted sources and overburdened sinks – has not been internalized by conventional economics. Environmentalists, ecologists and ecological economists have realized that growth is not a panacea.

If one agrees that the macroeconomy is a subsystem embedded in an ecosystem that is finite, non-growing and materially closed, then wouldn't one expect the macroeconomy to have an optimal scale relative to the total ecosystem – a scale beyond which its growth is uneconomic?

The governing spirit of mainstream economic theory is to deny any important role to nature or environment. Ecological economics posits that the environment is central in its support of the human economy. Ecological economics (Box 2.3) – the science of sustainability – recognizes that the macroeconomy is a subset of the global ecosystem. Neoclassical environmental and resource economics do not see the economy as a subsystem; consequently, they have no concept of the scale of the economy relative to the ecosystem, nor of the metabolic throughput by which the human economy lives off the global ecosystem. The sea changes referred to above the new scarcity and the discipline of ecological economics realize that the human economy subset has expanded in scale so much as to impair the source and sink capacities of the surrounding ecosystem.

Technical improvements in resource efficiency by themselves will simply lower the relative cost of using a resource, which will stimulate further uses. If doubled fuel efficiency causes us to travel twice as much, and thus nullify the technical improvements, it will have been for naught. Efficiency is more miles per gallon. Frugality is using fewer gallons. A policy of 'frugality first' stimulates efficiency. A policy of 'efficiency first' does not stimulate frugality – indeed, it fosters the perception that frugality has become less necessary. With lower resource prices even efficiency becomes less necessary.

The goal of sustainability, then, is not by itself sufficient. We must seek an optimal scale of the macroeconomy relative to its containing and

---

BOX 2.3   POTTED HISTORY OF ECOLOGICAL ECONOMICS

Most contemporary economists do not agree that the United States and other economies are heading into uneconomic growth. They largely ignore the issue of sustainability and trust that because we have come so far with growth, we can keep on going *ad infinitum*. Yet concern for sustainability has a long history, dating back to Adam Smith in 1776 and John Stuart Mill's famous chapter 'Of the stationary state' (1848), which Mill, unlike other classical economists, welcomed.

1776	Adam Smith described what he called the stationary state.
1798	The Reverend Thomas Malthus also analyzed the stationary state.
1848	John Stuart Mill's classical term, a 'stationary state of population and capital,' in his *Principles of Political Economy*, book 4, chapter 6: 'Of the stationary state.'
1936	John Maynard Keynes wrote about steady-state or 'quasi stationary community.'
1965	James Meade's *The Stationary Economy*.
1972	Donella Meadows et al., *Limits to Growth*.
1973	Herman Daly's *Toward a Steady-state Economy*.
1974	Roefie Hueting's *New Scarcity and Economic Growth: More Welfare through Less Production?* (*Nieuwe schaarste en economische groei. Meer welvaart door minder produktie?*)
1977	Herman Daly's *Steady State Economics*.
1987	Herman Daly and Bob Costanza invented 'ecological economics' while they were together at Louisiana State University, Baton Rouge.
1989	Herman Daly and John Cobb, *For the Common Good*.
1989	Daly and Costanza founded ISEE.
1989	First annual conference of ISEE (held at the World Bank, Washington, DC).
1989	*International Society of Ecological Economics Journal* first issued.
1991	Robert Costanza published *Ecological Economics: The Science and Management of Sustainability*, essentially the proceedings of ISEE's first annual congress.
1992	Meadows et al., *Beyond the Limits*.
1997	Robert Costanza et al.'s *An Introduction to Ecological Economics*.
2004	Daly and Farley's textbook, *Ecological Economics*.
2008	The first international 'degrowth' conference, Economic De-growth for Ecological Sustainability and Social Equity, was held in Paris in March (see Hueting, 2010).
2008	The Commission on Growth and Development released its final report, *The Growth Report: Strategies for Sustained Growth and Inclusive Development*.

---

sustaining envelope, the ecosystem (Figure 2.1). The concept of an optimal scale of the macroeconomy does not exist in current macroeconomics because, as we have seen, the macroeconomy is conceived as the whole. But in fact the macroeconomy is a part of a larger whole, the ecosystem. The

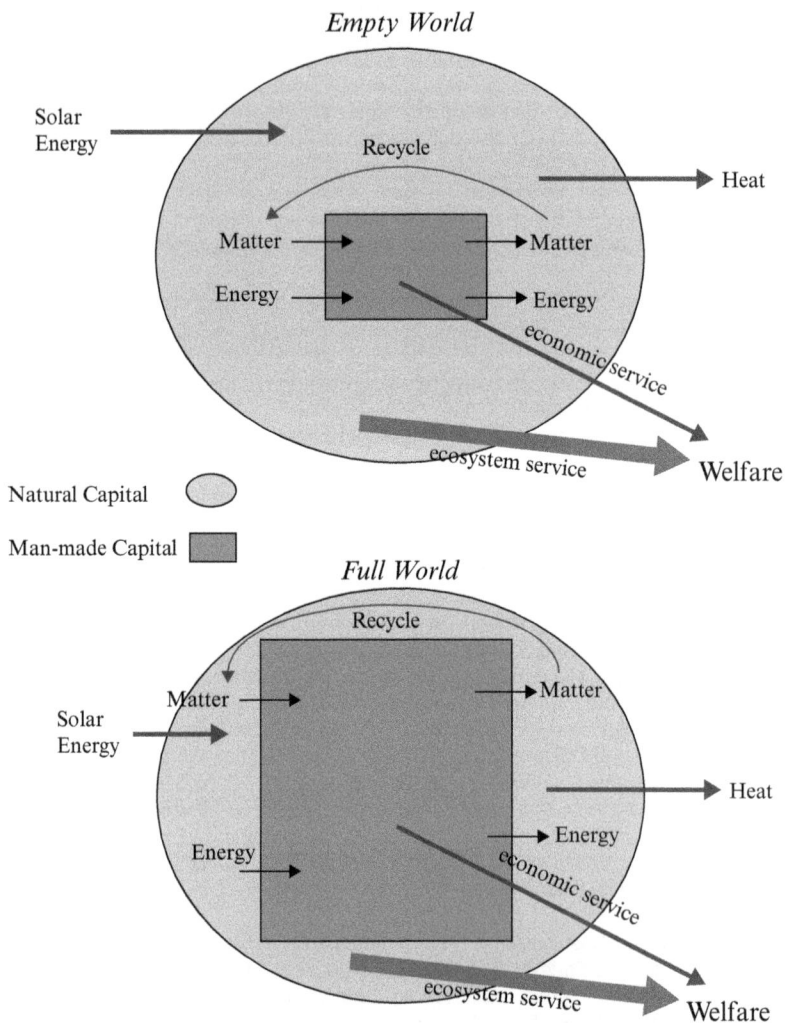

Figure 2.1   A 'macro' view of the macroeconomy

physical expansion of the economic subsystem encroaches on the rest of the whole and incurs an opportunity cost. At some point, perhaps already passed, it is possible that the extra opportunity cost of disrupted environmental services resulting from encroachment will begin to exceed the extra production benefits. In other words, we will have reached and passed the optimal scale of the macroeconomy relative to the ecosystem. So-called 'economic growth' (growth of the economic subsystem) would then in reality have become uneconomic growth – literally growth that costs us more than it benefits us at the margin.

A policy of sustainable development first aims at an optimal scale of the economy relative to the ecosystem. One of the features of an optimal scale is that it is sustainable – that is, the source and sink demands of the resource throughput necessary to sustain that scale are within the regenerative and assimilative capacities of the ecosystem. Second, once the scale of the resource throughput is limited, the distribution of ownership of this newly-scarce function must be decided. In the case of petroleum we know specifically who owns the sources in most cases, but not who owns or uses the sinks. A just distribution must be decided politically. In third place, after we have a socially defined sustainable scale and a just or at least acceptable distribution of ownership of sources and sinks, then we can allow the market to determine the efficient allocation of resources among competing uses.

2.4 SOME SOLUTIONS

2.4.1 Stop Counting the Consumption of Natural Capital as Income

Because income is by definition the maximum amount that a society can consume this year and still be able to consume the same amount next year, sustainability is built into the very definition of income. But the productive capacity that must be maintained intact has traditionally been thought of as man-made capital only, excluding natural capital. We have habitually counted natural capital as a free good. This might have been justified in yesterday's empty world, but in today's full world it is anti-economic. The error of implicitly counting natural capital consumption as income is customary in three areas: (1) the *System of National Accounts*; (2) evaluation of projects that deplete natural capital; and (3) international balance of payments accounting.

2.4.2 Maximize the Productivity of Natural Capital

Maximize the productivity of natural capital in the short run, and invest in increasing its supply in the long run. Economic logic requires that we behave in these two ways toward the limiting factor of production – maximize its productivity and invest in its increase. Those principles are not in dispute. Disagreements exist about whether natural capital is really the limiting factor. Some argue that man-made and natural capital are such good substitutes that the very idea of a limiting factor, which requires that the factors be complementary, is irrelevant. So the question is: are man-made capital and natural capital basically complements or substitutes? It is sufficiently clear to common sense that natural and man-made capital are fundamentally complements and only marginally substitutable.

In the past, natural capital has been treated as superabundant and priced at zero, so it did not really matter whether it was a complement or a substitute for man-made capital. Now remaining natural capital appears to be both scarce and complementary, and therefore limiting. For example, the fish catch is limited not by the number of fishing boats, but by the remaining populations of fish in the sea. Cut timber is limited not by the number of sawmills, but by the remaining standing forests. Pumped crude oil is limited not by man-made pumping capacity, but by remaining stocks of petroleum in the ground. The natural capital of the atmosphere's capacity to serve as a sink for carbon dioxide (CO_2) is likely to be even more limiting to the rate at which fossil fuels can be burned than is the source limit of remaining fossil fuels in the ground.

In the short run, raising the price of natural capital flows by taxing throughput will give the incentive to maximize natural capital productivity. Investing in natural capital over the long run is also needed. But how do we invest in something that by definition we cannot make? If we could make it, it would be man-made capital! For renewable resources we have the possibility of fallowing investments, or more generally regeneration by 'waiting' in Alfred Marshall's sense of allowing this year's growth increment to be added to next year's growing stock, rather than consuming it. Fallowing is investment in short-term non-production in order to maintain long-term yields. Slow or reduce the exploitation in order to let the renewable resource grow. This conforms to the economic definition of investment, namely, a reduction in present consumption in order to increase a future capacity to consume. As fallowing is investment without growth, current economics barely acknowledges the power of fallowing; lack of growth is tantamount to the end of progress.

For non-renewables we do not have the fallowing option. We can only liquidate them. So the question is how fast do we liquidate, and how much of the proceeds can we count as income if we invest the rest in the best available renewable substitute? And of course, how much of the correctly counted income do we then consume, and how much do we invest?

Humanity has to shift to a steady-state economy, one in which demands on the ecosystem's sources and sinks would remain safely in bounds. For example, logging must be kept within forest regeneration rates. Greenhouse gas emissions must be kept within the capacity of the ecosystem to absorb them. That implies shifting economic policy from a focus on boosting growth, where the scale of physical demands on ecosystems would perpetually increase; to development, meaning humanity would have to learn to make wiser use of a modest and more stable level of materials taken from the environment.

2.4.3 Tax Throughput

It makes no sense to tax what you want more of (income, labor, capital gains) instead of what you want less of (depletion, pollution). Therefore, tax energy and material extraction and pollution, not income. Tax labor and income less, and resource throughput more. Such eco-taxes could be revenue neutral during a transition period so as not to increase the total tax burden. In the past it has been customary for governments to subsidize resource throughput to stimulate growth. Thus, energy, water, fertilizer and even deforestation are even now frequently subsidized. Now it is necessary to go beyond removal of explicit financial subsidies to the removal of implicit environmental subsidies as well. 'Implicit environmental subsidies' mean external costs to the community that are not charged to the commodities whose production generates them. Costing ecosystem services in cost-benefit analysis of extraction activities also would help.

2.4.4 Get the Price Right

Getting prices right helps with efficient allocation. But a different scale just results in a different set of efficient prices for that scale, just as a different distribution also results in a different efficient allocation. A sustainable scale and a just distribution both must be socially and politically determined and imposed as constraints on the market, which can only then determine proper allocative prices. Sustainable scale and fair distribution cannot be discovered by the market. They have to be politically imposed on the market. Only then will efficient allocation really be worth pursuing.

2.4.5 Separate Allocation, Distribution and Scale

These three are separate problems.

First, neoclassical economics has dealt mainly with allocation (the apportionment of scarce resources among competing commodity uses – how many resources go to produce beans, cars, haircuts and so on?). A good allocation is efficient – in the sense that no reallocation can increase anyone's welfare without decreasing the welfare of someone else. Properly functioning markets allocate resources efficiently in this sense (called Pareto optimality).

Second, this concept of efficient allocation presupposes a given distribution (the apportionment of goods and resources among different people – how many resources embodied in beans, cars and so on, go to you, how many to me?). A good distribution is one that is just.

The third issue is scale, or the physical size of the economy relative to the ecosystem that sustains it. How many of us are there and how many beans, cars and so on do we each get on average, and how large are the associated matter-energy flows relative to natural cycles?

A good scale is sustainable. A sustainable scale, like a just distribution, cannot be determined by the market – both are conditions that the market must take as given, which must be politically imposed on the market, and subject to which the market finds the efficient allocation and corresponding prices.

Economists' legitimate concern with efficient allocation should not be allowed to obscure the critical presuppositions regarding just distribution and sustainable scale. It is fair to say that neoclassical economists accept this reasoning as far as distribution is concerned, but not for scale. If someone urges lower energy prices as a way to help the poor, economists rightly say, 'no: that will distort the allocative function of prices – better to help the poor by redistribution of income to them.' Yet economists seem to think that manipulating prices will solve the scale problem – if we just get prices right then the market will move us to the optimal scale. But then why not apply the same logic of just 'getting prices right' to distribution, for example? Why not internalize the cost of poverty by subsidizing wage goods and taxing luxury goods, and let the 'right prices' lead us to the optimal distribution?

There are good reasons for not trying to solve the distribution question by 'right prices,' but those reasons also prevent right prices from solving the scale problem. What are the 'right prices,' anyway? Are they the ones that give us the optimal allocation, the optimal distribution and the optimal scale, all at the same time? That would be lovely, but it runs afoul of logic. Nobel economist Jan Tinbergen set forth a basic principle: for every independent policy goal, we need an independent policy instrument. The logic is analogous to that of simultaneous equations. For every variable to be solved for, we need a separate equation. Is our goal optimal allocation? Fine, then supply equals demand pricing in competitive markets can be our policy equation. We also want just distribution? Fine, but we need a second policy instrument (not prices again). We also want a sustainable scale? Fine, now we need a third policy instrument (not prices yet again). Let us by all means keep prices and markets for solving the allocation problem.

Now what are our independent instruments for solving the distribution and scale problems? Following the logic of cap-and-trade, which conforms nicely to Tinbergen's rule, scale is set by ecological criteria of sustainability by setting aggregate quotas (caps); distribution is set by ethical criteria of fairness effected by distribution of ownership of the quotas; and that leaves only allocation to be settled by efficiency criteria effected through market prices.

How is it that economists accept the distributive precondition for efficient prices, but apparently not the analogous scale precondition? That may simply be because they have not thought much about scale. Sometimes scale is treated as infinitesimal – the economy is thought to be very small relative to the ecosystem, which consequently is considered infinite and non-scarce.

2.4.6 Focus on Development, Not Growth

Trying to define sustainability in terms of constant GDP is problematic because GDP conflates qualitative improvement (development) with quantitative increase (growth). The sustainable economy must at some point stop growing, but it need not stop developing.[9] There is no reason to limit the qualitative improvement in design of products, which can increase GDP without increasing the amount of resources used. The main idea behind sustainability is to shift the path of progress from growth, which is not sustainable, toward development, which presumably is.

What economists usually mean by growth is growth in GDP. And GDP is the difficult case. Is it physical or non-physical; quantitative or qualitative? Actually it is the conflation of both just referred to. GDP is measured in value units. Part of value is certainly physical – goods are physical, and even services are always provided by something or somebody for some period, and therefore have a physical dimension. The other part of value could increase forever, but that would be inflation, and no one wants to count inflation as growth. Economists take pains to calculate real GDP in order to estimate changes in physical growth, and eliminate changes in price levels.

Certainly Keynes defined the growth of the world economy to which the World Bank would be dedicated, in physical terms: 'By expansion we should mean increase of resources and production in real terms, in physical quantity, accompanied by a corresponding increase in purchasing power' (quoted in Rich, 1994, p. 55). Although this is the dominant meaning of growth, it is possible to have GDP growth without growth in aggregate throughput if the mix of goods shifts from high resource-intensive to low resource-intensive commodities. But this is a self-limiting process; it is a very small part of what economists and politicians have in mind when they seek economic growth. What is the best growth policy for the North to adopt for itself to help the South overcome poverty? Should the North grow as fast as possible so it can provide markets in which the South can sell its exports, and accumulate capital to invest in the South? How fair is it for the North to suck up the South's natural resources and count this as higher GDP of the South? Reforming national accounts is a must so natural resource user cost is internalized in the price (El Serafy, personal communication 2009).

The North should continue its welfare and efficiency growth but stop its throughput growth in order to free resources and ecological space for the South to grow enough to overcome poverty and achieve sufficiency before also stopping its throughput growth. The North should accept the consequences for its GDP growth, whatever they are.

It is clear that the World Bank has effectively opted for the North as well as the South to grow as fast as possible, although without ever explicitly asking whether growth is a qualitative improvement or simply an increase in quantity. The World Bank should explicitly ask that question. The closest it has come to doing so is the question we were invited to debate in March 2004 in preparation for the World Development Report on 'Sustainability,' *Can We Grow Our Way to an Environmentally Sustainable World?*

Is it the world, or the process of economic growth, that should be sustained? Development economists want to sustain growth – that is, a process, not a state of the world. Ecological economists would like to sustain the world in a state of economic and ecological sufficiency. The attempt to sustain growth will be inimical to that end. Beyond some point growth in production and population will begin to increase social and environmental costs faster than it increases production benefits, thereby ushering in an era of uneconomic growth – growth that on balance makes us poorer rather than richer, that increases 'illth' faster than it increases wealth. There is evidence that the United States and other Organisation for Economic Co-operation and Development (OECD) nations have already reached such a point.

What will it take for contemporary economists to adopt ecological economics? Probably a breakdown of current global capitalism, provoked by destruction of the supporting ecosystem. The crisis would destroy the legitimacy of standard growth economics. By analogy, Keynesian economics would have got nowhere without the Great Depression. Internal consistency is good, but correspondence with external facts is better.

2.4.7 Focus on Domestic Markets Before International Trade

Globalization refers to global economic integration of many formerly national economies into one global economy, mainly by free trade and free capital mobility, but also by easy or uncontrolled migration. It is the effective erasure of national boundaries for economic purposes. Part of the solution is to move away from the ideology of global economic integration by free trade, free capital mobility and export-led growth, and move toward a more nationalist orientation that seeks to develop domestic production for internal markets as the first option, having recourse to international trade only when clearly much more efficient.

Global interdependence is celebrated as a self-evident good. The royal road to development, peace and harmony is thought to be the unrelenting conquest of each nation's markets by all other nations. The word 'globalist' has politically correct connotations, while the word 'nationalist' has come to be pejorative. This is so much the case that it is necessary to remind ourselves that the World Bank exists to serve the interests of its members, which are nation states, national communities – not individuals, corporations or even non-governmental organizations (NGOs). It has no charter to serve the one-world-without-borders, cosmopolitan vision of global integration – of converting many relatively independent national economies, loosely dependent on international trade, into one tightly integrated world economic network upon which the weakened nations depend for even basic survival.

The model of international community on which the Bretton Woods institutions rest is that of a 'community of communities,' an international federation of national communities cooperating to solve global problems under the principle of subsidiarity. The model is not the cosmopolitan one of direct global citizenship in a single integrated world community without intermediation by nation states. To globalize the economy by erasure of national economic boundaries through free trade, free capital mobility and free, or at least uncontrolled, migration is to wound fatally the major unit of community capable of carrying out any policies for the common good. That includes not only policy for purely domestic ends, but also international agreements required to deal with environmental problems that are irreducibly global (for example, atmospheric CO_2 accumulation, ozone depletion). International agreements presuppose the ability of national governments to carry out policies to support them. If nations have no control over their borders they are in a poor position to enforce national laws, including those necessary to secure compliance with international treaties.

Cosmopolitan globalism weakens national boundaries and domestic economic policy, and the power of national and subnational communities, while strengthening the relative power of transnational corporations. Since there is no world government capable of regulating global capital in the global interest, and since the desirability and possibility of a world government are both highly doubtful, it will be necessary to make capital less global and more national. That is an unthinkable thought right now, but take it as a prediction – ten years from now the buzz words will be 'renationalization of capital' and the 'community rooting of capital for the development of national and local economies,' not the current shibboleths of export-led growth stimulated by whatever adjustments are necessary to increase global competitiveness. 'Global competitiveness' (frequently a slogan substituting for thought) usually reflects not so much a real increase in resource productivity as a standard-lowering competition to reduce wages, externalize environmental and social costs, and export natural capital at low prices, while calling it income.

Economists should reflect deeply on the words of John Maynard Keynes: 'I sympathize therefore, with those who would minimize rather than those who would maximize economic entanglement between nations. Ideas, knowledge, art, hospitality, travel; these are the things which should of their nature be international. But let goods be homespun whenever it is reasonably and conveniently possible; and, above all, let finance be primarily national' (Keynes, 1936, p. 403).

2.4.8 Climate Disruption

Climate disruption results mainly from the 'more growth forever' that conventional economic policy seeks unquestioningly. Climate change is a massive negative side-effect of growth. Lord Stern (2006) calls it the biggest externality the world has ever known. Climate change could uproot six million people annually by mid-century.

The limiting factor for the throughput of petroleum is no longer the man-made capital of drilling equipment, pipelines, tankers, refineries and combustion engines – and perhaps not even declining stocks of subterranean oil. Even more limiting is the sink capacity of the earth (atmosphere, soils, vegetation, oceans) to absorb the CO_2 resulting from petroleum combustion. Sink capacity is also natural capital. Economic logic says we should economize on and invest in the limiting factor. Economic logic has not changed, but the pattern of scarcity has. More and more it is remaining natural capital that now plays the role of limiting factor. We have been very slow to change our economic policies accordingly and refocus our economizing and investing on natural capital. Instead we have treated natural capital as a free good and accounted its drawdown as income, rather than unsustainable capital consumption. To avoid a write-off on the falling value of excess man-made capital that should result from the increasing scarcity of its complementary factor (natural capital), we continue to increase the rate of drawdown of natural capital, hoping for future geological discoveries and technical advances.

Ecological economics grapples with the (recent) scarcity of environ-mental functions or scarcity of sources and sinks. Communities have long faced local scarcities. The difference now is that these scarcities are regional and global. There is no new frontier. How total rents are determined and divided between source scarcity and sink scarcity is a technical problem that economists have not tackled because natural resources have not been considered important, and until recently pollution has been dismissed as an externality. Economists have focused on capturing source rents through property rights, then internalizing the external sink costs of pollution through taxes. Only recently has a theoretical discussion emerged of prop-erty rights in atmospheric sink capacity – whether these should be public or private, the extent to which trade in such rights should be allowed and so on. As an initial rule of thumb we might assume that since the sink side is now the more limiting function, it should be accorded half or more of the total throughput scarcity rents. In other words, sink rents should be at least as much as source rents.

2.4.9　The 2009 Economic Meltdown

This is really not a 'liquidity' crisis as it is often euphemistically called. It is a crisis of overgrowth of financial assets relative to growth of real wealth – pretty much the opposite of too little liquidity. Financial assets have grown by a large multiple of the real economy. It should be no surprise that the relative value of the vastly more abundant financial assets have fallen in terms of real assets. Real wealth is concrete; financial assets are abstrac-tions (Box 2.4). Basically they are liens on future real assets that are based on expectations of future real growth. That is to say, they are in real terms

---

BOX 2.4　WHAT ALLOWED FINANCIAL ASSETS TO BECOME SO DISCONNECTED FROM REAL ASSETS?

First, our fractional reserve banking system allows pyramiding of the money supply (see chapter by John Cobb in this volume).

Second, buying stocks and derivatives on margin allows a further pyramiding of the financial on top of the real.

Third, credit card debt expands the supply of quasi-money, as do other financial 'innovations' that were designed to circumvent regulation of commercial banks.

Important in all this is our balance of trade deficit that has allowed us to consume as if we were really growing, combined with the willingness of our surplus trading partners to lend the dollars they earned back to us by buying treasury bills – more liens on future growth. Some of us have for a long time been saying that this behavior was unsustainable. Maybe we were right.

debts or liabilities. The term asset is very misleading. Liens on the future are monetary assets to the owner, but are real liabilities to the society that has to grow in real wealth to redeem those liens. Can the economy grow fast enough in real terms to redeem the massive increase in liens? In a word, no. The general realization that the answer is no, even though no one publicly admits it, is what caused the crisis.

The problem is not too little liquidity, but too many worthless or devalued liens on the future. Growth in US real wealth is restrained by increasing scarcity of natural resources, both sources, like oil depletion, and sinks, like absorptive capacity for greenhouse gas, as well as spatial displacement, and also increasing inequality of distribution of income.

Marginal costs of real (not financial or abstract) growth now are likely to exceed marginal benefits, so that real physical growth makes us poorer, not richer. To keep up the illusion that growth is making us richer, we have multiplied financial assets almost without limit, conveniently forgetting that these so-called assets are nothing but liens on future growth in real wealth that is very unlikely to happen.

Peak oil also contributed to the current crisis. The spike in oil prices to greater than $140 per barrel and the spike in gasoline prices it caused was a trigger to expose the house of cards that the housing market had become. The recession eased demand and brought oil prices down, but if the 'stimulus' packages work, then demand will outstrip supply again, another oil price spike, and another recession. This may be the way we approach steady state, with damped oscillations as we bump up against energy and climate constraints (Costanza, personal communication 2009).

NOTES

1. Degrowth is an equitable downscaling of production and consumption that increases human well-being and enhances ecological conditions at the local and global levels, in the short and long term.
2. Growth is usually measured as an increase in real GDP or real GDP per capita. It is a poor measure of income and not a measure of wealth (a stock concept) at all (Victor, personal communication 2009).
3. An antonym for wealth, illth (coinage attributed to John Ruskin) is defined as economic and social activities that lead to no social good, such as pollution and depletion; all environmental changes harming humanity; a social 'bad.' (Also see the antonym of 'wealth' in the *Oxford English Dictionary*.)
4. From here on, growth refers to increases in GDP and in throughput unless otherwise stated. The productivity of activities with a big throughput has increased enormously, so consequently has their contribution to GDP growth (and their burden on the environment). On the other hand, activities with low or negligible throughput (piano-playing) have little or no increase in productivity, so their contribution to GDP growth (and burden on the environment) is small or zero (Hueting, 2010).
5. Externality or more strictly an external cost: as we move from an empty to a full world the

box labeled 'externalities' has grown very large and important. Indeed, nowadays the very capacity of the earth to support life is treated by neoclassical economists as an externality. Surely before reaching that point we should rethink and reshape our economic vision so that vital matters are internal to our theory and only trivial issues are external. But so far the priority of the neoclassicals has been to preserve the model by classifying whatever doesn't fit as an 'externality.' In the empty world, one could with some justification say 'mere' externality. In the full world, externalities are often much more important than what remains internal. The monetary valuation of ecosystem services is a start. We won't destroy what we value. The valuation of ecosystem services is a way to tackle the standard neoclassical externalities problem.

6. Neoclassical economist Robert Solow concedes this point, when he spoke to *Harper's Magazine*'s Stephen Stoll: 'There is no reason at all why capitalism could not survive without slow or even no growth. I think it's perfectly possible that economic growth cannot go on at its current rate forever. This does not mean that productivity will cease to increase our quality of life; it means that people might find it increasingly costly to turn productivity into the kinds of things they are now accustomed to buying with their earnings. It is possible, says Solow, that the United States and Europe will find that, as the decades go by, either continued growth will be too destructive to the environment and they are too dependent on scarce natural resources, or that they would rather use increasing productivity in the form of leisure ... There is nothing intrinsic in the system that says it cannot exist happily in a stationary state' (Stoll, 2008, p. 92).

7. Sustainability semantics: the abstract noun 'sustainability,' the adjective 'sustainable' and the past participle 'sustained' are all less informative than the transitive verb form 'to sustain,' which grammatically requires us to name both a subject and an object. It is good to be mindful that what is being sustained is the physical wealth of the economy (including the population), and what is doing the sustaining is the finite, non-growing biosphere. It is helpful also to say what sustainability is not. Neoclassicals try to define sustainability in terms of non-declining utility between generations. This is a non-starter for two reasons: first, utility is unmeasurable; second, utility cannot be bequeathed. Even if we could measure utility well enough to judge whether it is non-declining, which we cannot, we still could not pass it on from one generation to the next. As any parent knows, you can only pass on things, not happiness. Future generations are always free to make themselves miserable with whatever we give them. Sustaining means using without using up, to use while keeping intact, while maintaining or replacing the capacity for future use. What is being sustained is ultimately the capacity to produce income. Income is in turn the maximum that a community can consume this year and still produce the same amount next year – that is, income is consumption that leaves productive capacity (capital in the broad sense) intact. Income is by definition sustainable consumption, as defined by Sir John Hicks. 'Unsustainable income' is not income at all but capital drawdown.

8. Frugality here means 'non-wasteful sufficiency, thrifty, provident, and economical in use,' rather than 'meager scantiness.'

9. Roefie Hueting (personal communication) points out that if growth means increase in GDP (which it should not mean) then it holds: *clean growth is degrowth*! See also Hueting (2010).

BIBLIOGRAPHY

Commission on Growth and Development (2008), *The Growth Report: Strategies for Sustained Growth and Inclusive Development*, Washington, DC: World Bank.

Costanza, R. (1989), 'What is ecological economics?', *Ecological Economics*, **1**, 1–7.

Costanza, R. (ed.) (1991), *Ecological Economics: The Science and Management of Sustainability*, New York: Columbia University Press.

Costanza, R. (1996), 'Ecological economics: reintegrating the study of humans and nature', *Ecological Applications: A Publication of the Ecological Society of America*, **6** (4), 978.

Costanza, R. (1997), *Frontiers in Ecological Economics: Transdisciplinary Essays by Robert Costanza*, Cheltenham, UK and Lyme, NH, USA: Edward Elgar Publishing, p. 491.

Costanza, R. (2009), 'Toward a new sustainable economy', *Real-World Economics Review*, **49**, 20–21.

Costanza, R. and H.E. Daly (1987), 'Toward an ecological economics', *Ecological Modelling*, **38**, 1–7.

Costanza, R. and H.E. Daly (1992), 'Natural capital and sustainable development', *Conservation Biology*, **6**, 37–46.

Costanza, R., B. Haskell, L. Cornwell, H. Daly and T. Johnson (1990), 'The ecological economics of sustainability: making local and short-term goals consistent with global and long-term goals', Working Paper No. 32, Environment Department, World Bank, Washington, DC.

Costanza, R., O.S. Bonilla and J. Martinez-Alier (1996), *Getting Down to Earth: Practical Applications of Ecological Economics*, International Society for Ecological Economics Series, Washington, DC: Island Press, p. 472.

Costanza, R., C. Perrings and C. Cleveland (eds) (1997a), *The Development of Ecological Economics*, Cheltenham, UK and Lyme, NH, USA: Edward Elgar Publishing, p. 777.

Costanza, R., J.C. Cumberland, H.E. Daly, R. Goodland and R. Norgaard (1997b), *An Introduction to Ecological Economics*, Boca Raton, FL: St Lucie Press, p. 275.

Costanza, R., M. Hart, S. Posner and J. Talberth (2009), 'Beyond GDP: the need for new measures of progress', *The Pardee Center Papers*, Boston, MA, **4**, 40.

Daly, H.E. (1968), 'On economics as a life science', *Chicago Journal of Political Economy*, **76** (3), 15–29.

Daly, H.E. (1970), 'Towards a stationary-state economy', *Yale Alumni Magazine*, May.

Daly, H.E. (1971a), 'A Marxian-Malthusian view of poverty and development', *Population Studies*, **2** (1), 25–37.

Daly, H.E. (1971b), 'The stationary-state economy: toward a political economy of biophysical equilibrium and moral growth', *Distinguished Visiting Lecture Series*, No. 2, September, University of Alabama.

Daly, H.E. (ed.) (1971c), 'Essays toward a steady-state economy', *CIDOC Cuaderno* No. 70, Centre Intercultural de Documentación, Cuernavaca.

Daly, H.E. (1972a), 'In defense of the steady-state economy', *American Journal of Agricultural Economics*, **54** (5), 945–54.

Daly, H.E. (1972b), 'Institutions necessary for a steady-state economy: three suggestions', *IDOC*, September.

Daly, H.E. (1973a), 'A model for a steady-state economy', in *Growth and Its Implications for the Future: Part 1*, Hearings before the Subcommittee on Fisheries and Wildlife Conservation and the Environment of the Committee on Merchant Marine and Fisheries, House of Representatives, 93rd Congress, First Session (1 May), Washington, DC, pp. 435–57.

Daly, H.E. (ed.) (1973b), *Toward a Steady-state Economy*, San Francisco, CA: W.H. Freeman, p. 332.

Daly, H.E. (1974a), 'Steady-state economics vs. growthmania: a critique of the orthodox conceptions of growth, wants, scarcity, and efficiency', *Policy Sciences*, **5** (2), 149–67.

Daly, H.E. (1974b), 'The economics of the steady state', *American Economic Review*, **62** (4), 15–21.

Daly, H.E. (1975), 'The developing economies and the steady state', *The Developing Economies*, September, 231–42.

Daly, H.E. (1976), 'The transition to a steady-state economy', in *The Steady State Economy*, Vol. 5, Joint Economic Committee of Congress, *U.S. Economic Growth from 1976 to 1986: Prospects, Problems, and Patterns* (12 vols), Washington, DC: US Government Printing Office, pp. 13–39.

Daly, H.E. (1977a), 'The steady-state economy: what, why, and how?', in D. Pirages (ed.), *The Sustainable Society: Implications for Limited Growth*, New York: Praeger Publishers, pp. 107–30.

Daly, H.E. (1977b), *Steady State Economics: The Political Economy of Biophysical Equilibrium and Moral Growth*, San Francisco, CA: W.H. Freeman, p. 185.

Daly, H.E. (1978), *Toward a Steady-state Economy: The Economics of Biophysical Equilibrium and Moral Growth*, 2nd edn, San Francisco, CA: W.H. Freeman.

Daly, H.E. (ed.) (1980), *Economics, Ecology, Ethics: Essays Toward a Steady-state Economy*, San Francisco, CA: W.H. Freeman, p. 372.

Daly, H.E. (1981), *Lo Stato Stazionario: l'economia dell'equilibrio biofisico e della crescita morale*, Firenze: Sansoni Editore, p. 250.

Daly, H.E. (1984). *A Economia do Século XXI*, Porto Alegre, Brazil: Mercado Aberto Editora, p. 116.

Daly, H.E. (1990), 'Sustainable development: from concept and theory to operational principles', *Population and Development Review*, Suppl., 19.

Daly, H.E. (1991a), *Steady-state Economics: 2nd Edition with New Essays*, Washington, DC: Island Press, p. 302.

Daly, H.E. (1991b), 'Sustainable development: from concept and theory to operational principles', in K. Davis and M.S. Bernstam (eds), *Resources, Environment, and Population: Present Knowledge, Future Options*, New York: Oxford University Press, pp. 25–43.

Daly, H.E. (1992), 'Allocation, distribution, and scale: towards an economics that is efficient, just, and sustainable', *Ecological Economics*, **6** (3), 185–93.

Daly, H.E. (1994a), Farewell speech (upon leaving the World Bank), available at http://www.eoearth.org/view/article/51cbedc67896bb431f693d6a/ (accessed 12 December 2015).

Daly, H.E. (1994b), 'Operationalizing sustainable development by investing in natural capital', in A.M. Jansson, M. Hammer, C. Folke and R. Costanza (eds), *Investing in Natural Capital*, Washington, DC: Island Press, pp. 22–37.

Daly, H.E. (1996), *Beyond Growth: The Economics of Sustainable Development*, Boston, MA: Beacon Press, p. 253.

Daly, H.E. (1999a), 'Globalization versus internationalization: some implications', *Ecological Economics*, **31**, 31–7.

Daly, H.E. (1999b), *Ecological Economics and the Ecology of Economics*, Cheltenham, UK and Northampton, MA, USA: Edward Elgar Publishing, p. 191.

Daly, H.E. (2002), 'Sustainable development: definitions, principles, policies', *Invited Address: Comments on the World Bank's (draft) 'World Development Report 2003'*, Washington, DC: World Bank, 30 April.

Daly, H.E. (2003), 'The illth of nations and the fecklessness of policy: an ecological economist's perspective', *Post-autistic Economics Review*, **22** (1), 7.

Daly, H.E. (2004), *Can We Grow Our Way to an Environmentally Sustainable World? A Debate*, Washington, DC: World Bank, 2 March.

Daly, H.E. (2005a), 'Economics in a full world: society can no longer safely pretend the global economy operates within a limitless ecosystem. Planners must think afresh about how to increase prosperity', *Scientific American*, **293** (3), 100–107.

Daly, H.E. (2005b), 'Economics in a full world', *IEEE Engineering Management Review*, **33** (4), 21.

Daly, H.E. (2006), 'Population, migration, and globalization', *Ecological Economics*, **59** (2), 187–90.

Daly, H.E. (2007), *Ecological Economics and Sustainable Development: Selected Essays of Herman Daly*, Cheltenham, UK and Northampton, MA, USA: Edward Elgar Publishing, p. 270.

Daly, H.E. (2008), 'Growth and development: critique of a credo', *Population and Development Review*, **34** (3), 511–18.

Daly, H.E. and J. Cobb (1989), *For the Common Good: Redirecting the Economy Toward Community, the Environment, and a Sustainable Future*, Boston, MA: Beacon Press, p. 482.

Daly, H.E. and R. Costanza (1987), 'Toward an ecological economics', *Ecological Modelling*, **38** (1–2), 1.

Daly, H.E. and J. Farley (2004), *Ecological Economics: Principles and Applications*, Washington, DC: Island Press, p. 454.

Daly, H.E. and R. Goodland (1992), 'Ten reasons why Northern income growth is not the solution to Southern poverty', *International Journal of Sustainable Development*, **1** (2), 23–30.

Daly, H.E. and R. Goodland (1994), 'An ecological-economic assessment of deregulation of international commerce under GATT', *Population & Environment*, Part 1, **15** (5), 394–427; Part 2, **15** (6), 477–503.

Daly, H.E. and E. Mishan (1975), in Edison Electric Institute (ed.), *Economic Growth in the Future: The Growth Debate in National and Global Perspective*, New York: McGraw-Hill, p. 423.

Daly, H.E. and K. Townsend (eds) (1993), *Valuing the Earth: Economics, Ecology, Ethics*, Cambridge, MA: MIT Press, p. 387.

Daly, H.E. and Á. Umaña (eds) (1981), *Energy, Economics and the Environment: Conflicting Views of an Essential Interrelationship*, American Association for the Advancement of Science, Boulder, CO: Westview Press, p. 200.

Daly, H.E., R. Goodland and S. El Serafy (1993), 'The urgent need for rapid transition to global environmental sustainability', *Environmental Conservation*, **20** (4), 297–310.

Daly, H.E., R. Goodland and J. Kellenberg (1994), 'Imperatives for environmental sustainability: decrease overconsumption and stabilize population', in N. Polunin and M. Nazim (eds), *Population and Global Security*, Geneva: United Nations Population Fund, pp. 87–99.

Hueting, R. (1974), *New Scarcity and Economic Growth: More Welfare through Less Production? (Nieuwe schaarste en economische groei. Meer welvaart door minder produktie?)* Amsterdam: Agon Elsevier.

Hueting, R. (2010), 'Why environmental sustainability can most probably not be attained with growing production', *Journal of Cleaner Production*, **18** (6), 525–30.

Jackson, T. (2009), *Prosperity Without Growth? The Transition to a Sustainable Economy*, London: Sustainable Development Commission.

Keynes, J.M. (1936), *The General Theory of Employment, Interest and Money*, London: Macmillan, p. 403.

Malthus, T.R. (1798), *An Essay on the Principle of Population, as it Affects the Future Improvement of Society; With Remarks on the Speculations of W. Godwin, M. Condorcet and Other Writers*, London: J. Johnson, p. 396, 3rd edn in 1806.

Martinez-Alier, J. and K. Schlüpmann (1987), *Ecological Economics: Energy, Environment, and Society*, Oxford: Basil Blackwell, p. 286.

Meade, J.E. (1965), *The Stationary Economy*, London: Allen & Unwin, p. 238.

Meadows, D.H., D. Meadows, J. Randers and W.W. Behrens (1972), *The Limits to Growth*, New York: Universe Books, p. 405.

Meadows, D.H., D. Meadows and J. Randers (1992), *Beyond the Limits. Confronting Global Collapse, Envisioning a Sustainable Future*. Post Mills, VT: Chelsea Green, p. 300.

Mill, J.S. (1848), *Principles of Political Economy with Some of Their Applications to Social Philosophy*, London: John W. Parker, 2 vols.

Polimeni, J.M., K. Mayumi, M. Giampietro and B. Alcott (2008), *The Jevons Paradox and the Myth of Resource Efficiency*, London: Earthscan, p. 184.

Porritt, J. (2009), *Living Within Our Means: Avoiding the Ultimate Recession*, London: Forum for the Future, Sustainable Development Commission, p. 39.

Prugh, T., R. Costanza, J. Cumberland, H. Daly, R. Goodland and R. Norgaard (1995), *Natural Capital and Human Economic Survival*, Solomons, MD: ISEE Press, p. 195, 2nd edn in 1999.

Prugh, T., R. Costanza and H.E. Daly (2000), *The Local Politics of Global Sustainability*, Washington, DC: Island Press, p. 173.

Rich, B. (1994), *Mortgaging the Earth*, Boston, MA: Beacon Press.

Smith, A. (1776), *An Inquiry into the Nature and Causes of the Wealth of Nations*, London: W. Strahan and T. Cadell, 2 vols.

Stern, N. (2006), *Stern Review: The Economics of Climate Change*, Cambridge: Cambridge University Press.

Stoll, S. (2008), 'Fear of fallowing: the specter of a no-growth world', *Harper's Magazine*, March, pp. 88–92, 94.

Victor, P.A. (2008), *Managing Without Growth: Slower by Design, Not Disaster*, Cheltenham, UK and Northampton, MA, USA: Edward Elgar Publishing, p. 272.

World Bank (2002), *World Development Report 2003: Sustainable Development in a Dynamic World*, Washington, DC: World Bank, p. 276.

3. Toward a sustainable and desirable future: a 35-year collaboration with Herman Daly

Robert Costanza

3.1 ENERGY AND THE ECONOMY

My connection with Herman Daly began several years before I met him. As a PhD student at the University of Florida studying under H.T. Odum, I was introduced to Herman's 1968 article 'On economics as a life science' (Daly, 1968) and his path-breaking books on steady state economics (Daly, 1973, 1977). Daly was held in high esteem by Odum as the only economist he knew who understood the basic interconnections between humans and the ecological systems that supported them and which they were embedded within. It seemed obvious that the human economy, as a subsystem of the larger global ecosystem, could not continue to grow indefinitely. Obvious to everyone, that is, except mainstream economists.

Teaching thermodynamics to economists was also the goal of Nicholas Georgescu-Roegen, whose book on the entropy law and the economic process (Georgescu-Roegen, 1971) was also on my reading list. Georgescu-Roegen was Herman's mentor during his PhD at Vanderbilt and Herman is still one of the few economists that understand thermodynamics and its implications for economics. That economists could (and continue to) ignore the laws of thermodynamics has always been a frustrating mystery to both of us.

Part of my PhD research at Florida had to do with quantifying and modeling energy flows through ecological and economic systems. I used input-output (I-O) analysis to do this, based on work being done at the time by Bruce Hannon and Robert Herendeen at the University of Illinois (Hannon, 1973, 1976, 1979). I modified the US I-O model being used at Illinois to include the energy costs of labor and government and inputs of solar energy and found that such an inclusion greatly improved the correlation between total (direct plus indirect) or 'embodied' energy costs and dollar value of output by sector. I presented these results at a job interview at Louisiana State University (LSU) for a position in the Coastal Ecology Laboratory. Herman, who was in the Economics Department at LSU at the time, attended the seminar. Herman liked this approach, I think partly because it was similar to what he had suggested in his 1968 paper mentioned above – to use an integrated I-O model to link ecological and economic systems. I got the job, no doubt partly due to Herman's favorable impression. Herman was also organizing a session at the upcoming American Association for the Advancement of Science (AAAS) meeting on 'Energy, Economics and the Environment' and invited me to present my energy I-O results there.

The AAAS meeting was in San Francisco that year. The session was well attended and the discussion lively. Alvaro Umaña, later to become the first Environment Minister in Costa Rica, was the co-chair of the session. He and Herman also co-edited a book including all the session papers (Daly and Umaña, 1981). I ended up with two chapters in the book (Costanza, 1981a, 1981b), one on the basic results of my I-O modeling and one in response to Herman's problems with interpreting these results as supporting an 'energy theory of value.' Herman and I have had a lively and ongoing friendly debate on this topic over the years. In the end, I don't think we are that far apart, but more on that in a bit. The thing I remember most about it was Herman's way of conducting the exchange. In this, and in most of his scholarly discussions, Herman has always assumed good will on everyone's part – that we should be investigating questions from all sides and searching for mutual enlightenment, not defending intellectual turf or jockeying for personal status or position. He has not always been right in this assumption about other people, but I learned much from his insistence on (and personal adherence to) civil discourse, even with those who do not themselves play by the same rules. There is no better exemplar of how scientific discourse *should* be engaged than Herman Daly.

Martha Gilliland, a former colleague at the University of Florida, had written an influential article on energy analysis that had been recently published in *Science* (Gilliland, 1975). Martha thought enough of my I-O results that she suggested sending a revised version of my paper to *Science*. I did that and got an immediate rejection without review. However, I thought this was a mistake and Herman agreed to write to the *Science* editors arguing that he thought the paper deserved to at least be reviewed. This, along with my own further arguments about the relevance of the paper, changed their minds and the article was sent out for review. It was reviewed favorably and ultimately accepted (Costanza, 1980).

This article used an 87-sector I-O model of the US economy for 1963, 1967 and 1973, modified to include households and government as endogenous sectors (so as to include labor and government energy costs) and direct inputs of solar energy. This allowed me to investigate the relationship between total direct and indirect energy consumption (embodied energy) and dollar value of output by sector. I found that dollar value of sector output was highly correlated ($R^2 = 0.85 - 0.98$) with embodied energy when this was calculated including the energy costs of labor and government, and solar inputs. There was almost no correlation when just direct energy consumption or embodied energy was calculated excluding labor and government energy costs and solar inputs were used. Thus, after making some necessary adjustments to estimates of embodied energy consumption in order to better assess total energy costs, I showed that the empirical link between embodied energy cost and dollar value of output by sector were rather strong.

Ecologists (including H.T. Odum) and physical scientists (including Frederick Soddy) had proposed an energy theory of value to either complement or replace the standard neoclassical theory of subjective utility-based value. It is based on thermodynamic principles in which solar energy is recognized to be the only 'primary' or net input to the global ecosystem. This theory of value represents, in a sense, a return to the classical ideas of David Ricardo and more recently Sraffa (1960), but with some important distinctions. The classical economists recognized that if they could identify a 'primary' input to the production process then they could explain exchange values based on production relationships. The problem was that neither labor nor any other single commodity was really primary since they all require each other for their production. The traditional primary factors (land, labor and capital) are really intermediate factors of production. The classical economists were writing before the science of thermodynamics had been fully developed. Energy – or, more correctly, free or available energy defined as the ability to do work – is not a typical commodity and has special characteristics that satisfy the criteria for a 'primary input':

1. Energy is ubiquitous.
2. It is a property of all the commodities produced in economic and ecological systems.
3. It is an essential input to all production processes – without energy, nothing happens.
4. Although other commodities can provide alternative sources for the energy required to drive systems, the essential property of energy (the ability to do work) cannot be substituted.
5. At the global scale, the earth is essentially a closed system in thermodynamic terms (only energy crosses the boundary), so at this scale it is the only primary input.

6. The classical three sources of exchange value (wages, profits and rent) are intermediate inputs in this global scheme and interconvertable using the primary energy input.

While my results reported in the *Science* paper seemed to support an energy theory of value, neither the natural scientists nor the economists liked that conclusion. Odum, for example, thought that money left out so many things that the correlation I showed couldn't possibly exist – that money was an inherently flawed measure and that embodied energy represented 'true' value. Economists thought that since energy (just another commodity in their view) was only one input it couldn't possibly correlate with dollars, and if it did it had to be an artifact of the calculation scheme (cf. Huettner, 1982).[1] I have a more nuanced explanation (Costanza, 2004). Energy (and earlier labor) theories of value are inherently based on relative production costs. Thus, it is more accurate to speak of energy cost or labor cost and not energy value or labor value. However, in well-behaved economic systems it is well known that cost and price will, in general but not in all cases, come to equilibrium. This is the essence of the basic ideas of supply and demand. On the other hand, economic I-O tables and gross domestic product (GDP) are also themselves 'cost-based' systems of accounts, which leave out much that is of value to supporting human well-being and quality of life. They also include many things that are of negative value (like the costs of natural capital depletion, crime and family breakdown). The fact that embodied energy cost and dollar cost are correlated implies that embodied energy is a good, comprehensive indicator of total (or true) costs, and it's use can be extended to pick up costs that are external to markets and not included in economic I-O tables or GDP. But *neither* GDP nor embodied energy are comprehensive measures of total value, in terms of contributions to sustainable human well-being (more on this later). On this interpretation of my results I think Herman and I can agree.

3.2 THE *ECOLOGICAL ECONOMICS* JOURNAL AND THE INTERNATIONAL SOCIETY FOR ECOLOGICAL ECONOMICS (ISEE)

Herman and I were both keenly interested in bridging the gap between ecology and economics and in creating a more transdisciplinary 'ecological economics' to understand and manage our world. While interest in creating an ecological economics dates back at least to the 1960s in the work of Kenneth Boulding (1966) and Herman (Daly, 1968) the first formal efforts to bring ecologists and economists together occurred in the 1980s.

The first of these was in 1982, when AnnMari Jansson organized a symposium in Saltsjöbaden, Sweden, funded by the Wallenberg Foundation on 'Integrating Ecology and Economics' (Jansson, 1984). The 48 participants at this meeting included many of those who would later be involved in establishing the *Ecological Economics* journal and in forming ISEE, including myself, Herman, Charles Hall, Bruce Hannon, AnnMari Jansson, H.T. Odum and David Pimentel; 17 of the participants from this meeting ultimately served on the editorial board of *Ecological Economics*.

While this first meeting was certainly stimulating for all involved, it also led to the perception that the gap between ecologists and economists had become quite large indeed. Part of the reason for this perception had to do with the specific ecologists and economists who were invited. The ecologists were mainly ecosystem ecologists while the economists (with the notable exception of Herman) were mainly mainstream environmental economists (that is, Ralph d'Arge, Partha Dasgupta, Karl-Goran Maler, Rick Freeman and Allen Kneese).

Partly as a response to this meeting, Herman and I (we were both still at LSU at the time) began to pursue the idea of starting a new journal. As a first step, we decided to edit a special issue of the journal *Ecological Modelling* on the topic of ecological economics (Costanza and Daly, 1987a), to test the water and see if there would be enough interest for a full journal. This special issue included invited contributions from several scholars who would later become central to the journal and to ISEE, including Cutler Cleveland, Robert Goodland, Richard Norgaard, David Pearce and Roefie Hueting. The special issue included an introductory article (Costanza and Daly, 1987b) that laid out both the need for and the basic agenda of ecological economics. The response to this special issue was sufficiently enthusiastic to warrant going forward with the creation of a new journal. The first book with 'ecological economics' in the title (Martinez-Alier, 1987) also appeared in this year, adding further momentum to the movement to start a journal.

After planning meetings in Lidingo, Sweden and Warsaw, Poland, involving AnnMari Jansson, Joan Martinez-Alier and Thomas Zylicz, a second workshop on 'Integrating Ecology and Economics' was held in Barcelona, Spain, on 26–29 September 1987, sponsored by the European Centre for Research and Documentation in Social Sciences. This meeting was organized by Joan Martinez-Alier, and included several individuals who had been at the earlier meeting in Sweden or who had contributed to the special issue of *Ecological Modelling*, along with several new people who would also figure prominently in ecological economics. In addition to Joan Martinez-Alier, other prominent attendees at the Barcelona meeting who had not been involved in the earlier activities included Charles Perrings, Martin O'Connor, Sylvio Funtowicz, John Proops, Jerry Ravetz, René Passet, Matthias Ruth and Enzo Tiezzi.

A consensus emerged from this meeting that the idea of creating a new journal was a good one and should be further pursued, with several of the papers presented at the meeting serving as initial submissions.

During 1987 and early 1988, Herman and I negotiated with several potential publishers for the journal, finally deciding on Elsevier Science. I took on the role of Chief Editor, with Herman, AnnMari Jansson and David Pearce as the initial Associate Editors and a broad ranging editorial board. The first issue was published in February 1989. The journal has been a huge success, progressing from an initial four issues per year to 12 issues per year by 1992, with an impact factor now ranking it in the top quarter of all academic journals. The journal now publishes a large number of articles across a broad range of transdisciplinary topics. In 2007 it published 277 articles, ranking it number 1 among 191 economics journals in this category and number 12 in terms of total citations. Among 52 Environmental Studies journals it ranked 2nd in total articles and 1st in total citations. Among 116 Ecology journals it ranked 10th in total articles and 33rd in total cites, reflecting the generally higher publication and citation rates in the natural versus the social sciences.

During the initial negotiations with Elsevier, it became clear that the only way to get reasonably priced subscriptions to the journal for individuals would be to form a society. Therefore, during 1988 the International Society for Ecological Economics (ISEE) was formed and incorporated in Louisiana, with myself as the first President. Shortly thereafter, both Herman and I left LSU. I moved to the University of Maryland and established the editorial office of the journal and the secretariat for ISEE there. Herman moved to the World Bank in Washington, DC.

A third workshop was held in La Valletta, Malta, in April 1988, again sponsored by the European Centre for Research and Documentation in Social Sciences on 'Environmental Training of Economists' that also helped to move the ecological economics agenda forward and provide initial submissions for the journal.

Once the journal was underway and ISEE was created, it was clear that we needed to have meetings of the society. I organized the first meeting of ISEE (with funding support from the Pew Foundation) in May 1990 in Washington, DC. Herman, along with Robert Goodland (one of the few ecologists working at the World Bank) convinced the Bank to provide in-kind support by donating meeting space. Holding the meeting at the World Bank raised its profile significantly. About 200 attendees were expected at the meeting, but almost 400 showed up. A report on the conference was carried in *Science* and the World Bank published a working paper that included all the abstracts from the talks at the conference along with a summary of the meeting (Costanza et al., 1990).

Since that first meeting in Washington, DC, ISEE has held biannual meetings in Stockholm, Sweden (1992); San Jose, Costa Rica (1994); Boston, USA (1996); Santiago, Chile (1998); Canberra, Australia (2000); Sousse, Tunisia (2002); Montreal, Canada (2004); New Delhi, India (2006); Nairobi, Kenya (2008); Oldenburg, Germany (2010) and Rio de Janeiro, Brazil (2012). The maximum attendance at these meetings has been over 1500.

3.3   THE SCIENCE AND MANAGEMENT OF SUSTAINABILITY

The Washington conference was followed by a three-day workshop at the Aspen Institute's facilities on Maryland's eastern shore, attended by 38 invited participants, most of whom were plenary speakers at the Washington conference. The result of this workshop was an edited volume representing the state and goals of the emerging field of ecological economics, the research agenda and policy recommendations (Costanza, 1991). Herman and I, along with Joy Bartholomew who facilitated the Aspen workshop, wrote the introductory synthesis chapter for the book (Costanza et al., 1991), laying out the consensus of the participants on the agenda for ecological economics. It is interesting to look back, almost 25 years later, at how this agenda has played out.

As far as I can tell, the first published use of the term 'natural capital' was in the 1991 book. One of the major section heads in the synthesis chapter was 'Valuation of Ecosystem Services and Natural Capital' and this topic has been a major one in ecological economics ever since. In 1992, Herman and I published a paper in *Conservation Biology*, defining the term 'natural capital' as 'a stock of natural ecosystems that yields a flow of ecosystem services into the future' (Costanza and Daly, 1992, p. 38) and further elaborating the concept. I also published a paper in a book that Herman, Robert Goodland and Salah El Serafy edited in 1992 elaborating on these themes (Costanza, 1992). At a recent check of the ISI web of science database (August 2013), since then there have been 527 journal articles published with 'natural capital' and 4177 with 'ecosystem services' in the topic field (this does not include books and book chapters).

The major research questions we identified in 1991 in the section on valuation of ecosystem services and natural capital were:

- How do we measure the value of ecosystem services and natural capital? Under what conditions can values be translated to single scales, for example, money, utility or energy?
- Do measures based on subjective preferences (contingent valuation, contingent referenda, willingness to pay) have any relationship to values based on ecosystem functioning and energy flows?
- What is the appropriate discount rate to apply to ecosystem services?
- What (or where) are the thresholds of irreversible degradation for natural resources?

These are certainly still the relevant research questions in this area today, and there has been an explosion of research on these questions. The questions listed in the other sections of the paper (titled: Sustainability: Maintaining Our Life-support System, Ecological Economic System Accounting, Ecological Economic Modeling at Local, Regional, and Global Scales, and Innovative Instruments for Environmental Management) also still ring true today, as do the policy and education recommendations that came out of the workshop.

The title of the 1991 book was *Ecological Economics: The Science and Management of Sustainability*. The term 'sustainability science' has taken off recently, with several new journals and degree programs structured around this theme.[2] Ecological economics has from the beginning tried to link this more comprehensive, whole systems science with how we manage our world to create a better, more sustainable and more livable one (Costanza, 2009).

3.4   POLICIES TO ACHIEVE A SUSTAINABLE AND DESIRABLE FUTURE

In 1994 Herman left the World Bank after six years of battling to have environmental concerns taken more seriously there. Through the diligent efforts of Peter Brown, my colleague at the University of Maryland in College Park at the time, Herman was recruited to be a professor there. I also recruited Herman to be the Associate Director of the Institute for Ecological Economics that I had founded at Maryland in 1991. At Maryland, we worked on several educational projects, including ecological economics courses, seminars and a Graduate Certificate in Ecological Economics that was finally approved in 1998.

Herman's farewell speech on leaving the Bank is now a classic (Daly, 1994). In it, he articulated four policy recommendations that have become central to ecological economics.

1. Stop counting the consumption of natural capital as income.
2. Tax labor and income less and tax resource throughput more.
3. Maximize the productivity of natural capital in the short run, and invest in increasing its supply in the long run.
4. Move away from the ideology of global economic integration by 'free' trade.

Let's take each of these in turn and review their current status.

1. The idea of moving beyond GDP as a measure of economic well-being (something for which it was never designed) to a more comprehensive measure that can account for the depletion of natural capital is something that Herman had long advocated. In 1989 he and John Cobb (Daly and Cobb, 1989) created the 'Index of Sustainable Economic Welfare' (ISEW) that did just that. The ISEW showed that in terms of welfare (rather than mere marketed income) the USA had been in a period of 'uneconomic growth' since 1975 – GDP was growing but it has become 'uneconomic' because well-being as measured by ISEW was not improving. The idea that economic growth – touted by the economic mainstream and especially the World Bank as the solution to *all* problems – had costs that could outweigh the benefits was heretical at the time. It is an idea that is finally gaining broad support, however, and many institutions are now questioning the dominance of GDP growth as a primary policy goal and searching for alternatives (Costanza et al., 2009). It is also clear from new research is psychology, neuroscience, sociology and a range of other disciplines that quality of life or well-being is a much more complex function than merely the more consumption of marketed goods and services the better, as reliance on GDP as a policy goal would indicate. In a recent transdisciplinary synthesis, we defined quality of life as the interaction of human needs and the subjective perception of their fulfillment, mediated by the opportunities available to meet those needs presented by the built, human, social and natural capital assets of the system (Costanza et al., 2008). New aggregate measures of quality of life are beginning to take this complex relationship into account to turn economics from 'the dismal science' into the 'science of happiness' (Layard, 2005).
2. The idea of ecological tax reform has also been gaining ground in the policy arena. The idea of taxing carbon emissions in some way[3] is now firmly on the political agenda, even in the USA. In 1996, Herman and I organized a workshop on ecological tax reform and produced a short consensus statement published in *BioScience* (Bernow et al., 1998). Our proposal consisted of the following elements:

- Levy taxes on air pollution (for example, particulates, carbon dioxide, ozone precursors and other noxious substances that are not effectively controlled).
- Rebate this revenue to the taxpayers in a way that would maintain a progressive tax structure.
- Phase the tax shift in gradually and predictably over a number of years to help ensure an orderly and low cost transition.
- Use a small portion of the tax revenues to provide transitional assistance for communities, workers and pollution-intensive industries that are strongly affected by the tax and to support the development of clean technologies.
- Address the implications for international competitiveness of those industries that are most affected by the tax.

Many of these elements are appearing in the carbon emission control ideas being proposed at both the national and international scale (cf. Barnes et al., 2008).

3. The idea of investing in natural capital, and valuing natural capital as a major contributor to human well-being is also gaining significant traction. A significant stimulus to this recognition was a paper (motivated in part by Herman's encouragement) that we published in *Nature* in 1997 (Costanza et al., 1997a).[4] We estimated (admittedly crudely and conservatively) the total value of global ecosystem services at $33 trillion per year, significantly larger than global GDP at the time. Herman reviewed this paper informally before we submitted it and gave us positive feedback and encouragement.

    The paper stimulated a broad range of reactions and discussion (Costanza et al., 1998), but it has stood the test of time and is now the second most highly cited paper in the environment area since its publication. In a later paper (Balmford et al., 2002) we estimated the benefit:cost ratio of investing in conserving remaining global natural capital at 100:1 – a great investment from society's point of view, especially considering that the Corps of Engineers funds dam building projects that have benefit:cost ratios of barely better than 1:1.

4. The mainstream idea that 'free' trade makes all parties better off, even though it ignores environmental and social externalities and other problems, has been challenged by Herman for years. As Herman has often pointed out, achieving the theoretical benefits from international trade depends on several assumptions about the nature of international markets and other institutions that simply do not hold. These assumptions include that there be: (1) no externalities; (2) stable prices; (3) equally dynamic comparative advantages; (4) no coercion in

production or exchange; and (5) no international mobility of capital. The current system lies very far from matching *any* of these conditions, but especially numbers 1 and 5. To actually make trade mutually beneficial and sustainable, the burden of proof should be shifted to the trading parties to demonstrate that adequate steps have been taken to assure that the conditions for sustainable trade are actually met as a *precondition* for trade (Costanza et al., 1995).

Herman and I, along with several other colleagues, elaborated these and many other ideas central to ecological economics in a series of books and papers in the late 1990s and 2000s (Costanza et al., 1997b, 2000; Prugh et al., 1995, 2000). In all of these joint projects, Herman has always been the perfect collaborator – using dialog and discussion to build consensus where possible, while not straying from his fundamental principles. These ideas continue to evolve, but it feels like the time has finally come for them to begin to be more broadly understood, accepted and acted upon to create the more sustainable and desirable future we all want.

3.5   JUST REWARDS: THE HEINEKEN PRIZE

Herman has received several awards and prizes over the years, but the one I remember best is the Dr A.H. Heineken Prize for Environmental Sciences, awarded to Herman by the Dutch Academy of Sciences in 1996 (see Costanza, 1997 for a longer description). I remember this one not only because I'm a lover of Heineken beer, but because I was asked to write a letter of support for Herman's nomination. This gave me the opportunity to summarize Herman's contributions as succinctly as possible and make the case for him receiving the prize. I think enough time has passed that I can reproduce the support letter here as a fitting ending and summary of this chapter.

February 11, 1996

Dr. Heineken Prize/Miliwukunde
attn: Prof. P. Nijkamp, Honorary Secretary
KNAW

I can think of no one in the world more appropriate for and deserving of the Dr. Heineken Prize for Environmental Sciences than Prof. Herman Daly. Daly has been steadily swimming against the stream for the last 20 years and the real value, magnitude, and brilliance of his contributions have only recently begun to be widely realized and appreciated. Daly's 'steady state economics' can honestly be pointed to as the intellectual progenitor of the sustainability movement, which has grown to be so important in recent years. Awarding him the Heineken Prize at this point in his career would both acknowledge and validate Herman's enormous past contributions, and give him the freedom and recognition necessary to pursue the even greater challenges of actually creating a sustainable society.

Daly was among the first economists to link the study of human systems and ecosystems, and to deal with them as an integrated whole, subject to a common set of physical and biological constraints. His 1968 article 'On economics as a life science' attempted to change the entire world view of economics. The importance of this shift in 'pre-analytic vision' cannot be overemphasized. It implies a fundamental change in the perception of the problems of resource allocation and how they should be addressed. Daly further elaborated on this theme with his work on 'steady state economics' which elaborated the implications of acknowledging that the Earth is materially finite and non-growing, and that the economy is a subset of this finite global system. Thus the economy cannot grow indefinitely (at least in a material sense) and ultimately some sort of sustainable steady state is desired. This steady state is not necessarily absolutely stable and unchanging. Like in ecosystems, things in a steady state economy are changing constantly in both periodic and aperiodic ways. The key point is that these changes are bounded and there is no long-term trend in the system.

Daly's work in steady state economics can be seen as one of the direct antecedents of ecological economics, an area of rapidly growing interest and importance. His more recent writings on natural capital and the meaning and measurement of economic welfare are particularly important. His 'Index of Sustainable Economic Welfare' has caused a major shift in thinking about wealth measurement. But to list all of Daly's achievements would be impossible in this short letter. Suffice it to say that Daly is an intellectual giant whose enormous contributions have not yet been adequately rewarded. What more fitting recipient of the Dr. Heineken Prize for Environmental Sciences.

Sincerely,

Robert Costanza

NOTES

1. Robert Herendeen and I investigated this latter claim and found it not to be true (Costanza and Herendeen, 1984).
2. For example, the journal *Sustainability Science* was launched in June 2006. Another scientific journal *SAPIENS* (*Surveys and Perspectives Integrating Environment and Society*) was launched in February 2007, and *Proceedings of the National Academy of Sciences* (PNAS) has launched a new section of their journal dedicated to sustainability science. A Google search for 'sustainability science' yielded over 700 000 hits on 11 May 2009. For comparison, a Google search for 'ecological economics' on the same day yielded over 1.5 million hits.
3. Cap and auction systems, where the permits are sold upstream (at the point where greenhouse gas emitting products enter the economy) is similar in effect to a tax, the major difference being that a cap sets the quantity and allows the price to vary, while a tax sets the price and allows the quantity to vary.
4. An interesting backstory is that we first sent the paper to *Science*. The editor there had the paper reviewed and received one positive and one negative review. He therefore declined to publish the paper, but recognized its importance and promised that when we did publish it, he would run a news story in *Science* about it, which he did.

REFERENCES

Balmford, A., A. Bruner, P. Cooper et al. (2002). Economic reasons for conserving wild nature. *Science* **297**, 950–53.

Barnes, P., R. Costanza, P. Hawken et al. (2008). Creating an earth atmospheric trust. *Science* **319**, 724.

Bernow, S., R. Costanza, H. Daly et al. (1998). Ecological tax reform. *BioScience* **48**, 193–6.

Boulding, K.E. (1966). The economics of the coming Spaceship Earth, in H. Jarrett (ed.), *Environmental Quality in a Growing Economy*. Baltimore, MD: Resources for the Future and Johns Hopkins University Press, pp. 3–14.

Costanza, R. (1980). Embodied energy and economic valuation. *Science* **210**, 1219–24.

Costanza, R. (1981a). Embodied energy, energy analysis, and economics, in H.E. Daly and A.F. Umaña (eds), *Energy, Economics and the Environment: Conflicting Views of an Essential Interrelationship*. Boulder, CO: Westview Press, pp. 119–46.

Costanza, R. (1981b). Reply: an embodied energy theory of value, in H.E. Daly and A.F. Umaña (eds), *Energy, Economics, and the Environment: Conflicting Views of an Essential Interrelationship*. Boulder, CO: Westview Press, pp. 187–92.

Costanza, R. (ed.) (1991). *Ecological Economics: The Science and Management of Sustainability*. New York: Columbia University Press.

Costanza, R. (1992). The ecological economics of sustainability: investing in natural capital, in R. Goodland, H.E. Daly and S. El Serafy (eds), *Population, Technology, and Lifestyle: The Transition to Sustainability*. Washington, DC: Island Press, pp. 106–18.

Costanza, R. (1997). Just rewards: Herman Daly, the Heineken Environmental Prize, and the Ecological Economics Best Article Award. *Ecological Economics* **22**, 1–4.

Costanza, R. (2004). Value theory and energy, in C. Cleveland (ed.), *Encyclopedia of Energy*, Vol. 6. Amsterdam: Elsevier, pp. 337–46.

Costanza, R. (2009). Science and ecological economics: integrating the study of humans and the rest of nature. *Bulletin of Science, Technology and Society* **29**, 358–73.

Costanza, R. and H.E. Daly (eds) (1987a). Ecological economics. *Special Issue of Ecological Modelling* **38** (1–2).

Costanza, R. and H.E. Daly (1987b). Toward an ecological economics. *Ecological Modelling* **38**, 1–7.

Costanza, R. and H.E. Daly (1992). Natural capital and sustainable development. *Conservation Biology* **6**, 37–46.

Costanza, R. and R.A. Herendeen (1984). Embodied energy and economic value in the United States economy: 1963, 1967, and 1972. *Resources and Energy* **6**, 129–64.

Costanza, R., B. Haskell, L. Cornwell, H. Daly and T. Johnson (1990). The ecological economics of sustainability: making local and short-term goals consistent with global and long-term goals. Environment Working Paper No. 32, The World Bank, Washington, DC.

Costanza, R., H.E. Daly and J.A. Bartholomew (1991). Goals, agenda, and policy recommendations for ecological economics, in R. Costanza (ed.), *Ecological Economics: The Science and Management of Sustainability*. New York: Columbia University Press, pp. 1–20.

Costanza, R., J. Audley, R. Borden et al. (1995). Commentary: sustainable trade. *Environment* **37** (10), 5, 38.

Costanza, R., R. d'Arge, R. de Groot et al. (1997a). The value of the world's ecosystem services and natural capital. *Nature* **387**, 253–60.

Costanza, R., J.C. Cumberland, H.E. Daly, R. Goodland and R. Norgaard (1997b). *An Introduction to Ecological Economics*. Boca Raton, FL: St Lucie Press.

Costanza, R., R. d'Arge, R. de Groot et al. (1998). The value of the world's ecosystem services: putting the issues in perspective. *Ecological Economics* **25**, 67–72.

Costanza, R., H. Daly, C. Folke et al. (2000). Managing our environmental portfolio. *BioScience* **50**, 149–55.

Costanza, R., B. Fisher, S. Ali et al. (2008). An integrative approach to quality of life measurement, research, and policy. *Surveys and Perspectives Integrating Environment and Society* **1**, 1–5, available at http://www.surv-perspect-integr-environ-soc.net/1/11/2008/ (accessed 12 December 2015).

Costanza, R., M. Hart, S. Posner and J. Talberth (2009). Beyond GDP: the need for new measures of progress. *The Pardee Papers* No. 4, The Frederick S. Pardee Center for the Study of the Longer-range Future, Boston University, Boston, MA, available at http://www.bu.edu/pardee/pardee-paper-004-beyond-gdp/ (accessed 12 December 2015).

Daly, H.E. (1968). On economics as a life science. *Journal of Political Economy* **76**, 392–406.

Daly, H.E. (1973). *Toward a Steady State Economy*. San Francisco, CA: W.H. Freeman.

Daly, H.E. (1977). *Steady State Economics: The Economics of Biophysical Equilibrium and Moral Growth*. San Francisco, CA: W.H. Freeman.

Daly, H.E. (1994). Farewell speech to the World Bank by Herman E. Daly. World Bank, Washington, DC, 14 January, in C.J. Cleveland (ed.), *Encyclopedia of Earth*. Washington, DC: Environmental Information Coalition, National Council for Science and the Environment, available at http://www.eoearth.org/view/article/51cbedc67896bb431f693d6a/ (accessed 12 December 2015).

Daly, H.E. and J. Cobb (1989). *For the Common Good: Redirecting the Economy Toward Community, the Environment, and a Sustainable Future*. Boston, MA: Beacon Press.

Daly H.E. and A.F. Umaña (eds) (1981). *Energy, Economics and the Environment: Conflicting Views of an Essential Interrelationship*. Boulder, CO: Westview Press.

Georgescu-Roegen, N. (1971). *The Entropy Law and the Economic Process*. Cambridge, MA: Harvard University Press.

Gilliland, M.W. (1975). Energy analysis and public policy, *Science* **189**, 1051–6.

Hannon, B. (1973). The structure of ecosystems. *Journal of Theoretical Biology* **41**, 535–46.

Hannon, B. (1976). Marginal product pricing in the ecosystem. *Journal of Theoretical Biology* **56**, 256–67.

Hannon, B. (1979). Total energy costs in ecosystems. *Journal of Theoretical Biology* **80**, 271–93.

Huettner, D.A. (1982). Economic values and embodied energy. *Science* **216**, 1141–3.

Jansson, A.M. (ed.) (1984). *Integration of Economy and Ecology: An Outlook for the Eighties*. Stockholm: University of Stockholm Press.

Layard, R. (2005). *Happiness: Lessons from a New Science*. New York: Penguin.

Martinez-Alier, J. (1987). *Ecological Economics: Energy, Environment, and Society*. Cambridge, MA: Blackwell.

Prugh, T., R. Costanza, J.C. Cumberland, H.E. Daly, R. Goodland and R. Norgaard (1995). *Natural Capital and Human Economic Survival*. Solomons, MD: ISEE Press (distributed by Chelsea Green and Sinaurer Presses).

Prugh, T., R. Costanza and H. Daly (2000). *The Local Politics of Global Sustainability*. Washington, DC: Island Press.

Sraffa, P. (1960). *Production of Commodities by Means of Commodities: Prelude to a Critique of Economic Theory*. Cambridge: Cambridge University Press.

PART II

Changing the paradigm: what is biophysically
possible, and how do humans behave?

4. Population, resources and energy in the global economy: a vindication of Herman Daly's vision

Jonathan M. Harris

4.1 INTRODUCTION

Herman Daly pioneered the concept of environmental macroeconomics (Daly, 1973, 1991a, 1991b, 1996). He famously argued that we have moved from an 'empty world' of resource abundance to a 'full world' of energy and resource limits (Daly and Farley, 2011, chapter 7). His insights, however, have generally been rejected or ignored by most mainstream economic analysts. From the point of view of neoclassical economic analysis, resource shortages are remediable through market flexibility and substitution, posing no threat to long-term exponential economic growth. In the absence of immediate crisis, standard economics has been able to maintain this 'optimistic' stance, dismissing population, resource and energy limits. But developments during the first decades of the twenty-first century indicate that it will be Daly's view, rather than that of the mainstream, that will be most important in shaping economic development in the coming century.

A review of global trends in the areas of population, food supply, non-renewable and renewable resources, and environmental impacts including global climate change indicate that the situation has changed significantly during the first decade and a half of the twenty-first century. Evidence of resource shortages and environmental impacts that was contentious prior to the year 2000 has become unarguable. From the point of view of the debate among economists, this is most significantly reflected in price trends. During the debate over resource limits during the second half of the twentieth century, the trump card of the neoclassical position has always been the contention that prices for food, non-renewable resources and energy were generally stable or falling. This, it was argued, indicated that substitution, innovation and resource discovery were overcoming the limits foreseen by Daly – and that this process might continue indefinitely.

Projecting declining price trends into the future was never justifiable, and it is now evident that these price trends have decisively reversed.

The most obvious and urgent environmental limit is climate change. Some analysts from a standard economics background, such as Nicholas Stern (2007), have come to realize that climate change requires profound changes in global economic growth patterns. The full implications of a transition away from fossil fuel dependence, though, have yet to be explored. As Daly foresaw, an energy economy based on high efficiency and renewable fuels cannot pursue the exponential growth path characteristic of the fossil fuel-dependent economy of the twentieth century.

The issues involved go well beyond the energy sector of the economy. Population growth and food supply also become critical. There are many interactions between the agricultural and energy systems; in addition to energy intensification in agriculture, demands for biofuels put pressure on the limited supply of agricultural land. Recent price spikes in food, fuels and minerals indicate the tremendous stresses placed on the global eco-system by the combination of population and economic growth in China, India and elsewhere. They also raise major issues of equity, as high prices for energy and food impact the poor disproportionately. Energy and food in particular tend to have inelastic demand, so relatively small restrictions on supply can lead to significant price increases.

It will not be possible to adjust to such stresses simply through market flexibility. It is already evident that large-scale government intervention will be needed to respond to climate change. Similar problems affect ecological systems such as forests and fisheries on a global scale. In this context, an activist environmental macroeconomics will be required to balance the requirements of equity and ecosystem sustainability. Either through planned adjustment or through crisis, it will be necessary to shift away from a macroeconomics of indefinite growth toward stabilization of population and reduction of resource throughput, as Daly has long advocated.

A significant literature has already developed around the concept of development without growth, or at least without growth in what Daly identified as 'throughput' – resource and energy input and waste output (Harris, 2007, 2009, 2013a, 2013b; Heinberg, 2007, 2011; Jackson, 2009; Victor, 2008, 2010). The task of accomplishing this shift, while preserving the reasonable expectations of the developing world for better conditions of life, will be immense. Standard economic theory may provide some insight into necessary tools, such as carbon trading, but it is the broader framework of Daly's ecological theory that provides the essential context for real solutions.

4.2   POPULATION AND FOOD SUPPLY

A favorite argument of those who contest the 'full world' concept has been that population problems are in effect taking care of themselves. With falling rates of fertility and population growth, world population will stabilize, according to this view, at manageable levels. Recent evidence on population growth shows this assertion to be questionable.

While population growth rates are indeed falling, the growth in total population means that the average annual increase has barely changed since reaching a maximum in the 1990s. According to the United Nations' (UN) median population projection, the net annual increase will decline in coming decades, but will not have stabilized by 2050 (Figure 4.1). This implies a net addition of 2–3 billion people above the current global population of 7 billion before stabilization. Further, the fastest addition to population is occurring in those areas that can least support it: sub-Saharan Africa and poorer parts of Asia and the Middle East. In sub-Saharan Africa, population is projected to at least double before stabilization (Table 4.1 – in the 'medium' and 'high' projection population continues to grow after 2050).

This population picture presents two types of problems, both of which were not a major factor during the period of exponential population and economic growth. First is the very real issue of carrying capacity, as global

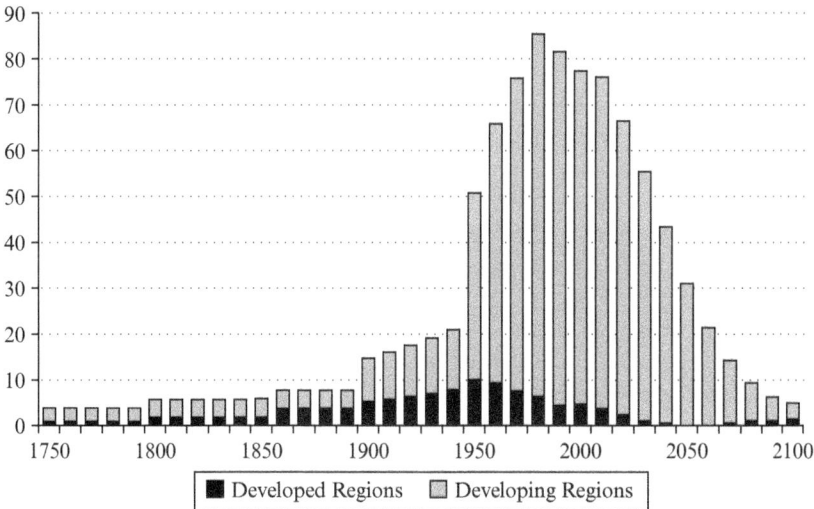

Source: United Nations Population Division (2010); medium variant: Repetto (1991).

Figure 4.1   Net annual increase in population by decade, 1750–2100

Table 4.1   Projected population growth for major world regions

| | 2010 population (million) | 2050 Population projections (million) | | |
Regions		Low fertility	Medium fertility	High fertility
Africa	1022	1932	2192	2470
Asia	4164	4458	5142	5898
Latin America and Caribbean	590	646	751	869
Europe	738	632	719	814
Northern America	345	396	447	501
Oceania	37	49	55	62
More developed regions	1236	1158	1312	1478
Less developed regions	5660	6955	7994	9136
World	6896	8112	9306	10614

Source: United Nations Population Division (2010).

population reaches levels that strain food and other essential life support systems (Figure 4.2). The other is the social problem of supporting a growing cohort of elderly people, an unavoidable result of population stabilization.

Slower population stabilization will make the first problem more acute, while faster stabilization will accentuate the second problem. In either case, as global population stabilizes, economic systems must adapt both to the greater food and resource requirements of larger populations and to their environmental and social impacts. This poses unprecedented challenges for macroeconomic policy, which has traditionally been oriented toward continuing exponential growth. The new realities of population will therefore demand new approaches to economic analysis and policy.

The first challenge posed by population growth is providing sufficient food. As Figure 4.2 shows, growth in grain production has barely kept up with population growth since the 1980s. So long as grain and other food prices remained stable, economists could argue that this slowdown was not evidence of resource constraints. Greater demand pressing on limited supply would lead to increased prices, and until recently food prices were stable or declining. But with the onset of the 'food crisis' in 2008, these price trends reversed to give a dramatic spike in food prices (Figure 4.3). Food prices again touched all-time highs in 2011, falling back in the 2012–14 period but remaining well above their previous lows around 2000 (FAO, 2014).

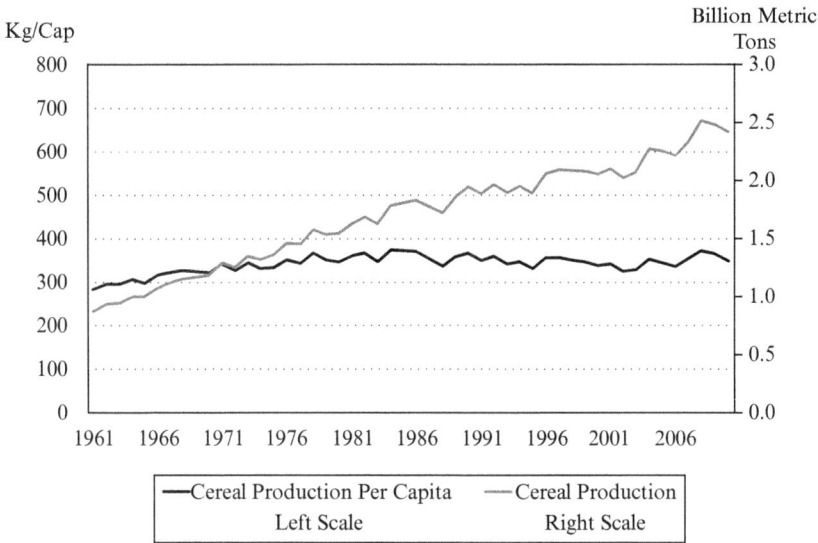

Source: World total cereal production: FAO (2011); population: World Bank (2011).

Figure 4.2   Absolute and per capita cereal production, 1950 to 2010

Increased food prices are partly attributable to a growing 'global middle class' with higher demands for meat and other luxury food products, and partly to demand for biofuels, which compete with food crops for limited arable land. The steady increase in land in cultivation from the 1950s to the 1980s, which helped to accommodate growing world food demand, has since slowed almost to a halt.[1] It appears that a higher price world food regime is a permanent change, not a temporary spike.

4.3   NON-RENEWABLE RESOURCES

The prices of non-renewable resources have also shown a recent uptrend that reverses a long-standing pattern of stable or declining prices (Figure 4.4). There have been previous periods, for example, the mid 1970s and the late 1980s, when price spikes led to some speculation that the long-term declining trend was over, but these previous price increases proved temporary. This may yet be the case with the current price spikes for many minerals, but while there has been some commodity price decline since 2013, prices are still well above 2000 levels.

A major factor in increasing prices for non-renewable resources is the

FAO Monthly Food Price Index, 1990–2012
(2002–2004 = 100)

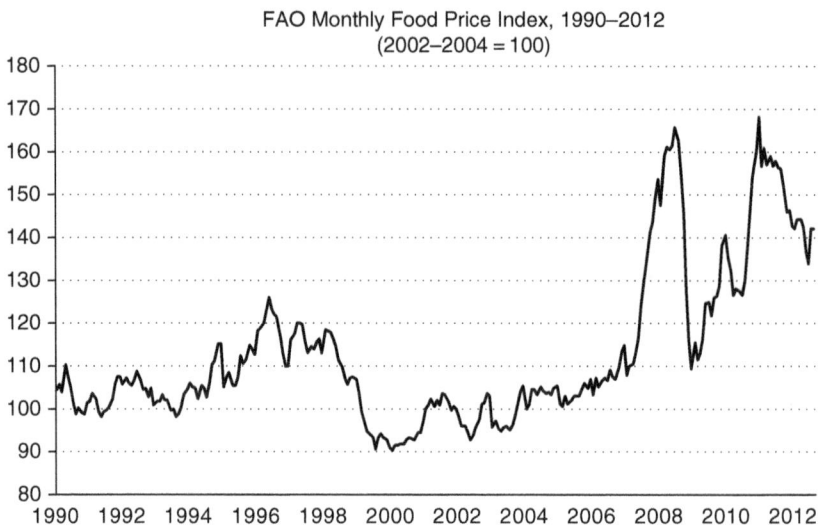

Source: FAO (2014).

Figure 4.3   Food Price Index, 1990–2012

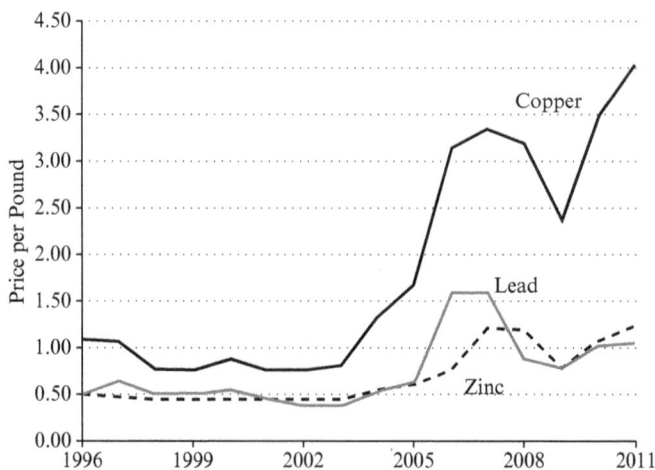

Source: USGS (2014).

Figure 4.4   Price trends for selected minerals (price per pound)

rapidly growing demand from fast-developing nations including China, India and Brazil. An increasing price trend for non-renewables is, of course, consistent with fundamental exhaustible resource theory as first set forth by Hotelling in the 1930s (Hotelling, 1931).[2] The theory, however, can be confounded by long periods and high discount rates: if exhaustion of a resource is not foreseen within the medium-term future, potential future shortages will not be reflected in current prices. Rising prices indicate that future shortages have begun to enter the consciousness of today's commodity traders. This does not mean imminent exhaustion of the entire resource, but rather a shift to more expensive extraction of lower-grade ores (Heinberg, 2011, chapter 3). These rising extraction costs are in turn associated with higher current or projected energy prices. Both higher extraction costs for energy resources themselves and the increased use of energy in lower-grade resource extraction contribute to this trend.

4.4   ECOSYSTEMS AND RENEWABLE RESOURCES

Ecologists identify a number of major areas in which current economic activities are systematically undermining the planet's long-term carrying capacity. These include:

- Erosion and degradation of topsoil; topsoil losses worldwide are currently estimated at 24 billion tons annually, with nearly 11 percent of the world's vegetated land suffering moderate to extreme degradation (Ehrlich et al., 2003).
- Overuse and pollution of fresh water supplies – a problem in virtually every country, reaching critical levels in China, India and parts of the former Soviet Union (Postel, 2003).
- Loss of biodiversity, with more species driven to extinction every year than at any time in the preceding 65 million years of planetary history (Hooper et al., 2012).
- Extreme climate fluctuations resulting in heat waves, drought, flooding and disruption of water supplies (IPCC, 2013).
- Collapse of fisheries and other overexploited ecosystems, with associated irreversible effects due to changes in species balance and invasive species.

Recent articles in *Nature* and *Science* suggest that these trends are approaching a 'tipping point' leading to an irreversible 'planetary-scale transition' (Barnosky et al., 2012; Steffen et al., 2015). This transition to a less diverse, less productive planetary ecosystem will have profound effects

Table 4.2   Declining major fisheries

Ocean area	Estimated annual potential (million tons)	Year potential reached	Decline from peak yield (%)
East Central Atlantic	4	1984	−22
Northwest Atlantic	4	1971	−38
Southeast Atlantic	3	1978	−53
West Central Atlantic	2	1987	−28
East Central Pacific	3	1988	−13
Northeast Pacific	4	1990	−12
Southwest Pacific	1	1991	−13
Antarctic	0.2	1980	unavailable
World	82	1999	unavailable

Source: FAO (1997); McGinn (1999).

for human well-being (Cardinale et al., 2012; Millennium Ecosystem Assessment, 2005a, 2005b). The prospect of ecological collapse should also have a major effect on principles of economic analysis. Economists have basically ignored macro-level ecological impacts, which are difficult to capture as 'externalities.' They can only adequately be addressed by considering Daly's principle of limits to economic scale. Clearly, this issue has now moved beyond a theoretical consideration for the future, and is a pressing immediate concern.

The broader ecosystem changes and their impact on human well-being can be difficult to quantify, but we can see a well-defined example of the phenomenon in fisheries. Many of the world's major fisheries have passed their peak sustainable yield, and are now in decline (Table 4.2). The global wild fish catch appears to have peaked around 1995 and has been stable or slightly declining since then (Figure 4.5). Expansion of aquaculture production has enabled overall output to keep up with population growth, but per capita catch has not increased since about 1970.[3] And of course many forms of aquaculture have significant environment problems, implying that this increase cannot continue indefinitely.

Fisheries thus provide a case study in approaching and reaching carrying capacity. It is possible that better fisheries management could prevent fishery collapse, but the essence of good fishery management is to limit catch to a level at or below sustainable yield. Even a global institution of good fishery practices (consistent with an economic principle of maximizing net social benefit) cannot expand fishery output much beyond current levels. For fisheries, as well as for an increasing number of ecosystems including inland water, forest and wetland biomes, human demand is

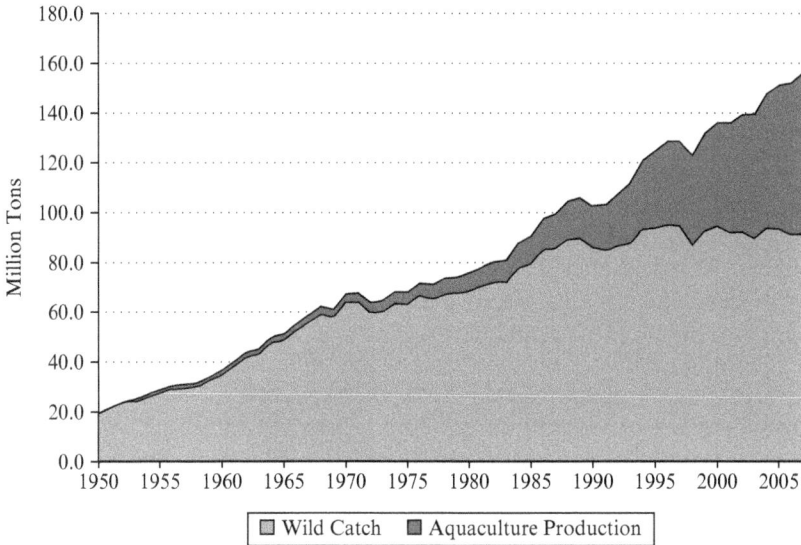

Source: FAOSTAT Statistical Database, http://www.fao.org/fishery/statistics/software/fishstat/en, updated February 2011 (accessed 1 December 2014).

Figure 4.5   Wild fish catch and aquaculture production

now clearly pressing up against carrying capacity on both regional and global scales. This suggests that Daly's concept of a 'biocentric optimum' taking into account ecosystem capacity, rather than an 'anthropocentric optimum' based on marginal costs and benefits, is essential for effective management of human/ecosystem interactions (Daly, 1996, chapter 2).

4.5   ENERGY AND CLIMATE

In the ecological perspective championed by Daly, energy and the entropic limits on energy use have a special importance, following the principles set out in Nicholas Georgescu-Roegen's fundamental work on energy and the economic process (Georgescu-Roegen, 1971). The entropy principle points to three essential limits on energy use: the planetary supply of non-renewable energy resources; the solar flux; and the ability of the ecosphere to absorb the wastes produced by energy consumption.

The first of these has received much attention in the recent debate over 'peak oil.' Estimates of 'ultimately recoverable' oil vary widely. Worldwide cumulative oil consumption is now about 1.1 billion barrels, and some analysts believe that there is only about another 1 trillion barrels of extract-able oil remaining. If this is true, we are at or close to a global peak, given well-established patterns of 'peak oil' for individual nations such as the USA. More optimistic estimates of ultimately recoverable oil, including natural gas liquids and 'unconventional' sources, would extend the period until the peak for at least several decades (Campbell, 2005; Campbell and Laherrère, 1998; Deffeyes, 2001, 2005; Hall and Klitgaard, 2012, chapter 15; Heinberg, 2007). Even if the more optimistic estimates of ultimately recov-erable oil prove true, the extension of the peak is dependent on the recovery of oil from unconventional sources such as shale and very deep water, which are generally higher-cost and have more severe environmental impacts.

The more binding constraint on energy use has to do with its waste products, in particular carbon dioxide. The lifetime of fossil fuels could in theory be extended significantly by increased reliance on coal and its derivatives. But of course coal, along with some kinds of unconventional oil, represents the dirtiest of fossil fuels. As Figure 4.6 shows, carbon emis-sions from fossil fuel use have risen steadily, with no sign of stabilization, let alone reduction. Despite numerous warnings from scientists, global economic growth remains tied to fossil fuels. Given the highly unequal

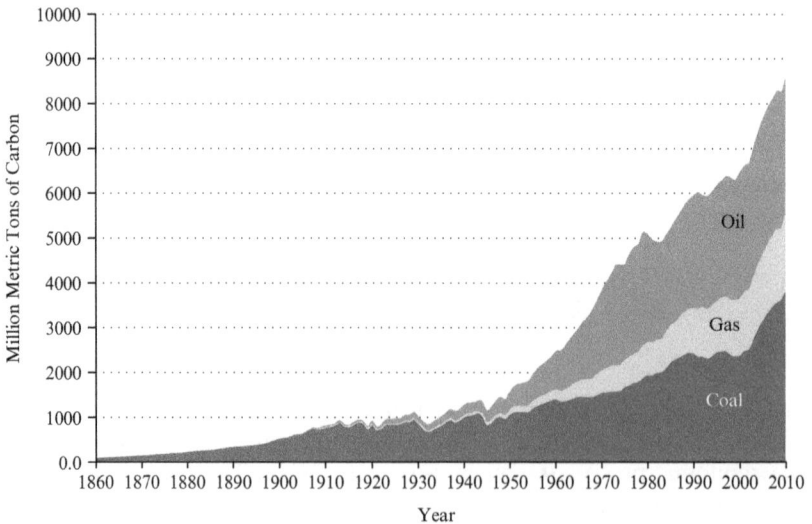

Source: http://cdiac.ornl.gov/trends/emis/glo.html (accessed February 2015).

Figure 4.6   Global carbon emissions from fossil fuel consumption, 1860–2010

distribution of per capita consumption and per capita emissions, there is certain to be further significant demand growth from the developing world in coming decades.

Despite numerous warnings from scientists, little has been done to internalize the true costs of carbon or to slow emissions growth. There is a huge disconnect between 'business as usual' and the recommendations of scientific groups such as the Intergovernmental Panel on Climate Change (IPCC). The IPCC has called for stabilization of carbon *accumulations* at no more than 450–550 parts per million, which requires drastic reduction in carbon *emissions*. Many scientists believe that even these targets are insufficient to keep warming below 2°C. Even at 2°C there is a possibility of catastrophic consequences such as destabilization of the Greenland ice sheet, causing up to 7 meters of sea-level rise (Hansen et al., 2007). Two scientific models including deep-sea warming have indicated that carbon dioxide (CO_2) emissions must fall to near zero by the mid twenty-first century to prevent temperature increases in the range of 4°C (7°F) by 2100 (Baer et al., 2009; Harris, 2009; IPCC, 2014; Matthews and Caldeira, 2008; Schmittner et al., 2008). Regardless of the accumulation target chosen, emissions must eventually fall to the natural planetary absorption capacity to stabilize at any level. Any carbon reductions even approaching these recommendations obviously imply major changes in patterns of global economic growth – again suggesting the essential role of Daly's concept of entropic limits.

An entropic perspective implies a massive transition away from fossil fuel dependence, with the use of fossil fuels strictly limited and a far more efficient economic system powered directly or indirectly from the flux of solar energy. One economic interpretation of this would be a strategy of 'decoupling' economic growth from energy use. In theory, economic growth could continue while energy use is reduced through greater efficiency, and carbon emissions further reduced by a transition to renewable energy sources. To a very limited degree, this is already occurring: economic systems are becoming somewhat more energy-efficient, and renewable power sources such as wind and solar are experiencing rapid growth.[4]

Theorists advocating 'prosperity without growth' argue that such 'decoupling has practical limits' (Hall and Klitgaard, 2012; Jackson, 2009; Victor, 2008). The deeply rooted dependence of current economies on fossil fuels offers opportunities for decoupling, but would require fundamental changes in the nature of growth – and in terms of energy and resource throughput, an end or reversal of growth – in order to achieve the kinds of carbon reduction targets suggested by the IPCC and other scientists. Decoupling is certainly needed, involving massive investment in energy efficiency and renewable supply systems, but these theorists suggest that reduced consumption and lifestyle changes are also essential, at least for the currently developed economies.

4.6   MACROECONOMIC THEORY PERSPECTIVES

In his essay, 'Elements of environmental macroeconomics' Daly suggests that the main requirement for macroeconomics to adapt to real-world limits is to adopt a macroeconomic goal of *optimal economic scale* to accompany goals of full employment, price level stability and distributive justice (Daly, 1991a, chapter 2). This would certainly represent a major shift away from the current structure of mainstream macroeconomics. Distributive justice does not rank high among standard macroeconomic goals, and any concept of scale is completely absent. What would it mean for macroeconomics to start, at last, to take Daly's proposition seriously?

One approach to answering this question is to modify macroeconomic growth models. There appears to be no reason why standard economic models, such as the Solow growth model, cannot be adjusted to take into account resource constraints. Interestingly, Solow himself has recently commented:

> There is no reason at all why capitalism could not survive with slow or even no growth. I think it's perfectly possible that economic growth cannot go on at its current rate forever . . . it is possible that the US and Europe will find that . . . either continued growth will be too destructive to the environment and they are too dependent on scarce natural resources, or that they would rather use increasing productivity in the form of leisure . . . There is nothing intrinsic in the system that says it cannot exist happily in a stationary state. (Robert Solow, quoted in Stoll, 2008)

Without an assumption of steady technological progress, Solow-type growth models converge to a steady state of constant output per worker (Solow, 1970). It is the assumption of technological progress that causes the model to exhibit continual growth in per capita income. Adding a resource constraint to Solow-type growth models can offset the effects of technological progress, leading to convergence to a steady state of output per worker. If population also stabilizes to a zero rate of growth, this will give an overall steady-state equilibrium.[5]

An alternative approach is to offset the effects of technological progress with a decreased input of labor time per worker (a shorter work day and/ or work week). This approach is central to the model presented by Victor (2008). This corresponds to Solow's suggestion above that increased productivity be taken in the form of leisure. This also harks back to speculation by J.S. Mill (1994) that satiation of material needs would lead to a cessation of economic growth – an outcome that Mill viewed as desirable.

There is thus no formal reason why macroeconomic models need to reflect an assumption of perpetual economic growth. This assumption, however, is deeply embedded in most approaches to macroeconomics, whether at the professional or textbook level. In practical terms, the main reason for this nearly universal acceptance of the necessity of economic growth has to do with the need to maintain employment. In real-life experience, whenever economic growth falters or temporarily reverses, as in a recession,[6] unemployment rises. The solution to unemployment is therefore widely seen as a resumption of economic growth. But this is a result of a perspective based on experience with current institutions and accepted economic policies.

In the current situation of a seriously depressed economy, Keynesian expansionary policies to promote a recovery may be essential, as advocated by Krugman (2012). But in the longer term, full employment does not necessarily depend on continued exponential growth. Full employment is possible in a steady-state economy, but it requires different institutions from those that prevail in current market economies (Victor, 2008, 2010).[7] The barriers to achieving well-being without economic growth, at least in advanced economies, are therefore political and institutional rather than economic.

A central issue for economic theory is whether more traditional Keynesian economic policies can be combined with a theory of resource and environmental limits to adapt to new realities. I have argued elsewhere that a 'green Keynesianism' is possible, and indeed essential, for adaptation of economies to carbon constraints and environmental sustainability (Harris, 2007, 2009, 2013a, 2013b). Specifically, I suggest that:

> There is a close complementarity between new Keynesian and ecological perspectives. While older Keynesian analysis was oriented towards promoting growth, a true Keynesian analysis of the relationship between investment and consumption does not depend on a growth orientation. What this analysis has in common with an ecological perspective is the rejection of market optimality assumed in classical models. Moving away from the neoclassical goal of intertemporal utility maximization allows for different, pluralistic economic goals: full employment, provision of basic needs, social and infrastructure investment, and income equity. These goals are compatible with environmental preservation and resource sustainability, whereas indefinite growth is not. But they require a revitalization of the sphere of social investment, seriously neglected (indeed often omitted completely) in standard models. (Harris, 2013a, pp. 33–4)

There is a good precedent for this approach in Keynes's own writings. In 'Economic possibilities for our grandchildren' Keynes envisioned an end to economic growth. He suggested that a different structure of economic incentives and values would be appropriate for a world in which material economic growth had ceased. In his essay on 'The end of laissez-faire,' he also recognized the importance of social direction of investment in achieving what he anticipated to be a better economic system: 'I believe that some coordinated act of intelligent judgement is required as to the scale on which it is desirable that the community as a whole should save . . . and whether the present organization of the investment market distributes savings along the most nationally productive channels. I do not think that these matters should be left entirely to the chances of private judgement and private profits, as they are at present' (Keynes, 1963, p. 173). Keynes also famously proclaimed that 'The outstanding faults of the economic society in which we live are its failure to provide for full employment and its arbitrary and inequitable distribution of wealth and incomes' (Keynes, 1964, p. 372) – a statement that seems to have particular contemporary resonance.[8]

Daly, like Keynes, recognizes the importance of orienting theory and policy toward goals of social investment and economic justice. Mainstream economic theory has moved far from this perspective. This is what makes mainstream theory an unreliable guide to responding to today's problems. The assumption of a self-regulating, self-adjusting economic equilibrium makes it essentially impossible to respond to problems like the need for a major energy transition or adjustment to a society with a stabilized population and a higher proportion of elderly. The Keynesian perspective transforms problems into solutions: massive investment in a clean energy transition, or in health and elder care services, generate employment and so appear not as net costs but as net benefits to society.

From the point of view of the developing world, an end to growth hardly seems like an encouraging prospect. But very different growth paths are possible. Investment in energy efficiency, renewable energy systems, clean water, basic health care, primary and secondary education, forest conservation and sustainable resource use and so on provide extensive possibilities for generation of employment without damaging the environment. In the long term, the growth of resource 'throughput' must end, but in the medium term a better goal is 'convergence,' with declining use in the global North, based on efficiency and lifestyle change rather than deprivation, and modestly increasing use in the global South.

Scientists have told us in no uncertain terms that unless we adapt our economic systems to planetary limits we face catastrophe before the end of the twenty-first century (Barnosky et al., 2012; Hooper et al., 2012; Matthews and Caldeira, 2008; Schmittner et al., 2008; Steffen et al., 2015). It is up to economists to respond, and there are plenty of options available in the microeconomic and macroeconomic toolkits if we choose to use them.

Neoclassical economics, despite its tunnel vision on many of the 'big' questions, may be effective in determining efficient solutions once better goals are identified. Keynesian economics provides avenues for infrastructure investment and employment generation that can be redirected to 'green' ends. The school of ecological economics inspired by Daly provides new forms of analysis more specifically appropriate for ecosystem functions and resource limits (see, for example, Costanza and Farber, 2002; Costanza et al., 2004; Malghan, 2010). By building on this rich legacy, the discipline of economics can contribute to, rather than retard, the process of finding solutions to the twenty-first century-challenges of population, environment, development and well-being.

NOTES

1. See Harris and Roach (2014, chapter 10) and http://faostat3.fao.org/ (accessed 1 December 2014) for data on arable land area.
2. See Harris and Roach (2014, chapters 5 and 11) for an exposition of the theory of non-renewable resources.
3. See Harris and Roach (2014, chapter 13); per capita catch has remained at about 16 kg per capita since 1970, after doubling from 8 kg per capita between 1950 and 1970.
4. See Harris and Roach (2014, chapters 12 and 17) for data on reduced energy intensity in industrial economies and expansion of renewable energy sources.
5. See Cleveland (2003) for an exposition of resource constraints in standard models of economic growth and review of relevant literature.
6. A recession is defined as 'a significant decline in economic activity spread across the economy, lasting more than a few months, normally visible in real GDP, real income, employment, industrial production, and wholesale-retail sales.' See http://www.nber.org/cycles.html (accessed 1 December 2014).
7. See also Lawn (Chapter 8 in this volume).
8. See Harris (2013b) for further discussion of the specific potential of 'green Keynesianism.'

REFERENCES

Baer, P., T. Athanasiou and S. Kartha (2009), 'The right to development in a climate-constrained world', in J.M. Harris and N.R. Goodwin (eds), *Twenty-first Century Macroeconomics: Responding to the Climate Challenge*, Cheltenham, UK and Northampton, MA, USA: Edward Elgar Publishing, pp. 75–114.

Barnosky, A.D., E.A. Hadly, J. Bascompte et al. (2012), 'Approaching a state shift in earth's biosphere', *Nature*, **486** (June), 52–8.

Campbell, C.J. (2005), 'The end of the first half of the age of oil', paper presented at the 5th ASPO (Association for the Study of Peak Oil and Gas) Conference, Lisbon, Portugal, available at http://www.cge.uevora.pt/aspo2005/abscom/ASPO2005_Lisbon_Campbell.pdf (accessed February 2015).

Campbell, C.J. and J. Laherrère (1998), 'The end of cheap oil', *Scientific American*, March, 78–83.

Cardinale, B.J., J.E. Duffy, A. Gonzalez et al. (2012), 'Biodiversity loss and its impact on humanity', *Nature*, **486** (June), 59–67.

Cleveland, C.J. (2003), 'Biophysical constraints to economic growth', in D. Al Gobaisi (ed.), *Encyclopedia of Life Support Systems*, Oxford: EOLSS Publishers.

Costanza, R. and S. Farber (2002), 'Introduction to the special issue on the dynamics and value of ecosystem services: integrating economic and ecological perspectives', *Ecological Economics*, **41**, 367–73.

Costanza, R., D. Stern, B. Fisher, L. He and C. Ma (2004), 'Influential publications in ecological economics: a citation analysis', *Ecological Economics*, **50** (3–4), 261–92.

Daly, H.E. (ed.) (1973), *Toward a Steady State Economy*, San Francisco, CA: W.H. Freeman.

Daly, H.E. (1991a), 'Elements of environmental macroeconomics', in R. Costanza (ed.), *Ecological Economics: The Science and Management of Sustainability*, New York: Columbia University Press, pp. 32–46.

Daly, H.E. (1991b), *Steady-state Economics*, Washington, DC: Island Press.

Daly, H.E. (1996), *Beyond Growth: The Economics of Sustainable Development*, Boston, MA: Beacon Press.

Daly, H.E. and J. Farley (2011), *Ecological Economics: Principles and Applications*, Washington, DC: Island Press.

Deffeyes, K.S. (2001), *Hubbert's Peak: The Impending World Oil Shortage*, Princeton, NJ: Princeton University Press.

Deffeyes, K.S. (2005), *Beyond Oil: The View from Hubbert's Peak*, New York: Hill and Wang.

Ehrlich, P.R., A.H. Ehrlich and G. Daily (2003), 'Food security, population, and environment', in D.E. Lorey (ed.), *Global Environmental Challenges of the Twenty-first Century: Resources, Consumption, and Sustainable Solutions*, Wilmington, DE: Scholarly Resources, pp. 15–36.

FAO (1997), *The State of World Fisheries and Agriculture*, Rome: Food and Agriculture Organization of the United Nations.

FAO (2011), *FAOSTAT*, Food and Agriculture Organization of the United Nations, available at http://faostat.fao.org/ (accessed 15 September 2011).

FAO (2014), *World Food Situation: FAO Food Price Index*, Food and Agriculture Organization of the United Nations, available at http://www.fao.org/worldfood-situation/foodpricesindex/en/ (accessed December 2014).

Georgescu-Roegen, N. (1971), *The Entropy Law and the Economic Process*, Cambridge, MA: Harvard University Press.

Hall, C.A.S. and K.A. Klitgaard (2012), *Energy and the Wealth of Nations: Understanding the Biophysical Economy*, New York and London: Springer.

Hansen, J., M. Sato, R. Ruedy et al. (2007), 'Dangerous human-made interference with climate: a GISS modelE study', *Atmospheric Chemistry and Physics*, **7** (9), 2287–312.

Harris, J.M. (2007), 'Reorienting macroeconomic theory towards environmental sustainability', in J.M. Gowdy and J.D. Erickson (eds), *Frontiers in Ecological Economic Theory and Application*, Cheltenham, UK and Northampton, MA, USA: Edward Elgar Publishing, pp. 36–52.

Harris, J.M. (2009), 'Ecological macroeconomics: consumption, investment, and climate change', in J.M. Harris and N.R. Goodwin (eds), *Twenty-first Century*

Macroeconomics: Responding to the Climate Challenge, Cheltenham, UK and Northampton, MA, USA: Edward Elgar Publishing, pp. 169–88, available at http://www.ase.tufts.edu/gdae/Pubs/wp/08-02EcologMacroEconJuly08.pdf (accessed 1 December 2014).

Harris, J.M. (2013a), 'The macroeconomics of development without through-put growth', in M.J. Cohen, H.S. Brown and P.J. Vergragt (eds), *Innovations in Sustainable Consumption: New Economics, Socio-technical Transitions, and Social Practices*, Cheltenham, UK and Northampton, MA, USA: Edward Elgar Publishing, pp. 31–47, earlier version available at http://www.ase.tufts.edu/gdae/publications/working_papers/index.html (accessed 1 December 2014).

Harris, J.M. (2013b), 'Green Keynesianism: beyond standard growth paradigms', in R.B. Richardson (ed.), *Building a Green Economy: Perspectives from Ecological Economics*, East Lansing, MI: Michigan State University Press, pp. 69–82.

Harris, J. and B. Roach (2014), *Environmental and Resource Economics: A Contemporary Approach*, 3rd edn, New York: Routledge, available at http://www.ase.tufts.edu/gdae/publications/textbooks/env_nat_res_economics.html (accessed 1 December 2014).

Heinberg, R. (2007), *Peak Everything: Waking Up to the Century of Declines*, Gabriola, BC: New Society Publishers.

Heinberg, R. (2011), *The End of Growth: Adapting to Our New Economic Reality*, Gabriola, BC: New Society Publishers.

Hooper, D.U., E.C. Adair, B.J. Cardinale et al. (2012), 'A global synthesis reveals biodiversity loss as a major driver of ecosystem change', *Nature*, **486** (June), 105–8.

Hotelling, H. (1931), 'The theory of exhaustible resources', *Journal of Political Economy*, **39** (April), 137–75.

IPCC (2013), *Climate Change 2013: The Physical Science Basis*, Intergovernmental Panel on Climate Change, available at http://www.ipcc.ch/ (accessed 1 December 2014).

IPCC (2014), *Climate Change 2014: Synthesis Report*, Intergovernmental Panel on Climate Change, available at http://www.ipcc.ch/ (accessed 1 December 2014).

Jackson, T. (2009), *Prosperity Without Growth: Economics for a Finite Planet*, London: Earthscan Publishing.

Keynes, J.M. (1963), *Essays in Persuasion*, New York: W.W. Norton & Co.

Keynes, J.M. (1964), *The General Theory of Employment, Interest, and Money*, New York: Harcourt, Brace.

Krugman, P. (2012), *End This Depression Now!*, New York and London: W.W. Norton.

Malghan, D. (2010), 'On the relationship between scale, allocation, and distribution', *Ecological Economics*, **69**, 2261–70.

Matthews, H.D. and K. Caldeira (2008), 'Stabilizing climate requires near-zero emissions', *Geophysical Research Letters*, **35** (27 February).

McGinn, A.P. (1999), 'Safeguarding the health of oceans', Worldwatch Paper No. 145, Worldwatch Institute.

Mill, J.S. (1994), *Principles of Political Economy and Chapters on Socialism*, edited with an introduction by J. Riley, Oxford and New York: Oxford University Press.

Millennium Ecosystem Assessment (2005a), *Ecosystems and Human Well-being: Synthesis*, Washington, DC: World Resources Institute.

Millennium Ecosystem Assessment (2005b), *Ecosystems and Human Well-being: Current State and Trends*, Vol. 1, Washington, DC: World Resources Institute.

Postel, S. (2003), 'Water for food production: will there be enough in 2025?', in D.E. Lorey (ed.), *Global Environmental Challenges of the Twenty-first Century: Resources, Consumption, and Sustainable Solutions*, Wilmington, DE: Scholarly Resources, pp. 51–70.

Repetto, R. (1991), *Population, Resources, Environment: An Uncertain Future*, Washington, DC: Population Reference Bureau.

Schmittner, A., A. Oschlies, H.D. Matthews and E.D. Galbraith (2008), 'Future changes in climate, ocean circulation, ecosystems, and biogeochemical cycling simulated for a business-as-usual CO_2 emission scenario until year 4000 AD', *Global Biogeochemical Cycles*, **22** (1), 1–21.

Solow, R.M. (1970), *Growth Theory: An Exposition*, New York: Oxford University Press.

Steffen, W., K. Richardson, J. Rockström et al. (2015), 'Planetary boundaries; guiding human development on a changing planet', *Science*, **347** (6223), doi: 10.1126/science.1259855.

Stern, N. (2007), *The Economics of Climate Change: The Stern Review*, Cambridge: Cambridge University Press, available at http://www.hm-treasury.gov.uk/ sternreview_index.htlml (accessed 1 December 2014).

Stoll, S. (2008), 'Fear of fallowing: the specter of a no-growth world', *Harper's Magazine*, March, p. 94.

United Nations Population Division (2010), *World Population Prospects: The 2010 Revision*, Population Division, Population Estimates and Projections Section, Department of Economic and Social Affairs, United Nations, available at http:// esa.un.org/unpd/wpp/index.htm (accessed 15 September 2011).

USGS (2014), *Historical Statistics for Mineral and Material Commodities in the United States*, US Geological Survey Data Series 140, available at http:// minerals.usgs.gov/ds/2005/140/ (accessed 1 December 2014).

Victor, P.A. (2008), *Managing Without Growth: Slower by Design, Not Disaster*, Cheltenham, UK and Northampton, MA, USA: Edward Elgar Publishing.

Victor, P.A. (2010), 'Ecological economics and economic growth', *Annals of the New York Academy of Sciences*, **1185**, 237–45.

World Bank (2011), 'Data', available at http://data.worldbank.org/indicator/ SP.POP.TOTL.

5. On limits

Arild Vatn

5.1 INTRODUCTION

Economics is first about scale, then about distribution and last about allocation. If we were to rank the core messages from the extensive work of Herman Daly, this would – despite the brute simplification – probably make it to the top. The issue of scale concerns the size of the economy compared to the capacities of the biosphere into which it is embedded. Hence, his position may be seen to pioneer the self-reflection of humanity at the stage of our development where the environmental consequences of human action have grown global. If we now provoke the failing of the biosphere to sustain our lives well, there would be no new place to go, no 'new frontier' for future generations to exploit.

Mainstream economic theory describes a world with unlimited options for substitution. It is moreover a position that is largely underpinning economic policy across the entire globe. Economic growth is a goal that goes unquestioned in most policy circles. Certainly, economic growth for those in poverty is morally unquestionable. However, its value as a basis for policy among the rich is far less obvious. Actually, it is rather such that we – the rich – should be more careful and leave as much space as possible for the poor who need to expand their consumption and hence the use of environmental resources.

So we should think seriously about limits. This chapter is about two kinds: those that are natural in the sense that they are characteristics of the physical and biological world in which we live, and those we have constructed. Moreover, our perceptions of limits may deviate from the reality of limits. Some natural limits may be seen as non-existent and some humanly constructed limits may be seen as 'natural' – that is, as something we cannot change. Hence, while natural resources and human needs are seen as unlimited among the mainstream, human motivation is limited to individual utility calculations only. When forming policies, it is crucial how we perceive our boundaries and capacities. We may try to do away with limits that cannot be surpassed and we might take as given limits that are only in our perceptions/that we actually can change.

In disentangling these issues, I shall start with the rather recent construction of a 'no limits' perspective in areas where natural or real limits nevertheless seem to exist. Next, I look at three sets of limits – the environmental, the social and human, and finally those of the economic system – discussing which are real and which are constructed implying that we also should be able to change them. I shall close with a discussion of ways to reduce the limitations we have constructed ourselves to make the hope for sustainability become real.

5.2   CONSTRUCTING 'NO LIMIT'

Mainstream economics has in a certain sense managed to remove resource limits from the agenda. In the world of this discipline there are no absolute limits, only relative ones. A few lines from Robert Solow illustrate my point:

> history tells us an important fact, namely, that goods and services can be substituted for one another. If you don't eat one species of fish, you can eat another species of fish. Resources are, to use a favorite word of economists, fungible in a certain sense. They can take the place of each other. That is extremely important because it suggests that we do not owe to the future any particular thing. There is no specific object that the goal of sustainability, the obligation of sustainability, requires us to leave untouched . . . Sustainability doesn't require that any *particular* species of fish or any *particular* tract of forest be preserved. (Solow, 1993, p. 181, emphases in original).[1]

The only real limit we face according to the prevailing orthodoxy is that of our capacity measured in the form of the budget constraint. By making the economy grow, that limit is shifted outwards and hence the only limit we face regards actually the speed of growth. How could the profession end up here?

5.2.1   Economics: How Did 'Nature' Disappear?

While economics is a rather new discipline, economic questions have certainly been of interest to people at 'all times.' It is well known that the Greek concepts *oikos/oikonomia* (*oikos*: house; *oikonomia*: house holding) form the origin of the concept of economics. According to Schumpeter (1954), *oikonomia* meant only practical wisdom of household management. While this is probably too narrow an interpretation (for example, Polanyi, 1968), it is important to note that for the Greek, the interdependency between humans and the physical nature was essential to the economic process – note also *oikos* as base for the concept of ecology. The Greek seems to have looked at the material aspects of the economy in quite static terms though. They emphasized issues concerning which soil was best for a specific type of crop, how much time was needed to take good care of a field and so on.

In the Western world, there is a long period from ancient Greece to the late medieval Europe where economics was not an important topic as a scholarly theme.[2] Economic thought first evolved into a more complete theory with the French Physiocrats of the middle eighteenth century. They saw natural resources in the form of land as the source of all wealth. Crossing the Channel we observe the establishment of classical economics a few decades later with the works of Smith, Ricardo and Malthus. While forming a broader theory of the economic process, land still played a crucial role in their analyses. These authors were active in the early stages of industrialization. The institutions of the economy became more and more separated from those of general societal life (Polanyi, 1944 [1957]). Hence, it is not difficult to understand that the development of economics as a separate discipline happened around the turn of the eighteenth century. It was also a period giving birth to unprecedented economic growth. The question whether this development could be sustained arose early on. Malthus (1803 [1992], 1836 [1968]) argued, as we know, that the productivity of land would become a constraint on future growth. Land was a fixed resource and the ability to increase its yields could not keep pace with population growth. Therefore subsistence costs would increase over time and growth would finally cease. Ricardo (1817 [1973]) emphasized that new land could be cleared for agriculture and that this would counteract the Malthusian poverty trap. However, new land was less productive, so even Ricardo concluded that growth had its limits.

Neither Malthus nor Ricardo included technological change in their analyses. Nor did they foresee the tremendous effect of expanded fossil fuel use on economic growth made possible by new technology. Mill, who was active some decades later, emphasized the role of technological change, and the focus shifted from looking only at land and labor as the main production factors to also including produced capital. Technology or produced capital counteracted the 'natural limits to growth' (Mill, 1848 [1965]). During his lifetime the use of minerals in the economy increased substantially, and he hence showed an interest in exhaustible resources like coal. His interest in the environment made him further include the value of nature as a source of inspiration and recreation in his writings. Finally, Mill may have been the first to advocate a steady state of the economy based both on ideas about the limits of nature and a perception of what would be a good life to live.[3] As part of that, Mill advocated rather radical ideas concerning redistribution of wealth.

The idea of limits to growth continued to be influential for some time even into the era of neoclassical economics. Jevons at least was interested in the issue. He was especially engaged in one of Mill's themes, the scarcity of coal or energy supply (Jevons, 1865 [1965]). He believed that progress would collapse as limited coal supplies were exhausted. Interestingly enough, he looked into potential alternative sources like wind, tide and bio-energy – issues that have resurfaced lately.

The worries soon vanished, however. Jevons was himself part of a movement shifting the focus from resources and production – the classical economist perspectives – to exchange processes – the neoclassical perspective. Land as a specific resource became relatively less important for the economy, and the standard production function in the neoclassical texts shifted over time to contain just capital and labor. Nature as a separate input and separate problem to worry about almost disappeared. It is easy to envisage that the tremendous changes in production capacity flowing from abundant availability of new sources of fossil fuels – especially oil – and continuous technological change influenced this.

When the Club of Rome launched the book *Limits to Growth* (Meadows et al., 1972) – bringing up again some of the Malthusian questions – the message was heavily countered by neoclassical economists such as Partha Dasgupta, Geoffrey Heal, Robert Solow and Joseph Stiglitz. Their argument was principally that the capability to replace natural resources with man-made capital could sustain unlimited growth (Dasgupta and Heal, 1974; Solow, 1974; Stiglitz, 1974). The rather curious thing was that the 'proof' delivered depended not on a thorough evaluation of the functioning of nature, but on using growth models with substitution elasticities between natural and man-made capital equal to or larger than one – for example, Cobb-Douglas technology – and making no distinction between stock-flow and fund-service resources.[4] These kinds of production functions had become conventions of the profession. Certainly, if the world was as these models describe, the conclusion would be obvious. While it seems like much of the conclusion ran from unsubstantiated assumptions about nature, one must acknowledge that 'history had shown' (compare with the previous citation from Solow) that growth had been possible despite the fact that we were running out of some resources. However, generalizing from this that there would always be a substitute available is a logical fallacy.

5.2.2 Human Nature as Unlimited

Economics also created its specific understanding of humans and their capacities. Over time it has – despite Mill's cautions – formulated a being not only with unlimited desires to consume, but also with unlimited mental capacity.

5.2.2.1 The creation of unlimited wants

Early economists like Smith, and we should also include Hume, were trained as philosophers and are normally described as philosophers as well as economists. In their work, different concepts of human virtues and vices play a central role. Old themes concerning what is a respectable life are abundant in their texts (O'Neill, 1998a). From the mid nineteenth century until the 1930s two core developments took place. First, hedonism and the concept of utility became central concepts in economics. Second, the concept of utility was transformed from a substantivist to a purely formal notion.

Utilitarianism/hedonism gained much of its position through the work of Jeremy Bentham (for example, Bentham, 1789 [1970]). He emphasized that what motivates humans is individual utility, the gain of pleasure and the avoidance of pain. This perspective gradually entered economics through the work of Mill, Jevons and Marshall. This seems not to have been an easy development. Mill had his own version emphasizing the various qualitative levels of pleasure – from lower to higher – and judging the morality of acts by their contribution to the happiness or greater good of all. The latter must be understood as opposed to the egoist interpretation of human action among hedonists. Similarly, Marshall noted some serious doubts about hedonism in his work. In a long footnote to his *Principles* he emphasized that: 'It has unfortunately happened that the customary uses of economic terms have sometimes suggested the belief that economists are adherents of the philosophical system of Hedonism or of Utilitarianism' (Marshall, 1890 [1949], p. 77). Kilpinen (1999, p. 188) emphasizes that the only thing Marshall manages to show is that 'economists are not professing hedonists in their *ethics*' (emphasis in original). In relation to this, one should note that Marshall was himself instrumental in changing the perspective of economic analyses from the broader concept of 'political economy' to that of 'economics.'

With emphasis on pleasure and pain, the focus shifted from seeing the human as an aspiring being to become a desiring one. As Holland (2002) emphasizes, the role of reason except the desire itself has then no place in understanding human choice – for example, the question of what desires I should have is made irrelevant. The price is high though as the model 'casts

our desires as somehow out of control . . . it makes no sense of deliberation, which is not a process of discovering what we want, but a process of
reflecting upon what there is most reason to want' (p. 23).

This development did away with old issues like self-restraint and mod-
eration that were virtues of the old paradigm. A process starting in the
1920s also removed any substantive content to the concept of utility. To
the 'old' neoclassical economists like Jevons, Marshall and Pigou, utility
had substantive content. While defined in subjective terms, it nevertheless
reflected concrete needs of physical and mental form. With the ordinalist
revolution in the 1920s and 1930s, the utility concept was emptied of any
such content. It was transformed into a formal concept – a pure ordering
without any reference to needs or mental states. Certainly, in such a structure the issue of satiation is irrelevant.

Whether the above developments influenced our move toward mass
consumerism or only reflects the economist understanding of that
process is hard to judge. What is clear, however, is that unlimited human
wants fits very well with a system aimed at growth. What is equally clear
is that unlimited wants is not an innate characteristic of humans. Rather,
it is a historic and institutional creation. Hunter-gatherers have not demonstrated any such abilities (for example, Gowdy, 1998). Their wants have
instead been rather fixed. They have typically been able to live sustainably
for tens of thousands of years without destroying their environments.
Hence, they have even been characterized as affluent societies (Sahlins,
1972) because they have managed to achieve a high amount of leisure
time. While one should be careful with romanticizing this form of life,
we note that unlimited wants is not a fundamental characteristic of
humanity.

5.2.2.2   The creation of unlimited capacities

The issue of the cognitive capacity of the human seems to be a rather
recent issue in economics. It becomes important not least when proving the
efficiency of competitive markets. Standard welfare theory as developed
in the 1930s and onwards was based on the assumption that agents had
full information and a capacity to handle this information rationally. As
these assumptions were increasingly challenged also within the economist
profession itself, we observed a move toward basing analyses more on
expectations – for example, rational expectations, Bayesian updating. This
made it possible to keep the main tenets of the economic model intact –
that is, the focus on maximization and equilibrium states that makes sense
only under certain assumptions about the information problem.[5]

These developments may have looked nice from within the profession,
but they were not more realistic than assuming full information. I believe

that Simon's (1979) summary of the debate on rational choice is very to the point when he states that:

> The axiomatization of utility and probability after World War II and the revival of Bayesian statistics opened the way to testing empirically whether people behaved in choice situations so as to maximize subjective expected utility (SEU). In early studies, using extremely simple choice situations, it appeared that perhaps they did. When even small complications were introduced into the situations, wide departures from the predictions of SEU theory soon became evident . . . the conclusion seems unavoidable that the SEU theory does not provide a good prediction – not even a good approximation – of actual behavior. (Simon, 1979, p. 506)

Using analyses based on full information or, for example, rational expectations makes it possible to develop models treating economic issues with highly sophisticated mathematical tools. The developments in economics since at least the 1930s have strongly emphasized 'rigor.' Using mathematical models is a way of ensuring 'rigor' in the meaning of being stringent and logical given the assumptions. Taking physics as the 'exemplar science' (Mirowski, 1989), it was maybe a 'necessary' move. On the other hand, the price was high as relevance had to be sacrificed concerning the assumptions.[6]

5.3 ON THE LIMITS OF THE BIOSPHERE

So far we have looked at how mainstream economics has made away with limits that are real. In the following I shall look at what research in other fields of inquiry – other disciplines – say about these issues. We will find that there may be crucial limitations that the economic model oversees, while there may also be limitations incurred that obstruct sensible responses to creating a sustainable future. Let me start with some observations concerning the kind of limitations that the biosphere represents.

The existence of physical limits is trivial. Our globe is a closed system. It carries a certain amount of matter that for practical reasons can be viewed as fixed. The inflow of solar energy per unit of time is given. Nevertheless, such limits are of little or no significance as long as the human species just uses small fractions of the resources. So, do we face any limits of practical importance?

The second law of thermodynamics states that in any isolated system entropy – disorder – is increasing. As the earth is not isolated, but a closed system, order can, however, be established by utilizing the inflow of low entropy sun energy. This is what has happened through the evolution of the biosphere over more than a billion years. This order has established itself by utilizing the low entropy energy from the sun and by exporting the necessary disorder produced through waste heat. This process has created a system of complementarities where what is a resource for one species becomes waste, which functions as a resource for other species. While non-equilibrium cycles of various kinds certainly exist, the macroscopic change of the biosphere as a consequence of this is very slow.[7] It is exactly this that has made it possible for the earth to become the scene for the creation and recreation of various interrelated life forms.

The entropy laws put a distinct limitation on change – also technological change. By increased ingenuity we may be able to create more order in favor of human consumption – that is, economic growth – in one part of the system – the economy – and at the same time ensure that the necessary disorder following this process is exported not only out of the economy, but also the biosphere. This does, however, demand that we acquire the necessary insights about the dynamics of the system. This amounts to being able to master the information stored in the present biosphere – all experience of the life system telling what are and what are not well-functioning expansion paths. It is an illusion to assume this to be possible. Moreover, we will most probably create new paths through the changes we make, paths for which the biosphere has no stored information.

The order established in the biosphere demands the reproduction of a vast number of complementarities. Loss of biodiversity reduces the biosphere's reproductive capacity. Increasing cycles beyond the capacity of the biosphere – for example, emissions of carbon dioxide (CO_2) and of nitrates – threaten its functioning. The problems are many. I shall illustrate with examples covering the two main types of challenges.

My first example is the working of photosynthesis. This is the process through which the life processes of the biosphere acquire the energy needed. Photosynthesis demands inputs of phosphorous to work. There is no substitute for this compound. Given this, phosphorous is a crucial input in, for example, agriculture/food production. While farmers may grow potatoes instead of wheat – compare with Solow – they cannot do so without phosphorous. Given the present magnitude of production needed, the level of erosion of soils and the fact that production and consumption are geographically separated, external inputs of the compound are necessary. The European Fertilizer Manufacturers Association (2000) has estimated that the production of this input will peak in 2040. Phosphorous is not lost. It is just made much less accessible when ending up in the world's oceans via various processes. The limit would appear in the form of our capacity to produce energy to retrieve phosphorous from sea water. The larger the energy requirements, the greater the transformation of the earth's surface/the biosphere would have to be to capture sun energy so that it can be used to recover phosphorous.

Second, the problem of species loss is not only about the loss of a specific consumption good for which a substitute can be found – compare again Solow's argument. The issue concerns first of all the capacity of the system to reproduce itself. In relation to this, the concept of resilience is crucial – that is, the capacity of a system to return to its original state after some external changes/shocks (Holling, 1973, 1986; Perrings, 1997).

The biosphere and its different ecosystems have over time developed a substantial level of resilience. Each ecosystem can be viewed as positioned within a basin – its attractor. External pressures/shocks may push the system toward the boundaries of the attractor – for example, a storm, increased influx of nutrients, emissions of pollutants. If the system is able to endure the pressure – it is significantly resilient against it – it will finally return to its original state if it is relieved of the stress. If the pressure is too heavy, the system will leave its attractor and the dynamics will change as when a lake undergoes eutrophication 'flip.' The result is a change in its dynamics including a very different balance between the species.

In a publication by Rockström et al. (2009) the authors try to estimate 'planetary boundaries within which we expect that humanity can operate safely. Transgressing one or more planetary boundaries may be deleterious or even catastrophic due to the risk of crossing thresholds that will trigger non-linear, abrupt environmental change within continental- to planetary-scale systems.' They define nine such boundaries while quantitative limits are set for seven of them. Of these, they argue that three have already been transgressed; for climate gas concentrations, rate of biodiversity loss and changes to the global nitrogen cycle. While they emphasize that the boundaries defined are rough – and one could ask if all are operating at the planetary level – their way of thinking shows very clearly what kind of issues we are up against. They are systemic and continuing to rely on the power of substitution is very problematic.

From the above understanding we see that what is critical is not so much the individual resources. The issue is the overall dynamics of the system. To get the focus right here, Daly's emphasis on throughput and the understanding of the economy as a subsystem of the biosphere is crucial (for example, Daly, 1977, 2005). Mainstream economics seems, so far, not to acknowledge this. Rather, the vast resilience of the biosphere may have caused ignorance about limits. So, while resilience is a good thing as it ensures some stability and offers space for some change, the danger lies in believing that what has worked so far will work for ever. What is typically expected is that we will push the system on a trajectory of no return long before any threshold effects can be observed.

That there is a limit is hence quite evident, but where it lies cannot be understood *ex ante*. While economics cannot deliver all the solutions for climate change and other future challenges, to make any significant contributions it must incorporate the principles of thermodynamics and the metabolic interdependence between the biosphere and the economic subsystem into its models.

5.4   ON SOCIAL AND HUMAN LIMITS

We noted in Section 5.2 that while mainstream economics sees wants as unlimited, human motivation is limited to maximization of individual utility. Both these perspectives are now fundamentally challenged – partly by economists themselves.

5.4.1   Social Limits to Consumption

The model of economic growth is based on the assumption that growth increases well-being. Already our discussion about the life of hunter-gatherers has cast some doubt about the generality of that assumption. Looking at the situation in 'consumption societies,' there are also some reasons to be cautious. Recent research on 'happiness' – for example, Layard (2005) – shows an interesting picture. In these studies, people are typically asked: 'All things considered, how satisfied are you with your life as a whole these days?' Repeatedly, these studies show that beyond an average level of gross domestic product (GDP) per capita of about $10 000–15 000, happiness thus measured does not seem to increase.

There are several issues related to what such studies can say about the quality of life – see for example, Aldred (2009). Nevertheless, the observation supports the idea that lower consumption – if necessary for sustainability – may not demand self-sacrifice in rich countries. The two main ideas used as explanations for the observation may, however, cast some doubt also about that conclusion. First, we have the so-called 'hedonic adaptation hypothesis' – for example, Frederick and Loewenstein (1999) – implying that people adjust to new levels of consumption. 'More' is only better if consumption continuously expands, as what was 'more' over time becomes the standard. Second, we have the idea of positional goods, where it is the relative position to others that counts for the subjective feeling of well-being and not the absolute level of consumption or income. The latter idea is not least elaborated by Hirsch (1977).

Both perspectives demonstrate that people in modern economies may be on some kind of a treadmill. It is not only that our wants have become unlimited. Getting more does not help. Certainly, falling behind others may make us worse off, so we may not have much of a choice if we want to live well. We must have more.

Another and quite different type of data supporting the importance of relative positioning is offered by Wilkinson and Pickett (2009). In a study of the OECD countries – that is, the richest countries – they find strong relationships between health and social problems, on the one hand, and income inequality, on the other. Their analyses cover a wide range of issues from literacy, life expectancy, obesity and homicide rates to trust and social mobility.

The Wilkinson and Pickett (2009) study is interesting also in that it is based on an evaluation of objective dimensions of life quality, not just subjective satisfaction levels. The objectivist understanding of well-being has a long history, going back at least to Aristotle. It discusses well-being in relation to human needs as opposed to preferences. Contrasting the subjectivist position of hedonism, it emphasizes an objectivist understanding of what it means to thrive. The focus is on the human as a certain kind of being with needs that follow from this. Living as a human being requires water, food of different kinds, shelter, but also friendship and other social relations to flourish (O'Neill et al., 2008). This tradition emphasizes that there are both lower and upper limits to satisfaction of needs. Addiction as well as non-satiation are both relevant issues. Moreover, needs are dominantly non-substitutable, hence the various goods and bads are not measurable along one dimension. This tradition emphasizes a pluralist perspective of what it means to live well.

As underlined by O'Neill (2008, p. 10): 'Beyond a certain point an increase in material consumption does not address central dimensions of the good life such as affiliation and may even be associated with losses in those dimensions. Where the new Aristotelians differ from the subjective welfare approaches is in the claim that policy needs to address these dimensions directly and not simply through subjective assessments. As such the approach is not prone to problems of adaptive preferences.'

In the present debate about breaking the logic of the above treadmill, one may distinguish between two main perspectives – that concerning false beliefs about what constitutes well-being and that concerning faulty institutions. According to O'Neill (2008), the former defines the solution in changing the beliefs about the nature of a good life, while the latter focuses more on the particular institutions under which people live and sees the problem of social disintegration and overconsumption as reflecting the dynamics and demands of institutions – for example, the market.[8]

5.4.2   A Wider View of Human Agency

The 'core' economic model of human behavior focuses on a 'monist' understanding of motivation – that of the selfish actor maximizing his or her utility. Disciplines like anthropology and sociology offer a much wider understanding of human action. Here not least the concept of meaning is heavily emphasized (for example, Geertz, 1973; Parkin, 1982). Similarly, there is a focus on norms – what is considered appropriate action in specific contexts (Scott, 1971). Such perspectives are also found in parts of political science – for example, March and Olsen (1995).

Recent research in experimental economics has also shown that people are willing to share in situations where there would be no individual gain from doing so (see Vatn, 2005, 2009) for a review of the literature on this). My reading of the findings is that human motivation depends heavily on the institutional context. Gowdy (1998) illustrates how the specific goals of the hunters and gatherers were reflected in their rules. Ostrom et al. (1994) document a wide variety of contexts where people choose to cooperate even when the individual would do better by defecting. The recent literature on 'crowding out' illustrates how introducing payments into situations where actions previously were driven by internal motivations or norms shifts motivations from, for example, sharing toward thinking about individual gain (for example, Frey, 1997; Gneezy and Rustichini, 2000; Vatn, 2009). The concepts of other-regarding behavior and reciprocity (Gintis, 2000) and the distinction drawn in the literature between the consumer and the citizen illustrate other similar ideas of plural rationalities and motivations. Even what is understood to be self-interest may be seen as influenced by institutions. As illustrated by O'Neill (1998b), the self-interest in modern occupations – that of a chief executive officer, a university professor, a bureaucrat – varies according to how the roles are defined as reflecting different objectives.

The characteristics of the physical environment in which people live make our actions necessarily interdependent. In the history of our civilization, we have therefore over and over again been confronted with situations where it has been necessary to define how we balance own and other people's interests and needs in situations where we depend on each other. In such a situation, it seems reasonable that developing the capacity of other-regarding behavior or social rationality would have been favorable (see Sober and Wilson, 1998, for similar reasoning).

Reviewing the literature, Hodgson (2007, p. 329) concludes that: 'Both modern experimental economics and game theory have revealed the limitations of all-purpose, context-independent rationality and pointed to the institutional influences on rationality itself.' There are two important observations to be made in relation to this. First, thinking always in individual incentive terms may actually aggravate problems. This was already observed by Daly and Cobb (1990) and has lately received further support – note Bowles (2008) point that policies designed for self-interested citizens may undermine moral sentiments.[9] One may argue that by fostering a narrow 'vision' of human agency, mainstream economics has been favoring policies that actually may create an agent that is less interested in ensuring sustainability through becoming more selfish. Second, at the same time the above findings open up a whole new set of opportunities for societies to organize and to handle problems related to ensuring sustainable developments. To the extent such a development demands cooperation and willingness to think in other-regarding terms, formulating institutions that support such 'visions' would be the way forward.

5.5   ON THE LIMITS OF OUR SYSTEMS

We live in a commercial society. Tremendous resources are going not only into production, but also into ensuring that what is produced is sold. A necessary side-effect of this is increased environmental pressures. We do, however, spend very few resources on understanding the potential medium to long-run effects of this. The 'eyes' of the system we have created are directed toward the market. It only sees expansion paths – new opportunities for growth. The problems are, however, not only the blind spots created concerning the future consequences of what we do now. Maybe more important is the fact that we have created a system that is not well adapted to do much about the challenges. The system offers us limited power to act sustainably.

5.5.1   Markets, Firms and the Environment

The role of mainstream economics is not that it influences so much how economies work. The important role is that of legitimizing certain systems or solutions. Given distributed rights, full information/rational expectations and zero transaction costs – the standard assumptions of economics – competitive markets could solve any allocation problem efficiently. Certainly, there is also the issue of distribution that needs to be tackled. That is, however, not a topic for economics. Hence, the normal advice of economists – assuming that distributional issues are tackled – is to advise allocation via markets.

There is merit to this conclusion. There are, however, also some serious problems. First, markets are themselves the origin of skewed distribution.

At present the 4–5 richest people on the globe own as much as the poorest 2 billion. The tendency to inequality follows from the dynamics of markets and the fact that the more you own, the more you can invest and hence not only earn income from your own labor, but also from savings. Poor people are trapped as they do not have the capacity to save. This situation puts high demands on redistribution policies as they will be running after a moving target. Moreover, it will imply 'taking' resources from somebody who has already inherited/earned them.

Second, securing the interests of future generations demands protecting their interests specifically by defining rights for them – that is, an asset transfer regime (cf. Bromley, 1989; Howarth and Norgaard, 1990). This is not normally acknowledged by the mainstream since markets in overlapping intergenerational models are also seen to deliver efficient allocations over time. The issue is, however, not about efficiency, but about equal or better living conditions along the time dimension. The efficiency criterion has nothing to say about that as observed by Daly on several occasions (for example, Daly, 1992, 2005).

Third, the policy advice of the mainstream when projected upon the world we live in is directly detrimental. It proposes institutional structures that reduce our capacity to handle future environmental problems rather than the opposite. Proposing solutions as if information problems were trivial – that is, full information or standard risk assessments – underestimates vastly the kind of problems we are facing. What typically characterizes decision-making in the field of the environment will be substantial levels of ignorance – compare with our previous emphasis on attractor shifts. Moreover, stakes might be high, so even in cases where we are able to establish enough information to treat uncertainties as risk, the standard model of expected utility cannot be defended (Elster, 1979).

Fourth, proposing solutions as if transaction costs are zero is very problematic. Bromley (1991) makes this very clear when emphasizing that splitting up the world into individual decision-making units – the championed competitive market – is also what maximizes environmental externalities by maximizing the number of borders across which costs (read: waste matter) may shift. Transaction costs are dependent on the type of institutional system in place. The competitive market – with all the potentials for 'internal' gains – establishes high, often insurmountable costs for handling the 'external costs' that by necessity have to appear in a world where the laws of thermodynamics rule.

Finally, proposing solutions as if preferences and motivations are context independent is also very problematic. Basically, if these are systems dependent – as emphasized in Section 5.4 – we need to discuss which system fosters the better preferences and motivations. I find this to be crucial in the case of sustainability, but the issue becomes invisible in the assumptions of the mainstream model. Three specific questions in relation to the above need to be highlighted:

- One concerns the issue of consistency about motivations in our models. Assuming that firms maximize profits implies that they will do so not only in markets, but also in the realm of external costs. Thinking in similar terms, Kapp (1971) emphasized that external costs are not 'accidental' side-effects. Rather, if one invests for profit-making, shifting costs to third persons or to society at large should be expected as long as it is not illegal.
- The other concerns the issue of perverted motivations. Given asymmetric information, there are lots of opportunities for acting opportunistically. This way, business norms about not withholding important information may erode as respect in capitalist societies seems not to be earned by acting properly, but by making money. Authors like Aglietta and Rebérioux (2005) and Waldfogel (2007) document increasing irresponsibility and decline in the moral standards of leaders of capitalist firms.
- The third concerns a 'systems drive' toward short-sightedness. Hence, Offer (2004, p. 358) emphasizes the observation that: 'In competitive market societies, the flow of innovation undermines existing conventions, habits and institutions of commitment. It reinforces the bias for short term.'

Mainstream economics acknowledges externalities and advises state regulations like environmental taxes to solve the problems.[10] This is indeed wise given the reduction in transaction costs that follows. What is not acknowledged is that what becomes efficient is nevertheless defined by the structure advised as if there would be no externalities. Due to the resilience of the biosphere, an environmental problem often first becomes visible long after the processes causing it were set in motion. More time may even be needed to prove who or what causes it. Despite the fact that this information is finally available, action may nevertheless not be warranted as it could be too costly compared to the gains from inaction. In that calculation, the potentially lost future income from the production causing the harm appears as a cost of regulation. Hence, investment decisions made under the assumption that no harm would be produced binds the decision about regulating when harm is finally proved. Moreover, the interests created both on the producer and consumer side – as an effect of the actual production – will next act as forces going against regulation on the political arena. Hence, a systematic asymmetry is created in the disfavor of the environment and future generations.

In relation to the above, we should also note that the system seems dependent on growth. Investment is an insecure business. Growth increases the chances of getting the 'necessary' payback on one's investments. Low or negative growth rates alarm the system and investors become afraid. Hence, less is invested and even more jobs are lost and so on. Because of this, the 'steady state' takes the form of a crisis putting a lot of stress on people. The recent 'financial' crisis strongly illustrates these dynamics.

The main remedy – Keynesian expansionism – responds to this downward spiral by increasing demand. While an effective remedy against the economic crisis – at least within limits – this medicine rather increases the long-run problem of sustainability. So we are caught between avoiding a short-run economic crisis and a long-run environmental one. While the latter will in the end cause a crisis of the economy itself, it is very difficult not to prioritize the short-run demands. Or is there a way forward where we transform the system so that it becomes possible to avoid this kind of choice?

5.5.2   Are There Ways to Reduce the Limitations of the Present System Making Us Able to Respect the Environmental Limits?

Herman Daly's insistence that we have to focus on the scale of the economy and regulate the throughput of material resources and energy is certainly a core remedy to establish a sustainable development path. The first step would therefore be to introduce limits to material resource use. This would help overcome some of the limitations of present *ex post* responses to upcoming harms. It would imply turning to an *ex ante* way of directing the metabolism between the economy and the biosphere. This will be a necessary and an adequate response to the fact that knowledge is limited and hence a way to make precaution operable.

Despite all its virtues, this solution will be difficult to establish under present conditions and would need other changes in the economic system to work. This has clearly been observed by Daly himself (see also Daly and Cobb, 1990), while different authors emphasize somewhat different remedies. I will close by sketching some ideas about what should be added to make a throughput regulation work.

First, we must take economic inequality much more seriously. This is not only so because of all the direct harm it creates for well-being. It is also because it is a driving force behind the treadmill of 'unsaturated consumption.' The main argument for accepting inequality is exactly its potential drive for growth. This is what rich countries need less of now.

In the present system, there is no limit as to how rich somebody can become. I find it very difficult to defend this. The situation is a function of the dominating forms of private property. Even those developing the defense of private ownership early on – for example, Locke (1690 [1988]) – did not look at it as a system to foster unlimited acquisition. The idea was rather contrary to that. Two premises were core in Locke's thinking. First, it was the mixing of own labor with nature that in his view was the basis for making something a person's property. Second, the premise was that 'there is enough, and as good left for others . . . As much as anyone can make use of to any advantage of life before it spoils; so much he may by his labour fix a Property in. Whatever is beyond this, is more than his share, and belongs to others' (Locke, 1690 [1988], p. 288).

While one might disagree with the first premise – that is, emphasizing rather that property is a social relation (Bromley, 1991) – the second does not seem to apply anymore in the way private property is instituted. In Locke's time, the fruits of land and labor could literally spoil, and having more than one could consume oneself did not make sense. Over time the relationship between property and covering one's needs has been 'relaxed.' The institution of private property is developed into many forms. One is the creation of the stock holding company and the institutions of shares. This structure has completely delinked the relationship between own labor and ownership or – more relevant here – between needs and the accumulation of wealth. Therefore, there is no limit anymore to how rich one can become. While the problems this creates for sustainable development is not necessarily an argument against private property – certainly not concerning the resources people need to make a living – it is a strong argument against property arrangements that in themselves do not establish any upper bounds on how much wealth it is possible to accumulate.

Second, we must look closer at what kinds of motivations an institutional system creates. As already emphasized, institutional structures may facilitate different kinds of motivations – for example, cooperative will instead of selfishness. While the most dynamic and powerful institutions of the present system are fueled by the profit motive, one could think of other solutions where choice was much more influenced by sharing and caring.

These insights open up several options that would be unthinkable given the view that preferences and motivations are context independent. Surpassing this constructed limitation offers the opportunity to create economic institutions built more on the role of cooperation, community and sharing. There are several potential gains in this. One would create less conflict between short- and long-term goals. It would be easier to get support for needed restrictions on scale, and it would be easier to institute a wider set of issues to be taken into consideration when doing economic choices. The latter is especially important in relation to the scale limitations emphasized above.

Regulating on scale implies regulating on quantities. There is, however, also a qualitative aspect to environmental disruptions following economic activity. The same amount of resources may provoke very different pressures on the environment dependent on what kind of products are made, what kind of waste is produced and where it is emitted. So added to limitations on scale, we need increased sensitivity in the system to potential effects of different transformations of the material throughputs. Some further state regulations beyond throughput restrictions may be needed to avoid problems. I think, however, that it will not be possible to be successful in this endeavor if economic agents themselves do not act in a cooperative way – that is, are themselves insensitive to the potential consequences of their own action. This observation points toward instituting both responsibility for environmental consequences and cooperative will at the level of the firm itself.

My last point concerns the need to establish reduced dependency on growth. One might argue that if restrictions on throughput are established and the qualitative aspect of production is treated well as discussed above, economic growth itself will represent no problem. I think this is too simple an analysis. My argument is two-sided. First, there is a conflict between having a system that is fundamentally dependent on growth and getting the necessary political support for establishing the quantitative and qualitative restrictions emphasized previously. It will be politically less doable simply because it will go against the interests of the economic agents as presently constructed – both owners and workers. Second, to the extent that growth is important to secure necessary investments and hence avoid sliding into recessions, politicians will find themselves continuously pressured to choose between economic and ecological crises. As already stressed, I find it utterly important to develop institutions that make it possible to avoid this kind of choice.

How would such institutions look? I think there are several options that should be explored. Fundamentally, this issue concerns the system of property rights and what it means to hold property and to invest. Presently, investment is dominantly motivated by profit considerations. As we have seen, this creates a conflict between the self-interest thus defined and long-run living conditions. One should rather create a system oriented at investing more directly into the well-being of individuals and communities – that is, 'for benefit' organizations. Alternatives here would involve an increased role for public property and community ownership. One could also think of various combinations of private and community ownership (see Vatn, 2012 and 2015 for further elaborations).

Actually, all the issues raised above – those on greater equality, more focus on cooperative will and investment for the future well-being of individuals and communities – point in the same direction. They point toward institutional change as the main strategy for solving urgent problems. They moreover point toward establishing institutions that foster other motivations and responsibilities than individual gain. While we might have thought this to be impossible after championing self-interest for more than two centuries, we see now that this endorsement is based on a far too limited understanding of human capacities.

5.6 CONCLUSION

The thrust of this chapter is that it all comes down to what limits we see and how we understand them. If we believe nature is limitless in the meaning that everything can be substituted for, human capacity to treat information is literally limitless too and costs of coordinating/transaction costs are zero, then the issue of sustainability is of scant interest. Problems, so to speak, take care of themselves. If we find nature to offer serious limitations for economic expansion, if our capacities to learn and coordinate are limited and if we depend on expansion to function both individually and systemically, then we are facing considerable challenges.

In this chapter I have argued that the solution to our problems lies very much in removing one limitation that simply seems to be unwarranted. That is the idea that humans are fundamentally selfish and that cooperation is possible only if it offers direct individual gains. Humans are social beings and, moreover, what motivates us is strongly influenced by the institutions we construct. Understanding what this means and understanding how we can expand our capacities in this domain is what is necessary for us to be able to respect the limits of a small celestial body – albeit being part of an unlimited cosmos.

NOTES

1. It should be noted that Solow in a rather recent interview with *Harper's Magazine* stated that: 'I think it's perfectly possible that economic growth cannot go on at its current rate

forever' (Stoll, 2008, p. 92). Hence, some doubt may exist regarding the far future, while Solow finds the limit of no relevance for today's policies.

2. There exist some minor works on mining and forestry. What is known can, however, be compiled in less than 100 pages. Note that our reference point here is the Western intellectual world. Sihag (2009) argues that the Indian Kautilya living 300 BC seem to have developed concepts coming close to those of European economics of the nineteenth century.

3. In Mill (1848), Book 4, chapter 6, titled 'Of the stationary state.' Given the context of this book, we should note that Herman Daly makes several references to Mill's work on this exact point – for example, Daly (1977) and Daly and Townsend (1994).

4. For a clarification of the importance of the latter, see, for example, Kraev (2002). He also discusses principal consequences of different formulations of the functional relationships between natural and man-made and natural capital – that is, Leontief, Constant Elasticity of Substitution (CES) and Cobb-Douglas production functions.

5. Certainly, if it is costly to produce and update information, the individual ends in an infinite regress on the issue of what are optimal information searching efforts. I agree with Knudsen (1993) emphasizing that an inextricable problem arises as soon as the cost of optimizing becomes part of the optimization calculus itself.

6. I do not by this imply that using mathematics need result in reduced relevance. More important is the specific interest among economists for (general) equilibrium modeling and the problems that more sophisticated or relevant assumptions concerning human choice pose for such models.

7. There are also other causes of such change, most notably genetic changes and changes in the inflow of sun energy per unit of time – the latter having increased quite substantially over the period since the earth was formed.

8. These discussions go back to different positions taken by Greek philosophers. Epicurus may be called the first hedonist with his emphasis on pleasure and absence of pain. He did nevertheless advocate simple living. Aristotle emphasized much more the importance of institutions – not least the difference between the forms of acquisition typical for the household economy and that of the market.

9. Bowles (2008) makes an explicit reference to Adam Smith and his *The Theory of Moral Sentiments* (Smith, 1759 [1976]), which is a more interesting, but much less acknowledged book than *The Wealth of Nations* (Smith, 1776 [1976]). While impossible to prove, one may wonder if the latter became much more famous simply because it 'served' the needs of the entrepreneurs of a burgeoning capitalism. For Smith the former book seems to have been more important. At least he rewrote it several times.

10. Mainstream economics both assumes zero transaction costs and argues for the need to establish specific environmental policies. This is curious. If transaction costs are zero and other mainstream assumptions apply, the so-called 'Coase theorem' rules. There is no need for state 'interventions' except defining rights. For more on this, see Vatn and Bromley (1997).

REFERENCES

Aglietta, M. and A. Rebérioux (2005), *Corporate Governance Adrift*, Cheltenham, UK and Northampton, MA, USA: Edward Elgar Publishing.

Aldred, J. (2009), *The Skeptical Economist: Revealing the Ethics Inside Economics*, London: Earthscan.

Bentham, J. (1789), *Introduction to the Principles of Morals and Legislation*, reprinted in 1970, London: Methuen.

Bowles, S. (2008), 'Policies designed for self-interested citizens may undermine "the moral sentiments": evidence from economic experiments', *Science*, **320**, 1605–9.

Bromley, D.W. (1989), 'Entitlements, missing markets and environmental uncertainty', *Journal of Environmental Economics and Management*, **17**, 181–94.

Bromley, D.W. (1991), *Environment and Economy: Property Rights and Public Policy*, Oxford: Basil Blackwell.

Daly, H.E. (1977), *Steady-state Economics*, San Francisco, CA: W.H. Freeman & Co.

Daly, H.E. (1992), 'Allocation, distribution, and scale: towards an economics that is efficient, just, and sustainable', *Ecological Economics*, **6**, 185–93.

Daly, H.E. (2005), 'Economics in a full world', *Scientific American*, **293** (3), 100–107.

Daly, H.E. and J.B. Cobb (1990), *For the Common Good: Redirecting the Economy Towards Community, the Environment and a Sustainable Future*, London: Green Print.

Daly, H.E. and K.N. Townsend (eds) (1994), *Valuing the Earth: Economics, Ecology, Ethics*, Cambridge, MA: MIT Press.

Dasgupta, P.S. and G.M. Heal (1974), 'The optimal depletion of exhaustible resources', in *Review of Economic Studies: Symposium on the Economics of Exhaustible Resources*, Vol. 41, Edinburgh: Longman, pp. 3–28.

Elster, J. (1979), 'Risk, uncertainty and nuclear power', *Social Science Information*, **18** (3), 371–400.

European Fertilizer Manufacturers Association (2000), *Phosphorous: Essential Element for Food Production*, Brussels: European Fertilizer Manufacturers Association.

Frederick, S. and G. Loewenstein (1999), 'Hedonic adaptation', in D. Kahneman, E. Diener and N. Schwarz (eds), *Well-being: Foundations of Hedonic Psychology*, New York: Russell Sage Foundation Press, pp. 302–29.

Frey, B.S. (1997), *Not Just For the Money: An Economic Theory of Personal Motivation*, Cheltenham, UK and Lyme, NH, USA: Edward Elgar Publishing.

Geertz, C. (1973), *The Interpretation of Cultures*, New York: Basic Books.

Gintis, H. (2000), 'Beyond *Homo economicus*: evidence from experimental economics', *Ecological Economics*, **35**, 311–22.

Gneezy, U. and A. Rustichini (2000), 'Pay enough or don't pay at all', *Quarterly Journal of Economics*, **115** (3), 791–810.

Gowdy, J. (ed.) (1998), *Limited Wants, Unlimited Means: A Reader on Hunter-Gatherer Economics and Environment*, Washington, DC: Island Press.

Hirsch, F. (1977), *Social Limits to Growth*, London: Routledge & Kegan Paul.

Hodgson, G.M. (2007), 'The revival of Veblenian institutional economics', *Journal of Economic Issues*, **XLI** (2), 325–40.

Holland, A. (2002), 'Are choices tradeoffs?', in D.W. Bromley and J. Paavola (eds), *Economics, Ethics and Environmental Policy: Contested Choices*, Oxford: Blackwell, pp. 17–34.

Holling, C.S. (1973), 'Resilience and stability of ecological systems', *Annual Review of Ecological Systems*, **4**, 1–24.

Holling, C.S. (1986), 'The resilience of terrestrial ecosystems: local surprise and global change', in W.C. Clark and R.E. Munn (eds), *Sustainable Development of the Biosphere*, Cambridge: Cambridge University Press, pp. 292–317.

Howarth, R.B. and R.B. Norgaard (1990), 'Intergenerational resource rights, efficiency, and social optimality', *Land Economics*, **66** (1), 1–11.

Jevons, W.S. (1865), *The Coal Question: An Inquiry Concerning the Progress of the Nation, and the Probable Exhaustion of Our Coal Mines*, reprinted in A.W. Flux (ed.) (1965), 3rd edn, New York: Augustus M. Kelley.

Kapp, K.W. (1971), *The Social Costs of Private Enterprise*, New York: Schoken Books.

Kilpinen, E. (1999), 'What is rationality? A new reading of Veblen's critique of utilitarian hedonism', *International Journal of Politics, Culture and Society*, **13** (2), 187–206.

Knudsen, C. (1993), 'Equilibrium, perfect rationality and the problem of self-reference in economics', in U. Mäki, B. Gustafsson and C. Knudsen (eds), *Rationality, Institutions and 'Economic Methodology'*, London: Routledge, pp. 133–70.

Kraev, E. (2002), 'Stocks, flows and complementarity: formalizing a basic insight of ecological economics', *Ecological Economics*, **43**, 277–86.

Layard, R. (2005), *Happiness: Lessons from a New Science*, New York: Penguin Press.

Locke, J. (1690), 'The second treatise of government', reprinted in P. Laslett (ed.) (1988), *Two Treatises of Government*, Cambridge: Cambridge University Press.

Malthus, T.R. (1803), *An Essay on the Principles of Population*, reprinted in D. Winch (ed.) (1992), Cambridge: Cambridge University Press.

Malthus, T.R. (1836), *Principles of Political Economy: Considered with a View to Their Practical Application*, reprinted in 1968, 2nd edn, New York: August M. Kelley.

March, J.G. and J.P. Olsen (1995), *Democratic Governance*, New York: The Free Press.

Marshall, A. (1890), *The Principles of Economics*, reprinted in 1949, 8th edn, London: Macmillan.

Meadows, D., D.L. Meadows, J. Randers and W.W. Behrens III (1972), *Limits to Growth: A Report for the Club of Rome's Project on the Predicament of Mankind*, New York: Universe Books.

Mill, J.S. (1848), *Principles of Political Economy: With Some of their Applications to Social Philosophy*, reprinted in 1965, Fairfield, NJ: A.M. Kelley.

Mirowski, P. (1989), *More Heat than Light: Economics as Social Physics, Physics as Nature's Economics*, Cambridge: Cambridge University Press.

O'Neill, J. (1998a), 'Self-love, self-interest and the rational economic agent', *Analyse & Kritik*, **20**, 184–204.

O'Neill, J. (1998b), *The Market: Ethics, Knowledge and Politics*, London: Routledge.

O'Neill, J. (2008), 'Living well within limits: well-being, time and sustainability', opinion piece for the Sustainable Development Commission, available at http://www.sd-commission.org.uk/publications/downloads/John_ONeil_thinkpiecel.pdf.

O'Neill, J., A. Holland and A. Light (2008), *Environmental Values*, London: Routledge.

Offer, A. (2004), *The Challenge of Affluence*, Oxford: Oxford University Press.

Ostrom, E., R. Gardner and J. Walker (1994), *Rules, Games, and Common-pool Resources*, Ann Arbor, MI: University of Michigan Press.

Parkin, D. (ed.) (1982), *Semantic Anthropology*, London: Academic Press.

Perrings, C. (1997), 'Ecological resilience in the sustainability of economic development', in C. Perrings (ed.), *Economics of Ecological Resources: Selected Essays*, Cheltenham, UK and Lyme, NH, USA: Edward Elgar Publishing, pp. 45–63.

Polanyi, K. (1944), *The Great Transformation: The Political and Economic Origins of Our Time*, reprinted in 1957, Boston, MA: Beacon Press.

Polanyi, K. (1968), *Primitive, Archaic and Modern Economies: Essays of Karl Polanyi*, ed. G. Dalton, Boston, MA: Beacon Press.

Ricardo, D. (1817), *The Principles of Political Economy and Taxation*, reprinted in 1973, Foreword by D. Winch, London: Dent.

Rockström, J., W. Steffen, K. Noone et al. (2009), 'Planetary boundaries: exploring the safe operating space for humanity', *Ecology and Society*, **14** (2), 32, available at http://www.ecologyandsociety.org/vol14/iss32/art32/.

Sahlins, M. (1972), *Stone Age Economics*, Chicago, IL: Aldine Atherton.

Schumpeter, J. (1954), *A History of Economic Analysis*, Oxford: Oxford University Press.

Scott, J.F. (1971), *Internalization of Norms: A Sociological Theory of Moral Commitment*, Englewoods Cliffs, NJ: Prentice-Hall.

Sihag, B.S. (2009), 'Kautilya: a forerunner of neoclassical price theory', *Humanomics*, **25** (1), 37–54.

Simon, H.A. (1979), 'Rational decision making in business organizations', *American Economic Review*, **69** (4), 493–513.

Smith, A. (1759), *The Theory of Moral Sentiments*, reprinted in E. Cannan (ed.) (1976), London: Methuen.

Smith, A. (1776), *An Inquiry into the Nature and Causes of the Wealth of Nations*, reprinted in 1976, Chicago, IL: University of Chicago Press.

Sober, E. and D.S. Wilson (1998), *Unto Others: The Evolution and Psychology of Unselfish Behavior*, Cambridge, MA: Harvard University Press.

Solow, R.M. (1974), 'Intergenerational equity and exhaustible resources', in *Review of Economic Studies: Symposium on the Economics of Exhaustible Resources*, Vol. 41, Edinburgh: Longman, pp. 29–45.

Solow, R. (1993), 'Sustainability: an economist's perspective', in R. Dorfman and N. Dorfman (eds), *Economics of the Environment*, New York: Norton.

Stiglitz, J. (1974), 'The optimal depletion of exhaustible resources', in *Review of Economic Studies: Symposium on the Economics of Exhaustible Resources*, Vol. 41, Edinburgh: Longman, pp. 123–37.

Stoll, S. (2008), 'Fear of fallowing: the specter of a no-growth world', *Harper's Magazine*, March, pp. 88–92, 94.

Vatn, A. (2005), *Institutions and the Environment*, Cheltenham, UK and Northampton, MA, USA: Edward Elgar Publishing.

Vatn, A. (2009), 'Cooperative behavior and institutions', *Journal of Socio-Economics*, **38**, 188–96.

Vatn, A. (2012), 'Environmental governance: the aspect of coordination', in E. Brousseau, T. Dedeurwaerdere, P.-A. Jouvet and M. Willinger (eds), *Global Environmental Commons: Analytical and Political Challenges in Building Governance Mechanisms*, Oxford: Oxford University Press, pp. 31–53.

Vatn, A. (2015). *Environmental Governance: Institutions, Policies and Actions*, Cheltenham, UK and Northampton, MA, USA: Edward Elgar Publishing.

Vatn, A. and D.W. Bromley (1997), 'Externalities: a market model failure', *Journal of Environmental and Resource Economics*, **9** (2), 135–51.

Waldfogel, J. (2007), *The Tyranny of the Market: Why You Can't Always Get What You Want*, Cambridge, MA: Harvard University Press.

Wilkinson, R. and K. Pickett (2009), *The Spirit Level: Why More Equal Societies Almost Always Do Better*, London: Penguin.

6. Toward a science-based theory of behavior: building on Georgescu-Roegen

John Gowdy*

[T]he real output of the economic process (or of any life process, for that matter) is not the *material flow* of waste, but the still mysterious *immaterial flux* of the enjoyment of life.
(Nicholas Georgescu-Roegen, 1974 [1976], p. 9, emphases in original)

Reality is infinitely various when compared to the deductions of abstract thought, even those that are most cunning, and it will not tolerate rigid, hard and fast distinctions. Reality strives for diversification.
(Fyodor Dostoyevsky, 1986, part 2, chapter 7, p. 305)

6.1 INTRODUCTION

Nicholas Georgescu-Roegen's contributions to economics have been widely recognized by the profession's top theorists. Paul Samuelson (1967, p. vii) praised Georgescu-Roegen as 'a scholar's scholar, an economist's economist.' His Festschrift published in 1976 contained contributions by four Nobel laureates – John Hicks, Jan Tinbergen, Simon Kuznets and Paul Samuelson. Georgescu did not attract a large following of students, partly because of the growing dominance of Walrasian[1] orthodoxy during the time he was at Vanderbilt University (1949–76) and partly because of his demanding personality. The lack of numbers, however, is offset by the quality of two of his students who went on to make internationally recognized contributions to economic science. One is Mohammad Yunus who went on to win a Nobel Peace Prize for his work in microfinance for the world's poorest, and the other is Herman Daly, winner of several major awards including the Heineken Prize and the Right Livelihoods Award, sometimes called the Alternative Nobel Prize.

Although he has made major contributions in the areas of environmental ethics and social justice, Daly is best known for his work extending

Georgescu's insights on the limits to growth and the importance of scale in the economic process. But for both Daly and Georgescu the central focus of economic analysis is the human actor. The purpose of this chapter is to explore some of the neglected contributions of Georgescu to utility theory and welfare economics that anticipated some of the revolutionary critiques of Walrasian economics being made by contemporary behavioral and neuroeconomists. I argue that the key assumption in Walrasian economics, emphatically rejected by Georgescu, is that economic behavior can be accurately described without reference to social context. Daly and Georgescu devoted their life's work to exploring the social nature of the economic process. Current work in behavioral economics, and perhaps even more importantly, neuroscience, has confirmed that it is the degree of social interaction that makes our species unique among mammals. The mathematical constraints of Walrasian economics make that framework virtually useless as a reliable guide to actual human behavior and effective public policy.

6.2   GEORGESCU-ROEGEN AND THE CURRENT IMPASSE IN ECONOMIC THEORY

Georgescu-Roegen is best known for his classic work *The Entropy Law and the Economic Process* (1971). The foundational impact of that work on ecological economics was the insight that economic activity ultimately depends on a limited and continually degrading stream of natural resources, particularly fossil fuel. However, it is sometimes forgotten that Georgescu's first love in economics was utility theory. A common view of Georgescu's work is that at the beginning of his career he was a standard neoclassical economist but later broke ranks with the publication of the *Entropy Law*. But in fact, from the start of his life as an economist he was critical of the approach of standard theory (Gowdy, 1985; Gowdy and Mayumi, 2001; Mayumi, 2001). Beginning in the 1930s he challenged the basic assumptions of Walrasian utility theory through his novel expositions of lexicographic preferences, the integrability problem, the importance of social norms and other-regarding preferences, and the limits of marginal analysis (Georgescu-Roegen, 1936, 1950, 1954). Today these ideas have reappeared in an interdisciplinary recasting of economics infusing hard evidence from behavioral economics and neuroscience.

Georgescu's analysis was guided by his insistence on the distinction between dialectical and arithmomorphic concepts. He used the word dialectical to describe phenomena having overlapping boundaries, for example, in the evolutionary change of one species (A) into another (B) there must exist intermediate forms that can be considered both A and B, or even both A and 'not A' (Georgescu-Roegen, 1967, p. 23). Dialectical relationships are the essence of real human relationships and real economic processes. Of course it is useful to use discrete distinctions in economic analysis. Analytical boundaries must be drawn somewhere. But to establish these boundaries arbitrarily – for example, by eliminating interactions between firms and between individuals – solely for mathematical tractability, and then to present them as general economic laws, is to violate basic norms of science. As argued below, drawing the analytical boundary of utility theory around the isolated individual strips away everything that makes human beings unique.

Today the boundaries of economic analysis are being expanded by exciting new research linking economics and the behavioral sciences. But the entrenchment of orthodoxy in economics is perhaps unparalleled in any other academic field. Silverberg (1990, quoted in DeCanio, 2003, p. 6) succinctly expresses the rigidity of the orthodox view:

> Perhaps nothing is more readily distinctive about economics than the insistence on a unifying behavioral basis for explanations, in particular, a postulate of maximizing behavior. The need for such a theory is not controversial; to reject it is to reject economics. The reason such importance is placed on the theoretical basis is that without it, any outcome is admissible; propositions can therefore never be refuted. Economists insist that some events are *not possible*, in the same way that physicists insist that water will never run uphill. Other things constant, a lower price will never induce less consumption of any good; holding other productive inputs constant. There are to be no exceptions. (emphasis in original)

But the 'laws' of economics are not like the laws of physics. Sometimes a lower price *does* cause a drop in demand because people use prices as an indicator of quality. Speculative demand increases when prices are rising, so there is a positive feedback loop between rising prices and rising demand. Sometimes a higher price *does* cause less of the good to be supplied as in the classic case of blood donations (Titmuss, 1971). Incentives include a lot more than price incentives. Sometimes price incentives can crowd out the public good and this fact should be acknowledged in economic theory and in formulating public policy (Frey, 1997).

A slightly more nuanced response than Silverberg's to behavioral research is to assert that if observed phenomena cannot be shoehorned into the mathematics of Walrasian economics then they are of no concern to economists. In an aptly titled essay 'The case for mindless economics,' Gull and Pesendorfer (2008, p. 5) write:

> Kahneman (1994) asserts that subjective states and hedonic utility are 'legitimate topics of study'. This may be true, but such states and utilities are not useful for calibrating and testing standard economic models. Discussions of

hedonic experiences play no role in standard economic analysis because economics makes no predictions about them and has no data to test such prediction. Economists also lack the means for integrating measurement of hedonic
utility with standard economic data. Therefore, they have found it useful to
confine themselves to the analysis of the latter.

In other words, if the real-world data do not match Walrasian assumptions
then they are of no use to economists. Georgescu discussed this antiquated
outlook in economics many years ago:

> At one end we find every form of positivism proclaiming that whatever the
> purpose and uses of dialectical concepts, these concepts are antagonistic to
> science: knowledge proper exists only to the extent to which it is expressed in
> arithmomorphic concepts. The position recalls that of the Catholic Church:
> holy thought can be expressed only in Latin. (Georgescu-Roegen, 1971, p. 50)

The Latin of contemporary economics is the mathematics of constrained
optimization and the dogma is that any approach that does not, or cannot,
use that technique is not economics. The analytical boundary of behavior
in the Walrasian system is drawn around an individual with fixed and
well-defined preferences isolated in space and time. Anything outside that
boundary is ignored.

The intractable difficulties present in the Walrasian system arise from
the inability of that system to allow any interactions among economic
agents – other than purely mechanical reactions like atoms bumping into
each other. In the two good (X and Y), two consumer (A and B) case, if
we modify even slightly the standard utility functions such that the utility
of each consumer depends on the fixed utility of the other consumer such
that,

$$U_A = f(X, Y, U_B) \text{ and } U_B = f(X, Y, U_A) \tag{6.1}$$

then the condition for Pareto optimality in exchange is (Henderson and
Quandt, 1971, p. 268):

$$[(\partial U_A/\partial X_A) - (\partial U_A/\partial X_B)] / [(\partial U_A/\partial Y_A) - (\partial U_A/\partial Y_B)] =$$
$$[(\partial U_B/\partial X_B) - (\partial U_B/\partial X_A)] / [(\partial U_B/\partial Y_B) - (\partial U_B/\partial Y_A)] \tag{6.2}$$

In the case of interdependent utility functions the condition for Pareto
optimality in consumption is *not* the equality of the marginal rates of
substitution (MRS) between the two consumers. However, the equality of MRSs is a necessary condition required to prove the efficiency
of competitive markets; that is, to establish that a perfectly operating

market economy will exactly duplicate the results of face-to-face barter-
ing (Gowdy, 2010). Of course it is easy to construct utility functions that
incorporate observed human behavior – loss aversion, reference dependent preferences, the endowment effect.[2] But such utility functions cannot
be used to construct the proof of the efficiency of competitive markets.
Thus, abandoning the requirement of self-regarding agents would mean
abandoning the basic ideological purpose of standard economics, namely,
to provide a rigorous analytical proof promoting the market economy as
the only viable institution to ensure the efficient allocation of society's
scarce resources. It is no wonder that neoliberal economists cling so des-
perately to the independent preferences assumption. Without the mathematical superstructure to hide behind, the ideological bias of Walrasian
orthodoxy would be clear.

Equations (6.1) and (6.2) still allow the construction of utility functions that may be smooth and continuous (and integrable). But Georgescu
(1936, 1973 [1976]) showed that integrability is without meaning unless
transitivity is assumed. Standard utility functions do not constitute a
preference field unless consistent binary preferences exist. Establishing the
axioms of revealed preference depends on assuming the validity of all the
characteristics of *Homo economicus.*

The basic tools of contemporary economic analysis – marginal valuation, relative prices as an indicator of value, the elasticity of substitution,
shadow prices – are driven by the mathematical requirements of constrained optimization, rather than by the careful and thoughtful analysis
of observed economic behavior. I once asked Georgescu why economists
were not more receptive to his ideas. His response was: 'Because I want to
take away their toys.' In his obituary essay about Georgescu, Daly (1994)
lamented the fact that his contributions have been met with 'deafening
silence' by mainstream economics. This is true not only of Georgescu's
work but also the contributions of numerous other economists who have
all but demolished the theoretical edifice of the Walrasian core, including Boadway (1974), Bromley (1990, 1998), Chipman and Moore (1978),
Scitovsky (1941) and many others.

Why haven't the theoretical intractabilities in the Walrasian system been
more widely acknowledged? One reason is the emphasis in contemporary
economics on technique to the neglect of epistemology. Well before the
widespread use of personal computers Georgescu (1971, p. 29) was concerned about the effects of easy computation on synthesis and analysis:

> It thus appears that the computer, just by being there, induces each one of us to
> record the fall of still another apple. Besides, even these records tend to become
> increasingly spurious, for the easy access to a computer center leads many

students to pay even less attention than before to the appropriateness of the statistical tools used in testing their particular models.

In the decades since Georgescu expressed his concern, the tendency in mainstream economics has been to push the emphasis on technique even further toward using ever more complicated statistical techniques rather than checking assumptions against reality. We are still waiting for a response to a question asked by Daly: 'Is there any example of a major question in economics that has been answered by econometric evidence?'

A positive effect of behavioral economics (so far at least) has been a return to concern about research design and the back-and-forth interplay between theory and evidence. This would please Georgescu who favorably referred to Pareto's observation that in order to form an accurate theory of choice, someone should follow consumers around and watch how they actually make decisions (Georgescu-Roegen, 1973 [1976], p. 314). This is more or less what behavioral economics and neuroeconomics has done over the past two decades.

It must be said that part of the blame for the impasse in economic theory lies not only with neoliberals but also with those associated with more progressive schools of economics. For example, much of the path-breaking work in economics is grounded in biology and evolutionary psychology. But there is a tendency among social scientists to dismiss any role for biology in human social processes (Gowdy et al., 2010; Hodgson, 2004). For Georgescu human biology was critical to understanding the economic process (Gowdy and Mesner, 1998). As argued below, bringing in biological explanations does not lead us to a crude form of sociobiology. On the contrary, current understandings of how the brain works confirm that (1) humans are uniquely social animals whose behavior is shaped by complex interactions between physical brain development and social conditioning and (2) human decision making depends crucially on our perceived relationship to others. Arguments for biological determinism are refuted by findings from modern biology (Wexler, 2006).

6.3   SOME KEY INSIGHTS FROM BEHAVIORAL ECONOMICS AND NEUROECONOMICS

If the Walrasian assumptions about human behavior (transitivity, non-satiation, strictly self-regarding behavior) are untenable, how can a suit-able alternative be constructed? Is it possible to create a realistic model of human behavior consistent across disciplines to inform economic theory and policy? The answer is a tentative 'yes' (Gintis, 2006). A number of insights from behavioral and neuroeconomics may be useful to inform economic theory and public policy.

6.3.1 Emotions are Not 'Irrational,' They Play an Essential Role in Human Decision Making

A commonly held view is that people strive to make rational decisions but are sometimes thwarted by their emotions. By contrast, the emerging view of cognition is that the human brain is a unified, highly evolved system with complementary, rather than conflicting (rational versus emotional) components.[3] Studies have shown that some people with neurological damage to the emotional part of the brain are incapable of making even simple decisions even though they can clearly describe the problems they are asked to solve and the consequences of each possible decision. More surprisingly, people with damage to a part of the brain called the ventromedial prefrontal cortex make decisions in accordance with the rational actor model. For example, most people would have difficulty making the following choice: 'You know that a carrier of a deadly airborne strain of Ebola is about to board a plane where he will share the same stale air with scores of strangers. Do you allow him to risk infecting fellow passengers or do you kill him if that is the only way to prevent him from getting on the flight?' (Swaminathan, 2007). Yet people with brain damage have no problem in answering the question. They would make the rational, utilitarian decision and kill the passenger. Further evidence that Walrasian rationality does not describe normal[4] human behavior is provided by an experiment by Shiv et al. (2005) described by Cassidy (2006).

> [W]hen people are confronted with ambiguity their emotions can overpower their reasoning, leading them to reject risky propositions. This raises the intriguing possibility that people who are less fearful than others might make better investors, which is precisely what George Loewenstein and four other researchers found when they carried out a series of experiments with a group of patients who had suffered brain damage. Each of the patients had a lesion in one of three regions of the brain that are central to the processing of emotions . . . The researchers presented the patients with a series of fifty-fifty gambles, in which they stood to win a dollar-fifty or lose a dollar. This is the type of gamble that people often reject, owing to loss aversion, but the patients with lesions accepted the bets more than eighty per cent of the time, and they ended up making significantly more money than a control group made up of people who had no brain damage.

Hazel Henderson (1996) may have been on the right track when she described neoclassical economics as a form of 'brain damage.'

6.3.2   There is No Sharp Distinction Between 'Brain,' 'Mind' and 'Society'

One of the most remarkable findings from neuroscience is the importance of socialization in human brain development. According to Brian Wexler (2006), an important idea to emerge from new knowledge about the sensitivity of the human brain to social inputs is the incredible diversity and variability among individuals resulting from environmental influences on brain development. Wexler (2006, p. 3) writes:

> There is an evolutionary advantage for life forms that reproduce sexually because mixing of genetic material from parents produces variety in their offspring. Thus, different individuals have different characteristics, which increases the likelihood that some members of the group will be able to function and reproduce even when the environment in which the group lives changes. In an analogous manner, the distinctive postnatal shaping of each individual's brain function through interaction with other people, and through his or her own mix of sensory inputs, creates an endless variety of individuals with different functional characteristics. This broadens the range of adaptive and problem-solving capabilities well beyond the variability achieved by sexual reproduction.

It has long been realized that humans are unique in the length of time required to raise an infant to maturity. The human brain continues to develop neurologically for years after birth and the way it develops depends critically on how a child is socialized. It is another way that variability can be introduced into the evolutionary mix. The ability to adapt customs and technology to changing conditions allowed humans to successfully compete for food resources with animals that depended on more purely genetic adaptation mechanisms. Humans alter the environment that shapes brain development to an unprecedented degree. Wexler (2006, p. 3) writes:

> These human alterations in the shared social environment include physical structures, laws and other codes of behavior, food and clothes, spoken and written language, and music and other arts . . . It is this ability to shape the environment that in turn shapes our brains that has allowed human adaptability and capability to develop at a much faster rate than is possible through alteration of the genetic code itself.

The importance of postnatal brain development in humans means that we have the innate ability to change our attitudes and ways of living. Today, the news is full of references to faith, identity and culture. We should not forget that all of these are flexible and negotiable.[5] The evolution of our 'social brain' also means that group norms can modify egoism for the good of the group (Frith, 2007; Grist, 2009). We have the innate potential both to reduce our pressure on the environment and adapt to the inevitable changes in the environment we have set in motion.

6.3.3   Most of Our Daily Decisions are Made Using Habits of Thought and Heuristic Shortcuts

Rational deliberation is a costly, time-consuming process. The human brain has a variety of ways to conserve on thinking and this has important policy implications. One of the most policy-relevant implications is the difference between 'opt-in' or 'opt-out' choices. For example, consider the statistics for different countries on organ donations (Table 6.1).

What accounts for the vast differences in donation rates in countries that are otherwise quite similar? The answer is simply that people in the four countries listed in Table 6.1 with low response rates are asked the question on their driver's application: 'Check the box below if you *want* to participate in the organ donor program.' People in the countries with high response rates were asked the question: 'Check the box below if you *do not want* to participate in the organ donor program.' We like to think of ourselves as rational decision makers in control of the choices we make. But in effect the person who designed the questions is really the one who made the choice about organ donations. Organ donation is a complicated moral decision and we would prefer not to think too much about it, so the fall-back, do-nothing-active choice is appealing.

The process of learning involves familiarizing ourselves with new information to the extent that we no longer have to consciously think about it when it comes up later. We make most decisions based on past experience. Habituation also has a neurological basis. Schultz (2002) measured the activity of neurons while thirsty monkeys sat quietly and listened for a tone that was followed by a squirt of fruit juice into their mouths. After a period of a fixed, steady amount of juice, the amount of

Table 6.1   Percent of drivers donating organs

Denmark	4%	France	100%
Netherlands	28%	Hungary	100%
Germany	12%	Poland	100%
United Kingdom	17%	Portugal	100%
Austria	100%	Sweden	86%
Belgium	98%		

Source: Ariely (2008).

juice was doubled without warning – the rate of neuron firing went from about 3 per second to 80 per second. As this new magnitude of reward was repeated, the firing rate returned to the baseline rate of 3 firings per second. The opposite happened when the reward was reduced without warning. The firing rate dropped but then returned to the baseline rate of 3 firings per second.

Humans become habituated both to higher levels of reward and lower levels. For public policy considerations this has good and bad implications as in the case of reducing consumption. On the one hand, consuming market goods can be a kind of addiction requiring ever increasing amounts to give us a constant level of satisfaction. On the other hand, behavioral results suggest that we can adjust to lower levels of material consumption and be just as happy as before.

6.3.4 The Degree of Human Cooperation is Unsurpassed Among Mammals

In the 1970s many economists became enamored with the 'selfish gene' idea in biology (Dawkins, 1976). To many conservatives it seemed to offer a 'natural,' 'scientific' justification for rational economic man and for free market economic policies (Manner and Gowdy, 2010). At that time theories of altruism in biology were in disfavor because there seemed to be no way around the fact that such behavior made an organism less fit compared to its non-altruistic competitors. But gradually biologists came to realize that pure altruism could emerge if such behavior gave a competitive advantage to a particular group. If competition existed between groups, then individual behavioral traits that conferred an advantage to the group could be selected. Once it was established that cooperative behavior (pure altruism) could have an evolutionary advantage, theories of group selection once again became acceptable to biologists (Wilson and Hölldobler, 2005; Wilson and Wilson, 2008). Cooperation depends in part on the ability to punish. It has been found that those societies with the highest degree of cooperative behavior are those having the most effective means of punishing those who violate social norms. Punishment effectively solves the free-rider problem (Henrich et al., 2006).

6.3.5 'Us' versus 'Them': The Robbers Cave Experiment

According to Alexander (1987), human ethics evolved from the long history of violent interactions among ancestral primate groups, which strengthened group cohesiveness. This is supported by asymmetric behavior reported in conflicts among apes and monkeys – conflict resolving inside the group, and extreme brutality to outsiders. Similarly, humans apply ethics asymmetrically to insiders and outsiders of the group they belong to. The most convincing examples of this are wars and religious and ethnic conflicts (de Waal, 1996; Wilson, 2002). Group cohesiveness has two faces, providing benefits to fellow group members and directing hostility toward outsiders.[6] Field (2001, p. 8) phrases it as: 'the ability to make common cause has a dark side: the control of within group conflict sometimes lays the foundation for violent attacks on outgroups. But the inclination is also what brings millions of people to the polls in democratic nations and is as much an underpinning of democracy as it is of totalitarianism.'

David Berreby (2005, chapter 8) describes a remarkable experiment illustrating both the negative consequences of 'them and us' behavior and also the ability of humans to redefine these categories. In 1954 Muzafer Sherif[7] and his colleagues at the University of Oklahoma conducted an experiment in group behavior at Robbers Cave camp in the mountains of eastern Oklahoma (Sherif et al., 1961). In the experiment 22 middle-class Caucasian boys enrolled in Oklahoma schools were divided into two groups of 11 boys each. Each group was assigned to a particular area with its own bunkhouse, mess hall and swimming hole. Each group was given the freedom to explore the area and organize itself as the group members chose. The groups chose names ('Rattlers' and 'Eagles'), designed their own logos and constructed various behavioral rules that established their own identities. During the first week, each group was unaware of the existence of the other group.

After the first week, each group was made aware of the other group. The reaction of each group toward the other was immediate and negative. Berreby writes:

> Among both bands, talk of 'our' swimming spot and 'our' field sprung up only after the boys knew there was another gang nearby. The feeling extended to everyone; fishermen and hikers passing through the state park would also cause the boys to fret about interference with 'our' territory. Their passionate sense of Eagleness and Rattlerdom was marking the entire human world. (Berreby, 2005, p. 170)

A week of arranged competition between the groups (baseball games, tug-of-war contests) made the rivalry between the two groups more intense and the sense of 'us versus them' even more pronounced.

> Fourteen days after they had arrived as strangers, then, these look-alike boys, all born around the same time, from look-alike households, had turned into two exclusive disdainful tribes, yelling 'dirty bums' and 'sissies' at their neighbors

whenever their paths crossed. It had all been 'experimentally produced from scratch' as Sherif put it. (Berreby, 2005, p. 173)

At this point, the results of the Robbers Cave experiment are discouraging. It seems that it is 'human nature' to automatically coalesce into hostile camps each with its own rules of conduct and defining characteristics of what is correct and incorrect behavior. 'Bad' human nature dominates our best intensions. But the third week of the experiment shows that the story of 'us and them' is not so bleak as popularly imagined.

During the third week Sherif initiated what he deemed to be the main objective of the experiment, namely, to disprove the 'original sin' view of human nature. Sherif initiated a number of activities that required the two groups to work together – repairing a broken faucet, raising money to rent a movie, getting a disabled truck going again. After a week of working together to solve common problems, the transformation of the 'us-them' mentality was remarkable.

> The last night, the boys decided they wanted to go to the camp's corral, where they roasted marshmallows. Then each group performed skits for the other. The next day was the last of the camp. At breakfast and lunch, the boys sat higgledy-piggledy, with no regard for Rattlerdom and Eagleness. The frequent opinion polls he was taking also told Sherif that attitudes were changing: overwhelmingly hostile sentiments about 'the others' had been replaced by overwhelmingly positive feelings. Meanwhile, the bands' ratings of their members had gotten somewhat less enthusiastic. It was as if the need to puff up their members had quieted, along with the urge to disparage the enemy. When they took seats on the bus for the trip home that afternoon, the boys ignored Rattler-Eagle lines completely. (Berreby, 2005, pp. 176–7)

Human history is full of accounts of horrible atrocities perpetuated by one group upon another. These groups may be based on real physical or ideological differences or they may be entirely arbitrary as in the Robbers Cave experiment. The good news is that the 'us-them' distinction is fluid and can be changed through communication, increasing familiarity with out-group members and the presence of some common challenge affecting all groups.

6.4   BEHAVIORAL ECONOMICS AND PUBLIC POLICY

Behavioral and neuroeconomics not only undermines the foundations of the Walrasian system but also lays new foundations based on a comprehensive, scientific description and explanation of human decision making. It is no longer tenable for economists to claim that the self-regarding, rational actor model offers a satisfactory description of economic behavior. Nor do humans consistently act 'as if' they obey the laws of rational choice theory. This simple insight undermines the prevailing neoliberal 'let the market take care of it' mentality dominating economic theory and policy (and having a major presence even in ecological economics). The implications for economic policy are enormous but have just begun to be explored. The current disarray of mainstream economics offers a huge opportunity for formally heterodox approaches to play a leading role in reshaping the economic approach to public policy. A few insights beginning to reach the mainstream are discussed below with reference to Georgescu.

6.4.1 The Centrality of Norms to Economic Behavior

One of Georgescu's most important papers was his 1960 article 'Economic theory and agrarian economics' on peasant economies (Georgescu-Roegen, 1960).[8] In that article he outlined his thesis that 'what characterizes an economic system is its institutions, not the technology it uses' (Georgescu-Roegen, 1960, p. 3). The peasant village was Georgescu's unit of analysis and that outlook shaped his ideas about institutions, entropy, self-organization and sustainable economic processes. Daly's modern conceptualization of ecological economics also stresses the importance of social norms on economic decision making, with his pre-analytic vision of economies as nested subsystems within social and cultural institutions, which in turn are subsystems of the larger containing and sustaining ecosystems.

Georgescu's way of thinking about self-organizing institutions and social norms are now almost mainstream. Akerlof's (2007) view on norms echoes Georgescu's although he loses much of the analytical rigor that Georgescu had by trying to shoehorn his insights into standard economic models. Stiglitz (2003) has been a vociferous critique of traditional development policies based purely on economic formalism without adequate appreciation of the specific cultures development policies were supposed to help. The award of the 2009 Nobel Prize in Economics[9] to Elinor Ostrom for her work on self-organizing institutions is the strongest signal yet that the intellectual orientation of economics is finally beginning to change.

6.4.2 Prices Cannot Accurately Represent the Value of Environmental Features

A critical debate is now taking place within ecological economics on the role of prices in environmental policy. The goal of Walrasian economic policy is to create the fictitious world of competitive equilibrium. A basic assumption is that relative prices can capture all the information needed to make socially optimal choices about resource allocation. Georgescu recognized the absurdity of this position.

> [T]here is no such thing as the cost of undoing an irreparable harm or reserving an irrevocable depletion, and since no relevant price can be set on avoiding the inconvenience if future generations cannot bid on this choice, we must insist that the measures taken for either purpose should consist of quantitative regulations, notwithstanding the advice of most economists to increase the efficiency of the market through taxes and subsidies. (Georgescu-Roegen, 1974 [1976], p. 33)

A growing body of evidence suggests that monetary incentives may have a perverse effect in terms of environmental policies. Contrary to the advice of many environmental advocates, placing prices on environmental features may be *incentive incompatible* with environmental goals. A growing body of evidence has shown that price incentives can crowd out the social good (Frey, 1997). In fact, *money itself* can be a deterrent to cooperative behavior. An often cited example is the finding that paying blood donors significantly reduces blood donations (Titmuss, 1971). A recent experiment found that the mere awareness of 'money' had a negative effect on sociality. Vohs et al. (2006) performed several experiments that compared various kinds of social behavior in groups of people that were first given reminders of 'money' with groups given a 'non-money' reminder. Participants were asked to unscramble jumbled words to make phrases. In the money group the phrases involved some concept of money, like 'a high-paying salary is important.' In the control group the phrases were neutral, like 'it is cold outside.' This reinforced thinking in terms of money in the experimental group but not the control group. The groups were then subjected to nine experiments designed to test the effects of exposure to money on 'self-sufficiency' and helpful behavior. In one experiment subjects were given $2 in quarters that they were told was left over from an earlier experiment. At the end of the word scrambling game they were offered the chance to put money in a box to denote to needy students. Those exposed to reminders of money gave substantially less to the charity. In another experiment subjects reminded of money were less likely to ask for help in performing a complicated task. In another test, subjects were asked to sit at desks and fill out a questionnaire. Some desks faced a poster with a picture of money, and others faced a poster showing flowers or a seascape. They were then asked to choose between a reward characterized as a 'group' or 'individual' activity; for example, individual cooking lessons versus a dinner for four. Those exposed to the money poster were more likely to pick individual activities. The authors summarize the results as follows:

> Relative to participants primed with neutral concepts, participants primed with
> money preferred to stay alone, work alone, and put more physical distance
> between themselves and a new acquaintance ... When reminded of money,
> people would want to be free from dependency and would also prefer that
> others not depend on them. (Vohs et al., 2006, p. 1154)

As the debates about biological diversity and climate change have made
clear, prices are a haphazard tool to use for environmental policy (Vatn and
Bromley, 1994). Correcting prices cannot be a substitute for correcting our
ethics toward future generations and the natural world.

> The only way to protect future generations, at least from the excessive consump-
> tion of resources during the present bonanza, is by reeducating ourselves so as
> to feel some sympathy for our *future* fellow humans in the same way in which
> we have come to be interested in the well-being of our *contemporary* 'neighbors.'
> (Georgescu-Roegen, 1974 [1976], p. 32, emphases in original)

We are now, collectively as a species, pushing the limits of the earth's
biophysical systems to support the current human population. Collective
action on a global scale is required to pull us back from the brink, and
such action will depend on our ability to redefine 'us' as the entire human
species. This is not to say that carbon taxes and other market-based instruments cannot buy us time. But merely tinkering with the market will not set
us on the path to sustainability.

6.4.3 Well-being Should Not be Equated to Income

Most economic models assume that social well-being can be equated with
per capita income. Psychologists have long argued that well-being derives
from a wide variety of individual, social and genetic factors. Economists
have also made significant contributions to the well-being literature
(Easterlin, 1974; Frey and Stutzer, 2002; Layard, 2005; Schor, 2010).
Recently a report commissioned by the government of France and headed
by Nobel laureate Joseph Stiglitz (Stiglitz et al., 2009) called for the abandonment of 'gross domestic product (GDP) fetishism' and the use of an
array of social and environmental indicators as a guide to public policy.
As Stiglitz pointed out, the *Report by the Commission on the Measurement
of Economic Performance and Social Progress* was made even more timely
by the financial meltdown that laid bare the ephemeral nature of financial accounting. According to Stiglitz, 'A focus on the material aspects
of GDP may be especially inappropriate as the world faces the crisis of
global warming. Should we "punish" a country – in terms of our measure
of performance – if it decides to take some of the fruits of the increase in

productivity from the advancement of knowledge in the form of leisure, rather than just consuming more goods?' (quoted in Kolbert, 2009).

Surveys, behavioral experiments and neurological analysis have identified key factors positively influencing well-being. These include health (especially self-reported health) (Ferrer-i-Carbonell and van Praag, 2002), close relationships and marriage, intelligence, education and religion (Frey and Stutzer, 2002). Age, gender and income also influence happiness, but not to the degree once thought. Some facts about income and happiness are now well established. First, people in wealthier countries are generally happier than people in poorer countries (Diener et al., 1995). But even this correlation is weak once basic needs are met and the happiness data show many anomalies. For example, some surveys show that people in Nigeria are happier than people in Austria, France and Japan (Frey and Stutzer, 2002, p. 35, table 2.2). Second, past a certain stage of development, increasing incomes do not lead to greater happiness. For example, real per capita income in the USA has increased sharply in recent decades but reported happiness has declined (Frey and Stutzer, 2002). Similar results have been reported for Japan and Western Europe (Easterlin, 1995). Studies of individuals also show a lack of correlation between increases in income and increases in happiness (Frey and Stutzer, 2002). Third, security seems to be a key element in happiness. This implies that large welfare gains would come from a focus on improving those things that increase individual security like health insurance, old age security, employment and job security. Fourth, mental health is a crucial factor in happiness. Frey and Stutzer (2002) and Layard (2005) argue, based on happiness survey results, for more public spending on mental health, especially for the very young since the first few years of a person's life play a large role in future happiness. If we want future generations to experience a high and sustainable level of welfare, we are likely to get high rates of return by investing in policies to ensure adequate child nutrition, health care, education and family counseling. Fifth, richer social relationships generally make people happier. This implies that welfare gains may be obtained from increased leisure time, and more public spending on social and recreational infrastructure. All of this research indicates that the policy focus on gross national product (GNP) growth as a means to increase welfare may be misplaced.

A missing element in modern behavioral economics is an appreciation of the evolutionary origins of human behavior. Like behavioralism in general, behavioral economics ignores evolutionary history and still tends to see behavior as a collection of blank slate 'anomalies.' An evolutionary framework could help organize the uncovered behavioral regularities into a systematic explanation of behavior. For example, 'fairness' seems to be a universal human attribute although it is manifested in different ways in different cultures. Humans have an incredible amount of behavioral and cultural flexibility but we do have an evolutionary history and genetic constraints. A useful metaphor is that human behavior is more like a coloring book than a blank slate. Neuroeconomics can help define the lines and the colors and how these change and reinforce each other.

6.5   WHAT CAN NEUROECONOMICS OFFER?

Georgescu's 'bioeconomics' (Georgescu-Roegen, 1977; Gowdy and Mesner, 1998) has been very influential in analyses of the production side of the economy. His elaboration of the insight that the human economy is a subset of the biophysical world is central to ecological economics. But his vision of bioeconomics also emphasized the fact that the humans are an evolved biological species. Behavioral economics and neuroeconomics can be seen as extending this vision, although both fields have yet to take a truly evolutionary approach (Wilson, 2010). The field of behavioral economics is still very new. Neuroeconomics is even younger, just a few years old, but it has the potential to change the face of economics even more than the behavioral revolution. We can categorize the contributions of neuroscience to behavioral economics going from 'certain' to 'speculative.'

6.5.1   Neuroscience has Confirmed the Results of Behavioral Experiments

Through functional magnetic resonance imaging (fMRI) neuroscience has confirmed the regularities uncovered by behavioral economics – loss aversion (Tom et al., 2007), reference dependent preferences (De Martino et al., 2009) and so on. These behavioral regularities are real. They have a physical, biological basis as well as a cultural basis. For example, in experiments monitoring brain activity as the Ultimatum Game (UG) is being played, it has been shown that both the emotional (the anterior insula) and the cognitive (dorsolateral prefrontal cortex) parts of the brain are activated when an unfair offer is received and that the anterior insula was activated when an unfair offer was rejected (Sanfey et al., 2003). Deciding whether or not to accept a UG offer is a complex process involving emotion, reason and socially conditioned standards of fairness.

6.5.2   Neuroscience has Provided an Increasingly Sophisticated Understanding of How the Human Brain Makes Economic Decisions

Different parts of the brain are involved depending on how the brain defines a particular decision and how these decisions are framed. When people discount the future, different parts of the brain evaluate the effects of future events depending on timing and the importance of the consequences. For example, hyperbolic discounting has been shown to be a consistent phenomenon and its existence has been confirmed and to some extent explained by neuroscience (Kim and Zauberman, 2009; Wittmann and Paulus, 2009). Evolutionary history also plays a role in the way humans and other animals discount. Like humans, bonobos and chimpanzees exhibit patience when given a choice between an immediate reward and waiting to receive a larger reward (Rosati et al., 2007).[10]

fMRI has also demonstrated that reactions to monetary rewards activate the same brain regions as primary enforcers like food (Elliot et al., 2003). But the reward system in the brain is complicated. Some parts of the brain distinguish between the size of the monetary reward while others respond only to its presence or absence.

> [D]ifferent components of human reward processing systems respond differently to monetary value. Regions including midbrain, striatum, and amygdala were more responsive to the presence or occurrence of reward than its value. Premotor cortex responded linearly to increasing reward value, perhaps reflecting the increasing potency with which larger rewards control goal directed behavior. (Elliot et al., 2003, p. 307)

6.5.3   Neuroscience has Confirmed the Existence of the Social Brain and Described Some of its Features

Other mammals are highly social animals with a variety of behavioral attributes evolved to facilitate social interaction. But humans are unique in their degree of sociability even among primates. In terms of how people react to information and how they make decisions, it's impossible to separate 'brain,' 'individual' and 'group.' A remarkable finding from neuroscience is the presence in the human brain of a kind of neuron (called Von Economo or spindle neurons) that are apparently present in order to make rapid decisions about other humans. Sherwood et al. (2008, p. 433) write:

> Based on the location, neurochemistry, and morphological characteristics of Von Economo neurons, it has been hypothesized that they transmit rapid outputs to subcortical regions (Allman et al. 2005). It is interesting that these

specialized projection neuron types have been identified in cortical areas that are positioned at the interface between emotional and cognitive processing. Given their characteristics, it has been speculated that Von Economo neurons are designed for quick signaling of an appropriate response in the context of social ambiguity (Allman et al. 2005). Enhancements of this ability would be particularly important in the context of fission-fusion communities, such as those of panids and possibly the LCA [last common ancestor], with complex networks of social interactions and potential uncertainties at reunions.

Von Economo neurons (VENs) are also found (in much lower numbers) in great apes and whales and dolphins, other highly intelligent species with complex social systems. In humans, most of these neurons are formed after birth, again pointing to the blurred line between heredity and socialization. It is hypothesized that these neurons help humans to adjust quickly to rapidly changing social situations.

We hypothesize that the VENs and associated circuitry enable us to reduce complex social and cultural dimensions of decision-making into a single dimension that facilitates the rapid execution of decisions. Other animals are not encumbered by such elaborate social and cultural contingencies to their decision-making and thus do not require such a system for rapid intuitive choice. (Allman et al., 2005, p. 370)

Like behavioral economics, neuroscience shows that the economic model of self-referential behavior strips away everything that makes humans unique.

6.5.4 Neuroscience has Identified the Importance of Homeostasis in Brain Structure and Function and This May be a Key to Understanding Sustainability

Homeostasis is a key phenomenon of living systems. It is the ability (or even the goal) of living systems to maintain balance through a complex, highly evolved system of interacting processes.

6.5.4.1 Homeostasis and the individual

One of the most interesting things about how the brain works is how it is intricately structured (physically, chemically, neurologically) to keep things in balance. Traditionally, economists have seen behavior in terms of 'satisfying preferences.' People know what they want and rationally choose the things that will best satisfy these wants. A more accurate way to look at 'wants' is to view them as one of several mechanisms to maintain 'balance' in the human mind and body. Camerer et al. (2005, p. 27) write:

As economists, we are used to thinking of preferences as the starting point for human behavior and behavior as the ending point. A neuroscience perspective, in contrast, views explicit behavior as only one of many mechanisms that the brain uses to maintain homeostasis, and preferences as transient state variables that ensure survival and reproduction. The traditional economic account of behavior, which assumes that humans act so as to maximally satisfy their preferences, starts in the middle (or perhaps even toward the end) of the neuroscience account. Rather than viewing pleasure as the goal of human behavior, a more realistic account would view pleasure as a homeostatic cue – an informational signal.

'Consumption,' for example, is one of many kinds of behavior that may move an individual toward, or away from, emotional balance. The goal, as Georgescu pointed out, is not to maximize utility but to enjoy life. There is much to learn here from reflective traditions in philosophy, psychology and even economics (Zsolnai and Ims, 2006).

6.5.4.2 Homeostasis and human societies

It can be argued that the goal of human societies and social rules is also homeostasis. Societies that are unable to maintain stability, either from external or internal stresses, are doomed to collapse (Diamond, 2005). Georgescu's work on peasant economies embodies this concept. For him, the village, community, not the individual, 'constitutes the analytical atom in the phenomenon domain of peasant sociology' (Georgescu-Roegen, 1965 [1976], p. 205). His choice function for the peasant was $\Omega = \Psi(Y; Y_s)$, where Y_s represents the society of the peasant village, showing the condition of reciprocity between village institutions and the individual. In the peasant village individual utility is a function not only of individual well-being (Y) but also of the well-being of the village (Y_s). Village institutions, he insisted, are designed to ensure continuity within a changing evolutionary framework including the ultimate dependence on biological processes subject to the entropy law.

'Viability' was the term Georgescu used for a sustainable economy. An economy was viable if (1) it uses technologies that do not draw down irreplaceable stocks and (2) it does not impair the ability of *fund* factors (labor capital and land) to maintain themselves through time. This implies, for example, that a society that does not maintain a balance in the everyday lives of its citizens is not sustainable.

6.6 CONCLUDING THOUGHTS

The insights of Georgescu-Roegen and Daly about economic behavior and the social nature of production may be out of step with prevailing economic orthodoxy but they have been confirmed by current findings of behavioral economics and neuroeconomics. The glue that holds the Walrasian system together is the rational actor model – the ideology that the economic process is driven by self-regarding, narrow rational individuals without social or biological context. This model is the current battleground for the heart and soul of economics. How the mainstream absorbs the behavioral revolution in economics will be the key as to whether neoliberal economic policies will continue to dominate the mainstream or whether economics can play a constructive role in the move to a sustainable, human-centered economic system.

Daly and Georgescu are best known for calling attention to biophysical constraints on economic activity. During the 1990s a vigorous debate erupted within ecological economics over the question of whether the goals of efficient allocation, just distribution and sustainable scale could be independently addressed (Daly, 1992; Malghan, 2010). Daly argued that they could be (Daly, 1991, 1992) and made a case that scale should be the primary focus of environmental policy (Malghan, 2010). Others (Prakash and Gupta, 1994; Stewen, 1998) argued for the interdependence of the three goals. Although this chapter focuses on behavior, the findings discussed above have profound implications not only for 'choices' but also for these broader policy goals of ecological economics. Phenomena such as the relative income effect suggest that policies to address scale should be integrated with distributional effects. Reducing consumption could actually increase well-being if we simultaneously move to increase non-positional activities such as leisure time and richer social relationships.

Many biophysical constraints manifest themselves as public goods problems, requiring collective action. If the overriding economic goal is efficiency, and if people are inherently selfish and narrowly rational, we have limited options for solving such problems, and we are forced to work within the market model. In contrast, if brains/minds/society and behavior are malleable, two important results emerge. First, by rewarding market institutions and thus reinforcing selfish behavior, we make it far more difficult to solve these problems. Second, behavioral research indicates that we can develop institutions that promote the cooperative behavior required to solve these problems. We have evolved to cooperate within our group, but less so between groups. In humans the 'group' is defined by cultural selection pressures. We now face problems that can only be solved by global cooperation. Appropriate institutions for solving these problems would punish non-cooperation, make cooperation the default behavior (Henrich et al., 2006) or bring people together to confront challenges that require cooperation (Berreby, 2005). The behavioral and neuroscience literature is reassuring in the sense that it opens up myriad possibilities for 'how to be human.'

NOTES

* Parts of this chapter are adapted from a background report prepared by the author for the Garrison Institute's 'Climate, Mind and Behavior' initiative and from a 2008 article, 'Behavioral economics and climate change policy' (Gowdy, 2008). The author would like to thank Josh Farley and Deepak Malghan for helpful comments on an earlier draft.

1. I use the term 'Walrasian' to refer to the mathematical model of economic activity – first formulated and developed by Walras, Pareto and Jevons in the late 1800s – that came to dominate economic analysis in the decades after World War II. This model – the general equilibrium system embodying the Fundamental Theorems of Welfare Economics (Feldman, 1987; Gowdy, 2004, 2010) – is central to every microeconomic textbook and continues to dominate public policy discourse in spite of a string of spectacular policy failures (Quiggin, 2010). Two core bundles of assumptions of the Walrasian system are embodied in the 'rational actor' model of human behavior and the model of 'perfect competition' among firms. Because of the mathematical requirements of constrained optimization, each of these models must preclude interaction among economic actors, whether among firms or individuals.

2. For examples, see chapter 11 on reference dependent preferences in Burkett (2006).

3. Although parts of the brain specialize in reacting to certain kinds of stimuli, there is no single brain system solely responsible for processing either emotions or reason (Frith, 2007; Glimcher et al., 2005). It is also true that initial emotional feelings can be modified by further reflection. In a study of racial prejudice it was found that negative responses of white people to pictures of black faces were significantly reduced if the pictures were shown for 525 ms rather than 30 ms. This reduction was associated with increased activity in the frontal cortex, a region of the brain associated with control and regulation (Cunningham et al., 2004; Frith, 2007). Emotional and cognitive parts of the human brain operate as an incredibly complex unified system to guide behavior.

4. Woody Allen gives a good definition of a normal person: 'Someone you don't know very well.'

5. For a wonderful account of this for the British in India, see William Dalrymple's *White Mughals* (2002).

6. A recent experiment looking at the effects of oxytocin sheds some light on the 'us versus them' phenomenon. Oxytocin is a neurotransmitter that promotes social bonding. De Dreu et al. (2010) found that oxytocin increased trust in an in-group prisoner's dilemma game. But it also increased the willingness to punish cheaters from outside groups. 'Our findings show that oxytocin, a neuropeptide functioning both as a neurotransmitter and hormone, plays a crucial role in driving in-group love and defensive (but not offensive) aggression toward out-groups' (p. 1408).

7. Sherif himself was almost a victim of the 'us-them' syndrome. In 1919, as a young boy he narrowly escaped being killed in the Greek massacre of Turks in the city of Smyrna in southeastern Turkey.

8. 'Economic theory and agrarian economics' is the only article reprinted in both *Analytical Economics* (Georgescu-Roegen, 1967) and *Energy and Economic Myths* (Georgescu-Roegen, 1976).

9. The Sveriges Riksbank Prize in Economic Sciences in Memory of Alfred Nobel.

10. Interestingly, bonobos are more tolerant of others and more cooperative than chimpanzees (Anderson, 2007; Hare et al., 2007) and this might be due to the retention of juvenile traits into adulthood (Wobber et al., 2010).

REFERENCES

Akerlof, G. (2007), 'The missing motivation in macroeconomics', *American Economic Review*, **97** (1), 5–36.

Alexander, R. (1987), *The Biology of Moral Systems*, New York: Aldine de Gruyter.

Allman, J., T. McLaughlin and A. Hakeem (2005), 'Intuition and autism: a possible role for Von Economo neurons', *Trends in Cognitive Science*, **9** (8), 367–73.

Anderson, J. (2007), 'Animal behavior: tolerant primates cooperate best', *Current Biology*, **17** (7), R242–4.

Ariely, D. (2008), 'We're all predictably irrational', Presentation at the Entertainment Gathering, Monterey, CA, 13 December, available at https://www.youtube.com/watch?v=JhjUJTw2i1M (accessed 13 December 2015).

Berreby, D. (2005), *Us and Them: The Science of Identity*, Chicago, IL: University of Chicago Press.

Boadway, R.W. (1974), 'The welfare foundations of cost–benefit analysis', *Economic Journal*, **84** (336), 926–39.

Bromley, D. (1990), 'The ideology of efficiency: searching for a theory of policy analysis', *Journal of Environmental Economics and Management*, **19** (1), 86–107.

Bromley, D. (1998), 'Searching for sustainability: the poverty of spontaneous order', *Ecological Economics*, **24** (2–3), 231–40.

Burkett, J. (2006), *Microeconomics: Optimization, Experiments, and Behavior*, Oxford and New York: Oxford University Press.

Camerer, C., G. Loewenstein and D. Prelec (2005), 'Neuroeconomics: how neuroscience can inform economics', *Journal of Economic Literature*, **43** (1), 9–64.

Cassidy, J. (2006), 'Mind games: what neuroeconomics tells us about money and the brain', *The New Yorker*, 18 September, available at http://www.newyorker.com/magazine/2006/09/18/mind-games-3 (accessed 13 Deember 2015).

Chipman, J. and J. Moore (1978), 'The new welfare economics 1939–1974', *International Economic Review*, **19** (3), 547–84.

Cunningham, W., M. Johnson, C. Raye, J. Gatenby, J. Core and M. Banaji (2004), 'Separable neural components in the processing of black and white faces', *Psychological Science*, **15** (12), 806–13.

Dalrymple, W. (2002), *White Mughals*, New York: Penguin Books.

Daly, H.E. (1991), 'Towards an environmental macroeconomics', *Land Economics*, **67** (2), 255–9.

Daly, H.E. (1992), 'Allocation, distribution and scale: towards an economics that is efficient, just and sustainable', *Ecological Economics*, **6** (3), 185–93.

Daly, H.E. (1994), 'On Nicholas Georgescu-Roegen's contributions to economics: an obituary essay', *Ecological Economics*, **13** (3), 149–54.

Dawkins, R. (1976), *The Selfish Gene*, Oxford: Oxford University Press.

De Dreu, C., L. Greer, M. Handgraaf et al. (2010), 'The neuropeptide oxytocin regulates parochial altruism in intergroup conflict among humans', *Science*, **328** (5984), 1408–11.

De Martino, B., D. Kumaran, B. Holt and R. Dolan (2009), 'The neurology of reference-dependent value computation', *Journal of Neuroscience*, **29** (12), 3833–42.

de Waal, F. (1996), *Good Natured: The Origins of Right and Wrong and Other Animals*, Cambridge, MA: Harvard University Press.

DeCanio, S. (2003), *Economic Models of Climate Change: A Critique*, London and New York: Palgrave Macmillan.

Diamond, J. (2005), *Collapse: How Societies Choose to Fail or Succeed*, New York: Viking.

Diener, E., M. Diener and C. Diener (1995), 'Factors predicting the well-being of nations', *Journal of Personality and Social Psychology*, **69** (5), 851–64.

Dostoyevsky, F. (1986), *The House of the Dead*, New York: Penguin Classics.

Easterlin, R. (1974), 'Does economic growth improve the human lot? Some empirical evidence', in P. David and M. Reder (eds), *Nations and Happiness in Economic Growth: Essays in Honor of Moses Abramowitz*, New York: Academic Press, pp. 89–125.

Easterlin, R. (1995), 'Will raising the incomes of all increase the happiness of all?', *Journal of Economic Behavior and Organization*, **27** (1), 35–7.

Elliot, R., J. Newman, O. Longe and J. Deakin (2003), 'Differential response patterns in the striatum and orbitofrontal cortex to financial rewards in humans: a parametric functional magnetic resonance imaging study', *Journal of Neuroscience*, **23** (1), 303–7.

Feldman, A. (1987), 'Welfare economics', in J. Eatwell, M. Milgate and P. Newman (eds), *New Palgrave Dictionary of Economics*, Vol. 4, London: Macmillan Press, pp. 889–95.

Ferrer-i-Carbonell, A. and B.M. van Praag (2002), 'The subjective costs of health losses due to chronic diseases: an alternative to monetary appraisal', *Health Economics*, **11** (8), 709–22.

Field, A. (2001), *Altruistically Inclined?* Ann Arbor, MI: University of Michigan Press.

Frey, B. (1997), 'A constitution for knaves crowds out civic virtues', *Economic Journal*, **107** (443), 1043–53.

Frey, B. and A. Stutzer (2002), *Happiness and Economics: How the Economy and Institutions Affect Well-being*, Princeton, NJ: Princeton University Press.

Frith, C. (2007), 'The social brain?', *Philosophical Transactions of the Royal Society B*, **362** (1480), 671–8.

Georgescu-Roegen, N. (1936), 'The pure theory of consumer behavior', *Quarterly Journal of Economics*, **50** (4), 545–93.

Georgescu-Roegen, N. (1950), 'The theory of choice and the constancy of economic laws', *Quarterly Journal of Economics*, **64** (1), 125–38.

Georgescu-Roegen, N. (1954), 'Choice, expectations and measurability', *Quarterly Journal of Economics*, **68** (4), 503–34.

Georgescu-Roegen, N. (1960), 'Economic theory and agrarian economics', *Oxford Economic Papers* (New Series), **12** (1), 1–40.

Georgescu-Roegen, N. (1965), 'The institutional aspects of peasant communities', reprinted in 1976, *Energy and Economic Myths*, San Francisco, CA: Pergamon Press, pp. 199–231.

Georgescu-Roegen, N. (1967), *Analytical Economics*, Cambridge, MA: Harvard University Press.

Georgescu-Roegen, N. (1971), *The Entropy Law and the Economic Process*, Cambridge, MA: Harvard University Press.

Georgescu-Roegen, N. (1973), 'Vilfredo Pareto and his theory of ophelimity', reprinted in 1976, *Energy and Economic Myths*, San Francisco, CA: Pergamon Press, pp. 307–49.

Georgescu-Roegen, N. (1974), 'Energy and economic myths', reprinted in 1976, *Energy and Economic Myths*, San Francisco, CA: Pergamon Press, pp. 3–36.

Georgescu-Roegen, N. (1976), *Energy and Economic Myths*, San Francisco, CA: Pergamon Press.

Georgescu-Roegen, N. (1977), 'Inequality, limits and growth from a bioeconomic viewpoint', *Review of Social Economy*, **35** (3), 361–75.

Gintis, H. (2006), 'A framework for the integration of the behavioral sciences', *Behavioral and Brain Sciences*, **30** (1), 1–61.

Glimcher, P., M. Dorris and H. Bayer (2005), 'Physiological utility theory and the neuroeconomics of choice', *Games and Economic Behavior*, **52** (2), 213–56.

Gowdy, J. (1985), 'Utility theory and agrarian societies', *International Journal of Social Economics*, **12** (6/7), 104–17.

Gowdy, J. (2004), 'The revolution in welfare economics and its implications for environmental valuation and policy', *Land Economics*, **80** (2), 239–57.

Gowdy, J. (2008), 'Behavioral economics and climate change policy', *Journal of Economic Behavior and Organization*, **68** (3–4), 632–44.

Gowdy, J. (2010), *Microeconomic Theory Old and New: A Student's Guide*, Stanford, CA: Stanford University Press.

Gowdy, J. and K. Mayumi (2001), 'Reformulating the foundations of consumer choice theory and environmental valuation', *Ecological Economics*, **39** (2), 223–37.

Gowdy, J. and S. Mesner (1998), 'The evolution of Georgescu-Roegen's bioeconomics', *Review of Social Economy*, **56** (2), 136–56.

Gowdy, J., C. Hall, K. Klitgard and L. Krall (2010), 'What every conservation biologist should know about economic theory', *Conservation Biology*, **24** (6), 1440–47.

Grist, M. (2009), *Changing the Subject*, Royal Society for the Encouragement of Arts, Manufactures and Commerce (RSA), available at https://www.thersa.org/globalassets/pdfs/blogs/nov28th2009changingthe-subjectpamphlet.pdf (accessed 13 December 2015).

Gull, F. and W. Pesendorfer (2008), 'The case for mindless economics', in A. Caplin and A. Shotter (eds), *The Foundations for Positive and Normative Economics*, Oxford: Oxford University Press, pp. 3–42.

Hare, B., A. Melis, V. Woods, S. Hastings and R. Wrangham (2007), 'Tolerance allows bonobos to outperform chimpanzees on a cooperative task', *Current Biology*, **17** (7), 619–23.

Henderson, H. (1996), *Creating Alternative Futures: The End of Economics*, West Hartford, CT: Kumarian Press.

Henderson, J. and J. Quandt (1971), *Microeconomic Theory: A Mathematical Approach*, New York: McGraw-Hill.

Henrich, J., R. McElreath, A. Barr et al. (2006), 'Costly punishment across human societies', *Science*, **312** (5781), 1767–70.

Hodgson, G. (2004), *The Evolution of Institutional Economics: Agency, Structure and Darwinism in American Institutionalism*, London and New York: Routledge.

Kahneman, D. (1994), 'New challenges to the rationality assumption', *Journal of Institutional and Theoretical Economics*, **150** (1), 18–36.

Kim, K. and G. Zauberman (2009), 'Perception of anticipatory time in temporal discounting', *Journal of Neuroscience, Psychology, and Economics*, **2** (2), 91–101.

Kolbert, E. (2009), 'Better measures', *The New Yorker*, 15 September, available at http://www.newyorker.com/news/news-desk/elizabeth-kolbert-better-measures (accessed 13 December 2015).

Layard, R. (2005), *Happiness: Lessons from a New Science*, New York: Penguin Press.

Malghan, D. (2010), 'On the relationship between scale, allocation, and distribution', *Ecological Economics*, **69** (11), 2261–70.

Manner, M. and J. Gowdy (2010), 'Group selection and the evolution of moral behavior: toward a coevolutionary foundation for public policy', *Ecological Economics*, **69**, 753–69.

Mayumi, K. (2001), *The Origins of Ecological Economics: The Bioeconomics of Nicholas Georgescu-Roegen*, London: Routledge.

Prakash, A. and A. Gupta (1994), 'Are efficiency, equity, and scale independent?', *Ecological Economics*, **10** (2), 89–90.

Quiggin, J. (2010), *Zombie Economics*, Princeton, NJ: Princeton University Press.

Rosati, A., J. Stevens, B. Hare and M. Hauser (2007), 'The evolutionary origins of human patience: temporal preferences in chimpanzees, bonobos, and human adults', *Current Biology*, **17** (19), 1663–8.

Samuelson, P.A. (1967), 'Foreword', in N. Georgescu-Roegen, *Analytical Economics*, Cambridge, MA: Harvard University Press, pp. vii–ix.

Sanfey, A., J. Rilling, J. Aronson, L. Nystrom and J. Cohen (2003), 'The neural basis of economic decision-making in the Ultimatum Game', *Science*, **300** (5826), 1755–8.

Schor, J. (2010), *Plenitude: The New Economics of True Wealth*, New York: Penguin Books.

Schultz, W. (2002), 'Getting formal with dopamine and reward', *Neuron*, **36** (2), 241–63.

Scitovsky, T. (1941), 'A note on welfare propositions in economics', *Review of Economic Studies*, **9** (1), 77–88.

Sherif, M., J. Harvey, J. White, W. Hood and C. Sherif (1961), *The Robbers Cave Experiment: Intergroup Conflict and Cooperation*, Middletown, CT: Wesleyan University Press.

Sherwood, C., F. Subiaul and T. Zadiszki (2008), 'A natural history of the human mind: tracing evolutionary changes in brain and cognition', *Journal of Anatomy*, **212** (4), 426–54.

Shiv, B., G. Loewenstein, A. Bechara, H. Damasio and A. Damasio (2005), 'Investment behavior and the negative side of emotion', *Psychological Science*, **16** (6), 435–9.

Silverberg, E. (1990), *The Structure of Economics: A Mathematical Analysis*, New York: McGraw-Hill.

Stewen, M. (1998), 'The interdependence of allocation, distribution, scale and stability – a comment on Herman Daly's vision of an economics that is efficient, just and sustainable', *Ecological Economics*, **27**, 119–30.

Stiglitz, J. (2003), *Gloablization and its Discontents*, New York: W.W. Norton.

Stiglitz, J., A. Sen and J.-P. Fitoussi (2009), *Report by the Commission on the Measurement of Economic Performance and Social Progress*, available at http://www.stiglitz-sen-fitoussi.fr (accessed 13 December 2015).

Swaminathan, N. (2007), 'Kill one to save many? Brain damage makes decision easier', *Scientific American*, 21 March.

Titmuss, R. (1971), *The Gift Relationship: From Human Blood to Social Policy*, New York: Pantheon Books.

Tom, S., C. Fox, C. Trepel and R. Poldrack (2007), 'The neural basis of loss aversion in decision-making under risk', *Science*, **315** (5811), 515–18.

Vatn, A. and D. Bromley (1994), 'Choices without prices without apologies', *Journal of Environmental Economics and Management*, **26** (2), 129–48.

Vohs, K., N. Mead and M. Goode (2006), 'The psychological consequences of money', *Science*, **314** (5802), 1154–6.

Wexler, B. (2006), *Brain and Culture: Neurobiology, Ideology and Social Change*, Cambridge, MA: MIT Press.

Wilson, D.S. (2002), *Darwin's Cathedral: Evolution, Religion, and the Nature of Society*, Chicago, IL: University of Chicago Press.

Wilson, D.S. (2010), http:/scienceblogs.com/evolution/ (accessed 13 December 2015). (Note: This site has several fascinating commentaries on economics and evolutionary theory.)

Wilson, D.S and E.O. Wilson (2008), 'Evolution "for the good of the group"', *American Scientist*, **96** (5), 380–9.

Wilson, E.O. and B. Hölldobler (2005), 'Eusociality: origin and consequences', *Proceedings of the National Academy of Sciences of the USA*, **102** (38), 13367–71.

Wittmann, M. and M. Paulus (2009), 'Intertemporal choice: neuronal and psychological determinants of economic decisions', *Journal of Neuroscience, Psychology and Economics*, **2** (2), 71–4.

Wobber, V., R. Wrangham and B. Hare (2010), 'Bonobos exhibit delayed development of social behavior and cognition relative to chimpanzees', *Current Biology*, **20** (3), 226–30.

Zsolnai, L. and K. Ims (eds) (2006), *Business Within Limits: Deep Ecology and Buddhist Economics*, Berlin: Peter Lang.

7. Denying Herman Daly: why conventional economists will not embrace the Daly vision

William E. Rees

7.1 INTRODUCTION: THE ILLUSION OF REALITY

This chapter contrasts key elements of the dominant neoliberal free market brand of economics with Herman Daly's steady-state ecological economics and provides a partial explanation of why the world prefers the former to the latter. To those who rigorously compare the two visions, there is little question that the Daly brand is more rational and better grounded in reality. Yet in half a century it has gained little traction in the minds of the public and policy makers alike.

This is no mere academic dispute. If pervasive influence is the measure, traditional neoliberal economists may well be the most universally acclaimed of performers on the global economic stage. Nevertheless, my starting premise is that for all the seeming elegance of their analyses, neoliberal economists are little better than master illusionists. The audience will therefore be excused for feeling betrayed – or merely silly – if the stage is left empty when the magician's mist of abstract equations has finally dissipated on the evening air.

Neoliberal economists should take no special offence at having their sleight-of-hand exposed. Technically speaking, all economists – even Herman Daly – are illusionists. In fact, everyone is. We can't help it. Humans necessarily conceive in metaphor and think from conceptual frames that may actually have little basis in reality. This is worth thinking about because metaphors, myths and models largely determine how individuals and whole cultures interact with each other and the rest of the material world. Indeed, my second premise is that the fate of civilization may well hinge on the content of contemporary conceptual models, particularly the economic models that give force and direction to both national and global development policy.

Some people may find the assertion that society is illusion-driven difficult to accept. Hard-headed practical people in particular will claim that their thoughts, politics and actions spring from 'real-world' experience; no mystical musings or whimsical abstractions interfere with *their* judgment. The problem with this is that humans actually have little truly direct experience of even physical reality. The best we can say is that we base our actions on seasoned perceptions – and seasoned perceptions, like all perceptions, are only elaborate models.

'But wait,' you protest, 'surely we experience the physical world directly through our five senses. Vision, hearing, touch, taste and smell have evolved precisely to enable us to navigate safely through the material world!'

On one level this is true and, by all the evidence, the process has worked fairly well. But consider for a moment what is involved with just our power of sight and, by inference, our other senses.

7.1.1   The Anatomy of Primary Illusion

Humans are visual animals with a well-developed optical system; vision is perhaps the most highly evolved of our senses. If you and I were sitting opposite each other at a well-lit table we would no doubt agree that each could 'see' the other (assuming, of course, that we are normally 'sighted'). Indeed, if encouraged, either could come up with a vividly elaborate verbal description of the other's physical being. (Add the interpretive freedom due artistic license and we might have the basis for an interesting party game!)

But would we actually be describing each other, the 'real (physical) thing'?

In fact, we would not. 'Seeing' does not provide the observer direct access to anything! We don't see objects per se, we detect light reflected off those objects, and this light contains only a tiny quantum of the total information about the object that might be revealed if we had sensory access to the entire electromagnetic spectrum.[1]

Fortunately, evolution has provided us with a very sophisticated instrument with which to extract that quantum of information. The human eye is a complex organ 'designed' to project a sharply focused image of perceived objects onto a light-sensitive tissue at the back of the eye called the retina. Thus, we can claim to experience reality at least indirectly as represented by tiny images-in-light dancing on the backs of our eyeballs.

But even this is not quite true. Our brains cannot decode light per se no matter how well focused and exquisitely detailed the retinal image (which, by the way, is upside-down). The retina must first encode the image into electrical impulses, the only form of 'data' that the brain can understand. The optic nerve then conveys the impulses to various parts of the brain for processing and interpretation and only when the signal finally (but seemingly instantaneously) arrives at the primary visual cortex do we actually experience 'seeing.' (That said, just how the brain assembles the continuous cascade of optical data into a coherently comprehensive, virtually real-time moving picture remains largely a mystery!)

What this technical romp reveals is that even our most vividly 'real' visual pictures are, in fact, nothing more (or less) than neural reconstructions of initially scanty data that are subsequently filtered by the mechanical eyeball and undergo at least two energy conversions in the retina before being fed to an unknown number of neuro-interpretive processes (all at what loss or tainting of information?) before finally emerging as sensory 'experience.'[2] In short, the sensory images that we use to regulate our interaction with the rest of the biophysical world (generally quite successfully) are mere feeble abstractions – and we often submit even these to subjective interpretation based on our previous education, socialization and personality. Bottom line? Humans routinely operate from sensory illusions that are woefully incomplete and distorted shadows of corresponding physical reality. Sometimes the imperfections and omissions are hazardous to life. We cannot see the camouflaged predator, taste the toxins in our food or sense the high-energy radiation that eventually gives us cancer.

All of which poses an interesting question: If the brain's reconstructions of the physical world are such partial representations, how much more ethereal and potentially dangerous are concepts, myths and models that are entirely socially constructed or that have few real-world touchstones? This is no trivial matter: a glance at the headlines reveals that religious dogma, political ideology, disciplinary paradigms (including economic paradigms) and all manner of cultural norms are more important determinants of how people behave as social beings than is their sensory experience.

7.2 SECONDARY ILLUSION AND DUELING PARADIGMS

All thinking about the world involves a degree of abstraction. Economics has taken this principle further than any other social science. (Wolf, 2010)

Existing economics is a theoretical system which floats in the air and which bears little relation to what actually happens in the real world. (Coase, 1997)

Which brings us back to economics. Economics used to be concerned with what people did with and on 'the land' to acquire the material basis of their own existence. The eighteenth-century 'Physiocrats' believed that land, particularly agricultural land, was the source of national wealth and valued agricultural labor as the means to extract it. Physiocracy, sometimes called the first body of organized economic thought, was also the last body of traditional economic thought to be so conceptually wedded to biophysical reality.

The divorce is virtually complete when it comes to the neoliberal market economics that dominates global development thinking today. 'Something strange happened to economics about a century ago. In moving from classical to neo-classical economics . . . economists expunged land – or natural resources' from their theorizing (Wolf, 2010). Land and resources were quietly dropped from mainstream production functions as capital (including finance capital) and knowledge came to be perceived as the principal sources of wealth and drivers of growth.[3]

This abstraction could be maintained historically: (1) because the undervaluation of nature relative to other factors of production (no one pays the earth for the resources we extract) means that in 'advanced' economies land and resources per se often contribute only marginally to gross domestic product (GDP) and (2) technology has succeeded until recently both in keeping the costs of extracting raw materials low and finding substitutes for some resources that have become scarce (for example, coal substituted for wood as the primary fuel of the Industrial Revolution; fish-farms increasingly substitute for wild fish stocks; fertilizer substitutes for depleted soil in industrial agriculture). Bottom line? Most contemporary economic models still float free from biophysical reality, blind to the energy and material flows essential for human existence and to the 'natural capital' stocks that produce them (Box 7.1).

7.2.1   The Economy as Self-fueling Machine

This blindness is the target for one of Herman Daly's most pointed challenges to mainstream thinking. Consider that mother of all conventional economic models, the 'circular flow of exchange value' (Daly, 1991a, p. 195). Economic textbooks typically feature a standard circular diagram of the economic process as 'a pendulum movement between production and consumption within a completely closed system' (Georgescu-Roegen, 1993, p. 75). Value embodied in goods and services flows from firms to households in exchange for spending by households (national product). A supposedly equal value, reincarnated in factors of production (labor knowledge, finance capital), flows back to firms from households in exchange for wages, rents, dividend and so on (national income).

Mainstream texts sometimes suggest that this stripped-down economy operates as a perpetual motion machine, generating a 'flow of output that is circular, self-renewing, self-feeding' (Heilbroner and Thurow, 1981, p. 127). From this perspective, economic growth is a spontaneous autocatalytic

BOX 7.1   THE CONSTANT CAPITAL STOCKS CRITERION FOR SUSTAINABILITY

Much contemporary discussion of 'sustainability' hinges on the concept of 'Hicksian income' after the British economist, Sir John Hicks. Hicks defined true income as the maximum level of consumption that an individual (or nation) can consume over a given time period while leaving wealth-producing capital intact (Hicks, 1946). In other words, living on true income means 'living on the interest' – not tempting poverty by depleting capital assets.

Hicksian income so defined is at the heart of the so-called 'constant capital stocks criterion for sustainability.' As might be expected, there are two competing versions (Victor, 1991). The dominant version reflects neoliberal economists' dismissal of the unique contributions of resources (particularly self-producing natural capital) to the economy and human well-being (Pearce and Atkinson, 1993; Victor et al., 1995). This so-called 'weak' version of the constant capital stocks criterion can be stated as follows: 'An economy is sustainable if the aggregate value per capita of its stocks of manufactured and natural capital (or the money-income derived from those aggregate stocks) remains constant or grows from one accounting period to the next.'

This definition obviously assumes the commensurability and substitutability of different forms of capital. As long as the aggregate market *value* of different forms of capital remains unchanged (or increases), society is deemed to be sustainable. It horrifies ecologists to observe that the weak sustainability criterion assumes all is well provided if the rising market value (that is, increasing scarcity value) of natural capital (or the income derived therefrom) increases to compensate for the depletion of the physical stocks.

Ecological economists therefore subscribe to an alternative 'strong' version of the constant capital stocks criterion as follows: 'An economy is sustainable if its physical stocks of both manufactured capital and natural capital per capita are held constant or grow in separate accounts from one accounting period to the next.'

By this definition, manufactured and natural capital are not commensurable and substitution is at best imperfect. Money valuation does not enter the picture. (Money is itself an abstraction.) Herman Daly has championed the idea that in many circumstances, manufactured capital and natural capital are complements not substitutes – more fish boats do not compensate for the collapse of the fish stock (for example, Daly, 1991a, chapter 13; Daly, 1994). Indeed, a moment's reflection reveals that some form of natural capital is a *prerequisite* for all forms of manufactured capital and their functioning.

Why does this dispute matter? Because self-producing 'natural capital' maintains the life-support functions of the ecosphere, the risks associated with its depletion are unacceptable and there may be no possibility for technological substitution. Meanwhile, the prevailing system of costs, prices and market incentives fails absolutely to reflect ecological scarcity or help determine appropriate levels of natural capital stocks. Even some fairly mainstream environmental economists have therefore observed that '*conserving what there is* could be a sound risk-averse strategy' (Pearce et al., 1990, p. 7, emphasis added).

process. All the more miraculous because the circular flows model makes no reference whatever to the energy and resources to which value is added to produce the goods and to generate the income flows that the model does represent, nor to the waste outflows the system generates: 'the circle flow is an isolated, self-renewing system with no inlets or outlets, no possible point of contact with anything outside itself' (Daly, 1991a, p. 196). Starting from self-generating flows and armed with bracing confidence in both market efficiency and human ingenuity, many mainstream economists face the challenges of global change with unabashed optimism.

7.2.2   The Economy as Super-organism

> In the later stages of economics, when we are approaching nearly to the conditions of life, biological analogies are to be preferred to mechanical (Marshall, 1925, p. 14).

If neoliberal economics casts the economy as lifeless machine, Daly's critique portrays it as living organism. He argues that studying the economic process in terms of self-generating circular flows without considering unidirectional throughput is akin to studying physiology in terms of the circulatory system with no reference to the digestive tract. One might as well ask engineering students to fathom how 'a car can run on its own exhaust' or biology students to accept that 'an organism can metabolize its own excreta' (Daly, 1991a, p. 197) (Box 7.2).

Daly's living system metaphor compares 'the basic within-skin life process of metabolism (anabolism and catabolism) with the outside-skin process of economics (production and consumption)' (Daly, 1968 [1980]). The value added by the metabolic process is the maintenance of life; the value added by the economic process is the maintenance and also the enjoyment of life. But in either case, 'the only *material* output is *waste*' (Daly, 1968 [1980], p. 251, emphases in original).[4]

Some readers might protest this last assertion. Is not the entire purpose and major output of the economy to produce useful (and sometimes not so useful) goods and services? So it would seem, but this is a limited, static view. It does not recognize that usable energy can make only a single pass through the economy. With useful work extracted, 100 percent of the degraded infrared residue radiates off the planet. As for material, only a fraction of the energy and material resources that enter the economy is actually converted to marketable products, and once these are consumed or worn out, the embodied material also joins the waste stream. Even with some recycling (which uses additional energy and at least some 'fresh' material), the *entire* stream of energy and resource inputs ultimately returns to 'the environment' as degraded waste.[5] Thus, from a purely

BOX 7.2   INTELLECTUAL RESCUE

Discovering Herman Daly's vision of the economy as living organism helped salvage my academic career. In the 1970s, not long after my arrival at the University of British Columbia (UBC) (as a card-carrying ecologist in a policy-oriented planning school) I had an occasion to present some early research ideas to an assembly of senior colleagues from across the campus. I was young, nervous and naïve, and had been struggling to adapt concepts from bio-ecology to land-use planning in ways that my students (mostly geographers and economists) could understand. I opted to present a crude model of the human carrying capacity of the Vancouver region (the Lower Mainland of British Columbia) pointing out that the region was already living well beyond its biophysical limits.

After my presentation (which was received politely enough) I was invited to lunch by a senior colleague who just happened to be a prominent resource econo-mist. Very gently, with the greatest of professional respect and courtesy, he advised me that should I persist in pursuing research on human carrying capacity, my academic career would likely be a Hobbesian 'nasty, brutish, and short.' He argued that economists had effectively negated all such neo-Malthusian thinking. Why should the population or economy of a given region or country be constrained by local shortages of anything? Any region could simply trade services or surpluses of resource 'a' for needed supplies of resource 'b,' thus freeing itself (and presum-ably its trading partners) from local limits to growth. And, in any event, technology could substitute for nature. He ended by suggesting that I bone up on trade theory, the power of the marketplace, the emerging service economy and technology's role in increasing 'factor productivity.'

My economist friend had delivered his verdict with intimidating assurance and conviction. These were new ideas for me. My formal training had not stretched far beyond the disciplinary boundaries of biology; I had never had so much as an introductory course in economics. I left the lunch deflated, discouraged and depressed, tail lodged firmly between my legs.

But there was something incomplete about my colleague's prescription. The farm-boy and ecologist in me could not conceive of a *Homo sapiens* so detached from nature. This question became the worm in the apple of my mind, gnawing away beneath the surface struggling to emerge. Even so, an embarrassing length of time passed (given the simplicity of the insight) before I had my 'eureka' experi-ence. Part of the problem was with the standard definition of carrying capacity as 'the average maximum population of a given species that can occupy a particular habitat without permanently impairing the productive capacity of that habitat.' Since humans engage in trade and are capable of increasing resource productivity, local limits apparently dissolve and economists could indeed argue that 'carrying capac-ity' had no useful meaning applied to humans.

But what happens if we invert the carrying capacity ratio? Rather than asking what population can be supported in a given area, the relevant – and answerable – question becomes how much ecosystem area is needed to support a given population on a continuous basis, *wherever on earth the land and water is located and whatever the technological sophistication of the population*. This simple shift in perspective re-established people's direct connection to 'the land.' It also led to my conceiving 'ecological footprint analysis' (EFA) as a tool to estimate the ecosystem area effectively appropriated by any specified population to produce the resources it consumes and to assimilate its wastes. Human carrying capacity was firmly back on the agenda.

But what really restored my confidence in studying *H. sapiens* as an ecologically significant species was encountering Herman Daly's insistence that the economy is indeed embedded in nature and that the economic process is subject to natural law, particularly the second law of thermodynamics. (A population's eco-footprint can also be defined as the photosynthetic surface required, on a continuous basis, to regenerate the biomass equivalent of the negentropy being consumed and dissipated by that population.) EFA has subsequently shown that most high-income consumer societies are running ecological deficits relative to domestic biocapacity and therefore living, in part, on imports. It also suggests that there is insufficient capacity elsewhere in the world to cover these deficits (only a few countries have surplus biocapacity). Trade has enabled the world as a whole to go into overshoot and, despite humanity's technological wizardry, the per capita eco-footprint is still expanding. As Herman Daly has long suggested, the human enterprise now grows by drawing down natural capital and the latter has become the scarce factor of production. This reality imposes formidable limits to growth.

'outside-the-economy' biophysical perspective, economic activity is clearly much more a consumptive process than it is a productive process.

7.2.3 Dissipating the Planet

This by no means exhausts the metaphor of the economy as super-organism. Seeing the economy as a generator of degraded energy and material cues us that, like all biological entities, the economy is subject to physical laws, particularly the second law of thermodynamics.

The second law is fundamental to all processes of energy and material transformation and is thus arguably the ultimate regulator of both biological and industrial metabolism. While the implications of this fact have been deemed irrelevant by neoliberal economists, Herman Daly (following his mentor Nicolas Georgescu-Roegen) has for decades led a small band of insurgents struggling to have the second law reflected in conventional analyses.

In its simplest form, the second law states that every spontaneous change in an isolated system increases the 'entropy' of the system (an isolated system cannot exchange energy or matter with its environment). In general, this means that the system becomes increasingly 'random' – energy dissipates, material concentrations disperse, gradients disappear. In short, with time, isolated systems become increasingly degraded in an inexorable, irreversible descent toward thermodynamic equilibrium. This is a state of maximum entropy in which nothing else can happen.

In recent decades, science has recognized that the workings of the entropy law apply also to open, far-from-equilibrium systems. *Any* complex differentiated system tends to unravel and run down. Despite all reasonable attempts at maintenance, every shiny new car eventually becomes worn out. And this is invariably a one-way trip – no rusted-out shell has ever spontaneously reacquired its show-room splendor.

Readers may be quick to point out the many apparent exceptions. A newly conceived fetus, an early succession ecosystem, the world's great cities, indeed, the entire human enterprise all prove that, rather than sink toward equilibrium, *living* systems actually gain in mass and complexity over time. How such systems subvert the second law long puzzled philosophers and scientists. Physicist Erwin Schrödinger resolved the conundrum only in 1945: 'The obvious answer is: By eating, drinking, breathing and (in the case of plants) assimilating . . .' Like any other system, 'a living organism continually increases its entropy – [that is, produces positive entropy] and thus tends to approach the dangerous state of maximum entropy . . . of death. It can only keep aloof from it, i.e. alive, by continually drawing from its environment negative entropy . . .' (Schrödinger, 1944 [1967], p. 70). ('Negative entropy' or 'negentropy' is free energy available for work.) In other words, organisms thrive by exchanging high-entropy outputs (waste) for low-entropy inputs (resources). However, second law inefficiencies also dictate that the organism's gain in negentropy is only a fraction of the increase in global entropy. As Daly asserts, this statement 'would hold verbatim as a physical description of the economic process' (Daly, 1968 [1980], p. 253).

The near-homology of living systems and the economy has acquired a sharper edge in recent years with the development of self-organizing holarchic open (SOHO) systems theory. Systems scientists have recognized that self-producing systems exist as loose overlapping hierarchical structures where each component subsystem ('holon') is contained by the next level up and itself comprises a chain of linked subsystems at lower levels (Kay and Regier, 2000). (Consider that an individual organism is part of a community embedded in an ecosystem, and itself comprises a descending hierarchy of subsystems from organs to cells.) The critical point is that at every level in the hierarchy, the relevant holon can develop and maintain itself *only* by using available energy and material (negentropy) extracted from its 'host' system one level up and by exporting degraded energy and material wastes (entropy) back into that host.[6] In effect, all thermodynamically open self-producing subsystems thrive – maintain themselves far-from-equilibrium – at the *expense* of their hosts (see Kay and Regier, 2000; Schneider and Kay, 1994a, 1994b, 1995).[7]

The highest earth-bound level in the SOHO hierarchy is the ecosphere, the macro-holon that comprises all subsidiary biomes, ecosystems and species. It follows that the structural and functional integrity of the ecosphere can be maintained only if the productivity and resilience of constituent ecosystems is sufficient to support indefinitely the development and maintenance of lower level holons (for example, all consumer organisms, the economy) and to assimilate/dissipate the ecosystems' aggregate entropic output.

Normally within ecosystems, the rates of resource imports and waste discharge by any subsystem (for example, a species population) fluctuate in the short term but are maintained by negative feedback within a range that is compatible with the overall rates of production and assimilation by the host ecosystem. Each lower holon therefore normally exists in a more or less 'steady-state' relationship with its host so the entire systems hierarchy retains its long-term structural and functional integrity. However, the hierarchical relationship among subsystems and their hosts contains the seeds of potential pathology (Rees, 2003). If any subsystem demands more than its host can produce, or discharges more waste than its host can assimilate, then further growth of that subsystem will necessarily deplete, degrade and dissipate higher levels in the systems hierarchy.

Now it is undeniable that the economy (which is really the material manifestation of human ecology) is an earthly entity, and therefore a subsystem of the ecosphere (actually, a subsystem of multiple ecosystems). But the two holons differ in one critical respect. The ecosphere evolves and maintains itself in a far-from-equilibrium steady state by assimilating and dissipating radiant energy from the sun, that is, an extra-planetary source of negentropy (and, effectively, the next highest level in the thermodynamic hierarchy). The economy, however, can grow and maintain itself only by extracting and degrading resources extracted from ecosystems. As noted, an unavoidable consequence of the second law is that when any given subsystem expands and complexifies (that is, rises further from equilibrium) its gain in negentropy is always less than the increase in global entropy.[8] It follows that, beyond a certain point, the expansion of the human enterprise *necessitates* the entropic depletion and dissipation of its host ecosystems (Table 7.1). Fisheries collapses, landscape degradation, soil erosion, tropical forest deforestation, biodiversity loss and so on are all symptoms of overconsumption by humans; marine dead zones, accelerated eutrophication, ocean acidification, ozone depletion, the toxic contamination of food webs, greenhouse gas accumulations (climate change) and so on are all symptoms of waste sinks filled to overflowing. SOHO systems framing clearly reveals today's perpetual growth economy to be an entropic black hole, thermodynamically positioned to consume and dissipate the ecosphere from within (Rees, 1999).

Table 7.1   A 'second law' comparison of human-less and human-dominated ecosystems

Ecosystems without humans	Human-dominated econo-ecosystems
Evolve and develop by assimilating, degrading and dissipating available solar energy (exergy) using photosynthesis and evapotranspiration.	Grow and develop by extracting, degrading and dissipating energy-rich 'resource stocks' that have accumulated in the ecosphere, including other species, entire ecosystems and fossil hydrocarbons.
Anabolic processes (production of biomass) marginally exceed catabolic processes (degradation and dissipation).	Catabolism (consumption and dissipation of energy and material resources) exceeds anabolism (the production of humans and their artifacts).
Biomass accumulation dominates; species proliferate, complexity increases; stocks of available energy and matter (resource gradients) accumulate.	Humans and their artifacts accumulate; ecosystems are simplified or eliminated, biodiversity declines; resource stocks are depleted and dissipated.
Materials recycle through ecosystems (biogeochemical 'nutrient' recycling); waste heat dissipates off-earth; the entropy of the universe increases.	Material wastes (economic throughput), often novel and toxic, accumulate in the ecosphere; waste heat dissipates off-earth; functional integrity of ecosystems is lost; the entropy of the ecosphere (ultimately the universe) increases.

7.2.4   The Problem of Scale and the Steady State

As Herman Daly has long recognized, the first corollary of any thermodynamic model of the economic process is the need to limit the scale (energy and material throughput) of the economic enterprise within the capacity of supporting ecosystems (for example, several chapters in Daly, 1991a; Daly and Farley, 2004). In theory, an economy has achieved its optimal scale or size at the point where the (diminishing) marginal benefits of material growth just equal the (rising) marginal costs – including the (currently unaccounted) costs of depleted natural capital, capital substitution and pollution. At this point the total net benefits of economic growth to date (total benefits minus total costs) is at a maximum and, as Daly originally noted – and is frequently moved to remind us – any further growth actually makes us 'poorer than richer' (for example, Daly, 1999). If intelligence and logic were the principal determinants of economic policy, the primary goal would be to ensure that growth slows as we reach the optimal scale and that the economy does not exceed this optimal size.

There is a problem, however – several actually. The facts that our measures of benefits are flawed (for example, GDP puts plus signs on both negative and positive entries), that we can neither identify nor monetize many of the costs (for example, who knows the present value of some future climate change cost of which we are as yet unaware but which may already have been triggered by historic and present actions?) and that changing circumstances constantly shift the exact 'location' of the optimal point, means that we could not actually perform a valid benefit/cost analysis of economic growth even if society were inclined to do so. But this in no way invalidates the basic point. There are real ecological and economic limits to sustainable global energy and material throughput. Politicians, heady from addiction to economic growth, should find it sobering that no mainstream economists can state with certainty that society is still below the optimal point and that numerous ecological economic indicators and biophysical studies suggest we may have long exceeded it (for example, Rockström et al., 2009; WWF, 2014).

The second corollary of economy-as-thermodynamic-process is that sustainability implies a steady-state economy. Our own bodies are steady-state systems in which the daily inflows of energy and matter are, on average, quantitatively equivalent to the outflows. (Of course, the *quality* is diminished by the extraction of negentropy from the inputs.) Thus, if 'we view capital as material extensions of the body, and we accept the fact that there are limits to the total number of human bodies supportable, then by the same logic we should recognize that the stock of extensions of human bodies is also limited and thus be led naturally to a steady-state perspective on the economy' (Daly, 1991a, p. 32).

The essential lesson is that after an initial phase of growth, all healthy living systems become steady-state systems, any propensity for further expansion constrained by negative feedback (for example, incipient resource scarcity, disease). The ecosphere as a whole is in approximate steady state limited by the constant solar flux and the geographically variable availability of water and nutrients. It follows that the economic subsystem, rapidly becoming the dominant subsystem of the ecosphere, must increasingly conform to the operational dynamics of the ecosphere *if it is to survive*. The operational dynamics of the ecosphere exemplify a dynamic steady state.

Which is not to be confused with a static state. The economy needn't cease developing, it must merely stop growing. With luck and good management it could hover indefinitely in the vicinity of its 'optimal scale' while steadily improving human well-being. There are no limits on the capacity of human ingenuity to better quality of life, only on the quantity of throughput available to do it. And even within that constraint, new firms and even whole industrial sectors could both develop *and* grow even as their thermodynamic equivalents in obsolete or 'sunset' industries are phased out. Because it draws so many logical threads together, Herman Daly's pioneering development and persistent advocacy of the steady-state economy is perhaps his greatest overall contribution.

7.2.5 The Quest for the 'Truer' Economy

> You may say, if you wish, that all reality is a social construction, but you cannot deny that some constructions are 'truer' than others. They are not 'truer' because they are privileged, they are privileged because they are 'truer.' (Postman, 1999, p. 76)

We have described two competing 'social constructions' or conceptual models of the workings of the economic process. The dominant neoliberal paradigm treats the economy as an independent entity, an open growing system whose productive cycle is virtually unconstrained by any biophysical reality outside itself. By contrast, ecological economists see the economy as an open, growing but also fully contained and dependent subsystem of the finite, non-growing and materially closed earth ecosystem (Daly, 1990 [1991]). This latter framing also recognizes that the bio-metabolism of the ecosphere and the industrial metabolism of the economy are both governed by inviolable biophysical laws. In the context of sustainability, the important question is which of these conceptual models provides a 'truer' representation of biophysical reality.

Who can dispute that in today's world the economy interacts with and seriously affects the productivity and behavior of ecosystems? Nevertheless, the mainstream economic models used to govern/regulate national economies and international development remain insensitive to the structure and function of the ecosystems upon which the economy draws, and of the time- and space-dependent processes that characterize ecosystem behavior. Indeed, the simple, reversible, mechanistic behavior of the economy implicit in mainstream models and derivative analytic tools (for example, benefit/cost analysis) is quite inconsistent with the complexity, irreversibility, lags, thresholds and positive feedback dynamics of the complex energy, information and ecosystems with which the economy interacts in the real world (Christensen, 1991). Even more remarkably, the modeled behavior is inconsistent with that of the real economies the models supposedly represent (as was clearly revealed, yet again, by the financial collapse of 2008). On all these grounds, a reasonable person would be justified in dismissing mainstream sustainability analyses as fatally illusory from an ecological perspective. The structural and relational assumptions framing the dominant economic models behind global development today disqualify them from generating useful insights into humanity's relationship with nature.

Contrast this with the relative structural integrity of the Dalyesque vision and the insights accessible to it. Seeing the economy as a growing dependent subsystem of the non-growing ecosphere enables one to surmise from the outset that at some point – even after accounting for human ingenuity – the economy will eventually be hobbled by scarcity and begin to suffocate in its own detritus. And what if the economy and the ecosphere really are far-from-equilibrium dissipative structures and the former is nested within the latter? This allows the equally rational conjecture that the ever-growing economy must inevitably degrade and dissipate the ecosphere in the manner of a malicious parasite. Virtually every so-called 'environmental' problem today, from collapsing fisheries and biodiversity loss, through peak oil and potential food shortages to contaminated food webs, accumulating greenhouse gases, climate change and ozone depletion is predictable or explicable from Daly's 'contained system' framing of the economic process.

Finally, ecological economics recognizes that complex systems – social systems, ecosystems and economic systems – are characterized by non-linear (discontinuous) behavior, particularly lags and thresholds. The latter represent 'tipping points' – if key variables of the system are pushed beyond these (by, for example, overexploitation) the entire system may 'flip,' potentially irreversibly, into a new stability domain where conditions are hostile to human purposes. (The collapse of the North Atlantic cod stocks in 1992 serves as a memorably tragic example – and warning.) Indeed, complex systems may have multiple possible equilibria or stable regimes whose existence is unknowable before the fact. These qualities together speak to the need to carefully monitor resource exploitation for any sign that the system is being over-stressed and to limit the overall scale of the human enterprise within cautiously safe limits.

Given present circumstances and global trends, Daly's organismic/thermodynamic model of the human enterprise is clearly less reassuring than the mainstream perspective. Nevertheless, one suspects that if ordinary people were given an opportunity to dissect and assess these two conceptual 'constructions,' most would judge Daly's version on the evidence as being a 'truer' representation of economy–environment relationships. Daly's construction is therefore the one that should be 'privileged' in the economic policy arena.

7.3 'THAT'S NOT THE RIGHT WAY TO LOOK AT IT'

Despite the growing cascade of data supporting this conclusion many practicing economists still do not agree. Their resistance has a cumulative history. Consider just one well-known example (Daly, 2008). The first draft of the World Bank's 1992 *World Development Report* (which focused on sustainable development) contained a diagram called 'the relation of the economy to the environment.' All it showed was a rectangle labeled 'economy' with an in-bound arrow labeled 'inputs' and an exit arrow labeled 'outputs.'

As senior economist in the Bank's environment department, it fell on Herman Daly to critique the draft. Daly observed that this drawing should be revised to include 'the environment.' As matters stood, the economy was exchanging inputs and outputs with nowhere. Always helpful, Daly suggested that the next version of the diagram show the economy as contained within a circle labeled 'ecosystem.' This would make clear that the economy was a subsystem, that the input arrow represented resources extracted from the ecosystem and that the output arrow represented waste returning to it as pollution. Daly suggested that this would stimulate fundamental questions, such as how large the economy could grow before it overwhelmed the total system.

The second draft of the report duly showed the original figure enclosed in a large unlabeled rectangle but this prompted Daly to complain that, incompletely labeled, the diagram changed nothing. The third draft omitted the diagram altogether. The Bank apparently recognized that something was wrong with that diagram but preferred to omit it rather than deal with the inconvenient questions it raised.

Sometime later Daly had an opportunity to question Lawrence Summers, Chief Economist at the World Bank (under whom the report was being written) about the same issue. Did the Chief Economist consider the question of the size of the economy relative to the total ecosystem to be an important one? Did he think economists should be asking the question: What is the optimal scale of the economy relative to the ecosphere? Summers' reply was 'immediate and definite: "*that's not the right way to look at it*"' (quoted in Daly, 1996, p. 6, emphasis added). Apparently, 'The idea that economic growth should be constrained by the environment was too much for the World Bank in 1992, and still is today' (Daly, 2008, p. 46).

Other rogue economists have advanced similar critiques of modern growth fetishism. According to Julie A. Nelson, economists show 'dogged allegiance to a narrow set of epistemological ideals, methodological framing and substantive assumptions' in their application of endogenous growth theory (EGT) (Nelson, 2005, p. 9). EGT explores the role of technological innovation and other sources in GDP growth, but 'no matter how tortured the logic, [the explanations] lead back to a source in economic fundamentals.' Apparently, the word 'endogenous' is a signal that the model is closed off from historical developments or other considerations that might undermine its validity. Evidence that violate its assumptions is set aside. 'And in line with the vast majority of economic theorizing about growth, the ecological implications of a ceaseless expansion of production are totally ignored' (Nelson, 2005, p. 9).

Mainstream economists are not doing much better in formally acknowledging the potentially devastating impacts of complexity theory on prevailing economic dogma. This makes economists and finance managers culpable in the 2008 collapse of the global finance system (Ormerod, 2010). The latest attempt to explain business cycles and 'booms and busts' from the 'rational agents using rational expectations' view of the world goes by the term 'dynamic stochastic general equilibrium' (DSGE) models. DSGE models contain all the key microeconomic assumptions of orthodox economic theory. Acting under the illusory fog thrown up by this framing, 'the authorities' assumed, falsely, that brokers and agents had used the 'correct' model in setting prices, that is, that the massive volumes of loans and debts being traded in the market had been 'priced rationally and hence optimally.' Had this been the case, and institution 'A' defaulted on a loan:

> sufficient provision via the optimal pricing of the loan [would have] been made to cover the loss arising from any such default. There was no need to tie up capital unnecessarily in liquid assets when it could be lent out at a profit. Across a portfolio of many such loans, the default of a single loan simply could not cause a problem. (Ormerod, 2010, p. 14)

The real economy, however, is a complex system that behaves little like a DSGE model whether or not its assumptions have been satisfied. Complex systems theory, specifically network theory, 'tells us that in an interconnected system, the same initial shock can, if we could replay history many times, lead to dramatically different outcomes.' Uncertainty is large and essentially irreducible. It may be that most of the time, 'shocks are contained and do not spread very far through the system. But in principle a shock of identical size can trigger a cascade of global proportions.' Unfortunately, as noted in other contexts, is that 'The economics profession in particular has become very insular and hostile to scientific work outside its own field.' Accordingly, 'economists are largely ignorant of the large amount of work carried out on cascades in interconnected systems by a whole range of disciplines over the past decades such as control engineers, computer scientists, physicists, and mathematicians.' Result? 'In the brave new world of DSGE, the possibility of a systemic collapse, of a cascade of defaults across the system, was never envisaged at all' (all quotes from Ormerod, 2010, pp. 14–15).

James K. Galbraith extends his critique of modern economics to include even the domain that it *does* purport to encompass. He argues that the empirical evidence 'flatly contradicts' the five leading ideas of modern economics and interprets this disconnect from the real world as evidence that 'modern economics . . . seems to be, mainly, about *itself*' (Galbraith, 2000, p. 1, emphasis in original). He goes on: 'But self-absorption and consistent policy error are just two of the endemic problems of the leading American economists. The deeper problem is the nearly complete collapse of the prevailing economic theory . . . It is a collapse so complete, so pervasive, that the profession can only deny it by refusing to discuss theoretical questions in the first place' (Galbraith, 2000, p. 4).

7.4   THE TRIUMPH OF ILLUSION

How can we explain this seeming abandonment of reason, the widespread hiding of heads in the sand? Humans pride themselves on being the best evidence that the universe is coming to self-awareness and intelligence. We claim to be a science- or at least a knowledge-based society. Why is it, then, that in so many domains, modern humans seem to act out of habit, ignore contrary data and happily embrace illusory fantasies?

Such illogical behavior could be part of a contemporary cultural trend. More than a half-century ago (at about the time economic growth began to push its way to prominence on the policy agenda) German philosopher Martin Heidegger observed that 'man today is *in flight from thinking*' (Heidegger, 1955 [2003], p. 89, emphasis in original). By 'thinking,' Heidegger did not mean the day-to-day calculative thought processes at which technological society actually excels. Rather, he believed that modern society was 'in flight' from the deeper kind of critical, questioning or, in his terms, 'meditative' thinking, the tool of philosophers and ordinarily contemplative people alike. Such generalized thoughtlessness (as reflected in the quality of the evening news?) is characterized by our failure to ponder, to observe, to question and even to show awareness of what is actually taking place around us and within us. From Heidegger's perspective, contemporary society is thus allowing to 'lie fallow' one of our great and most uniquely human abilities. With intellectual blinkers on, the world is being swept away in the techno-material tide, guided, if at all, by careless whims and sheep-like adherence to prevailing myth and ideology.

On the other hand, perhaps nothing has changed. Heidegger may merely be observing most people for what they are. And it seems people have always been lazy thinkers, preferring skillful illusionists to realists in politics as in art. Consider French behavioral psychologist Gustave Le Bon's observation in his 1895 classic study of 'group-think':

> The masses have never thirsted after truth. They turn aside from evidence that is not to their taste, preferring to deify error, if error seduce[s] them. Whoever can supply them with illusions is easily their master; whoever attempts to destroy their illusions is always their victim. (Le Bon, 1895 [2001])

Le Bon's observation is no mere curiosity. The 'deification of error' and resultant behavioral inertia (or deviance) at the top can determine the fates of nations. Pulitzer Prize winning American historian, Barbara Tuchman, details the tragic effects of self-delusion on entire societies through millennia in her 1984 classic, *The March of Folly*. According to Tuchman, 'folly' involves 'the pursuit of policy contrary to the self-interest of the constituency or state involved.' To qualify as true folly a particular course of action must be pursued even though a 'feasible alternative course of action [is] available.' In addition, the action or policy must generally be 'that of a group' (not merely an individual leader) and 'persist beyond any one political lifetime' (Tuchman, 1984, p. 5). So defined, political folly or 'wooden-headedness':

> plays a remarkably large role in government. It consists in assessing a situation in terms of preconceived fixed notions [for example, ideology] while ignoring any contrary signs. It is acting according to wish while not allowing oneself to be deflected by the facts. (Tuchman, 1984, p. 7)

My point? Le Bon and Tuchman are describing seemingly universal perceptual blocks and behavioral intransigence – even in the face of imminent danger – that are exhibited by people who have developed deeply entrenched systems of belief that have long shaped and directed their lives. (More on this to follow.)

Let's return to the present context but assume that the global community is *not* perceptually handicapped, that is, we are able to act decisively in a spirit of collective engagement and high intelligence in the face of global ecological change. This means that national and global policies for sustainability would have to be consistent with the scientific evidence that ecosystems and the climate system are in stress, including the fact that the human enterprise is currently in a state of overshoot (drawing down even self-producing natural capital and filling critical waste sinks to overflowing). The world would also have to recognize: (1) that the economy is a dependent subsystem of the ecosphere subject to thermodynamic laws, that is, for the economy to grow and maintain itself 'far-from-equilibrium', it necessarily 'feeds' on its supportive ecosystems and uses them as waste dumps and (2) there are limits to the regenerative and assimilative capacity of ecosystems. Corollary: for sustainability, there must be caps on aggregate energy and material flows and thus constraints on the scale of the material economy so that it operates safely within the means of nature. Let's also assume that as good global citizens, we express our compassion for others – basic equity considerations require formal recognition that today's levels of gross material disparity are intolerable.

In these circumstances, rich countries would accept that it is their responsibility to initiate programs to *shrink* their national economies toward a globally viable energy and material steady state (à la Herman Daly). North Americans, for example, would have to reduce their ecological footprints by about 76 percent, from around 7 global average hectares (gha) per capita to our 'fair earth-share' of 1.7 gha (Rees, 2006; WWF, 2014). Such contraction at the top is necessary to make room for needed growth in the developing world given that earth is a finite planet already in overshoot (Rees, 2008; Victor, 2008). These may seem to be unreasonable demands and impossible goals, but analysis shows that we actually have the technology to enable a 75–80 percent reduction in energy and (some) material consumption (von Weizsäcker et al., 2009) while improving quality of life in both rich and poor countries. (Remember that people in wealthy countries were actually happier on average with less than half of today's average per capita income.) In any case, as Daly and other analysts have shown, aggregate global growth itself has already likely become uneconomic and self-defeating.

The most politically plausible alternatives to such a 'steady state with redistribution' strategy are the status quo or some technologically engineered variant. But if our best science is correct, the increasingly likely outcome of these alternatives is ecostemic collapse, resource wars and geopolitical chaos. This dismal outcome underscores that it is actually in everyone's long-term interest to give up on continuous material growth and learn to share the earth's existing bounty. For what may be the first time in human history, *individual and national self-interest has converged with humanity's collective interests* (Rees, 2008).

Of course, as matters stand, 'steady state with redistribution' is off the table.[9] Instead, the dismal alternative is in play. Far from considering a planned economic contraction, all national government and mainstream international organizations (for example, the United Nations and the World Bank) subscribe to a mythic vision of unlimited global expansion inspired by neoliberal economics, fueled by globalization and expanded trade, and inflated by overweening confidence in efficiency gains and technological hubris. Popular support is assured by the single most successful program of social engineering in history, the purposeful global promulgation of consumer culture. A multi-billion dollar 'public relations' and advertising sector has converted virtually whole nations of potentially engaged citizens into passive consumers.[10] Little wonder that the concept of 'contraction' does not resonate in society's collective consciousness – it is not the narrative people have been conditioned to hear. In effect, we live from a socially constructed materialistic world model sustained by the smoke, mirrors and pixie dust sent aloft by professional illusionists of all stripes, prominent among whom are growthist economists.

To be fair, growth-based economics has been remarkably successful in improving the material well-being of a significant minority of the human population in what started out as an 'ecologically empty' world (Daly, 1991b). This provides superficial support for the prevailing mode of thinking. Why spoil what could be a luxury cruise for all if human ingenuity promises to maneuver the ship around any shoals thrown up in what is now an 'ecologically full' world? Privileged elites with the greatest personal stake in the status quo thus sit at the Captain's Table and insist we stay our course through the fog of illusion; middle-class passengers, even those nervous about the voyage, seem willing to sacrifice uncertain but major long-term gain (that is, global survival) to avoid the certain but minor short-term pain of having to adapt their lifestyles; and the folks in steerage have little choice but to go along for the ride, clinging hopefully to the expansionist myth as to a life-raft in effective denial of their lived reality.

7.5   EXPOSING THE ROOTS OF DENIAL

> No one is immune to it; in some respects it is the foundation of our lives. Magical thinking is a universal affliction. We see what we want to see, deny what we don't. (Monbiot, 2010)

How can we explain this behavioral conundrum? What motivates the perversely illogical politics described by Le Bon, Tuchman and others? Whenever people possess knowledge that should be powerfully motivating or profess a strong commitment to some belief or social ethic yet persistently ignore or violate it, there is a good possibility that some innate predisposition is unconsciously directing their actions (Pinker, 2002). This section argues that not only do illusory social constructions confound human intelligence, but that genetically determined 'biological drives . . . can [also] be pernicious to rational decision-making . . . by creating an overriding bias against objective facts . . .' (Damasio, 1994, p. 192).

Understanding the innate predispositions that affect individual and group behavior requires reference to the evolutionary biology of cognition. The latter involves both the evolved structure (nature) and the experiential development (nurture) of the human brain. First, consider that the human brain is a complex organ with a long and complex evolutionary history. Indeed, MacLean (1990) argued that the organization of the human brain roughly recapitulates three broadly overlapping phases of vertebrate evolution. Successive anatomical developments were added to and integrated with pre-existing structures, thus retaining original functions while enhancing the organism's overall fitness. In effect, the human brain has three quasi-independent subsystems each having distinct functions, memory, 'intelligence' and limitations:

1. The reptilian brain (the brainstem and cerebellum) is the seat of sensory perception and related coordinated movement; autonomic functions associated with the body's physical survival (for example, circulation and breathing); instinctive social behavior (for example, pertaining to territoriality, social stature, mating and dominance). It also executes the fight or flight response and controls other mainly hard-wired instinctive behaviors.
2. The limbic (or paleo-mammalian) system is the primary locus of emotions (for example, happiness, sorrow, pleasure, pain) and related behavioral responses (for example, sexual behavior, play, emotional bonding, separation calls, fighting, fleeing). It is also the location of affective (emotion-charged) memories and the source of value judgments and informed intuition.
3. The neo-cortex (neo-mammalian or 'rational brain') is the most recent (and least experienced) addition, but occupies over two thirds of the human brain by volume. It is the seat of consciousness and the locus of abstract thought, reason, logic and forward planning; it controls voluntary movement and actions.

Of course, the normal healthy brain acts as an integrated whole – the three sub-brains are inextricably interconnected, each continuously influencing the others. The emergent behavior and overall personality of the individual is therefore generally a seamless melding of thoughts, emotions and instincts. However, since awareness springs largely from the neo-cortex the individual may not be conscious that she or he is also under the influence of neural and chemical (hormonal) stimuli originating in other parts of the brain.

This interplay of motivations is of more than passing interest. It implies that *H. sapiens* is inherently a conflicted species. In some circumstances, emotional/instinctive predispositions (for example, overt aggression, passionate hatred, abject fear, sensual desire) originating beneath consciousness may well override reason and when this happens the individual may not be aware that a 'lower' part of the brain has seized control. Sometimes we crave the emotional boost that comes from being certain even when we are dead wrong (Burton, 2008)! Even if our actions are guided *mainly* by emotions, we often lie to ourselves (rationalize) that we are being entirely reasonable. Everyone is aware of situations in which *endogenous* factors generate irreconcilable tensions between our rational minds and our emotional/instinctive control centers. The 'circumstances' can range from trivial to life-changing. What dieter has not found himself or herself unable to resist that third helping from the all-you-can-eat buffet? The statistics on marital infidelity are witness enough to the frequency with which people's conscious will and professed morality yield to raw sex drive and emotions when the opportunity arises. Whether reason or emotion/ instinct wins out in a particular case depends on myriad factors including previous experience (for example, socialization, education and religious training) and the native personality of the individual. The main point is that whether or not one is conscious of what is going on, 'There are indeed potions in our own bodies and brains capable of forcing on us behaviors that we may or may not be able to suppress by strong resolution' (Damasio, 1994, p. 121).

Irresolvable conflict may also develop between the individual's sense of stability and *exogenous* factors. In these circumstances the universal human predisposition to lie may come into play. People are often not psychologically equipped to bear the burden of reality. Confronted by an overwhelming problem with no satisfying solution at hand, the natural human reaction is to paper it over, to lie about it to ourselves and to others. In some situations lies are psychologically necessary 'because without them many deplorable acts would become impossibilities' (Jensen, 2000, p. 2). (The same would apply to stupid or irrational acts.) Psychologist Dorothy Rowe suggests that 'Lying gives us the temporary delusion that our personal and social worlds are intact, . . . above all, that we are not likely to overwhelmed by the uncertainty inherent in living in a world we can never truly know' (Rowe, 2010, p. 29).

Perhaps the most complex and consequential form of self-deception is deep systemic denial by whole subgroups within society. Consider the well-funded and highly organized climate denial movement or continuing over-the-top resistance to the fact of evolution on the part of the religious right[11] (see MacKenzie, 2010). Systemic denial generally emerges in situations where an individual's or group's core beliefs and values are under siege. It is clearly reflected in such phenomena as unyielding loyalty to the established order of things in the face of overwhelming contrary data (for example, economists' continued defense of growth-based economics) or in situations where there is clear acknowledgment of 'a dire problem yet no volition to address it' (Pratarelli and Aragon, 2008) (for example, the failure of the November 2009 Copenhagen climate change conference).

This form of denial actually has a physical basis and involves yet another layer of nature/nurture interaction. Recent studies in human cognition show that in the course of individual development, repeated sensory experiences and continuous exposure to fixed cultural norms (for example, religious doctrines, political ideologies and disciplinary paradigms) literally help to shape the brain's synaptic circuitry in quasi-fixed patterns that reflect and embed those experiences. In short, *H. sapiens* has evolved in such a way that the brain is pre-adapted *to record for playback* critical beliefs and behavioral norms shared by members of the individual's group. (The automatic inscription in juvenile brains of tribal/cultural norms that have proved successful to date would presumably be highly adaptive in a relatively static biophysical environment.) The critical point in the present context is that once a synaptic circuit has formed, people tend to seek out *compatible* beliefs and experiences to reinforce the associated cultural pre-sets and, 'when faced with information that does not agree with their [preformed] internal structures, they deny, discredit, reinterpret or forget that information' (Wexler, 2006, p. 180).

Cognitive neurobiology thus provides a multi-layered bio-social basis for understanding individual behavioral intransigence and wider cultural inertia in the context of accelerating global change. Once a person's synaptic pathways are well entrenched and adapted to particular circumstances it is difficult for that individual to accept subsequent changes in their socio-cultural or biophysical environments. Even when one accepts that 'reprogramming' is necessary, the process can be lengthy and unpredictable. Re-establishing cognitive consonance between people's programmed perceptions and new environmental realities thus requires that all parties engage wilfully in the restructuring of their own neural pathways and psychological states (Wexler, 2006).

In these circumstances, achieving sustainability may require that global society engage in a world program of social re-engineering. There may be no other way to assert humanity's collective intelligence and reason over people's predisposition to defend the status quo. Certainly creating a global mindset receptive to planned dramatic change is the only way to implement anything like the 'steady state with redistribution' strategy for sustainability outlined earlier.[12]

As part of the above, we will certainly have to discard many of the 'pre-analytic visions' associated with the political ideologies, religious doctrines and academic paradigms that are helping to create the (un)sustainability crisis. Consider the dominant conception of the economy as an open, growing, self-producing system floating free from the biophysical world. This vision is so fundamentally at odds with Herman Daly's more realistic vision of the economy as an open, growing but fully contained and totally dependent subsystem of the non-growing ecosphere, that no reconciliation is possible. However, fully consistent with denial, or perhaps the subconscious need for familiar certainty, mainstream economists have generally tended 'to deny, discredit, reinterpret or forget' the Daly alternative rather than accept the collapse of their fundamental models. Given the pace of global change, Max Planck's interpretation of the general problem is particularly sobering:

> a new scientific truth does not triumph by convincing its opponents and making them see the light, but rather because its opponents eventually die, and a new generation grows up that is familiar with it. (Planck, 1949, p. 33)

(Of course, even this won't turn the trick if the universities keep churning out thought-clones of Lawrence Summers rather than Herman Daly think-alikes.)

7.6 EPILOGUE: HERMAN DALY AND CULTURAL EVOLUTION

I started out by arguing that humans have no choice but to live according to socially constructed models of reality and that, in the unconscious construction of these abstractions, we tend to be seduced by 'magical thinking.' I have also argued that this is not necessarily a hopeless situation – society could choose to engage in the *conscious* rewriting of its core cultural narratives. Certainly we need a new deliberately structured model of the economy that recognizes both humanity's de facto ecological niche as a consumptive 'dissipative structure' and people's complex relationships in community.

We already consciously create physical and abstract models in many domains of human activity from architecture to zoology. Invariably, the purpose is to simplify certain aspects of reality while retaining the essential character and behavior of the entity being modeled. We hope that understanding how carefully constructed models behave when we manipulate key variables or parameters will provide reliable insights into how the real world might behave under similar circumstances. This is why good experimental science proceeds cautiously, continuously testing its assumptions and hypotheses against the real world. When a hypothesis fails, scientists restructure the model accordingly, each time hoping to nudge the model's behavior closer to that of the reality it purportedly represents.[13]

It is worth noting too that bio-evolution proceeds in precisely this 'trial and error' fashion. In effect, every genetic mutation represents an experimental 'hypothesis' about the relevant organism's environment. Mutations that increase an individual's survivability or 'fitness' are retained and accumulate in its offspring, that is, in future 'models' of the organism. Failed hypotheses are 'selected out' and eventually disappear from the population.

Shouldn't society apply this understanding of both the creative role of models and the evolutionary process to the great economic experiment presently playing out in the material world? As we test the neoliberal economy against external reality, we are performing an uncontrolled and potentially dangerous experiment in human evolution. However, as the results come in we are showing little willingness to adapt the model to its 'environment.'

This is particularly disappointing. The fact that human evolution is more driven by cultural than by biological factors gives us a potential advantage over other species. It is common knowledge that 'genes' are the basis of biological evolution. Genes are heritable bits of genetic information that interact with 'the environment' to determine the physical and behavioral phenotype (the 'appearance') of the individual. Less familiar is the concept of 'memes.' Memes are heritable units of cultural information – persistent myths, economic models or working technologies – that influence the 'phenotype' of the society of concern (Dawkins, 1976). Memes are thus the basis of cultural evolution; they have a leg-up over genes in that memes can spread rapidly among living individuals in the *same* generation or population. This means that human evolution, particularly the cultural component, is potentially much faster than biological evolution.

But only potentially. Memes, like genes, are subject to natural selection. If a previously successful meme or meme complex (for example, growthist economics) becomes maladaptive under changing environmental circumstances it may be eliminated by that environment. Thus, while memetic evolution is theoretically faster than the genetic variety, it may not always be fast enough. Whole cultures that refused to abandon maladaptive meme complexes – core values and beliefs – have foundered and collapsed (see Diamond, 2005).

With this in mind, a truly rational society would quickly adopt Herman Daly's steady-state economics on the evidence that neoliberal economics is about to be 'selected out' and that the Daly brand provides a better map of contemporary biophysical reality. Simply put, steady-state economics offers humanity superior fitness and greater survival value.

While we're at it, we might consider improving the social dimensions of economic life. In addition to logical intelligence, humans also have unmatched capacity for empathy (with both other people and species), to exercise moral judgment and to use all of these traits in planning for their future. Neoliberal economics ignores most dimensions of human intelligence, eschews moral and ethical considerations and dismisses long-term planning. Once again, by contrast, Herman Daly's political economy displays all these qualities in abundance (see Daly and Cobb, 1994) and all are necessary if global civilization is to achieve an equitably sustainable 'steady-state' relationship with the ecosphere.

Wake up world! It would be a tragic irony if modern *H. sapiens*, that self-proclaimed pinnacle of self-conscious intelligence and earthly evolution, were to be unceremoniously ejected by the ecosphere because of a lingering, maladaptive propensity for political and economic folly based on self-deception and 'magical thinking.'

NOTES

1. There is a vast amount of electromagnetic energy out there that is not accessible to our senses but is as 'real' as what we can detect. For example, the signals of virtually every radio and television program being broadcast for hundreds of kilometers around and every cell-phone conversation in the vicinity are passing through your body unsensed right now. (Fortunately, one can only suppose.)
2. See Regal (1990) for a detailed description of how 'reality is always being tampered with by our nervous systems' and how 'the construction of internal [that is, 'subjective'] reality is a continual process in the human brain' (which Regal refers to as 'The Illusion Organ').
3. This will seems odd to non-economists, because most people still participate in 'the economy' to acquire the material basis of their own existence.
4. This perspective has spawned the entire subdiscipline of 'industrial metabolism' stimulated largely by the work of another renegade economist (and physicist) Robert U. Ayres (see Ayres and Simonis, 1994; Ayres and Warr, 2009).
5. The quantities can be prodigious. By the late 1990s, material waste output ranged from 11 metric tons per person per year in Japan to 25 metric tons per person per year in the United States. When so-called 'hidden flows' were included – flows resulting from economic activity but which do not actually enter the production process, such as soil erosion, mining overburden and earth moved during construction – total annual waste material output increased to 21 metric tons per person in Japan and 86 metric tons per person in the United States (WRI, 2000). That's 86 000 kilograms (198 598 lbs) every year for every man, woman and child in the latter country!
6. Because self-producing systems maintain themselves 'far-from-equilibrium' by degrading and dispersing imported energy and matter, they are called 'dissipative structures.' Prigogine suggested that distance from equilibrium would become as essential a variable in thermodynamic descriptions of nature as temperature is in classical equilibrium thermodynamics (Prigogine, 1997, chapter 2).
7. In some cases, host systems can thrive without (some of) their subsystems – the ecosphere would persist in the absence of humans, for example. In others, the subsystems and 'hosts' exist in a state of mutual dependence – think of the relationship between the nervous system and the entire body.

8. Even photosynthesis converts only about 2 percent of available solar energy ('exergy') into biomass (negentropy); the rest is dissipated into space as low-grade infrared (heat) radiation, mostly through evapotranspiration. The negentropy gain by the ecosphere is trivial compared to the entropy gain of the universe.
9. And is likely to remain so. What military or economic superpower has ever voluntarily relinquished its privileged position in the geopolitical hierarchy? For that matter, even most ordinary citizens as presently 'programmed' would see such a plan as a threat to their survival and respond accordingly.
10. To this extent, Heidegger was right – the corporate sector has exploited both humans' natural tendency to intellectual laziness and their hidden wants and fears to sideline meditative thinking from the public domain.
11. Many levels of motivation are at play. For big oil and coal, for example, it may seem rational in the economic short term to turn the public against effective carbon emissions reduction policies, but if the climate science is correct this strategy of denial is against everyone's longer-term interests.
12. Those who recoil at the thought of social engineering for the common good should keep in mind that the present generation has already been socially engineered for the corporate good. The alternative is to wait until widespread disaster knocks large numbers of people off their comfortable cognitive perches. This will also force them to reconstruct their internal 'realities' (perceptions) but in much less agreeable ways.
13. It has been argued that economist do the opposite, asking the real world to conform to their models!

REFERENCES

Ayres, R.U. and U.K. Simonis (1994), *Industrial Metabolism: Restructuring for Sustainable Development*, Tokyo: United Nations University Press.

Ayres, R.U. and B. Warr (2009), *The Economic Growth Engine: How Energy and Work Drive Material Prosperity*, Cheltenham, UK and Northampton, MA, USA: Edward Elgar Publishing.

Burton, R.A. (2008), *On Being Certain: Believing You Are Right Even When You're Not*, New York: St Martin's Press.

Christensen, P. (1991), 'Driving forces, increasing returns, and ecological sustainability', in R. Costanza (ed.), *Ecological Economics: The Science and Management of Sustainability*, New York: Columbia University Press, pp. 75–87.

Coase, R. (1997), Interview with Ronald Coase, Inaugural Conference, International Society for New Institutional Economics, St Louis, USA, 17 September, available at http://www.coase.org/coaseinterview.htm (accessed 19 July 2010).

Daly, H.E. (1968), *Journal of Political Economy*, **67** (3), 392–406, reprinted in H.E. Daly (ed.), 1980, 'On economics as a life science', in *Economics, Ecology, Ethics: Essays Toward a Steady-state Economy*, San Francisco, CA: W.H. Freeman, pp. 238–52.

Daly, H.E. (1990), 'Sustainable development: from concept and theory towards operational principles', *Population and Development Review* (special issue), reprinted in H.E. Daly (1991), *Steady-state Economics*, 2nd edn, Washington, DC: Island Press, pp. 241–60.

Daly, H.E. (1991a), *Steady-state Economics*, 2nd edn, Washington, DC: Island Press.

Daly, H.E. (1991b), 'From empty world economics to full world economics: recognizing an historic turning point in economic development', in R. Goodland,

H.E. Daly and El Serafy (eds), *Population, Technology and Lifestyle: The Transition to Sustainability*, Washington, DC: Island Press, pp. 23ff.

Daly, H.E. (1994), 'Operationalizing sustainable development by investing in natural capital', in A.-M. Jansson, M. Hammer, C. Folke and R. Costanza (eds), *Investing in Natural Capital*, Washington, DC: Island Press, pp. 22–37.

Daly, H.E. (1996), *Beyond Growth: The Economics of Sustainable Development*, Boston, MA: Beacon Press.

Daly, H.E. (1999), 'Uneconomic growth in theory and in fact', The First Annual Feasta Lecture, Trinity College, Dublin, 26 April, available at http://www.feasta.org/documents/feastareview/daly.htm (accessed 28 July 2010).

Daly, H.E. (2008), 'Special report: economics blind spot is a disaster for the planet', *New Scientist*, **2678**, 46–7.

Daly, H.E. and J.B. Cobb, Jr (1994), *For the Common Good*, 2nd edn, Boston, MA: Beacon Press.

Daly, H.E. and J. Farley (2004), *Ecological Economics: Principles and Applications*, Washington, DC: Island Press.

Damasio, A. (1994), *Descartes' Error: Emotion, Reason and the Human Brain*, New York: Avon Books.

Dawkins, R. (1976), *The Selfish Gene*, Oxford: Oxford University Press.

Diamond, J. (2005), *Collapse: How Societies Choose to Fail or Succeed*, New York: Viking Press.

Galbraith, J.K. (2000), 'How the economists got it wrong', *The American Prospect*, **11** (7), 14 February.

Georgescu-Roegen, N. (1993), 'The entropy law and the economic process', in H.E. Daly and K. Townsend (eds), *Valuing the Earth: Economics, Ecology, Ethics*, Cambridge, MA: MIT Press, pp. 75–88.

Heidegger, M. (1955), 'Discourse on thinking: memorial address', reprinted in M. Stassen (ed.) (2003), *Martin Heidegger: Philosophical and Political Writings*, trans. J.M. Anderson and E.H. Freund, The German Library, London: Continuum International Publishing Group, pp. 87ff.

Heilbroner, R. and L. Thurow (1981), *The Economic Problem*, New York: Prentice Hall.

Hicks, J.R. (1946), *Value and Capital*, 2nd edn, Oxford: Oxford University Press.

Jensen, D. (2000), *A Language Older than Words*, New York: Context Books.

Kay, J.J. and H. Regier (2000), 'Uncertainty, complexity, and ecological integrity', in P. Crabbé, A. Holland, L. Ryszkowski and L. Westra (eds), *Implementing Ecological Integrity: Restoring Regional and Global Environment and Human Health*, NATO Science Series IV: Earth and Environmental Sciences, Vol. 1, Dortrecht: Kluwer Academic Publishers, pp. 121–56.

Le Bon, G. (1895), *The Crowd: A Study of the Popular Mind*, reprinted in 2001, Kitchener, Canada: Batoche Press, available at http://socserv.mcmaster.ca/econ/ugcm/3ll3/lebon/Crowds.pdf (accessed 19 July 2010).

MacKenzie, D. (2010), 'Whose conspiracy? Special report on "denial"', *New Scientist*, **2760**, 38–41.

MacLean, P. (1990), *The Triune Brain in Evolution: Role in Paleocerebral Functions*, New York: Plenum Press.

Marshall, A. (1925), *Memorials of Alfred Marshall*, ed. A.C. Pigou, London: Macmillan.

Monbiot, G. (2010), 'Towering lunacy', *Guardian*, 17 August, available at http://

www.monbiot.com/archives/2010/08/16/towering-lunacy/ (accessed 18 August 2010).

Nelson, J.A. (2005), 'Rationality and humanity: a view from feminist economics', Working Paper 05-04, Global Development and Environment Institute, Tufts University, Medford, MA.

Ormerod, P. (2010), 'The current crisis and the culpability of macroeconomic theory', *Twenty-First Century Society*, **5** (1), 5–18.

Pearce, D.W. and G.D. Atkinson (1993), 'Capital theory and the measurement of sustainable development: an indicator of weak sustainability', *Ecological Economics*, **8**, 103–8.

Pearce, D.W., E. Barbier and A. Markandya (1990), *Sustainable Development: Economics and Environment in the Third World*, Cheltenham, UK and Northampton, MA, USA: Edward Elgar Publishing.

Pinker, S. (2002), *The Blank Slate: The Modern Denial of Human Nature*, New York: Viking.

Planck, M.K. (1949), *Scientific Autobiography and Other Papers*, trans. F. Gaynor, New York: Philosophical Library.

Postman, N. (1999), *Building a Bridge to the 18th Century*, New York: Vintage Books.

Pratarelli, M.E. and C.M. Aragon (2008), 'Acknowledging the "primitive origins of human ecological dysfunction": a view toward efficacy and global ecological integrity', *Globalization*, **8** (1), 1–17, available at http://globalization.icaap.org/content/v8.1/Pratarelli_Aragon.pdf (accessed 29 July 2010).

Prigogine, I. (1997), *The End of Certainty: Time, Chaos and the New Laws of Nature*, New York: The Free Press.

Rees, W.E. (1999), 'How should a parasite value its host?', *Ecological Economics*, **25**, 49–52.

Rees, W.E. (2003), 'Economic development and environmental protection: an ecological economics perspective', *Environmental Monitoring and Assessment*, **86** (1/2), 29–45.

Rees, W.E. (2006), 'Ecological footprints and bio-capacity: essential elements in sustainability assessment', in J. Dewulf and H. Van Langenhove (eds), *Renewables-based Technology: Sustainability Assessment*, Chichester, UK: John Wiley and Sons, pp. 143–58.

Rees, W.E. (2008), 'Human nature, eco-footprints and environmental injustice', *Local Environment – The International Journal of Justice and Sustainability*, **13** (8), 685–701.

Regal, P.J. (1990), *The Anatomy of Judgment*, Minneapolis, MN: University of Minnesota Press.

Rockström, J., W. Steffen, K. Noone et al. (2009), 'A safe operating space for humanity', *Nature*, **461**, 472–5.

Rowe, D. (2010), 'Liar, liar: why deception is our way of life', *New Scientist*, **2765**, 28–9.

Schneider, E.D. and J.J. Kay (1994a), 'Complexity and thermodynamics: toward a new ecology', *Futures*, **26**, 626–47.

Schneider, E.D. and J.J. Kay (1994b), 'Life as a manifestation of the second law of thermodynamics', *Mathematical and Computer Modelling*, **19** (6–8), 25–48.

Schneider, E.D. and J.J. Kay (1995), 'Order from disorder: the thermodynamics of complexity in biology', in M.P. Murphy and L.A.J. O'Neill (eds), *What is Life: The Next Fifty Years – Reflections on the Future of Biology*, Cambridge: Cambridge University Press, pp. 161–72.

Schrödinger, E. (1944), *What is Life?*, reprinted in 1967, Cambridge: Cambridge University Press, available at http://whatislife.stanford.edu/LoCo_files/What-is-Life.pdf (accessed 21 December 2015).

Tuchman, B. (1984), *The March of Folly*, New York: Alfred A. Knopf.

Victor, P.A. (1991), 'Indicators of sustainable development: some lessons from capital theory', *Ecological Economics*, **4**, 191–213.

Victor, P.A. (2008), *Managing Without Growth: Slower by Design, Not Disaster*, Cheltenham, UK and Northampton, MA, USA: Edward Elgar Publishing.

Victor, P.A., E. Hanna and A. Kubursi (1995), 'How strong is weak sustainability?', *Economie Appliquée*, **48** (2), 75–94.

von Weizsäcker, E., K. Hargroves, M. Smith, C. Desha and P. Stasinopoulos (2009), *Factor 5: Transforming the Global Economy through 80% Increase in Resource Productivity*, London and Droemer: Earthscan.

Wexler, B.E. (2006), *Brain and Culture: Neurobiology, Ideology and Social Change*, Cambridge, MA: Bradford Books, MIT Press.

Wolf, M. (2010), 'Why were resources expunged from economics?', *Wolfexchange*, London: *Financial Times*, available at http://blogs.ft.com/martin-wolf-exchange/2010/07/12/why-were-resources-expunged-from-neo-classical-economics/ (accessed 13 July 2010).

WRI (2000), *The Weight of Nations: Material Outflows from Industrial Economies*, Washington, DC: World Resources Institute, available at http://pdf.wri.org/weight_of_nations.pdf (accessed 26 July 2010).

WWF (2014), *Living Planet Report 2008*, Gland, Switzerland: Worldwide Fund for Nature.

PART III

Changing the goals: what is socially,
psychologically and ethically desirable?

8. The importance of a just distribution in a 'full' world

Philip Lawn

8.1 INTRODUCTION

My aim in this chapter is to argue that distributional equity, which ought to be a mandatory objective at any time, becomes an even more important consideration in a 'full' world – that is, in a world where human-made capital becomes the abundant factor and remaining natural capital becomes the limiting factor. To do this, I shall focus on the ecological economics position that achieving sustainable development requires the resolution of three distinct policy goals. They are: (a) ecological sustainability (ensuring the rate of throughput is no greater than the ecosphere's regenerative and waste assimilative capacities); (b) distributional equity (ensuring the distribution of income and wealth is fair and just); and (c) allocative efficiency (ensuring the incoming resource flow is allocated to product uses with the highest use value) (Daly, 1996).

There are, nevertheless, two other aspects that are critical to achieving sustainable development. In the first instance, and following Tinbergen (1952), the resolution of each of the three policy goals requires the application of a separate policy instrument. In other words, it is impossible to kill more than one policy bird with one policy stone.[1] The policy instruments required are:

- quantitative restrictions on the rate of resource throughput to achieve ecological sustainability
- taxes and transfer payments to achieve a just distribution of income and wealth
- relative prices determined by supply and demand forces in competitive markets to achieve allocative efficiency.

In the second instance, it is important to address the three policy goals in the order presented above – namely, ecological sustainability first, distributional equity second and allocative efficiency last. It makes no sense to try and resolve the allocation problem first and then make adjustments to ensure the incoming resource flow is both ecologically sustainable and distributionally just. Since the allocation process involves the relative division, through exchange, of the incoming resource flow among alternative product uses, it is too late to adjust the physical volume of the resource flow should it be unsustainable. In addition, since an individual's command over the allocation of the incoming resource flow depends on his or her ability to pay for the means to satisfy needs and wants, it is too late to adjust the distribution of the incoming resource flow among alternative people, following its allocation, should it be inequitable.[2]

Apart from this obvious sequencing imperative, resolving the policy goals in the above order extends market internalization beyond the mainstream imposition of depletion/pollution taxes. This is because the suggested policy sequence internalizes ecological and distributive limits, not just spillover costs.[3] In doing so, it paves the way for markets to facilitate a macroeconomic adjustment towards an optimal scale, and by this I mean a scale that is not only sustainable and just, but one where economic welfare – the difference between the benefits and costs of economic activity – is maximized. Conversely, an 'efficiency first' strategy is unlikely to prevent an economy from growing beyond its optimal scale because any increase in efficiency will give the appearance that the frugality required to achieve ecological sustainability is less necessary (Daly, 2007). Increased efficiency can also give the false impression that redistribution is less necessary given that greater efficiency implies the generation of more wealth from a given rate of resource throughput that most observers assume will automatically trickle down to the poor.

In bringing these three policy goals to attention, it is worth noting that mainstream economists have focused almost exclusively on efficient allocation – largely because of the falsely held assumption that allocative efficiency can achieve ecological sustainability – whereas ecological economists have focused mainly on sustainable scale. One might excuse ecological economists for this given the importance of sustainability and the fact that it is a poorly understood concept. Nevertheless, I believe that ecological economists must devote more time and effort to the issue of a just distribution at both the national and international levels. Following a brief explanation as to why we should concern ourselves with distributional equity, I shall then outline some of the policies that need to be implemented to achieve an intra- and internationally just distribution of income and wealth.

8.2 WHY IS A JUST DISTRIBUTION IMPORTANT?

A just distribution of income and wealth is important for an obvious reason – society is morally obliged to ensure that each and every citizen has access to the basic necessities of life.[4] Yet fairness goes much deeper than this since it is incumbent upon society to limit the order-of-magnitude difference in the income and wealth of its richest and poorest citizens. This aspect of equity has virtually been ignored, as evidenced by the massive increase in the order-of-magnitude difference between the pay of chief executives and average factory workers.[5] There are also few if any public campaigns to support the introduction of maximum income limits that would require the imposition of a 100 per cent marginal tax rate on incomes beyond a certain income threshold. This is somewhat surprising given that, in my view, incomes beyond a certain level effectively amount to an *economic rent*[6] and almost every undergraduate economics textbook portrays economic rents as unearned income that should be taxed away (confiscated) and redistributed.[7]

There is another good reason why an equitable distribution of income and wealth is important. It relates to the impact of a growing economy and the eventual need, at least in the minds of many ecological economists, for policy-makers to abandon the growth objective and initiate the transition towards a steady-state or non-growing economy.[8] The standard means of improving the well-being of a nation's citizens is to physically grow the economy. Ecological economists are happy to concede that the near continuous growth of industrialized economies since World War II has increased the material well-being of the average person in most industrialized nations. The doubt that ecological economists harbour is whether the increase in material possessions has always rendered the average citizen in these countries better off.

There are two reasons why ecological economists raise this doubt. The first pertains to a theoretical argument first expounded by Daly (1973). The second, which has emerged more recently, pertains to a growing weight of empirical evidence that appears to support Daly's theoretical argument. The theoretical argument itself is based upon a number of psychological, existential and biophysical principles, and I do not wish to elaborate on these principles in this chapter.[9] In a nutshell, ecological economists believe that as the economy grows relative to the finite, non-growing ecosphere that supports it, the marginal benefits of growth gradually decline while the marginal costs of growth steadily increase. Eventually a physical scale is reached where the marginal benefits and the marginal costs of growth equate. At this point, the economy arrives at its optimal scale, meaning that any further growth of the economy becomes 'uneconomic' insofar as it increases costs, usually of a social and environmental kind, more than it increases benefits, usually of an economic kind. Hence, growth beyond the optimum has the effect of lowering people's well-being even though it may increase their possession of material goods.

To make matters worse, the optimal macroeconomic scale is likely to be reached much sooner than most people envisage. It is generally believed that if there is such a thing as an optimal scale, it will not be encountered until the economy arrives at its maximum sustainable scale (that is, at a scale in keeping with the ecosphere's long-run carrying capacity).[10] However, it is because the cost of lost ecosystem services rises dramatically as an economy approaches its ecological limits – irrespective of whether they are reflected in markets – that an optimal scale is reached well before an economy arrives at its maximum sustainable scale. As a consequence, the former is likely to be a scale considerably smaller than the latter.

Of course, efficiency-increasing technological progress has the potential to increase the marginal benefits and lower the marginal costs of an increment of growth. This, in turn, can increase the physical size of both the optimal and the maximum sustainable scale of a nation's economy (Lawn, 2007). The problem here, however, is that biophysical factors severely limit humankind's capacity to reduce the marginal costs of growth. Biophysical factors also restrict how large an economic system can become before it is rendered unsustainable. But even if the technological potential exists to increase the size of the optimal scale, it is of little consolation if a nation's economy is already much larger than the optimum. In such circumstances, a nation must reduce the physical scale of its economy in order to increase the economic welfare enjoyed by its citizens.

This last point leads me to the second reason why ecological economists doubt whether the more recent growth experienced in industrialized nations has translated into an increase in human well-being. In the late 1980s, an Index of Sustainable Economic Welfare (ISEW) was developed by Daly and Cobb (1989) based on an earlier welfare index calculated for the USA by Nordhaus and Tobin (1972). The ISEW, which is now more commonly referred to as a Genuine Progress Indicator (GPI), is designed to measure and compare the benefits and costs of a growing economy. The GPI is therefore a useful indicator of where a nation's economy might be in relation to its optimal scale (Lawn, 2007; Lawn and Clarke, 2008; Lawn and Sanders, 1999). Presumably, if the GPI is rising, this indicates that a nation's economy is smaller than the optimum and that whatever growth is occurring is 'economic'. Conversely, if the GPI is declining, this suggests that the optimal scale has been surpassed and that the growth of the economy is 'uneconomic'.

In virtually every instance where the GPI has been calculated for an industrialized nation, the GPI, after rising in unison with gross domestic product (GDP), has either declined or stagnated (Jackson and Stymne, 1996; Kubiszewski et al., 2013; Max-Neef, 1995). Because the general downturn in the GPI occurred during the 1970s for some countries (for example, USA, UK and Australia), or the 1980s for others (for example, Sweden and the Netherlands), most industrialized nations appear to have long surpassed their optimal scale. As such, the well-being of many people in the industrialized world has probably been declining or stagnating for some time.

What is even more alarming is that the economies of many industrialized nations also appear to have exceeded their maximum sustainable scale. Studies based on a comparison between a nation's ecological footprint[11] and available biocapacity reveal that most of the world's industrialized countries have an ecological deficit (Wackernagel and Rees, 1996; Wackernagel et al., 1999).[12] Thus, more than having to reduce the physical scale of their economies to increase economic welfare (that is, move towards an optimal scale), industrialized nations need to undergo a phase of degrowth to again operate sustainably.[13]

Given what appears to be an urgent need to reduce the physical scale of the economy, it is clear that industrialized countries will be unable to rely upon growth as a means of improving the material well-being of their poorest citizens. They will have to rely heavily on the redistribution of income and wealth. Increased efficiency – in particular, value-adding in production – will also be of assistance, but greater efficiency cannot be acquired at will. Moreover, as already highlighted, technical efficiency is subject to severe biophysical constraints.[14]

Another important equity consideration arises if a society or nation elects to make the transition towards a steady-state economy and the transition requires a phase of degrowth. In these circumstances, distributional equity will be critical to minimize whatever pain may ensue. For example, innovative policies will need to be devised to keep unemployment and absolute poverty levels low as the economy diminishes in size. If this cannot be achieved, society may regard the resultant rise in poverty and unemployment too repugnant to accept, in which case it may reject the transition to a steady-state economy and revert to a growth objective. I shall have more to say about the policies to prevent escalating unemployment and poverty levels soon.

The final issue I want to raise relates to some disturbing new evidence regarding the sustainable economic welfare of a number of poor nations. I mentioned above that the GPI of wealthy nations has either fallen or stagnated since the 1970s–1980s. Somewhat remarkably, the GPI of the majority of these countries ceased to rise once their per capita GDP reached approximately Int\$15 000–20 000.[15] This led Max-Neef (1995) to put forward a threshold hypothesis – the notion that when a nation's per capita GDP reaches a certain level, its GPI is likely to fall. As unwelcome as this news was to growth-obsessed rich countries, it was good news for poor nations. With per capita GDP far short of the income threshold, poor countries could grow their economies safe in the knowledge that, for some time at least, it would translate into rising levels of sustainable economic welfare.

Alas, this does not seem to be the case. A book has been released revealing the results of a GPI study of seven nations in the Asia-Pacific region (Lawn and Clarke, 2008). Three of the nations are high-income countries – Australia, New Zealand and Japan; four are low-income countries – China, India, Thailand and Vietnam. Of the four low-income countries, two of them, China and Thailand, are already experiencing a decline in their per capita GPI. This is despite their per capita GDP being well short of the income threshold.[16] As for India and Vietnam, the per capita GPI of both countries is still rising but at a considerably lower rate than their per capita GDP. Moreover, because environmental costs in India and Vietnam are increasing significantly and likely to rise strongly in the near future, the per capita GPI of these two nations is liable to fall very soon.

What are the reasons for this apparent contraction in the threshold level of GDP? There are many, but the main factor appears to be the much higher marginal cost of growth in a full world. If one considers the initial growth phase of the world's richest countries, it took place in a relatively 'empty' world. Resources were plentiful and easy to access. Competition for resources in global resource markets was comparatively weak. In addition, waste sinks were relatively uncommitted and therefore readily able to absorb and assimilate much of the waste that was generated. Hence, the marginal cost of growth was quite low for the early growth-movers.

A completely different situation exists today. Oil is now sourced from distant deserts and deep ocean waters. China and India are now actively competing with Europe and North America for base commodities. Meanwhile, the global ecosphere struggles to cope with the growing discharge of carbon dioxide (CO_2) into the atmosphere. As a consequence, the marginal cost of growth is considerably higher for growth latecomers than it was for the world's richest nations at the equivalent stage of development.

What does this mean? Firstly, unless appropriate action is taken, low-income countries may never reach the level of well-being currently enjoyed by the world's industrialized nations. Secondly, rich nations not only need to quell their growth to increase their own levels of economic welfare, they must, from an equity perspective, cease to grow their economies in order to provide the 'room' that low-income countries need to enjoy a phase of welfare-increasing growth (Lawn and Clarke, 2008). Should rich nations do this, it would amount to an indirect form of redistribution, although, as we shall see, much more needs to be done than this on the redistribution front.

8.3　POLICIES TO ACHIEVE A JUST DISTRIBUTION

Given the aforementioned, it is quite clear that policies need to be implemented to achieve distributional equity both within and between nations. Equity between nations will be the more difficult to accomplish since it will require the relative equalization of wages, conditions of employment and environmental standards in an upwards direction across the world (that is, will require the conditions in the South to gravitate towards those of the North). Efforts to pull standards and conditions upward are important for obvious poverty-alleviation reasons. They are also important given that the forces of globalization have a tendency to exert downward pressure on standards – a so-called race to the bottom – and therefore must be adequately dealt with to achieve a genuine and desirable form of distributional equity.

8.3.1　Policies to Achieve Distributional Equity Within Nations

So long as disparities exist between countries in terms of their material wealth and productive capacity, the policies to achieve distributional equity within nations will differ from country to country. In low-income countries, where the capacity to meet the needs of the poor is limited, achieving distributional equity is likely to be confined to ensuring each person has access to the basic necessities of life. Conversely, in high-income countries, achieving distributional equity is likely to extend to the poor having access to some luxury goods and services. Considerations of a just disparity between rich and poor are also apt to arise in high-income countries given that one's relative income in a wealthy nation appears to impact more on individual welfare than one's absolute income (Abramowitz, 1979; Easterlin, 1974).

Putting aside the issue of how large a minimum income should be, a number of different methods have been recommended to guarantee its provision. Some observers have proposed a Basic Income Guarantee, which effectively amounts to a universal transfer payment to each and every citizen regardless of one's contribution to society (Atkinson, 1995; Baetz, 1972; Clark and Kavanagh, 1996; Van Parijs, 2004). Others have argued for something similar, but in the form of a negative income tax (Daly, 1991; Friedman, 1962; Tobin, 1966).

Because of concerns about the macroeconomic impact of a Basic Income Guarantee, a group of economists have recently put forward the concept of a Job Guarantee (Cowling et al., 2006; Mitchell and Watts, 2004; Tcherneva, 2006; Wray, 1998). The Job Guarantee is a demand-side policy where the government acts as an employer-of-last-resort to absorb all workers displaced by the private sector (Mitchell and Watts, 2004). Under a Job Guarantee, any person unable to secure employment in the private sector or conventional public sector is automatically offered a Job Guarantee occupation.

An important feature of the scheme is the payment of a minimum hourly award wage to satisfy the basic needs of full-time Job Guarantee employees and their dependents. The payment of a minimum wage also means that the government avoids having to compete with the private sector up the wage scale for labour. This ensures there is no disturbance of the private wage structure. As an added bonus, the minimum wage set by the government establishes a price-stabilizing wage floor for the entire economy (Mitchell and Muysken, 2008).

Advocates of the Job Guarantee believe that a number of factors make it the best means of providing a minimum income. Firstly, because the Job Guarantee ties the receipt of income to work, it overcomes any concern that may arise in relation to worker incentives and welfare dependency. Secondly, advocates of the Job Guarantee argue that a Basic Income Guarantee amounts to an indiscriminate form of Keynesian pump-priming that, if introduced, would trigger periodic phases of demand-pull and cost-push inflation. Because the inflationary spiral would then have to be countered by a contractionary macroeconomic response, Job Guarantee advocates believe that a Basic Income Guarantee would generate high rates of unemployment (Cowling et al., 2006). Conversely, a Job Guarantee would head off any inflationary pressure in two main ways. In the first instance, it would provide the demand expansion necessary to achieve full employment – no more, no less. Hence, it would not be indiscriminate in nature. In the second instance, it would employ the same inflation-control mechanism as the 'non-accelerating-inflation rate of unemployment' (NAIRU) approach that is widely adopted by most national governments. The NAIRU is an unemployment rate that, when achieved, is accompanied by a constant inflation rate. An increase in real GDP that reduces the unemployment rate below the NAIRU leads to non-productivity-related wage rises and an accelerated rate of price inflation (Dornbusch and Fischer, 1990). It is because of widespread concerns about inflation that contractionary macroeconomic measures are commonly implemented whenever the unemployment rate falls to something approximating the NAIRU. The unfortunate consequence of a NAIRU-based approach to macroeconomic policy is plain for all to see – it results in a permanent pool of sacrificed labour, the majority of which are society's most vulnerable and disadvantaged citizens.[17]

The inflation-control mechanism associated with the Job Guarantee is referred to by Mitchell and Watts (2004) as a 'non-accelerating inflation buffer employment ratio' or NAIBER. It works in the following manner. Firstly, assume that a NAIRU policy is being employed and exists at a 6 per cent unemployment rate.[18] The Job Guarantee scheme is then introduced to eliminate all but frictional unemployment. Because the scheme necessitates an increase in government spending, it boosts aggregate demand and real GDP. Let's assume that demand-pull inflationary pressures begin to emerge within the economy. Fearing the impact of inflation, the government dampens private sector activity by employing monetary policy instruments to raise interest rates.[19] As a consequence, the percentage of the labour force employed in the private sector declines while the percentage employed at the minimum wage under the Job Guarantee scheme increases. Provided the interest rate is appropriately manipulated, the ratio of Job Guarantee workers to private sector employees rises until the inflation rate is again stabilized. Inflation control and full employment are simultaneously accomplished and the NAIBER is attained.

Of course, advocates of the Basic Income Guarantee are likely to respond by contending that full employment is unnecessary if each citizen is guaranteed a minimum income upfront. They may even go further and argue that any high rate of unemployment arising from the introduction of a Basic Income Guarantee is also irrelevant. However, evidence suggests that unemployment, by eroding human capital and reducing one's capacity to engage in a market economy, significantly impedes one's ability to realize the full spectrum of human needs – in particular, the need to become fully actualized in what one is capable of becoming (Maslow, 1954). It has therefore been argued that a guaranteed access to paid employment constitutes a basic human right that can only be upheld if a full employment policy is adopted (Burgess and Mitchell, 1998). I wholeheartedly support this view and believe that ecological economists must give employment considerations greater attention than they have in the past. A Job Guarantee is a policy initiative well worth investigating.

Having said this, there is a concern that I have recently raised in relation to the Job Guarantee (Lawn, 2009). Let's assume that a nation is situated on an ecological precipice and there are no constraints imposed on the rate of resource throughput to keep it within the regenerative and waste assimilative limits of the ecosphere. If a Job Guarantee is introduced to eliminate unemployment, it would initially increase real GDP and tip a nation's economy into unsustainable territory. At first blush, it would seem that the Job Guarantee is inconsistent with achieving ecological sustainability. This may not be the case. Assume, instead, that throughput constraints have been imposed and exist in the form of a comprehensive cap-and-trade system.[20] Should a Job Guarantee be introduced, the ensuing demand stimulus would not translate into a higher yet unsustainable level of real GDP. It would lead to an increase in the price of resource permits – a consequence of a rise in the demand for resources relative to a constrained resource supply. This would raise the cost of production, increase goods prices, lower the real money supply (M/P) and push up interest rates. The rise in interest rates would deflate private sector spending and reduce private sector employment. With a Job Guarantee in place, the workers laid off in the private sector would obtain Job Guarantee occupations. Thus, even in circumstances where ecological limits render the stimulation of aggregate demand untenable, the Job Guarantee would ration paid work to the extent required to achieve and maintain full employment (Lawn, 2009). Hence, the Job Guarantee would serve as an invaluable distributional device in a full world.

Some observers would no doubt object to the idea of a portion of the labour force being 'forced' out of the private sector and into a lower-paid Job Guarantee occupation (that is, the NAIBER would initially be higher than the NAIRU). I have to admit that this is a potentially undesirable aspect of the Job Guarantee. However, consider the following. Firstly, having some people employed on a lower income is more equitable than having a great deal more people permanently unemployed under a NAIRU policy stance. Secondly, the higher resource costs induced by a cap-and-trade system would presumably: (a) stimulate the development and uptake of resource-saving technology; and (b) facilitate the allocation of the incoming resource flow to higher value-adding forms of production. In other words, higher resource costs would increase labour productivity over time. I believe this would result in the NAIBER being considerably lower than the NAIRU in the long run, which is an undeniably better outcome on all fronts.

The final point I would like to make relates to population growth. Clearly, in view of the ecological limits to growth, population numbers must eventually be stabilized along with the stock of human-made goods. However, it is also important to control population growth given that distributional equity is made exceedingly more difficult to achieve if population numbers are rapidly rising. There are, of course, many countries with low fertility and immigration rates. For these countries, population growth control is not a critical domestic concern. But for those nations with high fertility rates (usually low-income countries) and others with high immigration rates (for example, the USA, Canada and Australia), population issues need to be taken more seriously than they are at present.

8.3.2   Policies to Achieve Distributional Equity Between Nations

As previously indicated, one of the best distributive actions that Northern countries can take is to cease expanding their economies to enable the South to enjoy a phase of welfare-increasing growth. Beyond this, high-income countries should increase the financial aid they provide to the world's low-income countries. At present, average spending on foreign aid per wealthy nation is 0.3 per cent of GDP (OECD, 2008). This is woefully inadequate. A target foreign aid rate of at least 0.7 per cent of GDP would be eminently more just.[21]

There are four main areas where increased aid money should be directed to reduce the current inequity between nations. Firstly, in view of the need for many poorer nations to control their population numbers, aid money should be used to fund population stabilization programmes in circumstances where governments lack the necessary fiscal capacity.

Secondly, many of the world's critical ecosystems (for example, rainforests, wetlands and coral reefs) are located in low-income nations where further GDP growth is required. These ecosystems will come under intense pressure at a time when preservation is more urgent than ever. While the preservation of ecosystems generates non-direct-use benefits for all nations, it denies the host country direct-use benefits. To promote ecosystem preservation, the governments of wealthier nations should distribute aid money to compensate low-income countries for the direct use benefits they would subsequently forego. The aid money could then be redistributed by the recipient country to the citizens most affected by the lack of direct ecosystem access. This could take the form of direct compensation or the establishment of a substitute industry (for example, tourism to replace logging).

Thirdly, aid money should be used to assist low-income countries to increase their investment in natural capital – that is, by funding reforestation projects, wetland restoration and rehabilitation programmes, and assisting farmers to adopt sustainable land management practices.

Finally, since rich countries would indirectly benefit from a reduction in the resource use intensity of the world's low-income nations, the former should establish a transfer programme to assist the latter in the uptake of resource-saving technology. This might best be achieved by allocating foreign aid money to subsidize and thus lower the purchasing price of expensive new technology.

I mentioned earlier that globalization forces have a tendency to exert downward pressure on standards that will need to be addressed to achieve a desirable form of distributional equity. The downward pressure on standards arises because, in a globalized economy characterized by the free mobility of capital, international trade is governed by the principle of *absolute advantage* (that is, the absolute cost of production).[22] In these circumstances, capital is free to move wherever the cost of production is lowest, whether it be the result of: (a) employing better trained and educated workers; (b) the use of more advanced technology; (c) lower wages and tax rates; or (d) lower compliance costs due to weaker environmental and workplace regulations. Unfortunately, as the cost of relocation has fallen over time, it is the disparity in tax rates, wages and environmental and workplace standards that is affecting the cost of production most. It is therefore these factors that are having the greatest influence on where transnational corporations locate their production activities.

Fearing the loss of industries and jobs to other countries, governments will often try to minimize the relocation impact of higher wages, higher corporate tax rates and more stringent environmental and workplace regulations in their country. As a consequence, globalization forces make it difficult for governments to introduce the policies needed to achieve sustainable development, including those that improve the equitable distribution of income and wealth both within and between nations.

How can this problem be ameliorated without unduly affecting international trade? One potential solution is to allow countries with similar wages, tax regimes and environmental standards to trade freely with each other yet impose 'green' tariffs on countries with lower standards. To work effectively, the tariff would need to represent the undesirable cost advantage that exists due to differences in standards, not because of a genuine difference in the efficiency of production.[23] Since there is enormous potential for a system of green tariffs to be abused, which could easily trigger a degenerative tariff war, the system would need to be overseen by an international organization. The World Trade Organization (WTO) would seem a likely candidate although this would require the WTO to revamp its current attitude towards international trade matters.

In many ways, the WTO ought not to be antagonistic towards green tariffs. Much of the WTO's rhetoric on international trade centres on its potential efficiency benefits. Yet international trade in the presence of externalized social and environmental differentials is impeding the efficient allocation of global resources. Quite understandably, antagonism towards green tariffs is very likely to come from those who would view them as a means by which Northern countries could maintain their wealth advantage over the world's poorest countries. There is no doubt that the system would make it more difficult for many low-income nations to export to the North. However, this additional difficulty may not be such a bad thing. Indeed, it may help to close the gap between rich and poor. Consider the following response by Daly when asked about the possible implications of internalizing social and environmental standards into the prices of Third World goods:

> Granted this makes it harder for poor countries to export – so does a decent minimum wage and the existence of free labour unions and the outlawing of child labour within the poor country. In my view it is not all bad to make it harder for poor countries to export to the US. It means that instead of planting all their land in bananas or fancy fruits and flowers for export, the poor country might have to plant more rice and beans for its own citizens. And to sell the rice and beans to its own citizens, it will have to worry about their purchasing power – about domestic jobs and decent wages, and the distribution of income within their country. And they might worry a bit less about cutting wages and social benefits in order to be more competitive in the global market, as they must do in the export-led model of development to which the IMF and WTO are so totally committed. Admittedly, less export revenue will be available to buy expensive toys for the elite, but even that might not be all that bad. Maybe they will begin to invest some of their surplus in their own country. (http://csf.colorado.edu/seminars/daly97/proceedings, accessed November 2008)[24]

In other words, by provoking the world's low-income nations to consider more seriously the income of its poorest citizens, a system of green tariffs would force its policy-makers to implement the measures that would improve the equitable distribution of income and wealth domestically. Furthermore, the ability to better compete in the global market would require low-income countries to become genuinely more efficient in production, not to become increasingly attractive pollution and/or cheap labour havens. This would help close the productivity gap between the world's rich and poor countries and eventually bridge the income disparities across the globe.

Another potential globalization solution involves limiting the international mobility of capital to reinstate *comparative advantage* as the principle governing international trade. This would also circumvent any cost advantage associated with lower social and environmental standards, although it probably would not encourage the raising of standards to the same extent as green tariffs. I have elsewhere outlined a so-called Import-Export (IMPEX) system of exchange rate management to limit the international mobility of capital (Lawn, 2007). Word limits prevent me from detailing the IMPEX system. What I can say is that the IMPEX system is not anti-trade, it is largely market-based, and it precludes the growth of foreign debts that have also played a crucial role in reducing the capacity of many low-income nations to protect their poorest citizens.

8.4   CONCLUDING REMARKS

Sustainable development not only requires resolution of the three policy goals of ecological sustainability, distributional equity and allocative efficiency, but for each goal to be addressed in the correct order and via the application of an appropriate policy instrument. Although most ecological economists hold this view, very few have dealt adequately with the equity goal. Many have chosen to focus on what is required to achieve ecological sustainability. As important as ecological sustainability is, particularly given that many countries have surpassed their maximum sustainable scale, this is a mistake. Ecological economists urgently need to demonstrate that the steady-state economy they have heavily promoted need not lead to increased poverty rates or demoralizingly high rates of unemployment. This will require powerful and well-reasoned arguments as to how, in a full world, distributional equity can be achieved both within and between nations. Should ecological economists and other like-minded activists fail in this regard, humankind is much less likely to make the necessary transition to a steady-state economy. But even if the transition to a steady-state economy is undertaken, the failure to achieve distributional equity – perhaps as a consequence of underestimating its importance – increases the probability that society will return to the growth objective. Given the gravity of the current situation, humankind can ill-afford the eventuation of either circumstance.

NOTES

1. See Chapter 13 in this volume for an alternative view, which argues that the policy instrument of capturing natural resource rent is sustainable, just and efficient.
2. Of course, ensuring a just distribution prior to the allocation process does not guarantee a just distribution following it. Hence, there is always the need for some further redistribution. But redistribution, following allocation, is much less disruptive and market distorting if the distribution of the incoming resource flow is equitable to begin with. Above all, the policy goals of ecological sustainability and distributional equity must be resolved prior to the goal of allocative efficiency.
3. Whereas the imposition of depletion/pollution taxes without having resolved the sustainability and distributional goals amounts to falsely relying upon the internalization of spillover costs to determine a sustainable rate of throughput and an equitable distribution of income and wealth, resolving the sustainability and distributional goals at the outset ensures, firstly, that these two critical goals are insulated from the subsequent allocation of the incoming resource flow, and secondly, that the allocation of the incoming resource flow is determined by price signals that reflect ecological and distributive limits. The price-influencing effect of prior throughput and distribution decisions is not a trivial matter. In the case of natural resources, it has been shown that resource prices do not necessarily rise as resources become increasingly scarce (Bishop, 1993; Hall and Hall, 1984; Lawn, 2007; Norgaard, 1990). This is because resource prices are unable to

reflect absolute scarcity until such time as resource flows are explicitly capped to reflect ecological limits. See also Vatn (Chapter 5 in this volume) for an interesting discussion on externalities.

4. See Vatn (Chapter 5, this volume) for a relevant discussion on the social limits to growth, and Gowdy (Chapter 6, this volume) for a discussion of the universal human concern for fairness and just distribution.

5. Daly (1996) reveals that in the USA, the order-of-magnitude difference between the pay of chief executives and average factory workers grew from a factor of 12 in 1960 to a factor of well over 100 by the 1990s. This difference has continued to increase, reaching 273 in 2012 (Mishel and Sabadish, 2013). In the two years following the official end of the great recession in the USA, the poorest 99 per cent in the USA suffered a decline in income, while 121 per cent of the income growth that defined the end of the great recession went to the top 1 per cent (Saez, 2013).

6. See Cobb (Chapter 11 in this volume) for a more detailed discussion of economic rent.

7. Upon airing this suggestion, I am usually asked what the maximum income should be. For some time, I replied with a stab-in-the-dark figure that, with all honesty, I could not rigorously justify. Having given this more thought, it would seem reasonable to me that a good starting point is the annual salary of a nation's president, chancellor or prime minister. After all, no one has greater responsibility. From my Australian perspective, this would mean an order-of-magnitude difference in the income of the richest and poorest of around 15 to 20 times (the prime minister's salary is approximately $350 000 per year; the average income in Australia is approximately $50 000 per year; and the income of Australia's poorest – old-aged pensioners with no other source of income – is approximately $20 000 per year).

8. A steady-state economy is one that does not physically grow (that is, production of new goods equals the consumption/depreciation of existing goods), but qualitatively improves in terms of its content of physical goods, the means by which goods are produced and maintained, and the purpose for which the goods are intended. For more on the steady-state economy, see Daly (1973, 1991), Lawn (2007), Dietz and O'Neill (2013) and Czech (2013), as well as Chapters 12–14 in this volume.

9. For more on this, see Daly (1973, 1991, 1996), Mishan (1967, 1980), Georgescu-Roegen (1971), Weisskopf (1971, 1973), Hirsch (1976), Lawn (2000, 2007) and Mill (1857).

10. It is not uncommon for the two terms to be confused and thus be used interchangeably.

11. A country's ecological footprint constitutes the area of land *required* to generate the renewable resources needed to sustain economic activity at its current level and to absorb the resultant wastes. The emphasis on renewable resources in the calculation of the ecological footprint arises because of the inevitable exhaustion of non-renewable resources. To determine if a nation's economy has exceeded its maximum sustainable scale, the ecological footprint is compared to its biocapacity. A nation's biocapacity is indicated by the quantity of land it has *available* to generate an ongoing supply of renewable resources and to absorb its own wastes. Ecological unsustainability (ecological deficit) occurs if a nation's ecological footprint exceeds its biocapacity.

12. It is claimed that countries with ecological deficits can operate sustainably by importing resources from countries with ecological surpluses. This is true. However, two points are worth bearing in mind. Firstly, the ecological footprint of the global economy currently exceeds the biocapacity of the planet (Wackernagel et al., 1999). That is, the global economy is already in ecological deficit. Therefore, while the ecological deficits of some countries can be 'resource balanced', not all can. Secondly, because the economies of many surplus nations are growing, so too are their ecological footprints. This means that ecological surpluses are declining across the world. Even if a debtor country is able to balance its ecological deficit via an arrangement with a surplus nation, can it rely upon this arrangement to maintain sustainability if the latter's surplus is shrinking over time and its own deficit is expanding?

13. Degrowth is a deliberate yet measured decrease in the physical scale of the economy. It is not the same as a failing growth economy (recession) insofar as it involves the

implementation of specific policy measures designed to reduce the scale of any economy in an orderly and least painful manner. Degrowth is a relatively novel concept that was recently explored at a conference organized by the European Society for Ecological Economics (see www.ecoeco.org/esee/degrowth conference, accessed November 2008). See also Martinez-Alier (Chapter 13 in this volume).

14. For example, the first and second laws of thermodynamics dictate that the matter-energy embodied in physical goods (Q) must be something less than the matter-energy embodied in the resources used in their production (R). That is, technical efficiency (E), which equals Q/R, must be less than a value of one. Hence, production can never be 100 per cent efficient. The first and second laws of thermodynamics also preclude the 100 per cent recycling of matter and the recycling of energy altogether.

15. Based on 2004 prices and exchange rates.

16. The per capita GPI of China and Thailand peaked when their per capita GDP was Int$5000 and Int$7500, respectively.

17. There are claims that, in more recent times, the NAIRU has fallen to levels that equate to full employment. The Centre of Full Employment and Equity (CofFEE) at the University of Newcastle, Australia, has shown that when underemployment and labour underutilization are taken into account, the real unemployment rate is approximately twice the official rate. In Australia, at a time when the Federal Government was claiming to have achieved full employment at an official unemployment rate of around 4 per cent of the labour force (late 2007/early 2008), CofFEE (CofFEE Labour Market Indicators, various) estimated that close to 8 per cent of the labour force was either unemployed or underemployed. It was also estimated that 70 per cent of underemployed Australians were working at least ten hours fewer than the desired number of work hours. In addition, around 1 per cent of the labour force had been unemployed for at least one year.

18. The NAIRU is typically around 6 per cent of the labour force in most industrialized countries.

19. In actual fact, the use of monetary instruments in most countries is conducted by central banks acting independently of the central government. Having said this, central banks invariably perform their monetary policy role with the aim of achieving a desired inflationary target band that is legislatively inscribed in the central bank's charter by the central government. Hence, as much as monetary policy is conducted by central banks, it is merely undertaken by central banks on the behalf of central governments.

20. For more on cap-and-trade systems, see Lawn (2007, chapter 11) and Daly (2007).

21. 0.7 per cent of GDP was the figure agreed to by wealthy donor countries at the United Nations General Assembly in 1970.

22. In the more traditional model of international trade (Ricardo, 1817), the governing principle is that of 'comparative advantage', which is determined by the relative cost of production. When international trade is governed by this principle, trade will generally be mutually beneficial for those engaged in the international transaction. However, for international trade to be governed by this principle, capital must be immobile, which it no longer is. Thus, the traditional argument in support of the mutually beneficial gains from international trade no longer holds. See Goodland (Chapter 2 in this volume) for more details.

23. Green tariffs would be protectionist in the sense they would protect hard-won social and environmental standards. But they would not be protectionist in the sense of protecting genuinely inefficient industries. If, following the internalization of lower social and environmental standards, the price of a Third World good is less than it is in a high-income country, the green tariff would not prevent the industry in the high-income country from being competed out of existence.

24. Taken from an Internet seminar that followed the release of Daly's book, *Beyond Growth* (1996).

REFERENCES

Abramowitz, M. (1979), 'Economic growth and its discontents', in M. Boskin (ed.), *Economics and Human Welfare*, New York: Academic Press, pp. 3–22.

Atkinson, A. (1995), *Public Economics in Action: The Basic Income/Flat Tax Proposal*, Oxford: Clarendon Press.

Baetz, R. (1972), 'The Nuffield Canadian Seminar and after: a personal view', in *Guaranteed Annual Income: An Integrated Approach*, Ottawa: The Canadian Council on Social Development.

Bishop, R. (1993), 'Economic efficiency, sustainability, and biodiversity', *Ambio*, May, 69–73.

Burgess, J. and W. Mitchell (1998), 'Employment, unemployment, and the right to work', *Australian Journal of Human Rights*, **4** (2), 76–94.

Clark, C. and C. Kavanagh (1996), 'Basic income, inequality, and unemployment: rethinking the linkage between work and welfare', *Journal of Economic Literature*, **30** (2), 399–407.

Cowling, S., W. Mitchell and M. Watts (2006), 'The right to work versus the right to income', *International Journal of Environment, Workplace and Employment*, **2** (1), 89–113.

Czech, B. (2013), *Supply Shock: Economic Growth at the Crossroads and the Steady State Solution*, Gabriola, BC: New Society Publishers.

Daly, H.E. (ed.) (1973), *Towards a Steady-state Economy*, San Francisco, CA: W.H. Freeman.

Daly, H.E. (1991), *Steady-state Economics: Second Edition with New Essays*, Washington, DC: Island Press.

Daly, H.E. (1996), *Beyond Growth: The Economics of Sustainable Development*, Boston, MA: Beacon Press.

Daly, H.E. (2007), *Ecological Economics and Sustainable Development: Selected Essays of Herman Daly*, Cheltenham, UK and Northampton, MA, USA: Edward Elgar Publishing.

Daly, H.E. and J.B. Cobb Jr (1989), *For the Common Good: Redirecting the Economy Toward Community, the Environment, and a Sustainable Future*, Boston, MA: Beacon Press.

Dietz, R. and D. O'Neill (2013), *Enough is Enough*, San Francisco, CA: Berret-Koehler Publishers.

Dornbusch, R. and S. Fischer (1990), *Macroeconomics*, 5th edn, New York: McGraw-Hill.

Easterlin, R. (1974), 'Does economic growth improve the human lot?', in P. David and R. Weber (eds), *Nations and Households in Economic Growth*, New York: Academic Press, pp. 89–125.

Friedman, M. (1962), *Capitalism and Freedom*, Chicago, IL: University of Chicago Press.

Georgescu-Roegen, N. (1971), *The Entropy Law and the Economic Process*, Cambridge, MA: Harvard University Press.

Hall, D. and J. Hall (1984), 'Concepts and measures of natural resource scarcity with a summary of recent trends', *Journal of Environmental Economics and Management*, **11**, 363–79.

Hirsch, F. (1976), *The Social Limits to Growth*, London: Routledge & Kegan Paul.

Jackson, T. and S. Stymne (1996), *Sustainable Economic Welfare in Sweden: A Pilot Index 1950–1992*, Stockholm: Stockholm Environment Institute.

Kubiszewski, I., R. Costanza, C. Franco et al. (2013), 'Beyond GDP: measuring and achieving global genuine progress', *Ecological Economics*, **93** (September), 57–68.

Lawn, P. (2000), *Towards Sustainable Development: An Ecological Economics Approach*, Boca Raton, FL: CRC Press.

Lawn, P. (2007), *Frontier Issues in Ecological Economics*, Cheltenham, UK and Northampton, MA, USA: Edward Elgar Publishing.

Lawn, P. (ed.) (2009), *Environment and Employment: A Reconciliation*, London: Routledge.

Lawn, P. and M. Clarke (2008), *Sustainable Welfare in the Asia-Pacific: Case Studies Using the Genuine Progress Indicator*, Cheltenham, UK and Northampton, MA, USA: Edward Elgar Publishing.

Lawn, P. and R. Sanders (1999), 'Has Australia surpassed its optimal macro-economic scale? Finding out with the aid of benefit and cost accounts and a sustainable net benefit index', *Ecological Economics*, **28** (2), 213–29.

Maslow, A. (1954), *Motivation and Personality*, New York: Harper & Row.

Max-Neef, M. (1995), 'Economic growth and quality of life', *Ecological Economics*, **15** (2), 115–18.

Mill, J.S. (1857), *Principles of Political Economy*, Vol. 2, London: John W. Parker.

Mishan, E. (1967), *The Costs of Economic Growth*, London: Staples Press.

Mishan, E. (1980), 'The growth of affluence and the decline of welfare', in H.E. Daly (ed.), *Economics, Ecology, and Ethics: Essays Toward a Steady-state Economy*, San Francisco, CA: W.H. Freeman, pp. 267–81.

Mishel, L. and N. Sabadish (2013), 'CEO pay in 2012 was extraordinarily high relative to typical workers and other high earners', Issue Brief No. 367, Economic Policy Institute, Washington, DC.

Mitchell, W. and J. Muysken (2008), *Full Employment Abandoned: Shifting Sands and Policy Failures*, Cheltenham, UK and Northampton, MA, USA: Edward Elgar Publishing.

Mitchell, W. and M. Watts (2004), 'A comparison of the macroeconomic consequences of Basic Income and Job Guarantee schemes', *Rutgers Journal of Law and Urban Policy*, **2** (1), 1–24.

Nordhaus, W.D. and J. Tobin (1972), *Is Growth Obsolete?* Economic Growth, National Bureau of Economic Research, No. 96, New York.

Norgaard, R. (1990), 'Economics of resource scarcity: a critical essay', *Journal of Environmental Economics and Management*, **19**, 19–25.

OECD (2008), *OECD Development Statistics Online*, Organisation for Economic Co-operation and Development, available at http://www.oecd.org/statistics (accessed 20 October 2008).

Ricardo, D. (1817), *Principles of Political Economy and Taxation*, Cambridge: Sraffa Edition.

Saez, E. (2013), 'Striking it richer: the evolution of top incomes in the United States (updated with 2011 estimates)', University of California-Berkley Working Paper, University of California, Berkeley, available at http://emlab.berkeley.edu/~saez/saez-UStopincomes-2011.pdf (accessed 27 July 2013).

Tcherneva, P.R. (2006), 'Universal assurances in the public interest: evaluating the economic viability of basic income and job guarantees', *International Journal of Environment, Workplace and Employment*, **2** (1), 69–88.

Tinbergen, J. (1952), *On the Theory of Economic Policy*, Amsterdam: North-Holland.
Tobin, J. (1966), 'The case for an income guarantee', *The Public Interest*, **4**, 31–41.
Van Parijs, P. (2004), 'Basic income: a simple and powerful idea for the twenty-first century', *Politics and Society*, **32** (1), 7–39.
Wackernagel, M. and W. Rees (1996), *Our Ecological Footprint: Reducing Human Impact on the Earth*, Gabriola Island, BC: New Society Publishers.
Wackernagel, M., L. Onisto, P. Bello et al. (1999), 'National natural capital accounting with the ecological footprint concept', *Ecological Economics*, **29** (3), 375–90.
Weisskopf, W. (1971), *Alienation and Economics*, New York: E.P. Dutton & Co.
Weisskopf, W. (1973), 'Economic growth versus existential balance', in H.E. Daly (ed.), *Towards a Steady-state Economy*, San Francisco, CA: W.H. Freeman, pp. 240–51.
Wray, L.R. (1998), *Understanding Modern Money: The Key to Full Employment and Price Stability*, Cheltenham, UK and Lyme, NH, USA: Edward Elgar Publishing.

9. Hicksian income, welfare and the steady state

Salah El Serafy

The range of Herman Daly's contributions to environmental economics has been extensive. I select here one topic upon which he pondered and successfully propagated among environmental economists. This is 'Hicksian income.' The estimation of national (or social) income, particularly the portion of it that derives from the exploitation of natural resources, is a subject that has occupied my thinking for some considerable time.[1] This chapter discusses Herman's 'Hicksian income,' and additionally touches on the related topic of 'steady state economics,' which I take to be Daly's most enduring interest. Another aspect of the same topic also reviewed is Daly's clear preference for viewing income estimates, not just as gauges of output, but as indicators of welfare. In this he has obviously been following Pigou but, surprisingly, as I hope to show below, Hicks also.

9.1 INTRODUCTION

Herman Daly popularized what he called 'Hicksian income' among environmentalists as well as others. Generally speaking, 'Hicksian income' is the standard concept of income as traditionally used by accountants and also by the more thoughtful economists.[2] Income, thus defined, must not contain any element of capital. To estimate income correctly, capital must remain intact. Here, keeping capital intact is a theoretical device for the estimation of income and does not entail a normative advocacy. Quite appropriately, Herman argued for extending the category of capital that must be kept intact to natural resources since they are obviously part of society's assets. In practice, the estimators of national income make no allowance for natural capital erosion, regularly inflating income estimates by including in them the proceeds of natural asset sales such as forest products, fish or mineral deposits, while turning a blind eye to their deteriorating stocks. This 'standard' practice is obviously a major estimation error of which most users of the national accounts seem to be unaware. But

Daly has had a wider interest going beyond the descriptive *ex post* estimation of income – a description that conflates income with 'output.' Such a conflation, in fact, is the general view held by national income statisticians who would deny vehemently that they are in the business of estimating 'welfare.' For instance, what the domestic product measures, they would claim, is simply the domestic 'output' as it is transacted in the marketplace. Put simply, without knowing the size of population or how individual incomes are distributed, a rise of gross domestic product (GDP) cannot be read as a rise of welfare. However, following essentially Pigou (1952), and also Hicks (albeit occasionally in the case of Hicks), Herman, with suitable qualifications, set out to interpret national income estimates as signifying the 'welfare' that the product sheds on the income recipients. Interpreting output as synonymous with welfare, however, is a complex matter and an attempt is being made here to disentangle this complexity.

The present chapter begins with Hicks's income as elaborated in his magnum opus, *Value and Capital* (Hicks, 1946) together with the variations or 'approximations' Hicks discussed around his central meaning of income.

This chapter strays out of the concept and measurement of income to dwell briefly on the not unrelated topic of 'steady state economics,' which is one of Daly's enduring interests. It will be shown that as there is a 'Hicksian income' there is also a Hicksian 'steady state,' and a Hicksian 'stationary state' – both of them having deep roots in classical economic thought. While obviously looking upon national income as a metric of output, Hicks entertained on occasion the view that it could also indicate welfare.

9.2   WHAT IS INCOME?

Income is a quantity received by an individual, a group or a nation that is usually recurrent. It ordinarily derives from wages, property rent, earned interest or profits. It is a flow that accrues per unit of time, and it is decidedly not a stock existing at a point of time. In *The Wealth of Nations*, Adam Smith used 'wealth' synonymously with an income flow – a usage that has misled some economists into thinking that Smith's wealth was other than the 'national income' of nations (Smith, 1776).[3] Historically, the accountants confronted the estimation of income before the economists, who came to the field much later – though with a great deal of analysis that manifested a somewhat different perspective. The accountants, to their credit, had initiated the notion of 'keeping capital intact,' not as a normative imperative, though this may not be discounted, but as a tool for a rough and ready estimation of the illusive quantity called income. In the late Middle Ages, the sea-faring merchants of the Mediterranean ports (both north and south) had asked their accountants to estimate how much of their revenues could be allocated to family consumption. The accountants' response was that enough from the receipts should be put aside for 'maintaining capital' before regarding any remainder as income. Needless to say, the merchants could, if they wished, save part of their income, adding it to capital for expanding the business. But the accountants, qua accountants, had no say on this 'managerial' matter; they were simply estimating income during a period that had become past.

Adam Smith recognized that wealth could not increase without additions to capital, such additions, he held, came only from thrift. This view dominated the thinking of the classical economists down to J.S. Mill, but when the turn of neoclassical economists came, and the variety of capital categories multiplied, defining the capital that must be kept intact in practice became almost impossible. By the time of Marshall we find several capital categories: auxiliary and instrumental capital; free and floating capital; social capital; circulating capital; fixed and overhead capital – among others. The problem of obsolescence added to the problem as machinery that had not physically depreciated became outmoded (Hicks, 1942). Economists including Pigou, Hayek and Hicks battled over the concept of 'keeping capital intact' in the 1930s, to conclude in effect that an *objective* notion of the intactness of capital, let alone its empirical calibration, was not possible. This was before natural resources in their almost infinite diversity were proposed as unquestionably part of society's capital (see below).

The correspondence between income and capital is obvious. Alfred Marshall, often recognized as the father of 'neoclassical economics,' reminded us that Adam Smith had said that 'a person's capital is that part of his stock from which he expects to derive income,' adding that 'almost every use of the term capital which is known to history has corresponded more or less closely to a parallel use of the term Income' (Marshall, 1920 [1947], p. 78). He also wrote: 'When capital ceases to increase, income likewise will stop growing' (Marshall, 1920 [1947], p. 78). Hence, seeking to keep capital intact should be seen as fundamental to income generation.

Relevant to both income, and the intactness of capital, is the proper valuation of end-period stocks that will be bequeathed to the next account period. For this purpose the accountants had devised a precautionary valuation rule with which the economists have not always been happy. This may be paraphrased: 'When in doubt opt for undervaluing rather than overvaluing this stock.' In other words, income should rather be underestimated than overestimated. In this respect the accountant functions as a guardian of 'sustainability,' but it is a shorter period sustainability, namely, from one accounting period to the next. If this rule were to be observed year after year, the short-term survivability of the enterprise (or the nation) could be made to extend over longer periods. Economists, however, have favored a different view – a view that has seeped into national accounting – placing a greater store on valuing stocks at *current* prices, and this in practice has frequently undermined the accountant's concept of sustainability.[4]

Most commonly, overestimated income must have included elements of capital – elements that should not be there in the first place.[5] The expression 'sustainable income' is usually a misnomer because the adjective 'sustainable' becomes redundant if income is properly estimated. Herman's invocation of the name of Hicks in this regard was indeed proper, and probably motivated by his intention to convince doubting economists of the solid economic foundations upon which the estimation of income should rest. Economists, whether they needed convincing or not, are the principal users of the macroeconomic magnitudes produced by national accounting. And it is remarkable that, with few exceptions, they take these magnitudes at their face value, proceeding to analyze them sometimes with ostensible sophistication. Economists would arrive at dubious interpretations of economic performance, often leading them to questionable policy recommendations.[6]

For many countries, the conventionally compiled national[7] accounts would need correction, but such a need is most acute where serious deterioration in natural resources is taking place and not captured in the accounts. The fact that the richer countries at present tend to derive most of their national income from manufactures and increasingly from services reduces for them the importance and urgency of reforming national accounting practices in the direction of 'Hicksian income.' Their national accounts are good enough for meeting their macroeconomic needs, both for indicating past performance and providing guidance for future policy. Having in most cases depleted the bulk of their natural capital in the process of industrialization, they, with some exceptions, tend to underestimate the value of what has come to be known as 'green accounting,' and appear even to oppose it. The poorer countries, on the other hand, whose economies depend on primary activities to a much greater extent, and whose conventional accounts often cry out for drastic adjustment, understandably carry little influence in the international forums that devise national accounting procedures. Even when certain developing countries have well-founded doubts about their own national estimates that are faithfully tailored on internationally devised standards, suspecting that the accounts falsify their performance and show them to be more prosperous than they actually are, they put up with the judgment of the national accounting 'experts' who, regrettably, include those employed by the United Nations. To this day, even the revenue obtained from the commercial extraction of natural resources (fish, timber, minerals inter alia) still appears in the standard accounts as 'income' with no allowance made in the flow accounts for the disinvestment associated with the observed decline in resource stocks (see Commission of the European Communities et al., 1993).[8]

9.3   ADJUSTING THE CONVENTIONAL ESTIMATES

Herman participated during the 1980s in the series of international workshops organized by the United Nations Environment Programme (UNEP) jointly with the World Bank.[9] Initially, the workshop participants were searching for a periodically reckoned 'number,' or index, capable of expressing environmental and natural resource deterioration. This, they thought, would impress citizens and politicians alike about the worsening state of the environment and thus spur remedial actions. After some hesitation the workshops settled down to considering the set of national income and product accounts as an excellent medium for meeting their purpose. The fact that income estimation depends on the principle of 'keeping capital intact' provided a major theme that gathered momentum during these discussions, with natural resources having to be recognized as part of society's capital.[10] The work accomplished at the workshops contributed in no small way to the 1993 revision of the United Nations' *System of National Accounts* (SNA) that had remained virtually unchanged for a quarter century.[11] Subsequently a number of meetings were held before the issuance of the new SNA, one of which was the important conference organized by the International Association of Research in Income and Wealth in Austria in 1991.[12] It should be stressed that the process of amending the accounts was viewed from the outset as slow and gradual, and would hopefully move in time, with further research and ingenuity, from being partial and tentative in the direction of comprehensiveness and robustness.

A selection of the contributions made during the UNEP-World Bank workshops was subsequently published, containing Herman's paper, 'Toward a measure of sustainable social net national product' (Daly, 1989). Herman's piece began with Hicks's basic concept of income (Hicks, 1946) that defined 'sustainable' income. The rock base on which Daly's income rested was netting out from the estimated gross product an allowance for the deterioration of natural resources – resources, here to be taken in their wider sense as 'sink' as well as 'source.' How much should be netted out, however, was not easy to determine and has remained a bone of contention.[13] The adjustment proposed by Daly included also the deduction from the conventional estimates of any 'defensive expenditure' undertaken to correct harmful side-effects of production and consumption. Interestingly, in that short piece Herman was looking at the national or domestic product (alias income) as *output* without any connotation of *welfare*. However, almost simultaneously in his joint book with Cobb (Daly and Cobb, 1994; first published in 1989) he was emphasizing national income as an indicator of *welfare*: a rise in estimated income suggested a rise of welfare and a drop suggested a decline. In that work, Herman and Cobb proceeded further to adjust the official national income estimates for the United States employing a number of deductions varying from losses of source resources to deterioration of amenities. This endeavor set in motion and reinforced already-begun efforts that viewed natural resource deterioration as welfare losses, with the result that both the adjusted income level and, quite often (but by no means always), its presumed growth had to be scaled down.[14]

In later publications, especially in tandem with his advocacy of 'stationary state economics,' Daly convincingly explained that the pursuit of unending growth, which most economists strongly favor, was untenable since the economy is a subset of a finite biosphere that is not expanding. Daly persisted in stressing the argument that the apparent benefits of economic expansion must be balanced against its costs in a truly Pigouvian manner that centered on welfare. For Pigou had said in the fourth edition of his *Economics of Welfare* (1932) that 'economic welfare . . . consists in the balance of satisfactions from the use of the national dividend . . . over the dissatisfactions involved in the making of it' (quoted in Hicks, 1981, p. 307).

9.4   HICKS'S INCOME

Hicks had given a lot of thought to the concept and estimation of income and written about it in several of his publications, but his chapter on 'Income' in *Value and Capital* (second edition 1946 that is used here) contains his most detailed thoughts on the subject. He would come back to the subject intermittently, finding something fresh to add in scattered *obiter dicta*, but most significantly in his seminal paper, 'The scope and status of welfare economics' (Hicks, 1975). However, it would be remiss to overlook his earlier book, *The Social Framework: An Introduction to Economics* (Hicks, 1952; first published in 1942), which was totally devoted to national income in theory and practice. In *The Social Framework*, he systematically elaborated the relevant macroeconomic concepts and examined their interconnections, including consumption, investment, factors of production, population, capital, the social product and foreign payments. He also faced up to the formidable task of sorting out a tabulation of the social accounts of the United Kingdom for 1938 and 1949 (the latter year appearing in the 1952 second edition) while explaining related quantities and definitions. In the process he went back and forth in time to offer comparisons, pointing out practical estimation difficulties and how he dealt with them. This was a brave exercise that revealed to the uninitiated how difficult it was (and still is) to come up with objective estimates, with a warning to users ignorant of the practical obstacles that have to be faced by national income statisticians.[15] It will be seen below that Hicks's views on income, while safely anchored in *Value and Capital*, were to receive in 1957 an intriguing interpretation by none other than himself – an interpretation of relevance to Herman's income work.

9.5   INCOME IN *VALUE AND CAPITAL*

The income chapter of *Value and Capital* consists of two parts: the main discourse (Hicks, 1946, pp. 170–81), followed by Notes to Chapter XIV (Hicks, 1946, pp. 181–8) – the latter analyzing income in conjunction with saving and investment together with a discussion of the interest rates to be used for capitalizing expected future income streams. In the wider scheme of *Value and Capital* the income chapter came at the conclusion of parts I–III, devoted to 'static' analysis, with Hicks intending the income discussion as a springboard to the dynamic analysis of the later parts. This attention to statics versus dynamics, it will be seen, sheds light on his income definitions. In statics, he asserted, 'the difficulty about income does not arise: a person's income can be taken without qualification as equal to his receipts' (Hicks, 1946, p. 172). Interestingly, he saw here a similarity between statics and the 'stationary state' of the classical economists, viewing that state as a branch of dynamic economics where everything had come to rest (Hicks, 1946, p. 172). The income chapter of *Value and Capital* also contained a consideration of the related concepts of 'saving, depreciation and investment' that Hicks insisted were 'not logical categories at all,' but merely approximations needed for 'prudent behavior' by the income recipient. After considering income from various angles he thought it pointless to seek a *precise* definition of income since that 'would put upon it a weight of refinement it cannot bear' (Hicks, 1946, p. 171). Something rougher, he maintained, was 'actually better.'

Hicks's analysis of income proceeded in steps, first offering a general definition he judged as 'basic' or 'central,' namely, 'the maximum value which he [the income recipient] can consume during a week and still expects to be as well off at the end of the week as he was at the beginning' (Hicks, 1946, p. 172). The use of the week was a Hicksian simplification so that nothing much could be expected to change during this short duration. Worthy of notice here is also the loose wording such as 'maximum *value*' (emphasis added), 'still expect,' 'as well off' – all rather vague but consistent with the roughness he attached to income estimation. Hicks then went on to discuss variations around this basic concept (which he named income number 1) calling them 'approximations' made by 'business men and economists alike.' He then introduced 'income number 2,' to be derived from the capitalized money value of an individual's prospective receipts. Noting its flexibility, however, since expectations of interest rates would vary, he concluded that that second definition was more appropriate to income from property than income from wages. At this juncture he went back to elaborate 'income number 1,' basing it explicitly on the maintenance of capital. 'Income No. 1 is the maximum amount which can be spent during a period if there is to be an expectation of maintaining intact the capital value of prospective receipts (in money terms)' (Hicks, 1946, p. 173), adding that income number 2 was theoretically 'a closer approximation to the central concept than Income No. 1.' But he also considered income number 3, which depends explicitly on price expectations. If prices are expected to rise, the income recipient must expect to be less well off at the end of the week and thus 'his' current income would be lower. That is because income is the maximum that a recipient can spend and still expect to be able to spend the same amount *in real terms* in subsequent periods. Hence, income number 3 is subject to 'indeterminateness' (Hicks, 1946, p. 175). Income number 4 enters the discussion with the introduction of 'durable consumption goods.' Here Hicks emphasized the distinction that should be made between 'spending' and 'consuming.' Income is the maximum amount that can be *consumed*, not just spent, while keeping capital intact. If part of the expenditure goes into acquiring durable consumer goods then expenditure will in this case exceed consumption. Only if acquisition of durable consumption goods anew matches the use (or consumption) of 'durables' acquired in the past will consumption and spending match. But if the old stock is being used up and there are no new acquisitions, the income recipient must be worse off.

All told, Hicks's approximations around the central concept of income yielded little extra illumination, and thus we were forced back onto the central definition that 'a person's income is what he can consume during the week and still expect to be as well off at the end of the week as he was at the beginning.' This is the definition that Daly has rightly embraced and named 'Hicksian income.'

It is interesting that the value of stocks (or accumulations) held by the income recipient receive no mention in Hicks's income chapter. Since his income period was short he could overlook changes in the unit value of stocks held at the beginning and end of the account period. With a longer period, however, he was of the opinion that stocks, both beginning and end, should be valued at current prices.[16] Stock valuation at current prices is the practice generally favored by economists, and this has been followed by the national income statisticians who have sometimes to go through tortuous exercises of 'reconciliation' to accommodate changes in stock values. The value of beginning-period stocks is unambiguously that of the previous period-end, and the stocks held at the end of the current period should be valued, according to the accountants, at their purchase prices or current market prices *whichever values are less*. Undervaluing end-period stocks is a precautionary measure that may underestimate income, but this brings no harm as it checks consumption and thus 'ensures' income sustainability. For national accounting, natural resources (as sources as well as sinks) must be viewed as part of society's capital that must be kept intact for the estimation of income – an argument that is to be found in Herman's paper (Daly, 1989) in Ahmad et al. (1989).[17]

9.6   INCOME FROM WASTING ASSETS

Embedded in Hicks's income chapter is the important notion that whichever of the 'approximations' to the concept of income we choose to use, the calculation of income consists in finding some sort of *standard stream* of values whose present capitalized value equals the discounted value of the stream of receipts that is actually in prospect. The present receipts should not be viewed as income, that is, what the income recipient would be receiving if he were getting a standard stream of the same present value as his expected receipts. He further stressed that any stream of values has a capitalized value that is the function of the rate of interest. In this respect, he put forward the important thought to be found on page 187 of *Value and Capital*, viz.:

> If a person's receipts are derived from the exploitation of a wasting asset, liable to give out at some future date, we should say that his receipts are in excess of his income, the difference between them being reckoned as an allowance for depreciation. In this case, if he is to consume no more than his income, he must re-lend some part of his receipts; and the lower the rate of interest is, the greater the sum he will have to re-lend in order for the interest on it to make up for the expected failure of receipts from his wasting asset in the future. (Hicks, 1946)[18]

It is remarkable that Hicks's insightful notion of income from wasting natural resources – a notion that inspired the user cost method of El Serafy (1981, 1989) – has yet to find expression in the official estimates of national income.

9.7   LATER HICKSIAN THOUGHTS ON INCOME

As previously mentioned, Hicks's view of income did not rest with *Value and Capital*. On at least two occasions he came back to explain or slightly modify what he had said there. This pertained in particular to the place of *income in time*, and the place of *income in growth theory*. In some sense he was qualifying what he had said about income in *Value and Capital*, and in another sense he wanted to justify what he thought were shortcomings of that earlier exposition.

In the Festschrift for Nicholas Georgescu-Roegen (Tang et al., 1976) Hicks contributed a chapter on 'Some questions of time in economics' (Hicks, 1976). Stressing the irreversibility of time, he referred to the valuation of stocks in social accounting, holding, rather oddly, that the value of the opening stock reflects in part the value to be expected for the end-period stock (Hicks, 1976, p. 136). Further, he repudiated the notion that all options open to a consumer could form a stable scale of preferences to be hierarchically ordered, and mapped by indifference curves. Hicks's frequent references to 'in time' and 'out of time' meant, respectively, a difference between a dynamic movement and a static snapshot, the latter to him being 'a stationary state' (Hicks, 1976, p. 139). He accused both himself and Keynes of 'muddling' in that they mixed statics and dynamics, specifically where Keynes considered liquidity as a stationary state phenomenon, viz.:

> Keynes's theory has one leg which is *in* time, but another which is not. It is a hybrid. I am not blaming him for this; he was looking for a theory which would be effective, and he found it. I am quite prepared to believe that effective theories always will be hybrids – they cannot afford to bother about difficulties which are not important for the problem in hand. (Hicks, 1976, p. 140)

In the same vein, Hicks looked back on his income chapter in *Value and Capital*, identifying what he thought were weaknesses common to him and Keynes, who, Hicks asserted, was merely expounding Marshall's short period analysis. The 'Keynes theory and *Value and Capital* theory were weak in corresponding ways. They both lacked, at one end, a satisfactory theory of *markets*; and at the other end, they lacked a satisfactory theory of *growth*.' Several pages later Hicks explained that his own 'steady state' was a 'growth equilibrium model' where the balance of macroeconomic variables, technology and investment (both autonomous and induced – see Hicks, 1950; emphasis added) was made to produce a constant rate of economic expansion. His alleged failure to develop a theory of markets in *Value and Capital* is not convincing: he simply assumed (he says) that prices were determined by demand and supply. In both these cases of self-criticism a fair critic would conclude that Hicks was exaggerating his own shortcomings, and may have been attempting to sketch future paths for others to further the development of economic theory.[19]

9.8   STEADY AND STATIONARY STATE ECONOMICS

The steady state and the stationary state have crept into the above text without adequate clarification. Daly's steady state is obviously different from that of Hicks, who disliked it intensely. It is not difficult to find out why. 'I shall not say much about Steady State Economics; for in spite of all that it has meant for the economics of the fifties and sixties, it is my own opinion that it has been rather a curse' (Hicks, 1976, p. 142). To him the 'stationary state' was even worse: it was moribund with no growth at all. Unlike the stationary state, Hicks's steady state was a dynamic process of a 'regularly progressive economy' with a *constant* rate of growth – an artifact he used for discovering the factors that could produce a constant growth rate following on from the models of 'Harrod and Domar (or perhaps . . . von Neumann).' How such steady growth might be achieved had also been Hicks's quarry in his book on the *Trade Cycle* (Hicks, 1950).

Looking further back it is interesting to see how earlier economists treated the subject. Adam Smith had described the stationary state as a state in which a country 'had acquired that full complement of riches which the nature of its soil and climate, and its situation with respect to other countries, allowed it to acquire; which could, therefore advance no further' (Smith, 1776 [1937], Book I, chapter IX, p. 94).[20]

Marshall picked up the theme (Marshall, 1920 [1947], Book 5, chapter V, pp. 2–4), calling the stationary state 'a famous fiction'.[21] To Marshall it was a monotonous state where all was predictable (Marshall, 1920 [1947], p. 810) with population stationary and the average age constant (Marshall, 1920 [1947], pp. 367–8), and the character of man himself was of constant quantity. Marshall contrasted the progressive reality around him with the stationary state world where

> every plain and single doctrine as to the relations between cost of production, demand and value is necessarily false: and the greater the appearance of lucidity

which is given to it by skilful exposition, the more mischievous it is. (Marshall, 1920 [1947], p. 368)

Analytically Marshall wanted a state that would illumine economic thought, believing that a stationary state was barren and sterile. But he also briefly attempted a relaxation of some of its rigid assumptions, mainly in respect of population and capital constancy, with a view to bringing it closer to reality and therefore rendering it more useful for economic analysis.

Between Smith and Marshall came John Stuart Mill from whom Herman took his cue.[22] It was Mill who had extolled the virtues of the stationary state (Mill, 1848, Book IV, chapter VI) hoping for a future where the progress of society would relax before the utmost physical limit had been reached. He pleaded for the enjoyment of solitude, the beauties of nature and the pursuit of moral and social progress instead of material advance. Echoes of the same sentiment are to be found in Keynes (1930 [1963]) as he also looked forward to a future when the economic problem had been largely solved, and humanity settled down to the pursuit of the higher ends of leisure and enjoyment, and when economics had become a humble vocation like dentistry.

After adopting Hicks's definition of *ex post* income Daly moved forward to confront the future of income change. Impelled by the dangers he saw in the unfettered expansion of economic activity advocated by most economists, he used his powers of persuasion in support of 'steady state economics' as an alternative to growth economics. Unlike Hicks, he dismissed future growth as untenable, whether at a constant or a variable pace. He argued convincingly that the scale of world production and consumption had reached or exceeded limits that the earth can ill afford. In this he touched a sensitive nerve among economists, who not only idolized growth for its own sake, but made it the principal – if not the sole – criterion of economic success. Daly's steady state is, however, a little vague on population. The classics had followed a Malthusian vision that expected population to be controlled by wages falling below subsistence. Daly's 1974 paper, admittedly put forward rather tentatively, talked of imposing 'population quotas' to restrain population increases, an idea Daly apparently took from Boulding (Daly, 1974, p. 19). Herman is clearer on this issue in Daly (1991, p. 17) where he advocated a physical population requiring births to offset inevitable deaths at low rather than high levels, with increased life spans. This is of course a sensitive subject to many and if I am not mistaken it has been left out of Herman's later writings.

9.9   A DIGRESSION ON VALUATION BY COST OR BY 'UTILITY'?

Writing on Pigou's notions of welfare, Hicks made a great deal of whether to value the social product by cost or by utility – a rivalry of valuation that has mostly escaped the notice of the statistical estimators – this despite the fact that national income estimates have sometimes been expressed 'at factor cost' in addition to the standard valuation by market prices. According to Hicks (1975), valuing the national product at cost goes back to the classics, notably Ricardo, when the product was valued by its labor inputs. Land, the other major factor of production at the time, was left out since rent was viewed as a 'surplus' to be determined only after the price of the product had been established. Nevertheless, it is obvious that output is produced *for a purpose*, and the purpose is doubtless to satisfy a want. Since a product gives out 'utility' it therefore made sense to consider valuing it by the welfare it imparts – a line of argument later strenuously championed by Pigou that could be traced back at least to W. Stanley Jevons, known to environmentalists as the author of *The Coal Question* (Jevons, 1865). While Jevons's name is usually associated with the marginalist revolution in economics in the last quarter of the nineteenth century, Hicks gives him more credit for leading (along with others, mainly the Austrians) a revolution that sought to shed the classical costing by labor inputs in favor of valuation by marginal utility.

Fundamentally, whether as output or welfare, should social income be valued by the cost of making it or alternatively by the 'utility' it is supposed to impart to the income recipients? Valuation at market prices, which is now the standard used in national accounting does in fact combine cost and utility in Marshall's two-blades-of-a-scissors manner. To Marshall it was futile to ask whether it is the upper or the lower blade of a pair of scissors that cuts a piece of paper: both do so simultaneously. Similarly, the two sides of the market – supply (cost) and demand (utility) – determine market price, and it is market prices that now dominate the valuation of national income estimates. For valuation purposes (especially the valuation of the non-transacted services of Nature (which Hicks does not specifically mention) Hicks elaborated Marshall's views and illuminated them thus:

> In a perfect market, prices are proportional to marginal utilities, and to marginal costs. Prices may therefore be regarded as reflecting *either* marginal Utilities *or* marginal costs; if all goods which entered into an economic aggregate were sold upon perfect markets, the prices at which they were sold could be taken to stand for marginal utilities, or for marginal costs, indifferently. If markets are not perfect, utilities and costs may diverge; price may diverge from either, or from both. If there is no market there is no price, but valuation in terms of utility or

in terms of cost may still be possible, though there is now no reason why those valuations should coincide. When we seek to set values on non-marketed commodities, it is the utility value or the cost value that we must be setting, but they will not (in general) be the same. In general . . . there are two principles of valuation, a utility principle and a cost principle, answering at bottom quite different questions. (Hicks, 1981, pp. 190–91; emphasis added)

Historically speaking, valuation by utility failed to gain acceptance, and cost, now clipped into shape by Marshall's scissors and expressed in market prices, became the mainstay of the new and blossoming discipline of national accounting. This made a comeback as a tool for financing the World War II effort, particularly in Britain and the United States. Economic resources had to be husbanded and carefully devoted to support the war in competition with domestic needs. The contributions of Keynes, Hicks, Kuznets, Meade and Stone were crucial for laying down the rules of income estimation that dominate national accounting today. National accountants would deny that they are measuring 'welfare' or utility at all, but merely estimating the market transacted output or product. It is interesting to note that Hicks and Kuznets debated national income concepts and valuation in the pages of *Economica* during the 1940s.[23] Hicks, it seems, wanted the national income to express both output and the welfare gained from it. As a clear indicator of Hicks's thinking of income as output (not as an index of welfare) he had proposed that per capita income should be based not on *total* population but only the *working* population (Hicks, 1952, p. 188). In this regard (as stated above) he lamented the fact that national income could not also express welfare.[24] For him income (*ex post*) was consumption plus investment, and this left behind Irving Fisher's view that investment should be dropped from income on the pretext that it did not contribute to current welfare.

9.10   MORE ON WELFARE

Herman's endorsement of Hicks's definition of income went only part of the way for he was more of a Pigouvian than a Hicksian. Hicks had expressed great doubts over the state of 'welfare economics' – a subject to which he had contributed a great deal, particularly as he urged the estimation of 'utility' ordinally rather than cardinally. To Hicks, economics was not ethics, though it bordered on ethics (Hicks, 1975, p. 311). On my part, I believed that in trying to reform national accounting the focus should primarily be on a more correct estimation of *output*. Welfare was only a derivative of output, and the joy it yielded depended on many factors absent from GDP and its cohorts. Just looking at GDP will not give you income

per capita, its distribution among recipients or the effort extended in producing it. But Herman's approach, adapted to cover such lacunae, proved
popular and gave fruit to subsequent efforts that set out to show that a
rise in GDP does not necessarily increase happiness. Counterbalancing
what Hicks had detected as the absence of cost in Pigou's social dividend,
Herman was to stress the negative impact of growth on the economy, in
fact using the eminently Pigouvian device of externalities.[25] The cost in
terms of congestion, noise, air and water pollution, resource depletion and
many others had to be balanced against apparent growth in order to show
that in many cases growth meant reduced welfare.

Here also Herman's focus on scale was an overarching concern: the
economic system is part of the physical ecological framework and cannot
possibly grow indefinitely without causing irreparable harm. Daly's work
in this area has reinforced as well as inspired the efforts of other scholars,
also dissatisfied with GDP as an indicator of sustainable welfare. These
have included the Index of Sustainable Economic Welfare (Daly and Cobb,
1994, pp. 443–507); the Ecological Footprint (Rees and Wackernagel,
1994); the Human Development Index (UNDP, 1990); the Genuine
Progress Indicator (Redefining Progress, 1995); and the Happy Planet
Index (NEF, 2006).

9.11   A KIND OF SUMMING UP

This chapter has attempted an assessment of Daly's contribution to the
propagation of the Hicksian concept of 'sustainable income' that has had
a great impact on *environmental* economics and is central to *ecological*
economics. Daly imbued Hicks's definition with a welfare tint, supporting
or inspiring the development of a number of welfare-oriented alternatives to conventional GDP. The discussion covered Daly's selection of one
from among a number of definitions of income elaborated by Hicks. A
comment was offered on Daly's steering of Hicks's income in the direction of Pigou: in other words, from a measure of sustainable *output* to an
indicator of sustainable *welfare*. This 'twist' was in fact in harmony with
Hicks's own leaning toward viewing national income as an indicator of
both output and 'welfare.' Since much of the environment falls outside the
market and since monetizing the environment's services defies adequate
measurement, Daly's stress on environmental losses being essentially
welfare losses must be regarded as an important contribution that has
found much appeal among environmentalists. Mainstream economists
and conventional national accountants, however, have remained skeptical,
particularly over conflating GDP with aggregate welfare. Pigou himself

had reservations about conflating his social dividend with welfare, but remained fast in conflating the two. Hicks himself was clearer (Hicks, 1975, p. 318; emphasis added), stating that: 'It is unconvincing to assure us, as he [Pigou] in substance does, that increase in the Social Product is *usually* a good thing.'

Given Daly's emphasis on the unfeasibility of maintaining endless economic expansion owing to the physical constraints imposed by the earth's ecological system, it is natural that he has been a strong proponent of what he put forward as 'steady state economics.' This chapter has touched on the concept of a steady state and its connections with output and income, comparing it to the earlier economic view of a 'stationary state' that can be found in Adam Smith and John Stuart Mill among others. The emergence of neoclassical economics as a 'science' to replace 'political economy' tilted economic inquiry toward pursuits that mimicked the physical sciences, permitting little discussion of 'ends' and allowing scant room for normative economics. Daly's focus on policy matters has been a refreshing drive to reopen consideration of the *purpose* of economic activity in an attempt to move economic thought once again in the direction of normative economics.

NOTES

1. Hicks had been the supervisor for my Oxford 1957 doctorate; we later corresponded on the topic of income.
2. Unlike Daly I never use the expression 'Hicksian income' myself since 'income,' properly estimated, would suffice.
3. It is rather important to stress this point because Professor Sir Partha Dasgupta of Cambridge, England, had made this error in his retirement address as President of the Royal Economic Society (Dasgupta, 2001).
4. Though Hicks had thought a great deal about accounting methods, he was under the impression that the 'value that is set upon the opening stock depends in part upon the value which is expected, at the beginning of the year, for the closing stock . . .' (Hicks, 1976, p. 136).
5. Overestimating income is dangerous in that it encourages consumption that would threaten the ability of the income recipient to maintain the same level of income in future. On the other hand, underestimating income is usually harmless in that it suppresses consumption and helps to build up capital to the benefit of 'sustainability.'
6. The January 2006 issue of the *Economic Journal* published an article by three Norwegian economists, 'Institutions and the resource curse' (Mehlum et al., 2006) where the authors used regression analysis to study failed 'growth' in so-called natural resource abundant countries using several dependent variables. They concluded that the quality of institutions was decisive for explaining the resource curse. I sent a comment to the *Economic Journal* and the authors explaining that the GDP numbers used in the analysis confused value added with resource sale proceeds: a decline in 'growth,' I argued, could reflect a reduction in extraction occasioned by the country running out of the resource or a prudent act of resource management. The authors had not been aware of the weakness of the GDP estimates they used (letter dated 13 March 2006) and

expressed interest in commenting on my views if they were published in the *Economic Journal*, which turned my comment down 'for lack of space.'

7.   I shall be using social accounting and national accounting interchangeably since they both have existed in the literature synonymously.

8.   An attempt is made in the *System of National Accounts, 1993* (1993 SNA) to construct natural 'asset accounts' showing new discoveries as additions and extraction as a deduction, but the asset accounts are not integrated in the income flows (Commission of the European Communities et al., 1993) – fortunately, however, since adding discoveries to income makes no economic sense. There is a brief discussion as to whether deduction for depletion should be 'total' or confined only to 'the user cost' (Commission of the European Communities et al., 1993, p. 517), but the matter was left to be determined outside the 1993 SNA in the so-called *System of Environmental-Economic Accounting* (SEEA; later known as *Integrated Environmental and Economic Accounting*) that was meant as a practical guide for the compilation of environmental satellite accounts. Though another version of the guide was issued in 2003, this also proved controversial.

9.   Two preceding workshops had been held in Geneva and Washington before I joined this initiative at the third workshop in Paris in 1985 and was elected rapporteur. I then chaired the fourth and fifth workshops held in Washington in 1986 and Paris in 1988. See appendix in Ahmad et al. (1989, pp. 93–5).

10. See Daly (1989), Daly and Cobb (1994) and chapter 7 in Daly (1996). See also El Serafy (1991).

11. The 1993 revision of the SNA introduced 'satellite accounts' for the environment that in effect left the main accounts largely unchanged, and despite much work since then the initiative for greening the national accounts (in value terms) seems to have come to a dead end, at least at the official level.

12. Selected papers presented at that conference were issued two years later in Franz and Stahmer (1993). This contained my paper, 'Depletable resources: fixed capital or inventories?' where I drew a distinction between depreciation and the using up of stock (El Serafy, 1993).

13. The near-consensus among advocates of green accounting reform has been to reduce the conventional macroeconomic magnitudes by the entirety of the estimated deterioration – a position I have objected to, recommending instead deducting only the 'user cost.' The hankering after what in effect is an over-correction often reduced the adjusted numbers to meaninglessness, a fact that has contributed to the stymieing of the whole reform initiative. On this, see El Serafy (1999, 2006).

14. See El Serafy (1993; 2006, p. 75, note 23).

15. See also Meade and Stone (1948).

16. Though his view that the valuation of opening stocks 'depends in part' upon the expected end-period value (Hicks, 1976, p. 136) seems at odds with his general position.

17. The same argument had been advanced with reference to petroleum in El Serafy (1979, 1981) and extended to cover natural resources generally in El Serafy (1991). See also El Serafy (1992).

18. It was this thought that guided me to formulate what became known as the 'El Serafy method' for estimating income from the revenue obtained in depletable resource extraction. See El Serafy (1981, 1989).

19. Hicks's self-criticism here may be compared to his partial repudiation of his famous IS-LM apparatus that he had put forward in 1937 to explain Keynes's *General Theory* (Keynes, 1936). See Hicks (1981).

20. Smith envisaged that in a stationary state profits would drop and wages decline sufficiently to quell population growth (Smith, 1776 [1937], Book I, chapter IX).

21. Schumpeter comments wryly that though it was a fiction, 'as a methodological fiction the stationary state was not at all "famous" in 1890' (Schumpeter, 1954, p. 966). Schumpeter in fact traces the stationary state back to Plato (Schumpeter, 1954, pp. 55–6).

22. In the classical economic literature writers would often use the expressions 'steady state' and 'stationary state' without clarifying the distinguishing features of each.

23. See especially Hicks (1940) and Kuznets (1948).
24. In the preface of *The Social Framework* (Hicks, 1952), Hicks acknowledged the help he received from Richard Stone (later Nobel laureate Sir Richard Stone) in piecing together the British national accounts (along Keynesian lines).
25. The role of externalities, however, remained limited in that to discuss them usefully there must be a presumption of some existing market 'to which they are external' (Hicks, 1975, p. 317, note 1).

REFERENCES

Ahmad, Y.J., S. El Serafy and E. Lutz (eds) (1989), *Environmental Accounting for Sustainable Development, A UNEP-World Bank Symposium*, Washington, DC: The World Bank.

Commission of the European Communities, International Monetary Fund, Organisation for Economic Co-operation and Development, United Nations and World Bank (1993), *System of National Accounts, 1993*, Brussels, Luxembourg, New York, Paris, Washington, DC: United Nations Publications.

Daly, H.E. (1974), 'The economics of the steady state', *American Economic Review*, Papers and Proceedings of the Eighty-sixth Annual Meeting of the American Economic Association, **64** (2), 15–21.

Daly, H.E. (1989), 'Toward a measure of sustainable social net national product', in Y.J. Ahmad, S. El Serafy and E. Lutz (eds), *Environmental Accounting for Sustainable Development: A UNEP-World Bank Symposium*, Washington, DC: The World Bank, pp. 8–9.

Daly, H.E. (1991), *Steady-state Economics*, 2nd edn, Washington, DC: Island Press.

Daly, H.E. (1996), *Beyond Growth: The Economics of Sustainable Development*, Boston, MA: Beacon Press.

Daly, H.E. and J.B. Cobb, Jr (1994), *For the Common Good: Redirecting the Economy Toward Community, the Environment and a Sustainable Future*, Boston, MA: Beacon Press.

Dasgupta, P. (2001), 'Valuing objects and evaluating policies in imperfect economies', *Economic Journal*, **111** (471), C1–C29.

El Serafy, S. (1979), 'Oil price revolution of 1973–1974', *Journal of Energy and Development*, **4** (2), 273–90.

El Serafy, S. (1981), 'Absorptive capacity, the demand for revenue and the supply of petroleum', *Journal of Energy and Development*, **7** (1), 73–88.

El Serafy, S. (1989), 'The proper calculation of income from depletable natural resources', in Y.J. Ahmad, S. El Serafy and E. Lutz (eds), *Environmental Accounting for Sustainable Development*, Washington, DC: UNEP-World Bank Symposium, pp. 10–18.

El Serafy, S. (1991), 'The environment as capital', in R. Costanza (ed.), *Ecological Economics: The Science and Management of Sustainability*, New York: Columbia University Press, pp. 168–75.

El Serafy, S. (1992), 'Sustainability, income measurement and growth', in R. Goodland, H.E. Daly and S. El Serafy (eds), *Population, Technology and Lifestyle: The Transition to Sustainability*, Washington, DC: Island Press for the International Bank for Reconstruction and Development and UNESCO, pp. 63–79.

El Serafy, S. (1993), 'Depletable resources: fixed capital or inventories?', in A. Franz and C. Stahmer (eds), *Approaches to Environmental Accounting*, Proceedings of the IARIW Conference on Environmental Accounting, Baden (near Vienna) and Heidelberg: Physica-Verlag, pp. 245–58.

El Serafy, S. (1999), 'Natural resource accounting', in J.C.J.M. van den Bergh (ed.), *Handbook of Environmental and Resource Economics*, Cheltenham, UK and Northampton, MA, USA: Edward Elgar Publishing, pp. 1191–206.

El Serafy, S. (2006), 'The economic rationale for green accounting', in P. Lawn (ed.), *Sustainable Development Indicators in Ecological Economics*, Cheltenham, UK and Northampton, MA, USA: Edward Elgar Publishing, pp. 55–77.

Franz, A. and C. Stahmer (eds) (1993), *Approaches to Environmental Accounting*, Proceedings of the IARIW Conference on Environmental Accounting, Baden (near Vienna) and Heidelberg: Physica-Verlag.

Hicks, J.R. (1940), 'The valuation of the social income', *Economica* (New Series), **7** (26), 105–24.

Hicks, J.R. (1942), 'Maintaining capital intact: a further suggestion', *Economica*, **9**, 174–9.

Hicks, J.R. (1946), *Value and Capital*, 2nd edn, Oxford: Clarendon Press.

Hicks, J.R. (1950), *A Contribution to the Theory of the Trade Cycle*, Oxford: Clarendon Press.

Hicks, J.R. (1952), *The Social Framework: An Introduction to Economics*, 2nd edn, Oxford: Clarendon Press.

Hicks, J.R. (1975), 'The scope and status of welfare economics', *Oxford Economic Papers*, **27** (3), 307–26.

Hicks, J.R. (1976), 'Some questions of time in economics', in A.M. Tang, F.W. Westfield and J.S. Worley (eds), *Evolution, Welfare and Time in Economics: Essays in Honor of Nicholas Georgescu-Roegen*, Lexington, MA: Lexington Books, Heath and Company, pp. 135–52.

Hicks, J.R. (1981), *Wealth and Welfare: Collected Essays on Economic Theory*, Vol. I, Cambridge, MA: Harvard University Press.

Jevons, W.S. (1865), *The Coal Question: An Inquiry Concerning the Progress of the Nation, and the Probable Exhaustion of Our Coal Mines*, London: Macmillan.

Keynes, J.M. (1930), 'Economic possibilities for our grandchildren', reprinted in J.M. Keynes (1963), *Essays in Persuasion*, New York: W.W. Norton, pp. 358–73.

Keynes, J.M. (1936), *The General Theory of Employment, Interest and Money*, London: Macmillan.

Kuznets, S. (1948), 'On the valuation of social income: reflections on Professor Hicks' article. Part I', *Economica* (New Series), **15** (57), 1–16.

Marshall, A. (1920), *Principles of Economics*, 8th edn, reprinted in 1947, London: Macmillan and Co.

Meade, J.E. and R. Stone (1948), *National Income and Expenditure*, 2nd edn, Cambridge: Bowes and Bowes.

Mehlum, H., K. Moene and R. Torvik (2006), 'Institutions and the resource curse', *Economic Journal*, **116** (508), 1–20.

Mill, J.S. (1848), *Principles of Political Economy with Some of their Applications to Social Philosophy*, 2 vols, London: John W. Parker.

NEF (2006), *The Happy Planet Index: An Index of Human Well-being and Environmental Impact*, London: New Economics Foundation.

Pigou, A.C. (1952), *Essays in Economics*, London: Macmillan and Co.

Redefining Progress (1995), 'Gross production vs. genuine progress', excerpt from *The Genuine Progress Indicator: Summary of Data and Methodology*, San Francisco, CA: Redefining Progress.

Rees, W.E. and M. Wackernagel (1994), 'Ecological footprints and appropriated carrying capacity: measuring the natural capital requirements of the human economy', in A.-M. Jansson, M. Hammer, C. Folke and R. Costanza (eds), *Investing in Natural Capital: The Ecological Economics Approach to Sustainability*, Washington, DC: Island Press.

Schumpeter, J.A. (1954), *History of Economic Analysis*, New York: Oxford University Press.

Smith, A. (1776), *An Inquiry into the Nature and Causes of the Wealth of Nations*, reprinted in 1937, London: Edwin Cannan.

Tang, A.M., F.W. Westfield and J.S. Worley (eds) (1976), *Evolution, Welfare and Time in Economics: Essays in Honor of Nicholas Georgescu-Roegen*, Lexington, MA: Lexington Books, Heath and Company.

UNDP (1990), *Human Development Report, 1990*, United Nations Development Programme, New York: Oxford University Press.

PART IV

Changing the rules: institutions for a
sustainable and desirable future

10. Ecological and Georgist economic principles: a comparison

Clifford Cobb

There are today a large number of schools of thought in economics that take as their starting point a critique of neoclassical economics. Yet, in their critique of the dominant mode of economic analysis, they do it homage.[1] They are like students arguing with the master, whom they acknowledge by their disputes.

The two-factor, highly formalized models that characterize neoclassical thought will be moved from the center to the periphery of economics only if the proponents of diverse schools of criticism begin studying each other's thought and building alternative paradigms that are as comprehensive as the one they seek to replace.

This chapter attempts to draw some connections between the principles of ecological economics and Georgist economics (named after Henry George). In order to engage in this dialogue, I will adopt a rather stylized view of both perspectives. My hope is not to offer a thorough explication of their differences and similarities, but merely to begin a process of looking for questions on which dialogue might be fruitful.

10.1 THE NATURE OF LAND

One feature that characterizes both Georgist and ecological economics is the centrality of land in all aspects of theory. When neoclassical economists claim that land has been of diminishing importance in the industrial era and the 'information age,' Georgists and ecological economists agree that what Herman Daly has called 'angel economics' is a dangerous and misguided fantasy. Nevertheless, in their understanding of the nature of land, these two strands of heterodox economics are poles apart.

Ecological economics considers land in bio-physical terms and in its particularity as complex ecological processes occurring at specific sites. It views land as both a resource for human use and a life-sustaining matrix. The key issue for ecological economics is defining the scale of human activity that will disrupt that matrix. Thus, when ecological economists examine the role of land in urban life or farming or forestry, they think largely in terms of the conflict between human activity and natural processes.

Historically, Georgist economics has treated nature purely as resource. When Henry George wrote in the late nineteenth century, before widespread understanding of the second law of thermodynamics, he adopted the view that the earth could sustain 100 billion people and a nearly infinite amount of physical transformation of the earth. Thus, Georgism began as an anthropocentric worldview. In Georgist economics, the central issue has been the liberal hope of human freedom, a world in which no human is allowed to dominate another. Land is important primarily as an intermediary in the struggle of humans for power and secondarily as the storehouse of potential wealth for humanity. The value of land (all of nature) is not derived from its physical characteristics, but rather as location relative to economic activity. This is not so different from the neoclassical view of land or space. The main difference is that Georgist economics takes that value seriously and reorients the entire framework of thinking by doing so.

Both perspectives (the ecological view of land as matrix of life and the Georgist view of land as matrix of human interactions) are neglected in neoclassical economics, which assumes that labor and capital work together in a kind of mathematical ether. Thus, while it would be possible to belabor the differences between the ecological and Georgist views of land, it is far more useful to note that both are relevant to solving the massive problems created by neoclassical theories that ignore both of them.

Both approaches risk becoming one-sided. The ecological approach to land risks becoming a purely physicalist approach (treating ecological complexity or negentropy as the only value worth considering), whereas the Georgist approach risks losing sight of the necessity of limiting human encroachment on fragile ecosystems, including the earth's climate. Thus, each needs the other to achieve balance.

10.2   GROWTH AND THE ENVIRONMENT

One topic on which balance is urgently called for is the assessment of benefits and costs of economic growth or increased scale. Georgists and ecological economists agree that growth creates severe problems, but they do not agree on what those problems are. For Georgists, economic growth has the positive effect of producing more goods and services and the negative effect of increasing pollution and inequality. The latter problems can be corrected, however, so Georgists favor a growing economy. By contrast, ecological economists regard increased scale of human activity as the primary culprit behind environmentally damaging activity and support a steady-state economy without growth of materials and energy consumption, but with increases in services and the quality of goods.

An appropriate balance of Georgist and ecological economics on the subject of growth is not some point along a continuum between high growth and zero growth. Instead, it requires taking account of the concerns of both traditions. In this section, the focus will be on the environment. In a later section, the problems of inequality will be addressed.

An intelligent approach to growth involves (1) distinguishing between the benign and harmful elements of growth and (2) designing policies based on those distinctions. Analyzing the elements of growth entails moving away from highly stylized views that lump diverse activities into single categories, such as IPAT (Impact = Population × Affluence [income/population] × Technology [impact/income]) or ultimate bio-physical limits on human activity. A crucial question that remains unresolved is the extent to which economic growth necessarily entails a higher volume of physical resource consumption, pollution and waste. Technically speaking, economic growth is an accounting device that records changes in the volume of human exchanges and interactions. Its impacts depend very much on the ratio of value produced per unit of energy consumed and on the institutional framework within which human interactions occur, particularly institutions related to property rights and the provision of public goods.

There are some environmental issues on which the problem of scale (the result of growth) appears to be almost the only factor worth considering. These are the sorts of issues that lend credence to the very generalized critiques of growth that have been made by ecological economists. For example, economic growth has historically entailed greater energy consumption, almost any source of which has some damaging effects. Except in the unusual case of Switzerland and Germany, which have achieved zero or negative energy-GDP elasticity,[2] respectively, most nations increase their energy consumption as their GDP rises (Fang and Chen, 2007). But the relationship is not fixed. In Organisation for Economic Co-operation and Development (OECD) countries, energy elasticity ranged between 0.6 and 0.9 from 1975 to 1995 (Energy Information Agency, 1995, p. 13, table 5), but it has fallen to 0.55 since 2000 (Gately and Huntington, 2001). In non-OECD countries, energy elasticity was in the range of 1.1 to 1.4 during the earlier period, but it has fallen dramatically since then (Energy Information Agency, 1995, p. 13, table 5). In 2005, India's had fallen to 0.8, and is expected to fall to 0.67 by 2021 (Krishnan, 2006).[3] China's energy elasticity rose briefly from an average of less than 0.6 in the 1980s to 1.5 in 2003–04, but then fell in 2005 to 1.02, and to 0.87 in 2006 (Logan, 2005).[4]

What is significant in this array of statistics is the variability in the relationship between energy use and growth of GDP. This demonstrates conclusively that there is no *necessary* connection between the two.[5] The linkage between economic growth and damage from energy use is thus institutional and based on *political* choices; it is not a purely natural relationship.[6] If energy taxes had long ago been set high and raised rapidly enough to offset the effects of higher incomes, capital could have substituted over time for energy in many contexts, and income growth could have continued.[7]

Of course, the idea that taxes on energy use should be introduced to forestall the effects of depletion presupposes a basic premise of ecological economics: future generations are likely to suffer if finite resources are rapidly consumed. The standard compensation that neoclassical economists offer their grandchildren is the promise that the future will be like the past six or seven decades, when cheap oil and highgrades of ore permitted the price of raw materials to fall. Neoclassical economists also offer technological optimism that technical change will fully offset depletion. Prudence and intergenerational equity, however, require that such resources be rationed over numerous generations rather than being largely consumed within a few generations.

If institutional reforms, including environmental taxes, can achieve far more efficient use of resources and increased exchange of low-impact services, then economic growth per se *may* not be an immediate problem. However, those reforms need to be tested to determine the extent to which altered price signals and changes in cultural norms will continue to permit economic growth while stabilizing or reducing energy and materials consumption.

The key to achieving a synthesis of economic growth and conservation may thus depend on the kinds of policies that are applied to achieve growth. Since the prerequisites of growth are still not well understood by economists, there is considerable latitude for error.

When energy is subsidized by some governments in the mistaken notion that energy and capital are the keys to rapid development, obviously those policies run counter to conservation. Similarly, tariffs designed to protect home industries may also serve to discourage investment in new technologies that use less energy than older production methods.

Just as foolish as policies designed to promote growth by wasting resources are misguided efforts to conserve resources by stunting growth through macroeconomic policies. If a government were persuaded by ecological economists to halt growth for the sake of the environment, how should they do so? That is an unanswered question. If monetary or fiscal restraints were applied in a sort of reverse Keynesianism of intentional efforts to reduce growth, the result would likely be not only declining disposable incomes (the intended effect?) but also massive unemployment (an unintended effect). Macroeconomic management designed to maintain economic stability and growth remains more an art than a science. If ecological economists recommend limiting economic growth, they need to define the precise mechanisms for doing so, in order to evaluate the full consequences of any proposal.

From a Georgist (and a neoclassical) perspective, it would be absurd to interfere with the forward momentum of an economy just to prevent side-effects of negative aspects of the economy. Lower disposable incomes would not necessarily reduce the most harmful impacts on the environment in any case. Targeting specific causes of harm would be more useful than broad-brush efforts to slow the economy as a whole. For example, pesticides are used heavily even in countries with low per capita incomes. Policies designed to slow growth will probably not reduce consumption of nickel-cadmium batteries compared to alkaline batteries or increase the chances of proper disposal of the waste products. In rural areas, poverty may lead to deforestation more rapidly than affluence. In general, the damage caused by an activity may have little connection with the value-added that is associated with it.

A targeted approach to damage prevention through the use of environmental taxes that internalize marginal external costs may be the one point on which ecological, neoclassical and Georgist economists already agree. Yet, agreement in principle does not run very deep when it comes time to act. Because of difficulty measuring damage to human health and to ecosystems in monetary terms, there are huge administrative and judicial obstacles to using environmental taxes that are high enough to change behavior (which is their purpose). First, there are obstacles to setting judicially permissible tax rates on sources of harm, beginning with the types of evidence of harm demanded in court and in legislative proceedings. The degree of certainty required about causation can only be obtained after bodies start to pile up, and even then no evidence is perfect. Second, there are problems of measurement and enforcement, particularly when harm is diffuse or occurs over prolonged periods. Third, existing companies prefer to be given tradable permits to pollute rather than having to pay for the right to do so. Thus, cap-and-trade systems start with a political advantage over taxation. For these and other reasons, the use of environmental taxes will continue to be honored more in the breach than in the observance. A precautionary principle that can legally define unforeseen risks but not stifle useful innovation has so far remained elusive, but without it, setting a fair price on pollution will happen only rarely.

Even if effective taxes on pollution or congestion can be designed, they address only a narrow range of types of damage from growth. A deeper principle is needed than 'taxing bads.' This is the point at which Georgist economics has something distinctive to offer, something more than taxes that internalize external costs.

The contribution of Georgism is sometimes reduced to one policy: the tax on site values. Yet, behind that policy lies a simple, but powerful, principle that is widely neglected: the best way to solve problems is through indirect means. To be indirect means that consequences are not self-evidently connected to causes. Taxing harmful substances to discourage their production or use is, by this definition, a direct policy. Income transfers to achieve more equal incomes is also direct. By contrast, Georgist policies have second-order and third-order effects on humans and the environment. Most of those effects have yet to be analyzed, but they are definitely indirect because they are not obvious upon inspection.[8]

Logically, one would expect that ecological economists would devise policy prescriptions that impose fewer impacts on nature than policies stemming from the Georgist view of land as location. Yet, logic does not always prevail in a world of paradoxical feedback loops. The central Georgist policy prescription is to tax all land at its full market value and to substitute that tax, to the extent possible, for all other taxes. Neither Henry George nor most of his followers in the twentieth century conceived of this tax as an environmental policy. They saw it as a way of achieving equitable growth.

Ironically, though, site value taxation may conserve land, water and other resources through indirect means more effectively than policies with that direct intention. For example, taxing the value of land has no direct effect on plans to develop land far from urban centers. Its effects on sprawl are entirely indirect. By encouraging intensive development in areas already built up, it simply reduces the demand for land in distant suburbs, exurbs or informal settlements (in developing nations). Under a regime of high taxes on land, vacant and underutilized land in urban centers would be effectively forced into production.[9] This does not require paving over parks. Big cities typically have from 10 percent to 30 percent developable land that is occupied by parking lots, dilapidated buildings or weeds and garbage. One- and two-storey buildings in areas where demand would support high-rises is another form of underutilization. By applying constant economic pressure to develop on those who currently hoard usable sites for speculative purposes, city centers and inner-ring suburbs would rise from their current decay, and the demand for development in distant suburbs would fall sharply.[10]

With such a tax in place, rising residential and job density at the urban core would dramatically reduce the pressure to develop farmland at the urban fringe, 30 or 40 miles from the urban center. Higher density would not only reduce development pressure in rural areas, it would also increase energy efficiency in the city by making transit service more affordable and reliable, thereby reducing dependence on private vehicles.

A similar tax on water rights in arid areas would reduce agricultural demand for water resources (shifting from water-intensive crops and encouraging drip irrigation, for example), and thus reduce the need to construct dams, with all of the problems they create for fish and other wildlife. With senior water rights holders abandoning their claims to water that is currently used wastefully, far more water would be available for in-stream flows in the summer.

In tropical countries with large landless populations, a tax on site values would force those holding large tracts of prime farmland, now used mostly for grazing, to transfer rights to those who would farm the land intensively. This would reduce the pressure by the landless to decimate the rainforest, which is rarely suitable for farming in any case.[11] Watersheds and habitat for unique species can be preserved only if the poor are not forced to use that land because the rich are hoarding the most productive land.

Georgist theory thus offers a model of development that indirectly and unintentionally reduces the conflict between growth and the environment. The incentive that promotes economic growth through intensification simultaneously reduces pressure on the environment caused by lateral expansion of human activity. Nor is the model based on the usual reasoning that claims that higher incomes permit more investment in anti-pollution equipment. No such assumption is required here. The Georgist model proposes that growth can reduce impacts over a broad range of environmental concerns, not just pollution.

Another benefit of the Georgist model of development in relation to environmental protection is the potential it brings for greater public acceptance of restrictions on damaging behavior. Fear of the unknown prevents change, and opportunities lessen fear. People are much more willing to give up what they currently hold dear if the opportunity exists to replace it without much trouble. Higher average wages and a lower rate of unemployment (resulting from higher turnover of capital goods) will make political dynamics more flexible (Gaffney, 1970).[12] Deadlocks that pit commercial interests against environmental values often seem permanent in a world of limited opportunities. Those deadlocks can be broken if economic opportunities abound.

The impact of Georgist policy on human population growth is one environmental consequence that is not clear. No form of economic theory has decisively shown which policies will arrest human population growth, short of famine and disease. Coercion was only marginally successful in a totalitarian society (China) and an abject failure in a democracy (India). Anecdotal evidence suggests, however, that policies giving women greater employment opportunities are successful in reducing fertility. Urbanization has also reduced fertility rates throughout human history. If those are the two most crucial variables in limiting fertility, then Georgist economics scores well by increasing employment opportunities for both men and women and by making cities more livable.

Although the indirect effects of Georgist policies will have enormous environmental benefits, it is important not to overstate this fortuitous outcome. There is an inherent conflict between the growth of human activity and the availability of undisturbed habitat for other species. Georgist policies would redirect growth in more positive ways and buy time to develop additional methods to control the disruptions caused by human societies. However, Georgist economics is not sufficient to save the planet. In order to be ultimately successful in creating a sustainable economy, Georgists need to learn about limits from ecological economists, and the latter need to learn from Georgists about policies that can achieve environmental goals through indirect means. Only by learning from each other can the limits of their respective domains of knowledge become apparent.

10.3   EQUITY

In the past two centuries, the central ideological debate between conflicting economic theories has been about the tension between private property and social equity. Capitalists have favored the former because it rewards personal initiative and increases productivity. Socialists have emphasized the latter, claiming that only public management and economic planning can avoid exploitation and gross inequality.

Ecological economists have tended to side with the capitalists in this debate.[13] In the almost canonical article 'Tragedy of the commons,' Garrett Hardin argued that resources treated as common property are subject to abuse and spoliation, and that private property is necessary to prevent the destruction of the earth (Hardin, 1968). Hardin later amended this view by distinguishing between a commons with open access and one with restricted access, but he will be remembered for the original defense of private property (Hardin, 1991).[14] Thus, common property may not be as indefensible as Hardin originally maintained. Yet, in the extensive literature on management of the commons by Elinor Ostrom, Bonnie McCay and others in the International Association for the Study of Common Property, the commons is little more than a broadening of the boundaries of private property.[15] A managed commons requires enforceable boundaries that prevent incursions from those outside the commons. According to this view, resources can be shared among members of a group, but sharing them more broadly, with an entire region, nation or the globe, invites disaster.

While private property solves the problems caused by open access, it creates another set of problems, particularly in a growing economy. As average incomes grow, the price of access to fixed resources grows even faster. That means owners grow wealthier, while those lacking property are forced to pay a larger portion of their incomes to survive. Asset ownership and property income become more concentrated over time, and poverty deepens for the landless. The poor suffer the most from this state of affairs, but there is damage to the health of all members of a society in which wealth is skewed (Daniels et al., 1999).[16]

Perhaps the most useful way of comparing ecological and Georgist economics on the question of equity is to consider different types of equity. I define three types (more may exist) as (1) intergenerational; (2) income and wealth; and (3) the dispersion of power.

10.3.1 Equity I: Integenerational Equity

A number of ecological economists have considered the issue of intergenerational equity (Howarth, 1998; Howarth and Norgaard, 1990, 1995; Lind, 1995; Padilla, 2002). They have proposed policies that would lead to a sustainable production of value from resources over hundreds or thousands of years. The basic moral principle involved in this analysis is that the use of resources to sustain affluence in the present should not diminish the affluence of future generations by depriving them of equivalent value from that stock of resources.

I make no effort here to discuss in depth the analysis by ecological economists of this issue. I presume most readers of this volume are already familiar with the writings of Daly and others about weak and strong forms of sustainability, which hinges on the question of how thoroughly capital can substitute for nature in the long-run production of economic value. I would note only that Daly's insights on these issues are among his most important contributions to the field of economics.

The topic of intergenerational equity has unfortunately been ignored by Georgist economists (and most other categories of economists as well). When Henry George wrote, the principle of entropy was not well known, and it has not played a significant role in the thought of his followers. As a result, the problem of resource depletion has not been an integral part of Georgist theory.

In fact, there is a tendency for ecological and Georgist economists to be

directly at odds on questions of conservation. Whereas ecological economists are likely to favor policies such as severance or stumpage fees that
raise the costs of extracting raw materials (including cutting of timber),
Georgists tend to recommend taxes on resources in situ, which has the
effect of encouraging more rapid extraction. This Georgist orientation
toward non-renewable resources is, however, a contingent view, not a necessary corollary of Georgist principles. Thus, it seems possible that some
meeting of minds between ecological and Georgist economics is possible
on questions of intergenerational equity.

10.3.2 Equity II: Income or Wealth Equity

The subject of intra-generational equity, or income and wealth distribution, has received far less attention within the field of ecological economics. Using the search engine at www.sciencedirect.com, only 12 articles
appeared in a search of the journal *Ecological Economics* for 'income
distribution' and no results were found for 'wealth distribution.' Of
those that did appear regarding income distribution, they were about
the environmental Kuznets curve, the effects on income distribution of
efficient pricing of resources or the Genuine Progress Indicator. None
dealt with constructive policies to improve income or wealth distribution.
Although one journal may not be entirely representative of the field of
ecological economics, it appears to reinforce the negative stereotype that
those concerned with the environment care more about plants and animals
than about humans.

Herman Daly has been one of the rare exceptions to the general
pattern.[17] He has addressed the issue of income distribution throughout
his career. In his book *Steady-state Economics* and again recently, Daly
called for the radical idea of both a lower *and* an upper limit on income.[18]
He recognizes that many of the conservation and anti-pollution taxes
recommended by ecological economists are regressive and thus require
some method of offsetting the burdens on the poor.[19] In *For the Common
Good*, Daly and Cobb did not propose to set an upper and lower limit on
incomes, but instead proposed both 'a combination of income and inherit-
ance taxes, . . . social dividends, worker ownership of business, and guaranteed employment' (Daly and Cobb, 1994, p. 331), plus a negative income
tax on low incomes, severance and pollution taxes, and application of the
quasi-Georgist transformation of the property tax to a two-rate tax that
would tax land more heavily than buildings.[20]

Daly calls for cap-auction-trade schemes to reduce use of resources or
waste sinks to a sustainable level. However, beyond the problem of the
regressivity of such proposals,[21] which he does at least recognize, there

is another serious problem of equity, which he does not acknowledge. Any system of property rights, whether it begins with a gift of rights or an auction of them, allows the owners to capture the subsequent increase in their value, which the owners do nothing to create. It also encourages hoarding that decreases new entrants to the field and thus stifles competition, which sustains inefficiency and high prices. A more equitable solution is a rising annual lease payment or some other provision for public capture of the unearned rise in the value of the resource. Despite his sensitivity to the plight of the poor, even Daly overlooks this fundamental point.[22]

The more important limitation of Daly's thought on the question of equity is that he tends to see the problem of wealth and poverty in terms of 'redistribution' rather than 'distribution.' That is to say, Daly, despite passing comments to the contrary, takes for granted a certain distribution of initial entitlements (property rights), from which flow inequalities in outcomes. When he discusses policy options, he thinks exclusively in terms of transferring income or wealth *after* the market has already caused its flows to be highly skewed. The possibility that modifying the basic ownership structure of assets by taxing site values is not an option he considers. When he does discuss rent taxation, he seems to think of it purely as a revenue-generating device.[23]

The question of how to achieve greater equity of incomes and wealth was one of two primary concerns of Henry George. (His other major concern was the efficient use of resources, particularly urban land. Because this dovetails with the efficiency orientation of neoclassical economics, many followers of George have emphasized these issues to the virtual exclusion of equity issues.)

The central Georgist policy prescription (a tax on site values) is designed to achieve greater equity, but in a way quite different from most proposals.[24] It is concerned not with equalizing income through after-tax redistribution, but with creating a more just distribution of income before taxes by altering the conditions under which exchange occurs. The purpose of the tax on site values (and an offsetting reduction in other taxes) is thus not to raise revenue that can be used to ameliorate poverty. Rather, the aim is to reduce income from unearned gains and to raise pre-tax wages. How a tax on site values would modify market conditions is more complex than can be explained adequately in this chapter, but I shall provide here a brief overview.[25]

To understand the effects of site value taxation, one must first recognize that every tax (on wages, sales, gross receipts and so on) already falls on economic rent or site values by reducing aggregate income. This is more easily recognized in reverse: a cut in the federal income tax shows up almost immediately as a rise in real estate prices, in the same way a farm subsidy is capitalized in a higher price for farmland. By increasing aggregate demand, a tax cut raises production of all commodities. Since all economic transactions occur at some location, the rise in production and sales leads in the final analysis to an increased demand for sites or locations, the supply of which is perfectly inelastic. Thus, increased aggregate demand causes the price of land to rise. The whole process works in reverse if income or sales taxes are increased. Since all taxes ultimately come out of rent or site values, it means that every current tax is a tax on site values *plus* a burden on or disincentive to productive activity.[26] To estimate the taxable value of land, the tax base would be the price of land *after* other taxes were reduced or eliminated.

Just as a reduction in other taxes would raise the price of land, the first-order effect of a tax on site values would be to reduce it. An annual tax of 30 percent on the value of land would transfer around 90 percent of the value of landholdings from private hands into public coffers.[27]

The effect of a site value tax on the distribution of wealth depends on the total value of land compared to other assets.[28] To develop an estimate of that value would require piercing the veil of paper assets (stocks, bonds, mortgages) to examine the underlying assets that give those paper assets their value. The framework of cost accounting is not designed to provide that information. A substantial portion of what an accountant deems to be 'profits' of corporations, partnerships and sole proprietorships are actually economic rents, that is, the value-added by the location of its offices, production facilities, warehouses and so on. Accounting practices further obscure the trail by conventionally assigning costs and revenues only as transactions occur and by recording land at its historic cost, not its market value, and certainly not its current annual contribution to realized income. Imputed income from non-depreciating assets (that is, land) therefore escapes notice entirely because there are no location-related transactions to record when someone buys a DVD at WalMart or visits a doctor. Yet, the location is an extremely important part of each of those transactions and adds value to them. (Even mail order warehouses are located in population centers, not the middle of the Nevada desert.) The information system (accounting procedure) simply fails to record the value added by land. As a result, corporate and government accounts vastly underestimate the contribution of land to the value of output, and until that is corrected, researchers must rely on indirect measures.[29]

My own very rough estimate is that the aggregate value of land in the United States is around seven or eight times the GDP,[30] whereas the net value of fixed reproducible capital is around twice the value of GDP. That would mean economic rent amounts to about 20–30 percent of national income and returns to fixed capital around one quarter that much. If site values constitute two thirds of the value of all fixed assets, against which stocks, bonds and mortgages are issued, then a tax of 30 percent on site values would reduce the value of those paper assets by around 60 percent (90 percent of 67 percent). Since the top 10 percent of wealth-holders hold 80 to 90 percent of those assets (Kennickell, 2006, p. 55, table A-4), the transfer of 60 percent of the value of those paper assets to the public would amount to a dramatic shift in wealth distribution. Wealth distribution in the United States would change from one of the most unequal in the world to one of the most equal. (The current Gini coefficient for net worth in the United States is around 0.8, comparable to Brazil and Zimbabwe before its collapse.)[31]

A radical reduction in the value of assets held by the richest members of society is part of the equalizing effect of a tax on site values. The other effect is the spur such a tax would be to wages.

The revolutionary claims made by Henry George are that (1) productive urban land is currently underutilized (as a result of satisficing instead of optimization – see footnote 14); (2) labor and capital are currently forced onto marginal urban locations that add less value than could be produced with the same inputs in better locations; (3) a tax on site values will encourage more intensive use of prime locations (for commercial, industrial or residential purposes); and (4) the result will be a general rise in productivity, leading to a rise in average wages and higher returns to capital equipment. Removing taxes on labor (starting with the payroll tax) would also provide low-income households with additional net income. All of these benefits to the working poor and the middle class occur because of the incentive effects of the site value tax and reduced taxes on labor, not from any redistribution of the revenues generated.

A Georgist economy would not provide everyone equal incomes or other results. Rather, the claim made here is that it would change the structure of opportunity, so that privilege would not be the basis of wealth and inequality.

10.3.3   Equity III: The Dispersion of Power

If we extend the analysis of equity into the arena of political power, the concentration of wealth and power among large corporations is cause for concern. The corporate (limited liability) form of organization and the legal difficulties of holding them accountable are not the chief reasons they have attained such power in the modern world. Instead, their power stems largely from their size, as measured by their assets. They are not monopolies in the strict sense of the word, and they may even face price competition from similar giants. Nevertheless, they dominate decision-making everywhere in the world because their concentrated economic power permits them to buy greater scientific expertise and legal talent than most public agencies can, and their political influence enables them to bend foreign policy to their bidding, including the overthrow of regimes they do not like (for example, the United Fruit Company in Guatemala, ITT in Chile).

Neither ecological nor Georgist economists have had much to say about this aspect of inequity.[32] Both tend to take industrial organization as a given. But, in fact, different methods of regulation and taxation will have an impact on the concentration of ownership by corporations.

The kinds of policies favored by environmentalists tend to favor large corporations over smaller companies. Regulation, cap-and-trade and auctioning of pollution rights all favor existing companies over challengers by raising barriers to entry to new companies and allowing existing companies to hoard their rights. Only pollution taxes that require full compensation for ongoing social costs are neutral with respect to the size of firms.

Georgist tax policy is not consciously designed to reduce the concentration of industrial and commercial ownership, but that would be the likely effect. A great deal of the power and size of large companies stems from their control of assets that generate economic rent. (That includes urban land, petroleum deposits, minerals, forests, fisheries, as well as patents and other intellectual property rights.) By definition, rents are cost-free income; they are what one does not have to work for. They are the surplus that derives from owning and excluding others from strategic locations, deposits or bodies of information. Rent-producing assets make possible the funding of researchers, legal teams and lobbyists that enable large firms to sustain their pre-eminent position. Treating economic rent as the primary source of tax revenue would not eliminate the excessive power of corporations, but it would curb it.

Large corporations (particularly resource companies such as oil, mining and timber companies) are also land- and capital-intensive. Large retailers and financial companies may not own natural resources or large amounts of equipment, but they have significant investments in real estate in the form of stores and branch offices. Consequently, large companies tend to have high ratios of capital per employee (Gaffney, 1976).[33] Even though corporations may complain about the effects of payroll and income taxes (since they partially fall on employers when labor demand is inelastic), taxes on wages give a comparative advantage to large companies and permit them to grow larger. That is because they hurt small, labor-intensive companies more than the big capital-intensive ones. Thus, a tax on site values will benefit small companies and discourage concentration of ownership by large ones.

10.3.4 Why Equity is Important for the Environment

Ecological and Georgist economists have much to learn from each other about equity. Both, however, need to understand that it is not merely a matter of justice or fairness for humans. All forms of equity are necessary preconditions for protecting the environment.

An example that captures this principle is a story Erik Eckholm told decades ago about a rural reforestation project in Ethiopia to control erosion and provide firewood to villagers (Eckholm, 1976, p. 109).[34] Landless laborers were hired to plant the seedlings. When the project managers went into the field to evaluate the success of the program, they discovered that many of the seedlings had been planted upside down. The laborers were not naïve; they were fully aware of what they were doing. They acted in that manner because they knew the benefits of the project would accrue to the landowners in the area, driving a deeper wedge between their own poverty and the wealth of the landowners.

If the problem of equity is ignored, the results are not only rising levels of poverty; efforts to achieve conservation will also be constantly thwarted. Wildlife preserves are a last ditch effort to sustain the habitat of endangered species. But a preserve can work only if peasants on surrounding land have the means of earning an adequate income legally. If the alternatives to poaching are sufficiently rewarding, they are more likely to respect the boundaries of the preserve and the rules against poaching.

The Green Revolution is another example of how inequity is associated with environmental damage. The introduction of new seed varieties raised yields. However, achieving those yields (a) reduced genetic variability among seeds; (b) increased use of pesticides, chemical fertilizers and mechanical tractors (displacing water buffalo); and (c) increased reliance on irrigation systems, which justified the construction of large-scale water projects that altered natural systems. At the same time, increased productivity raised the price of land and displaced millions of peasants, leaving them landless and forced to pay higher rents to landlords.

10.4 DESIGNING SOLUTIONS

The point of deepest philosophical conflict between ecological and Georgist economics is one that has only been hinted at thus far. It seems possible that specific issues about natural limits, economic growth and equity can probably be resolved if there is agreement about methodology. In that regard, there is a methodological dispute that may stand in the way of any synthesis between ecological and Georgist economics.

The key issue is whether it is possible for a single policy instrument to do double duty. Herman Daly, representing ecological economics, answers resoundingly in the negative. Georgist economics begins with the premise that a single policy can bring about more benefits than we can imagine. Ecological economists stand in a tradition beginning with Malthus that emphasizes scarcity, trade-offs and TANSTAAFL.[35] Georgists stand in the tradition of multiplying loaves and fishes to feed the multitude and the principle that some trade-offs are merely a result of lack of imagination.

Daly throws down the gauntlet in *Valuing the Earth: Economics, Ecology, Ethics*, where he declares, 'The basic rule that for every independent policy goal we must have an independent policy instrument has been emphasized by Professor Jan Tinbergen[36] but seems to have been forgotten in recent discussion. Yet we all recognize "you can't kill two birds with one stone" at least if they are flying independently. If they are flying in tandem or sitting on the same fence, then one might manage to do it. This book argues, among other things, that we need a third stone because the birds are flying independently. The "birds" are the three goals of allocation, distribution, and scale. The first two have a long history in economic theory and have their two specific policy instruments. The third, scale, has not been formally recognized and has no corresponding policy instrument' (Daly and Townsend, 1993, p. 1).

The reason this is such a fundamental principle for Daly only becomes apparent when one reads the article in *Land Economics* from which this chapter in *Valuing the Earth* is drawn. In the earlier journal article, Daly explains:

> An example of the confusion that can result from the non-recognition of the independence of the scale issue from the question of allocation is provided by the following dilemma (Pearce et al. 1989: 135). Which puts more pressure on the environment, a high or a low discount rate? The usual answer is that a high discount rate is worse for the environment because it speeds the rate of depletion of nonrenewable resources and shortens the turnover and fallow periods in the exploitation of renewables. It shifts the allocation of capital and labor toward projects that exploit natural resources more intensively. But it restricts the total number of projects undertaken. A low discount rate will permit more projects to be undertaken even while encouraging less intensive resource use for each project. The allocation effect of a high discount rate is to increase throughput, but the scale effect is to lower throughput. Which effect is stronger is hard to say, although one suspects that over the long run the scale effect will dominate. The resolution to the dilemma is to recognize that two independent policy goals require two independent policy instruments – we cannot serve both optimal scale and optimal allocation with the single policy instrument of the discount rate (Tinbergen 1952). (Daly, 1991, pp. 257–8)

Something odd is going on here. The pre-analytic vision behind Tinbergen's rule is one in which reality is divided up into pieces that conform to our categories, with each category having its own form of optimality. That fragmentation contradicts Daly's criticism of the fallacy of misplaced concreteness and his religious vision of the world.[37] In the example he chooses, the discount rate is effectively a function of the long-term interest rate that emerges from quadrillions of decisions made within markets; it can hardly be deemed a policy instrument at all. Central banks can set short-term rates, but no one has yet learned the secret of managing long-term rates. Since there are a large number of moral trade-offs associated with high and low interest rates (with more than allocative efficiency and optimal throughput at stake), it is perhaps best that long-term rates are determined through complex social patterns, not by conscious design.

In fact, governments are limited to extremely few levers in trying to manage human societies: taxes, subsidies, monetary policies, regulations and direct service provision (including military action). After a century, we still know little about the second- and third-order effects of most of those policy instruments, and in some cases, we are still trying to fathom the first-order effects. We certainly know even less about the potential for interaction among the second- and third-order effects and the ways in which different agencies and jurisdictions of government work at cross-purposes with each other.

Tinbergen's notion that there needs to be a one-to-one correspondence between goals and policy instruments makes perfect sense in a world represented by simultaneous equations, but it quickly loses its relevance in the world of administrative non-compliance, incentive and disincentive effects, confused information signals, complex feedback loops and unforeseen consequences. There is nothing linear about the effects of policy instruments once they dip their toes in the stream of history. Indeed, it is surprising that Tinbergen's rule would ever have entered the field of ecological economics. As Ropke says about the origins of the discipline, '*Systems thinking* in a broad sense was shared baggage for several of the initiators, particularly those coming from the natural sciences, but also for some of the economists' (Ropke, 2005, p. 267, emphasis in original).

Georgist philosophy presupposes no artificial boundaries that separate policies and outcomes into separate and distinct bundles. The primary claim by Georgists, in fact, is that its primary policy instrument, a tax on site values, will not only increase equity in a society, but it will also improve efficiency (by making the land market less lumpy and subject to hoarding). As Henry George wrote in 1880:

> What I have done in this book . . . is to unite the truth . . . of Smith and Ricardo to the truth perceived by . . . Proudhon and Lassalle; to show that laissez faire . . . opens the way to a realization of the noble dreams of socialism. (Preface to the fourth edition of *Progress and Poverty*)

In short, George's aim was to synthesize rather than compartmentalize. This runs directly counter to the logic of the Tinbergen-Daly rule that each policy can have only one effective outcome.

The followers of George have noted the dual-purpose nature of his conclusions – namely, that site value taxation solves at least two problems simultaneously, without sacrificing one benefit for the other. However, there has been little effort to extend this finding from the particular case to a more general principle.

For George himself, the general principle was that nature is benign and ultimately favors symbiosis over competition, if human institutions conform to natural principles. This conforms with the view of micro-biologist Lynn Margulis that symbiogenesis or co-evolution between bacteria and host is more important than competition in determining adaptive capacity and differential survival rates in evolutionary development (Margulis, 1970).

Another interpretation of the general principle in Georgist thought is that trade-offs may be unnecessary in some synergistic systems. Biodynamic farming may be both more productive and less dependent on chemical inputs than more conventional farming methods. Historically, urbanization beyond a certain threshold made populations more disease resistant *and* more economically productive (McNeill, 1998). Taxes on greenhouse gases that are used to offset other consumption or payroll taxes may have a 'triple dividend,' reducing climate change, more equitably distributing income *and* promoting economic growth. (The validation or disconfirmation of the 'double dividend hypothesis' depends largely on whether the economist evaluating the topic was funded by an oil company or a public institution.)

Since any claim that it is possible to overcome a specific trade-off is so often met with skepticism, assertions of synergistic effects, particularly in the social sciences, are rare. That is precisely why a multi-disciplinary effort is needed to investigate this phenomenon with an open mind. If nature is going to give us something for free, it is foolish to continue operating as if a trade-off between two values is necessary.

10.5 CONCLUSION

Ecological and Georgist economics tend to define themselves in opposition to neoclassical economics and to ignore each other. It is time they began to learn from each other as well as from other 'alternative' versions of economics such as Austrian, Institutional, post-Keynesian, binary and others.

Georgists and ecological economists definitely agree on one subject: the need to reintroduce the importance of land in economics. They differ profoundly on the meaning of land, however. The proper response from both sides is to learn respect for the perspective of a potential ally. Since their primary foci are different (a sustainable environment for ecological economics; social justice for Georgists), they are not in conflict with each other. It should be possible to reintroduce land in more than one way into economic discourse.

Regarding the question of growth and its impact on the environment, there are surely differences between ecological and Georgist economists at the level of theory. Ecological economists have a strong presumption against economic growth; Georgists have far fewer compunctions about embracing growth without any reservations. Nevertheless, the policies proposed by Georgists may actually be more effective in preventing the damage caused by economic growth than the policies favored by ecological economists.

Both ecological and Georgist economists are concerned with issues of equity, but they differ greatly in what sorts of equity they emphasize. Ecological economics focuses on intergenerational equity, and Georgists focus on present-day inequities in wealth. Neither has a theoretical model about inequities of power, and neither seems particularly interested in the connection between inequity and environmental damage. Thus, not only could they learn from each other, each has new areas of research that could prove fruitful on unexplored topics.

Methodologically, ecological and Georgist economists differ on a key issue – the Tinbergen rule that each policy goal requires a separate policy instrument. Speaking for ecological economists, Herman Daly has repeatedly argued for the Tinbergen rule. Georgist economists question the validity of the rule, for if it were true, the synthetic possibilities of George's thought (reconciling the goals of efficiency and equity) would be lost.

Finally, it is important to remember that ecological and Georgist economics (and many other branches of human understanding) are not rivals for intellectual loyalty. Each contains some element of truth, which we ignore at our peril. If we are to use knowledge to solve problems, that goal can only be achieved by transcending the artificial barriers that so often stand between competing theoretical perspectives.

NOTES

1. Referring to institutional or evolutionary economics, Spash and Villena (1998, p. 26) assert that 'there has been a tendency for the institutional literature to centre upon

presenting criticisms of the neo-classical approach, rather than suggesting constructive alternatives' (cited in Ropke, 2005, p. 279). The same problem plagues other forms of heterodoxy in economics.

2.   The percentage change in energy consumption associated with 1 per cent change in gross domestic product (GDP).

3.   See also *A Strategy for Growth of Electrical Energy in India*, Department of Atomic Energy (India), http://dae.nic.in/?q=node/123 (accessed 16 December 2015).

4.   See also Zhang and Zheng (2008, p. 99).

5.   However, the decline in energy elasticity has been due more to changes in the fuel mix – shifting from coal to petroleum and natural gas – than to energy-conserving technical innovation. As oil and gas prices rise, and substitution becomes more costly, elasticities will presumably decline more slowly (Kaufman, 1992).

6.   The fact that energy intensity (energy use per unit of income) is more than twice as high as in developing countries attests to the importance of institutions, particularly accurate market signals, in achieving economic efficiency (Energy Information Agency, 2004, p. 25, figure 25).

7.   Ecological economists are not the only ones to question whether growth can continue without a commensurate increase in energy consumption. Neoclassical economists also tend to think of productivity in physical terms and presume that growth is tied to cheap energy. The connection between the 'oil price shocks' of 1974 and 1979 and subsequent recessions became an article of faith among most economists. However, the evidence does not bear out that conclusion. Examining disaggregated industry data for the United States, Germany, Japan and the United Kingdom, Bohi found these countries experienced varying consequences from the 1973–74 and 1979–80 shocks. For example, Japan managed to avoid a recession after the 1979–80 oil price shock even though the other three countries did not. In addition, employment and capital formation were no more affected in energy-intensive sectors of the four economies than other sectors. Rather than oil shocks causing unemployment and other symptoms of recession, Bohi concluded that restrictive macroeconomic policies, designed to prevent inflation, were responsible (Bohi, 1989, 1991; Bohi and Toman, 1996, pp. 50–51; Helliwell, 1988). Brazil's experience also contradicted common sense expectations during the oil price shocks (Wachsmann et al., 2009).

8.   Another example of an indirect effect is the rise in death rates that resulted from limiting speed limits on interstate highways to 55 miles per hour from 1974 to 1995. The paradox is solved if one considers increased use of two-lane rural highways, which are more dangerous than divided highways. The net effects of the 55 mph limit are hotly contested, and my aim is not to enter the debate. My point is simply that shifts among types of highways *may* have led to counterintuitive consequences, thus exemplifying an indirect effect. It also reveals that indirect effects are often contrary to common sense.

9.   A mathematical demonstration of the effects of land-value taxation on development can be found in Tideman (1999). Intuitively, the response to a tax on site values can be seen in the following example. If a vacant one-acre parcel at the center of the city is worth $10 million, the annual rental value of the land will be about $300 000. Imagine the land is currently occupied by a blacktop parking lot (no structure) yielding $180 000 per year (about $500 per day) or an abandoned building yielding no revenue. The owner may continue this way indefinitely, even though the owner loses the opportunity cost of developing the site or selling to someone else. Market forces will not drive out the inefficient owner who underutilizes the site. However, if the local government imposes a tax of just 6 percent on the land, the market price of the lot will fall to $3.33 million (through a capitalization process), and the tax will be $200 000 per year. Whether the land is used as a parking lot or an abandoned building, the owner will have to expend cash to keep it. Either way, the tax will effectively force the owner to build or sell.

10.   Some economists believe the tax on land is purely neutral. They agree that a reduced tax on buildings will encourage development, but they doubt that a tax on bare land would promote development. They argue that any tax on infra-marginal income will

not affect behavior. That view presupposes (1) that the only relevant incentive from a tax is the price effect, not the income or liquidity effects, and (2) that all property is currently developed to its highest and best use. The second premise is decisive. This precisely parallels a debate in the 1990s between engineers and economists over whether a tax on energy use would encourage investments in energy conservation. Economists argued that a tax would not promote conservation because profitable cost-saving investments would have been made already. Operations research engineers had plenty of anecdotal evidence of tens or hundreds of millions of dollars of untapped conservation investments with internal rates of return from 20 percent to 50 percent per year. In the end, theory won out over empirical evidence. However, it was the wrong theory. Herbert Simon's concept of 'satisficing' or 'bounded rationality' suggests that economic actors do not seek out all profit-making opportunities, but instead optimize solely within a restricted set of options (by 'look[ing] for satisfactory choices instead of optimal ones') (Simon, 1979, p. 501). In the absence of external pressure (competition or taxes), managers and property owners do *not* consider all opportunity costs and do *not* make the effort to take advantage of all profitable opportunities. As a result, when a tax is applied, managers seek to reduce the tax as efficiently as possible by investing in high-yield energy conservation projects (in the case of an energy tax) or by investing in income-yielding development (in the case of a tax on site values). That is why both of those taxes have beneficial social effects.

11. Only some 6 percent of the soils in the Amazon basin do not offer serious limitations to agriculture (Fearnside, 1990).

12. Gaffney (1970) has explored a variety of second- and third-order effects of Georgist policy. The increase in the turnover of capital as a result of site value taxation is one of his most original and distinctive contributions. Briefly, the tax on site values works in the following manner. A high tax rate would encourage more efficient use of urban sites, which would entail shorter periods between renovation or rebuilding on any site. First, that would mean building on vacant buildable sites, which does not include parks. Vacant lots constitute anywhere from 5 percent to 25 percent of a city's area. Second, it would encourage restoring of old buildings or tearing them down and building new ones. Higher turnover of capital simply means more construction per unit area per year. That results directly in more jobs for construction and maintenance, and other secondary jobs, the number depending on the local multiplier effect (which would also rise because less money would leak out as rent to absentee landlords in other jurisdictions). The basic principle is that long-lived capital is labor-saving; short-lived capital (based on high turnover) increases the demand for labor. Greater demand for labor strengthens the power of labor and increases opportunities for the average member of society.

13. See, however, Vatn (Chapter 5), Gowdy (Chapter 6) in this volume for arguments in favor of cooperation, collective action and common ownership. Such arguments are increasingly common among ecological economists.

14. It is not an accident that this essay by Hardin appears in a book edited by a Georgist. In private correspondence with the editor, reproduced on page viii of the volume, Hardin wrote, 'I have known . . . of Henry George's work for a long time and always thought it a shame that he could not have been born two centuries earlier and laid out the ground rules for the development of the New World.' (Here Hardin ignores the fact that the optimist William Godwin, a precursor in some ways of George, was the foil against which Thomas Malthus wrote in the late eighteenth century. Even John Locke, writing two centuries before George in his *Second Treatise*, betrayed more sympathy for universal claims on the commons than Hardin.)

15. Their treatment does not make the commons *merely* an extension of private property. Their work shows common property is in fact superior to private ownership in managing resources with mobility (herds of land animals, fisheries, groundwater and so on) or resources requiring long-term institutional stewardship based on local knowledge systems. My aim is not to denigrate work on common property. My purpose is solely to indicate the limits of its applicability.

16. In the United States, income inequality accounts for about one quarter of the difference in mortality rates between states, after controlling for differences in state median income. See Kennedy et al. (1996) and correction in *British Medical Journal* (1996, **312**, p. 1194). See also Vatn (Chapter 5) in this volume.

17. In reference to the field of ecological economics, Ropke (2005, p. 267) says: 'Considering the interests of future generations, the scale of the economy has to be limited, and therefore, the issue of *equity and distribution* comes to the fore. Because of the environmental limits, the poor cannot be cared for by continuing economic growth, so the ethical challenge to take care of other human beings calls for an increased focus on redistribution.' This statement accurately reflects an ongoing concern of Daly, but it is hard to find any evidence of it among ecological economists outside his writing.

18. 'If we must stop aggregate growth because it is uneconomic, then how do we deal with poverty in the SSE [steady-state economy]? The simple answer is by redistribution – by limits to the range of permissible inequality, by a minimum income *and* a maximum income' (Daly, 2008, p. 4, emphasis in original).

19. 'The regressivity of . . . a consumption tax could be offset by spending the proceeds progressively, by the limited range of inequality [between permissible upper and lower incomes], and by the fact that the mafia and other former income tax cheaters would have to pay it. Cap-auction–trade systems will also increase government revenue, and auction revenue can be distributed progressively' (Daly, 2008, p. 8).

20. The idea of a one-to-ten ratio of low to high incomes is discussed as the desired aim of political evolution, but not a currently acceptable proposal.

21. Any policy that raises consumer prices functions as an excise tax. An excise tax is steeply regressive with respect to current income, and somewhat regressive with respect to permanent income.

22. However, Daly and Farley (2010) recognize the potential for speculation and rent capture with cap-and-trade schemes, and call instead for a system of 'cap and rent,' based on frequent auctions and no subsequent trading.

23. Again, in his 2010 textbook, Daly repeatedly discusses rent taxation as a policy for promoting the just distribution of wealth and resources, explicitly citing Henry George. See below for a discussion of the problems associated with Daly's insistence that each policy instrument should be associated with only one goal.

24. Site value taxation is not the only policy prescription that derives from Georgist analysis. Another major source of unearned income stems from the monopoly power created by patents and copyrights. George himself favored copyrights but believed that patents should be eliminated. A more balanced Georgist approach to intellectual property would be to protect all forms of it as private property but to limit the monopoly aspects of it to a few years (perhaps five or ten), then to impose a progressively increasing fee that would either encourage licensing of the information or transfer into the public domain. The aim should be to balance the private aspect of innovation (the 'romantic' idea of single authorship of ideas) with the social nature of intellectual creation. This would also raise the cost of holding information off the market that would be socially beneficial if more widely available.

25. A good starting point is Harrison (1998). Also see numerous articles by Mason Gaffney at www.masongaffney.org (accessed 12 December 2015) and work on deadweight losses of taxes on productivity by Nicolaus Tideman and Florenz Plassman (in Harrison, 1998, pp. 146–74).

26. Why then have societies not shifted all taxes directly to the base of site values and bypassed all of the deadweight loss associated with other taxes? The answer lies in the distribution of burdens. A tax on site values falls solely on landowners. (Tax shifting depends on some degree of elasticity of supply.) A tax on wages or consumption falls on others as well as the landowner, and enhances the relative power of landowners. To begin to understand the politics of competing tax bases in actual historical conditions, one might compare the New England democracy that relied heavily on the property tax since the seventeenth century with the Southern plantation economy that impoverished

working people by avoiding direct taxation of property. The landed aristocracy of Latin America, like the slaveocracy of the southeastern United States, also assiduously avoided taxes on land, and still does.

27. A tax on the market price of land leads to a reduction of that price and thus to the value of the asset for those who own it. The price, after tax is, Price = Annual Rent/(real interest rate + tax rate). If the real interest rate is 3 percent, then a tax of 12 percent on the price of land will reduce the price by approximately 83 percent (because x/0.15 is approximately 83 percent less than x/0.03) relative to a situation in which there is no tax. What remains will be capitalized as the market price at which land would trade. If the tax rate on site values were 27 percent, the tax would capture about 90 percent of the rent, and market price would be 10 percent of the price in the absence of any tax.

28. The reader should be mindful that 90–95 percent of site values is concentrated in urban areas, not in the vast expanses of farms and forests, which have low value per acre. A single acre of land in midtown Manhattan has the same market value as a thousand acres of Midwestern farmland.

29. Most economists assume that land is not of great significance in an industrial or information-based economy. That bias is reinforced by official statistics, which are based on faulty methodology. To begin with, no official estimate of economic rent takes into account the value of land that is captured by existing taxes. That factor alone means the estimates are inaccurate not just marginally, but by one or two orders of magnitude. Gaffney (2009) discusses other aspects of the deeply flawed methodology by which the national income accounts and studies by Raymond Goldsmith have estimated aggregate rent.

30. I estimated that ratio as part of a project carried out at Redefining Progress in 1995, in which we sought to estimate the capacity of all 'green taxes' to replace existing taxes in the state of California. The potential revenues from site value taxes were larger than all other environmental taxes (air, water pollution, water rights, congestion pricing, noise, solid waste) by an order of magnitude. Our report was never published since the foundation that financed the preliminary work is financed almost entirely from site rents and presumably did not like our conclusions; so they cut off funding. The method for estimating site values involved working from official statistics of property value in California and adjusting for biases in assessment related to Proposition 13, a 1978 amendment to the Californian Constitution that placed limits on both assessed value and tax rates of real property. Extrapolating those findings to a national level involves estimating the capitalized value of the impact of all federal taxes on site values. (This is a crucial step that has been left out of most other efforts to estimate the taxable capacity of sites.) I readily acknowledge the imprecise nature of the results, but I would contend that they are more accurate in terms of order of magnitude than official estimates or Goldsmith's estimates, on which so many economists rely. As Keynes is reported to have said, 'It is better to be vaguely right than precisely wrong.' (The actual source for this statement was probably Wildon Carr, a philosopher who was a contemporary of Keynes.)

31. See Kennickell (2006, p. 10, table 4) for the Gini coefficient for wealth in the United States.

32. An exception is the discussion of problems associated with unequal power in Daly and Farley (2010, p. 447).

33. According to Gaffney (1976, pp. 113–14), 'Factor mix also tends to change with size of business and wealth of individuals. As a broad statistical truth, the application of labor to property tends to be regressive. The larger holdings use less labor per unit of property value.' Since large firms use more site value on average than smaller firms (measured by net worth) to generate a dollar of income, a tax on site values would fall more heavily on large firms than small ones. That would cause large firms to sell some of their landholdings to smaller firms that use land more intensively. One of Gaffney's main points in this essay, however, is that reduced taxes on labor have a similar effect by encouraging higher turnover of capital per unit of land and labor, thereby creating an economic advantage for firms that are relatively small and labor-intensive.

34. Eckholm's (1976) story is derived from an account in Thomas (1974, p. 307).
35. TANSTAAFL is the acronym for 'There ain't no such thing as a free lunch.'
36. The reference is to Tinbergen (1952).
37. Perhaps this subdivided world would make sense if reality were comprised of 'windowless monads' (as Leibniz proposed) or if reality operated according to the disjointed empiricism of Hume or the Ding-an-sich presupposition of Kant, but in the Whiteheadian worldview of organic inter-connections, which was the leitmotif of *For the Common Good*, that sort of splintering of reality is problematic.

REFERENCES

Bohi, D.R. (1989), *Energy Price Shocks and Macroeconomic Performance*, Washington, DC: Resources for the Future.
Bohi, D.R. (1991), 'On the macroeconomic effects of energy price shocks', *Resources and Energy*, **13**, 145–62.
Bohi, D.R. and M.A. Toman (1996), *The Economics of Energy Security*, Boston, MA: Kluwer Academic.
Daly, H.E. (1991), 'Towards an environmental macroeconomics', *Land Economics*, **67** (2), 257–8.
Daly, H.E. (2008), *A Steady-state Economy*, London: Sustainable Development Commission, available at http://www.sd-commission.org.uk/data/files/publications/Herman_Daly_thinkpiece.pdf (accesssed 12 December 2015).
Daly, H.E. and J.B. Cobb, Jr (1994), *For the Common Good*, Boston, 2nd edn, MA: Beacon Press.
Daly, H.E. and J. Farley (2010), *Ecological Economics: Principles and Applications*, Washington, DC: Island Press.
Daly, H.E. and K.N. Townsend (1993), *Valuing the Earth: Economics, Ecology, Ethics*, Cambridge, MA: MIT Press.
Daniels, N., B. Kennedy and I. Kawachi (1999), 'Why justice is good for our health: the social determinants of health inequalities', *Daedelus*, **128** (4), 215–51.
Eckholm, E. (1976), *Losing Ground*, New York: W.W. Norton.
Energy Information Agency (1995), *International Energy Outlook*, US Department of Energy.
Energy Information Agency (2004), *International Energy Outlook*, US Department of Energy.
Fang, J.M. and J.C. Chen (2007), 'Empirical analysis of CO_2 emissions and GDP relationships in OECD countries', *Sci-Tech Policy Review*, **1** (1), 37–60.
Fearnside, P. (1990), 'Reconsideração do cultivo contínuo na Amazônia', *Revista Brasileira de Biologia*, **50** (4), 833–40.
Gaffney, M. (1970), 'Tax-induced slow turnover of capital, I.', *American Journal of Economics and Sociology*, **29** (1), 25–32.
Gaffney, M. (1976), 'Toward full employment with limited land and capital', in A. Lynn, Jr (ed.), *Property Taxation, Land Use and Public Policy*, Madison, WI: University of Wisconsin Press, pp. 99–166.
Gaffney, M. (2009), 'The hidden taxable capacity of land: enough and to spare', *International Journal of Social Economics*, **36** (4), 328–411.
Gately, D. and H.G. Huntington (2001), 'The asymmetric effects of changes in

price and income on energy and oil demand', *Working Papers 01-01*, C.V. Starr Center for Applied Economics, New York University.

George, H. (1879), *Progress and Poverty*, reprinted in 1979, New York: Robert Schalkenbach Foundation, available at http://schalkenbach.org/library/henry-george/p+p/ppcont.html (accessed 12 December 2015).

Hardin, G. (1968), 'Tragedy of the commons', *Science*, **162**, 1243–8.

Hardin, G. (1991), 'Tragedy of the *unmanaged* commons: population and the disguises of providence', in R.V. Andelson (ed.), *Commons Without Tragedy*, London: Shepheard-Walwyn, pp. 162–85.

Harrison, F. (ed.) (1998), *The Losses of Nations*, London: Shepheard-Walwyn.

Helliwell, J.F. (1988), 'Comparative macroeconomics of stagflation', *Journal of Economic Literature*, **26**, 1–28.

Howarth, R.B. (1998), 'An overlapping generations model of climate-economy interactions', *Scandinavian Journal of Economics*, **100**, 575–91.

Howarth, R.B. and R.B. Norgaard (1990), 'Intergenerational resource rights, efficiency, and social optimality', *Land Economics*, **66** (1), 1–11.

Howarth, R.B. and R.B. Norgaard (1995), 'Intergenerational choices under global environmental change', in D.W. Bromley (ed.), *Handbook of Environmental Economics*, Oxford: Basil Blackwell, pp. 111–38.

Kaufman, R.K. (1992), 'A biophysical analysis of the energy/real GDP ratio: implications for substitution and technical change', *Ecological Economics*, **6**, 35–56.

Kennedy, B.P., I. Kawachi and D. Prothrow-Stith (1996), 'Income distribution and mortality: cross-sectional ecological study of the Robin Hood index in the United States', *British Medical Journal*, **312**, 1004–7.

Kennickell, A.B. (2006), *Currents and Undercurrents: Changes in the Distribution of Wealth, 1989–2004*, Washington, DC: Federal Reserve Board, available at http://www.federalreserve.gov/Pubs/oss/oss2/papers/concentration.2004.5.pdf (accessed 12 December 2015).

Krishnan, N.R. (2006), 'To power 7–8% GDP growth', *Business Line*, 9 May, available at http://www.thehindubusinessline.com/2006/05/09/stories/2006050900491000.htm (accessed 12 December 2015).

Lind, R.C. (1995), 'Intergenerational equity, discounting, and the role of cost-benefit analysis in evaluating global climate policy', *Energy Policy*, **23** (4–5), 379–89.

Logan, J. (2005), 'Statement of Jeffrey Logan, Senior Energy Analyst and China Program Manager, International Energy Agency', in *EIA 2005 Annual Energy Outlook: Hearing before the Committee on Energy and Natural Resources, United States Senate, One Hundred Ninth Congress, First Session*, 3 February, Washington, DC: US Governmernt Printing Office, available at http://purl.access.gpo.gov/GPO/LPS60425 (accessed 12 December 2015).

Margulis, L. (1970), *Origin of Eukaryotic Cells: Evidence and Research Implications for a Theory of the Origin and Evolution of Microbial, Plant, and Animal Cells on the Precambrian Earth*, New Haven, CT: Yale University Press.

McNeill, W. (1998), *Plagues and Peoples*, Garden City, NY: Anchor Press.

Padilla, E. (2002), 'Intergenerational equity and sustainability', *Ecological Economics*, **41** (1), 69–83.

Ropke, I. (2005), 'Trends in the development of ecological economics from the late 1980s to the early 2000s', *Ecological Economics*, **55** (2), 262–90.

Simon, H.A. (1979), 'Rational decision making in business organizations', *American Economic Review*, **69** (4), 493–513.

Spash, C.L. and M.G. Villena (1998), 'Exploring the approach of institutional economics to the environment', *Environment Series*, **11**, Department of Land Economy, University of Cambridge.

Thomas, J.W. (1974), 'Employment creating public works programs: observations on the political and social dimensions', in E.O. Edwards (ed.), *Employment in Developing Nations*, New York: Columbia University Press, p. 307.

Tideman, N. (1999), 'Land value taxation is better than neutral: land taxes, land speculation, and the timing of development', in K.C. Wenzer (ed.), *Land Value Taxation: The Equitable and Efficient Source of Public Finance*, Armonk, NY: M.E. Sharpe, pp. 109–33.

Tinbergen, J. (1952), *On the Theory of Economic Policy*, Amsterdam: North Holland Press.

Wachsmann, U., R. Wood, M. Lenzen and R. Schaeffer (2009), 'Structural decomposition of energy use in Brazil from 1970 to 1996', *Applied Energy*, **86** (4), 578–87.

Zhang, Y. and C. Zheng (2008), 'The implications of China's rapid growth on demand for energy and mining products imported from Australia', *Economic Papers: A Journal of Applied Economics and Policy*, Economic Society of Australia, **27** (1), 95–106, available at http://onlinelibrary.wiley.com/doi/10.1111/j.1759-3441.2008.tb01029.x/abstract (accessed 16 December 2015).

11. Making money

John B. Cobb, Jr

11.1 WHAT IS MONEY?

Everyone knows that money is important. In some sense we all 'know' what it is. We have some of it in our purses or wallet and more in our bank accounts. We use it to pay for things we want. We keep some in the bank so as to be sure that we will be able to pay for things later. Since the bank will give us currency when we ask for some of our money back, we think of the money that it holds for me as being an extension of what we carry with us. The fact that generally we use checks and credit cards rather than cash does not seem significant.

Many of us have assumed that the paper money in our pockets is made by the government. We see that it consists of 'Federal Reserve notes,' but we have assumed that the Federal Reserve is part of the government. We earned it by working, and we spent some and saved some for a 'rainy day.' Basically we have understood money as a medium of exchange.

We have supposed that the bank accepts our money partly for safe keeping but also in order to lend it to others. It pays us a little interest and charges the borrowers more. That has seemed reasonable and proper. If we have quite a lot of savings, we may lend some to a business or to governments in order to receive a higher rate of interest. Obviously, this is a different function of money, but we think of it as an extension of the use as a medium of exchange.

We try, when it is not 'raining,' to spend less than we earn so as to be ready for the 'rain.' It seems that other people and organizations should do so as well. For example, we suppose that except in emergencies, businesses and governments should also stay out of debt.

Although many of us have thought in these ways, we have also seen that the real world functions quite differently. Businesses are constantly borrowing money, and national governments increase their debts year after year with no obvious harm. Most of us give up trying to understand and leave matters to the experts.

11.2   MONEY AS DEBT

Although I knew that I did not understand these things, I did not realize quite how mysterious they were until I worked with Herman Daly on what became *For the Common Good* (Daly and Cobb, 1989). We employed Whitehead's idea of 'the fallacy of misplaced concreteness' as a basis for critiquing a number of the ways that standard economic theory employs its concepts. This fallacy is to treat abstractions as if they corresponded to what is fully actual. For example, economists speak of *Homo economicus*. This term designates those aspects of human desires and activities that seem most relevant to behavior in the marketplace.[1] As long as this abstractness is fully recognized, this concept can be quite useful. But the tendency is to think that by using this abstraction, conclusions can be drawn about all human behavior in the marketplace, and even about human behavior in general. This mistakenly attributes concreteness to the abstraction. In fact, the same people who for some purposes can be understood as *Homo economicus*, for other purposes are better understood as *Homo politicus* or *Homo religiosus*. And the full actuality of individual people is not captured even when all of these abstractions are combined.

Money would seem to be an excellent illustration of the fallacy of misplaced concreteness; since we so easily view it as something that is valuable in itself, when in fact it has no 'use value' at all; so I asked Daly to draft a chapter on it. His reply was that nobody knows what money is; so he was not ready to attempt such a chapter. The book originally appeared with no discussion of money.

This seemed a striking lack in a book on economics, and it increasingly bothered me. On the other hand, this was not a topic on which I had the slightest possibility of writing the initial draft. So I twisted Daly's arm, and when we prepared a second edition, the most important change was the addition of an 'afterword' on money.

Whereas most chapters of the book are joint products so that we could not divide the book into his chapters and mine, my contribution to this 'afterword' consisted only of asking questions for clarification. The idea that money is debt was quite new to me as was the idea that commercial banks create money. My questioning led Daly to helpful clarifications, but the ideas it contains are mine only in the sense that Daly has persuaded me that they are basically true.

Daly taught me that banks can lend the same money over and over again and that in making each loan the banks increase the money supply. Of course, repayment reduces it. I now understand that the amount of money created by the loan is sufficient only to repay the principal, whereas the loan must be repaid with interest. The amount of interest may be as much as, or even more than, the loan itself.

Speaking in this way may be misleading since it does not make sense if we are considering a single loan. Obviously, the loan is not literally paid back with the money that is loaned. That money may be used to expand a business, the profits from which are used to pay both principal and interest month by month for many years. As long as the expansion of the business is successful, the owners not only make their payments but also increase their income.

To understand the problem of finding the money to pay the interest, we do better to think of all the money that the banks collectively lend in a particular year. The amount of money put in circulation is the amount of the principal of the loans. Now suppose that this amount was roughly constant year after year. In that case the amount needed to pay back the principal on all existing loans is being pumped into the economy, but there is nothing left to pay the interest. Some borrowers may have plenty with which to pay, but it is not possible that all do so. Unless additional money is pumped into the economy through additional loans, so that the money supply is growing, there will not be sufficient money in circulation for all borrowers to pay the interest on their loans, leading them to default. This means that the economy as a whole can flourish only as there is substantial growth in the money supply, created by increasing lending. This seems to work well during times of expansion. There are plenty of borrowers and banks make numerous loans, thus providing the funds by which to repay previous loans with interest.

On the other hand, when the new money does not suffice for repayment with interest, loans are not repaid. Banks respond by tightening credit. The money supply ceases to grow, and more loans fail. The dependence of the economy on bank loans causes a recession to feed upon itself, just as growth stimulates growth. In other words, creation of money by banks exacerbates the problems of cyclical growth and contraction.

Daly has emphasized that the human economy operates in the context of the inclusive planetary economy. The latter is not growing. Much increase in product is possible by technological improvements *without* increasing use of planetary resources. Standard economics teaches that scarcity leads to rising prices and this triggers technological improvements or substitution of more plentiful resources. Often this works, but there are limits, and price signals do not guarantee wisdom in replacing scarce supplies.

The reaching and surpassing of limits is in the news today with respect to oil. The demand for oil rises, but to increase production in order to meet the demand it is necessary to extract dirtier, less accessible oil with ever-higher environmental costs. Part of the problem is temporary, due to

political and military disturbances, for example. Also some oil is being left
alone for environmental reasons. But few now question that supply will be
unable to keep up with growing demand. The price is rising, and over the
next years will almost certainly rise more. Some who have seen this coming
have begun seeking substitutes and finding technological solutions. The
pace now quickens.

However, the response thus far illustrates the tendency to solve one
problem while creating others. Oil can be made from crops such as corn.
The enthusiasm for ethanol has led to a shift from producing crops for
food to producing crops for ethanol. But this 'solution' to the problem of
'peak oil' has precipitated or exacerbated the shortage of food. Ironically,
in the past, food shortages were avoided by the Green Revolution, which
has greatly increased the use of petroleum in agriculture. Now so much oil
is used in the farming by which ethanol is produced that the net gain in fuel
is not impressive, while the reduction in food production is causing vast
suffering among the global poor.

The evidence strongly supports Daly's insistence on the reality of limits
against the standard economic view of inexhaustibility of resources.
Almost everyone now recognizes also that the capacity of sinks to deal
with our wastes has already been exhausted in so far as the gases responsible for global warming are concerned. There are limits to how much the
human economy can grow. The level of consumption of Americans could
not possibly be generalized to the global human population. It is true that
there are types of economic growth that are not limited, but to aim at
growth in general hastens the coming of catastrophe. The proper goal is
'development' understood as the real improvement of the situation.

Daly has recognized that our economy as currently organized requires
growth. He comments that it is like an airplane that has to move in order
to stay in the air. But he argues that there could be an economy like a
helicopter, one that could stay still while meeting all human needs. As I
have begun to understand the monetary system, I have become convinced
that this must be radically changed if we are to move toward a steady-state
economy.

11.3   IS THERE AN ALTERNATIVE?

Currently almost all the creation of money is by commercial banks lending
money into existence. This is why Daly and others have said that, today,
money is debt. The banks must continuously increase the money supply in
order for this system to work. That requires growth. If banks were nationalized so that the profit from creating money came into the government's

coffers, there might be many advantages. But if the banks continued to charge interest, the system would still require growth. The goal of a steady-state economy could still not be reached.

There has always been another way in which the money supply can be increased. That is by the government spending new money into existence. This money is not to be repaid and requires no interest. If the government decides to improve the infrastructure, for example, it can pay those who do the work and supply the material with new money. There is no increase in debt and hence no requirement of interest. It is worth noting that the US Federal government is essentially spending money into existence right now, albeit in a roundabout fashion. Under its quantitative easing policy, the Federal Reserve is currently (March 2014) buying about $40 billion per month in US Treasury notes. The Federal government must pay these back with interest, but by law, the Fed returns 94 percent of all profits to the US government. In effect, the Fed is helping the US government spend money into existence.

This does not mean that taxes are never needed. If the government spends more money into existence than is required by the economy, there will be inflation. Some governments have caused runaway inflation in this way. Just as repaying a loan reduces the money supply loaned into existence by banks, paying taxes reduces the money supply spent into existence by government. There is then a need for taxes to avoid inflation. They can also be used for redistributive purposes. Taxes can also discourage use of scarce resources and encourage the development of alternatives. But to whatever extent the increase of the money supply by the banks is reduced, a similar increase in government spending of new money is not inflationary. Private banks have reduced their lending since the start of the 2007 financial crisis, while continuing to collect loan repayments to the extent possible, thus reducing the money supply. This explains why the Fed's quantitative easing policies in recent years have not caused inflation. Further, since this money is interest-free, there is no need to expand the money supply in order to provide funds for future payments.

To overcome the problems caused by the payment of interest on loans, one might propose that we follow the biblical mandate and forbid all interest. However, there will always be a need for borrowing money, and despite the problems connected with it, there are good reasons for charging the borrower interest.

Maintaining a system in which money is loaned at interest does not have to mean continuing to create money in this way. It is possible for people to pool their surplus funds for the purpose of lending them at interest, and it is possible for institutions to manage these. This does not increase the money supply. Limiting their loans to the amount of their deposits would not end the need for the creation of new money to pay the interest. But it would avoid the need to pay interest on the money borrowed to pay the interest. The money expansion would be interest-free. Over time this would reduce the need to borrow, or at least it would stabilize this need at a more or less constant level. A financial system of this sort could operate within a steady-state economy.

Lending institutions of this kind could be run by the government, and around the world many are. However, one argument against national-izing all banks is that then all borrowing would have to be from one source, the government. Favoring those who support the government would probably follow. In money-lending, as in other fields, competition is desirable.

Governments at all level can participate in creating money. North Dakota has a state bank, and currently a number of other states are con-sidering creating such banks. Ellen Brown leads a national movement that presents state banks as a solution to many of the financial problems that plague most of the other states.

There are also experiments in local currencies that operate outside the dollar system altogether. When we consider the possible collapse of the current financial system, experiments like these assume an importance far beyond their current size. They offer a way of making exchange pos-sible beyond barter when the official currency loses its usefulness or is too scarce.

However, I will focus this discussion on what can be done at the national level to help governments at other levels. Advocates of shifting away from the debt economy propose that the Federal government make long-term loans to state and local governments, especially for infrastructure, without interest.

Currently local governments recognize many needs that they cannot afford to fulfill. The infrastructure backlog grows steadily. Interest-free Federal loans would quickly reverse this unsustainable situation. This would also make it possible to employ many of the now jobless in socially needed work.

For example, a city may see the need for a subway to reduce depend-ence on automobiles and reduce congestion. Suppose the cost will be a billion dollars, and revenues can be expected to be sufficient to make pay-ments of $30 million a year. A commercial loan over 20 years at 6 percent will require annual payments of $85 million. The city cannot afford the subway even if economists calculate that the citizens will save more than that from reduced need for private cars, reduced pollution and time saved. If, however, the national government provides a 50-year loan charging only the cost of managing the loan, payments will be closer to $20 million a year. The subway can be built with money that is gradually spent into existence. (I depend for these figures on Priestman, 2008, p. 4.)

11.4   THE STORY OF MONEY CREATION IN NORTH AMERICA

The questions about who creates money and how it is created should be a part of mainstream political discussion. In this chapter I will supplement what I learned from Daly with what I have learned from Ellen Hodgson Brown's *The Web of Debt* (Brown, 2008) about how money creation in the United States came to be completely privatized and, therefore, how money came to be equivalent to debt. If a financial system in which money is debt cannot be fitted into a steady-state economy, an alternative should be considered.

Brown (2008) shows that in the earlier history of the European settlement in North America, the importance of how money was created was much more widely recognized than it is now. Some of the American colonies before the Revolutionary War created money and attained considerable prosperity thereby. Benjamin Franklin was a major proponent of this style of financing government expenditures. In 1764 the Bank of England persuaded the British Parliament to forbid the colonies to issue their own money. This had severe economic effects, which had more to do with revolutionary feeling than the small tax on tea.

The Continental Congress financed the American Revolution by creating money. In the end, the Continental currency lost its value, and this means of financing governmental expenditures lost favor. 'Not worth a Continental' became a common description of what was worthless. However, some who have studied what happened note that part of the British strategy was to destroy the value of the Continental currency by flooding the market with counterfeit. This strategy certainly made a major contribution to the decline of the value of the currency.

Abraham Lincoln financed the Civil War by issuing greenbacks. This was 'fiat' money, similar to that issued by the Continental Congress. It was spent into existence and created no debt. Again there was considerable inflation during the war, but whether inflation would have been less if Lincoln had borrowed the money from banks instead is by no means clear. Since during war much productive facility is directed away from the general economy, some inflation is hard to avoid.

Opponents of 'greenbacks' were aided by the 'common sense' view, which they cultivated and promoted, that money should be backed up by some physical reality with real value. Gold was the preferred back-up of the banks. Because of the scarcity of gold, money creation was restricted. A major political issue was whether the United States should shift from the gold standard to the silver standard. William Jennings Bryan campaigned tirelessly for this change that, he thought, probably correctly, would make money more plentiful and ordinary people more prosperous.

Public opinion had been against a central bank, but a banking crisis in 1907 opened the question to serious discussion. This crisis may have been manipulated by the bankers themselves. In any case, to take advantage of the new public mood, in 1910 leading bankers met on Jekyll Island and drafted proposals for a central bank that would be largely controlled by Wall Street. However, neither Congress nor the president was ready to implement the plan at that time. Woodrow Wilson was friendlier to banking interests; so his election in 1912, also partly engineered by the bankers, created a more favorable situation.

Congressional support depended on approval by Bryan who was deeply suspicious of the bankers. The bankers proposed a new bill just before Christmas in 1913. Its language was very technical and confusing, and Bryan was duped into thinking that 'the right of the government to issue money is not surrendered to the banks; the control of the money so issued is not relinquished by the government' (Brown, 2008, p. 125). With his support, 'the Federal Reserve Act' was passed on 22 December 1913. It was signed by Wilson the next day. At the time, Wilson did not fully understand the implications of the bill. Before he died, he said: 'I have unwittingly ruined my country' (Brown, 2008, p. 126).

Bryan and Wilson are not the only ones who have been misled into thinking that the Federal Reserve Bank is an arm of the US government. In fact, it consists of 12 regional banks owned by the commercial banks in each region. These banks jointly own the whole system. The Federal Reserve Bank of New York owns 53 percent of the stock, and of course the Federal Reserve Bank of New York is controlled by the largest banks there.

What led Bryan to think that the creation of this system did not transfer power over the economy to the commercial banks was in part that the Secretary of the Treasury and the Comptroller of the Currency both sat on the Board. In fact, commercial banking interests were clearly in control.

Franklin Roosevelt blamed the banks in large part for the Depression and changed this pattern of governance of the Federal Reserve. He replaced the existing structure with a seven-member board of governors appointed by the president. This in principle gives the elected administration considerable power, although to protect the board from undue political influence, members were appointed for 14-year terms. Roosevelt himself used his power to appoint persons who would not undercut his program, and assuming that the Board would work with him, he increased its powers.

There were congressmen at the time who called vigorously for the issuance of money by the Federal Treasury to replace borrowing from the banks. Roosevelt, however, did not use the legal power of the Treasury to spend money into existence as had the Continental Congress and Lincoln. Instead, following the desire of the banks, he financed his efforts to spend the nation out of depression by taxes and borrowing. This pattern has been followed by subsequent administrations and, as a result, the national debt, which was $15 billion in 1931, nearly 15 percent of gross domestic product (GDP), is now approaching $17 trillion in 2013, or nearly 75 percent of GDP. Roosevelt's acts left the Federal Reserve Board strengthened, but he failed to overcome its close connection with the New York banks.

No subsequent administration has tried to spend money into existence instead of borrowing from the banks and paying them interest, although there are indications that Kennedy contemplated some such move shortly before his assassination. In any case, one of the first acts of Johnson on assuming the presidency after Kennedy's assassination was to take the government completely out of the money-making business by replacing all Treasury notes with those of the Federal Reserve System. The take-over by the banks was then complete.

The Bank of Canada, in contrast, is an agency of the government. Through it, Canada paid the costs of World War II in large part by creating money, and it financed social programs in the subsequent years in the same way. However, the influence of the banks has led to severely circumscribing governmental money creation in Canada as well, so that the government's ability to maintain the services that it earlier offered is in question. Bankers complain that for the government to spend money into existence is inflationary, and they have persuaded the legislature to limit this practice.

Once the government turns over money creation to the banks, it becomes one borrower among others. However, its debt is endlessly rolled over. The problem is only that the interest must be paid. If the budget had not vastly expanded, it would have been totally overwhelmed by payment of interest on the national debt. Here again the debt system requires a growing economy in order to continue. Even so, the cost of interest payments is growing more rapidly than either the economy as a whole or the budget as a whole.

Matters are further complicated by the fact that more and more of the debt is owed to other countries, which thereby gain considerable power over our national finances. If China stopped buying US debt, and especially if it unloaded its huge holdings, the results would be highly inflationary. The dollar would rapidly lose much of its value. Since the value of Chinese holdings would shrink with the dollar, and since the United States would no longer be able to buy the products of Chinese factories, China is not eager to ruin us. But it has a huge threat to hold over our heads in the power games that nations play. Also, the interest on the debt exacerbates the American balance of payments deficit.

11.5   CONCLUSIONS

I have argued that ending the power of the banks to create money and reassuming the government's ability to do so is required in order move toward a steady-state economy. Obviously that argument will not move many, especially among economists, to support this change. As of now, the steady-state economy does not have a mass following!

For this reason it is important to emphasize that there are other reasons for making this move. Massively increasing the national debt each year is not sustainable. Neither is the neglect of the nation's infrastructure. Nor, I think, is the concentration of wealth in fewer and fewer hands. If it became widely recognized that these problems are caused, or at least exacerbated, by the privatization of the creation of money, the possibility of governments retrieving that power might become a topic of public debate. That would be a gain. If the financial condition of the nation becomes sufficiently critical, even the national administration might lead in taking the needed steps.

Many might favor this move precisely for the sake of renewing the growth of the economy. The question of how to use the new economic possibilities would be a quite separate issue. Nevertheless, the situation would be far more favorable for this second discussion. At least the outlines of the further changes that would be needed for this purpose would be discernible in that context. In a world in which the consequence of transgressing limits has become inescapably visible, there would be a chance of getting a hearing for these next steps.

NOTE

1.   See Vatn (Chapter 5 of this volume), Gowdy (Chapter 6) and Rees (Chapter 7) for further discussions on *Homo economicus* and human behavior.

REFERENCES

Brown, E.H. (2008), *The Web of Debt: The Shocking Truth About Our Money System and How We Can Break Free*, Baton Rouge, LA: Third Millennium Press.

Daly, H.E. and J. Cobb (1989), *For the Common Good: Redirecting the Economy Toward Community, the Environment, and a Sustainable Future*, Boston, MA: Beacon Press.

Priestman, R. (2008), 'Municipal cash crunch', *COMER (Journal of the Committee on Monetary and Economic Reform)*, **20** (6), 4.

PART V

The steady-state economy

12. The steady-state economy

Peter A. Victor

12.1 INTRODUCTION

Among Herman Daly's many contributions to ecological economics none is likely to have a greater and more lasting significance than his analysis of and advocacy for a steady-state economy. As is typical of so much of his work, Professor Daly has been inspired by and built on the work of predecessors including most notably John Stuart Mill, Frederic Soddy and Nicholas Georgescu-Roegen. But he has also brought his own imagination and insights as well as his remarkable capacity for expressing complex ideas in simple terms. It is fair to say that he has virtually single-handedly ensured that the steady-state economy remains an alternative to be considered in discussions of the future possibilities for the economy and society.

In this chapter we trace the main strands of the history of the steady-state economy. In summarizing the ideas of various writers we consider their definitions of a steady-state economy, noting what is to be held steady, the case they make for a steady-state economy and their proposals for policies and operational principles, to use Professor Daly's phrase.

This historical review of a steady-state economy provides the context for an account of this author's investigations into the macroeconomic conditions for a steady-state economy, based on several simulation models, two of which are highlighted in this chapter. The first is a simple model of the US economy in which long-range (100-year) scenarios are explored showing relationships between economic growth, energy prices and possible transitions from non-renewable energy sources to renewable ones. The second model is a more detailed, medium-term (30-year) simulation model of the Canadian economy that generates macroeconomic scenarios in which the rate of economic growth is reduced ultimately to zero but where important economic, social, environmental and fiscal objectives are achieved.

Many questions about steady-state economics remain including, for example, its compatibility with capitalism in one form or another. As we proceed further into the twenty-first century we will have to address these questions or face the unpalatable consequences of striving for continued economic growth in a world that mounting evidence shows is being stressed beyond its limits. Fortunately, with the contributions of Professor Daly and others as a springboard we have a fighting chance for success.

12.2 A SHORT HISTORY OF THE STEADY-STATE ECONOMY

John Stuart Mill was not the first economist to write about the steady-state economy (which he called the stationary state), but he was among the first to contemplate it with pleasure rather than distaste as Adam Smith, Thomas Malthus and David Ricardo had done before. In his *Principles of Political Economy* first published in 1848 (Mill, 1848 [1970]), Mill devoted an entire chapter to the stationary state defined by him as 'a stationary condition of capital and population', which he pointed out did not imply a 'stationary state of human improvement' (Mill, 1848 [1970], p. 116). According to Mill, 'in the richest and most prosperous countries' the arrival of the stationary state would soon follow 'if no further improvements were made in the productive arts, and if there were a suspension of the overflow of capital from those countries into the uncultivated or ill-cultivated regions of the earth' (Mill, 1848 [1970], p. 111).

Mill regarded the prospect of the stationary state positively for several reasons that resonate today and which have found their way into more current treatments, including those by Professor Daly. In his own much quoted, eloquent language Mill writes:

> I am not charmed with the ideal of life held out by those who think that the normal state of human beings is that of struggling to get on; that the trampling, crushing, elbowing, and treading on each other's heels, which form the existing type of social life, are the most desirable lot of human kind, or anything but the disagreeable symptoms of one of the phases of industrial progress . . . the best state for human nature is that which, while no one is poor, no one desires to be richer, nor has any reason to fear being thrust back, by the efforts of others to push themselves forward. (Mill, 1848 [1970], pp. 113–14)

Mill was careful to note that in the 'backward countries . . . increased production is still an important object' and argued that 'in those most advanced, what is economically needed is a better distribution, of which one indispensable means is stricter restraint on population' (Mill, 1848 [1970], p. 114). However, he gave few details of how such restraint was to be implemented.

In making the case for the stationary state Mill stressed the disadvantages of too many people even if they enjoy a good material living standard. 'A population may be too crowded, though all be amply supplied with food and raiment. It is not good for man to be kept perforce at all times in the presence of his species. A world from which solitude is extirpated, is a very poor ideal . . .' (Mill, 1848 [1970], p. 115). One can only wonder what Mill would say if confronted with a world of over seven billion rising to more than nine billion human inhabitants, a large and increasing proportion of which are in continuous electronic communication.

With respect to the stationary state, technology (which Mill called the 'industrial arts') and time spent working, Mill anticipated later writers when he said:

> there would be . . . as much room for improving the Art of Living, and much more likelihood of its being improved, when minds ceased to be engrossed by the art of getting on. Even the industrial arts might be as earnestly and as successfully cultivated, with this sole difference, that instead of serving no purpose but the increase of wealth, industrial improvements would produce their legitimate effect, that of abridging labour. (Mill, 1848 [1970], p. 116)

It would be a considerable stretch to say that Mill anticipated much of the current environmental arguments for a steady-state economy that have become so central among more recent contributors. Yet we are reminded of such modern analytical tools as the ecological footprint (Wackernagel and Rees, 1996) and the human appropriation of the net products of photosynthesis (HANPP) (Haberl et al., 2007) when Mill wrote that there is not

> much satisfaction in contemplating the world with nothing left to the spontaneous activity of nature; with every rood of land brought into cultivation, which is capable of growing food for human beings; every flowery waste or natural pasture ploughed up, all quadrupeds or birds which are not domesticated for man's use exterminated as rivals for his food, every hedgerow or superfluous tree rooted out, and scarcely a place left where a wild shrub or flower could grow without being eradicated as a weed in the name of improved agriculture . . . (Mill, 1848 [1970], p. 116)

Mill concluded his remarkable chapter on the stationary state with a thought for the future saying, 'I sincerely hope, for the sake of posterity, that they [the population] will be content to be stationary, long before necessity compels them to it' (Mill, 1848 [1970], p. 116).

Karl Marx is far more well known for his analysis of capitalism and his prediction of its ultimate collapse than he is for what he had to say about steady-state economics. In the mid nineteenth century, while mainstream economists were concerning themselves with the conditions for and implications of single and multi-market static equilibria, Marx devoted his attention to the dynamics of capitalism. He used the concept of 'repro-duction', the process by which an economy, and more broadly, a society, recreates the conditions at the end of each time period necessary for it to continue to the next. His analysis of capital accumulation and the declin-ing rate of profit in a growing capitalist economy led him to conclude that eventually capitalism would fail to reproduce the conditions required for its ongoing existence.

As a prelude to this analysis Marx analysed the requirements for 'simple reproduction': workers receive a wage sufficient to reproduce themselves and the owners of capital replace worn out capital but do not expand it. Burkett (2004) argues that Marx was well aware of the 'natural condi-tions' required even for simple reproduction and he takes issue with those who claim that Marx was just as guilty of abstracting the economy from its dependence on the biosphere as mainstream economists.[1] Within the larger discussion of steady-state economics we learn from Marx that there is value in discerning which economic, social and environmental condi-tions must be recreated and which can be varied without compromising the fundamental requirements of a steady-state economy. Not only must the economic system be capable of reproducing itself, it must do so in a way that is consistent with reasonably stable social and environmental systems.

Like Marx, John Maynard Keynes contemplated the steady-state economy without using this particular terminology. Unlike Marx, Keynes thought that the steady-state was a very real possibility for those living in the second quarter of the twenty-first century, some 100 years after he wrote his essay: 'Economic possibilities for our grandchildren' (Keynes, 1930 [1963]). Considering economic growth in Britain since 1580, when Drake stole Spanish treasure, Keynes concluded that: 'assuming no impor-tant wars and no important increase in population, the *economic problem* may be solved, or be at least in sight of solution, within a hundred years' (Keynes, 1930 [1963], pp. 365–6, emphasis in original).

Keynes did not define what he meant by 'important' with respect to war and population, but World War II and more than a tripling of the world's population since 1930 likely qualify. Accordingly, we might extend his pro-jection of when the economic problem could be solved somewhat further into the twenty-first century, but that is really not the point. Rather it is that Keynes anticipated the dramatic increases in economic output result-ing from technological change and recognized that 'the economic problem is not – if we look into the future – *the permanent problem of the human race*' (Keynes, 1930 [1963], p. 366, emphasis in original).

In contemplating the future, Keynes was concerned about '*technologi-cal unemployment* . . . unemployment due to our discovery of means of economising the use of labour outrunning the pace at which we can find new uses for labour' (Keynes, 1930 [1963], p. 364, emphasis in original). As it turned out his own prescriptions for maintaining full employment set out some years later in *The General Theory of Employment, Interest and Money* (Keynes, 1935) helped prevent this scenario from being realized, at least to the extent he forewarned and in the time frame he considered.

More pertinent to the subject of this chapter are the concerns expressed by Keynes about all the changes in work habits, moral codes, 'all kinds of social customs and economic practices, affecting the distribution of wealth and of economic rewards and penalties, which we now maintain at all costs, however distasteful and unjust they may be in themselves, because they are tremendously useful in promoting the accumulation of capital, we shall be free, at last to discard' (Keynes, 1930 [1963], pp. 369–70). In particular, 'The love of money as a possession – as distinguished from the love of money as a means to the enjoyments and realities of life – will be recognised for what it is, a somewhat disgusting morbidity, one of those semi-criminal, semi-pathological propensities which one hands over with a shudder to the specialists in mental disease' (Keynes, 1930 [1963], p. 369).

Keynes's view of the steady-state economy was one of abundance and not in any respect a response to the need to bring economies into some sort of balance with the rest of nature, a theme that Mill had discussed nearly 100 years earlier. Nonetheless, Keynes's observations of the challenges presented by an adjustment to such circumstances are a valuable reminder of difficulties likely to be faced in a transition to a steady-state economy.

The day has long passed since economics was called the 'dismal science' in part at least because of Malthusian expectations that the human population would outrun food production. These days it is fair to say that natural scientists are more readily persuaded than most economists of the ultimate requirements for economic growth to come to an end because of resource and environmental constraints. This is especially true of those with a background in the life sciences where carrying capacity is a widely used concept that is understood to limit the growth of populations. Humans of course are a biological species as well as a social one, so the argument goes that we must also be subject to some sort of carrying capacity limit. Whether or not this applies to growth of the economy as well as to population is a complex question. Its answer depends on the definition of what is growing, possibilities for substitution among whatever may become scarce and the role of technology in enhancing the earth's carrying capacity for humans.

One natural scientist who contributed to the discussion of the steady-state economy was the geologist M. King Hubbert. Hubbert is best known for his work on peak oil and his prediction published in 1956 that oil production in the lower 48 states in the US would peak in 1970 (Hubbert, 1956). In 1974 Hubbert appeared before a Subcommittee on the

Environment of the Committee on Interior and Insular Affairs in the US House of Representatives. In his testimony he stated that 'a system is said to be in a steady-state when its various components either do not change with time, or else vary cyclically with the repetitive cycles not changing with time' (Hubbert, 1974, p. 2). Hubbert contrasted the steady-state with the 'transient' state when 'various components are undergoing noncyclical changes in magnitude, either of increase or decrease' (Hubbert, 1974, p. 3). He used these concepts to describe the historical transition of human societies from a steady-state to a transient state made possible by the utilization of fossil fuels.

Taking the long view, from 5000 years in the past to 5000 years in the future, Hubbert argued that 80 per cent of all fossil fuels combined 'coal, oil, natural gas, tar sands, and oil shales' (Hubbert, 1974, p. 7) would be consumed within a span of about 300 years and that we were already well into this brief period: 'the epoch of the fossil fuel era can be but an ephemeral and transitory event – an event, nonetheless, that has exercised the most drastic influence so far experienced by the human species during its entire biological existence' (Hubbert, 1974, p. 8).

Hubbert went on to argue that 'the exponential phase of the industrial growth which has dominated human activities during the last couple of centuries is drawing to a close . . . [because] it is physically and biologically impossible for any material or energy component to follow the exponential growth phase . . . for more than a few doublings, and most of those possible doublings have occurred already' (Hubbert, 1974, p. 10). Interestingly, in his testimony Hubbert admitted to having changed his mind about nuclear power based on fission as a substitute for fossil fuels since 'it represents the most hazardous industrial operation in terms of potential catastrophic effects that has ever been undertaken in human history' (Hubbert, 1974, p. 8).

Hubbert concluded by saying that since 'our institutions, our legal system, our financial system, and our most cherished folkways and beliefs are all based upon the premise of continuing growth . . . it is inevitable that with the slowing down in the rates of physical growth cultural adjustments must be made' (Hubbert, 1974, p. 10). However, it is not clear on whether Hubbert welcomed these adjustments, as Mill might have done, or whether he simply thought they were inevitable.

Kenneth Boulding made several contributions to our understanding of the dependence of economies on the biosphere in which they are embedded. His seminal essay, 'On the economics of the coming Spaceship Earth' (Boulding, 1966), is the most well known and deservedly so since it provides a remarkably effective outline of what was later to become the framework of ecological economics. As I have written elsewhere:

In 11 short pages Boulding gave an account of the economy and its relation to the environment that distinguished between open and closed systems in relation to matter, energy, and information; described the economy as a sub-system of the biosphere; considered the significance of the second law of thermodynamics for energy, matter and information and the extent to which they are subject to entropic processes; argued that knowledge or information is the key to economic development; noted that fossil fuels are a short-term exhaustible supplement to solar energy and that fission energy does not change this picture; considered the prospects for much better use of solar energy enhanced perhaps by the biological revolution; argued that human welfare may be better understood as a stock rather than a flow; presented an ethical basis for conservation; acknowledged that human impacts on the environment have spread from the local to the global; observed the limited contribution that corrective taxation might play; and commented that technological change has become distorted through planned obsolescence, competitive advertising, poor quality, and a lack of durability. Boulding summed up his analysis by comparing a 'cowboy' economy which is designed to maximize throughput (for which GNP is a rough measure) with a 'spaceman' economy in which stocks are maintained with minimum throughput. (Victor, 2010, p. 237)

Boulding alluded to steady-state economics when he said that 'the closed earth of the future requires economic principles which are somewhat different from those of the open earth of the past' (Boulding, 1966, p. 9) and expounded on these in his paper. He developed his ideas further in a paper devoted specifically to a consideration of the 'stationary state' (Boulding, 1973) that he described as 'an integral part of the "economic imagination"' (Boulding, 1973, p. 89). In this paper Boulding stressed that 'the quality of the stationary state depends almost entirely on the nature of the dynamic functions relating the stocks to the flows . . .' and that 'all stocks, of course do not have to be stationary at the same time' (Boulding, 1973, p. 92). He also distinguished among a number of 'quasi-stationary states in which some elements of the system are stationary while others are not' (Boulding, 1973, p. 92). Harking back to Mill, Boulding described one such state as having 'a stationary population and a stationary capital stock with . . . a change in the character of the capital stock . . .'. However, in connecting this to 'a larger throughput and a larger production and consumption with the same overall size of the capital stock' (Boulding, 1973, p. 92) this particular quasi-stationary state does not fully embody all of the different economic principles a spaceship economy would seem to require.

Perhaps the most important point that Boulding made in his treatment of the stationary state is that 'no matter what element in the system is stationary . . . the critical question concerns the nature of the controlling mechanism which keeps it so' (Boulding, 1973, p. 92). Such mechanisms may be draconian (for example, forced population control) or more passive, even voluntary, or according to Boulding, they might engender 'mafia-type societies in which government is primarily an institution for redistributing income toward the powerful and away from the weak' (Boulding, 1973, p. 95). This is a warning to be heeded as we move from discussing the rationale for a steady-state economy to its implementation: 'the problem of building political and constitutional defences against exploitation may emerge as the major political problem of the stationary state' (Boulding, 1973, p. 95). Anticipating Hubbert, Boulding concluded his comments on institutional considerations with a trenchant comment on existing institutions and their compatibility with the stationary state: 'precisely because existing institutions – political, economic, educational and religious – have exhibited survival value in a very rapidly progressing society, their survival value in a slow or stationary society is an open question' (Boulding, 1973, p. 100).

In his 1966 paper, Boulding included a paragraph or two about the second law of thermodynamics, increasing entropy and economics. He was not the first to make this link. As Professor Daly has pointed out (Daly, 1996), Fredric Soddy did so 40 years earlier (Soddy, 1926) but nobody noticed or if they did, thought it important. This began to change with the publication of Nicholas Georgescu-Roegen's magisterial treatise, *The Entropy Law and the Economic Process*, in which he argued forcefully for the relevance of the second law of thermodynamics to an understanding of economic processes (Georgescu-Roegen, 1971). Georgescu-Roegen's account of this law has engendered considerable debate, especially over his attempt to refute its interpretation as a statistical improbability and his application of the law to matter as well as energy. Nonetheless, he succeeded in convincing many ecological economists of the need to include the second law of thermodynamics in their analytical tool-box. Some, such as Professor Daly, have used it as part of their rationale for a steady-state economy (Daly, 1996), a position with which Georgescu-Roegen was not entirely in agreement. Georgescu-Roegen described those from Malthus onwards who 'were set exclusively on proving the impossibility of growth' as being 'deluded by a now widespread, but false syllogism: since exponential growth in a finite world leads to disasters of all kinds, ecological salvation lies in the stationary state' (Georgescu-Roegen, 1980, p. 66). He challenged this position on three grounds. First, any rate of growth, positive, zero and even negative, depletes a fixed stock of resources and so this process must eventually end. Second, if the steady-state is understood as an open thermodynamic steady-state then Georgescu-Roegen pointed to the special conditions and delicate balance that must hold for such a steady-state to endure. Third, he questioned the plausibility of mechanisms by which technological change manages to compensate for a declining resource base, all the while with the capital stock remaining constant, whatever that may mean.

Georgescu-Roegen ended his discussion of the steady-state economy by challenging the assumption of Mill and others that intellectual activities might flourish in a steady-state by pointing to many contrary historical examples, 'the Middle Ages, for one, of quasi-stationary societies where arts and sciences were practically stagnant' (Georgescu-Roegen, 1980, p. 68). Yet despite his withering criticism of the steady-state, Georgescu-Roegen offered a menu of policy directions derived from 'bioeconomic' principles that are very similar to those proposed by others who still find virtue in the steady-state. Summarizing and paraphrasing Georgescu-Roegen (1980, pp. 69–72), these policy directions include:

- Cessation of the production of all instruments of war, *not only war itself*.
- Aid the underdeveloped nations to arrive as quickly as possible at a good (not luxurious) life.
- Gradually lower the human population to a level that could be adequately fed only by organic agriculture.
- Until either solar energy becomes a general convenience or controlled fusion is achieved, all waste of energy should be avoided and, if necessary, strictly regulated.
- Cure ourselves of the morbid craving for extravagant gadgetry.
- Eliminate fashion, emphasize durability.
- Make durable goods even more durable by designing them to be repairable.
- Come to realize that an important prerequisite for a good life is a substantial amount of leisure spent in an intelligent manner.

One other contribution to steady-state economics that has had a lasting impact is *The Limits to Growth* (Meadows et al., 1972). This short book described a simulation model of 'the world system' and some of the scenarios that it generated include several in which the system collapses some time in the twenty-first century. In one such scenario, 'the "standard" world model run, [which] assumes no major changes in the physical, economic, or social relationships that have historically governed the development of the world system, . . . the behaviour mode of the system . . . is clearly that of overshoot and collapse' (Meadows et al., 1972, p. 124). Other scenarios based on different assumption showed how the system could be stabilized, at least over the duration of the model run (that is, to 2100), approximating a steady-state.

The Limits to Growth was subjected to an immense amount of criticism and is often dismissed out of hand today incorrectly as having been proved wrong (see Victor, 2008, pp. 89–94 for more discussion). And yet when comparing what actually happened in the world since *The Limits to Growth* was published with the scenarios described in the book, Turner observes '30 years of historical data compare favourably with key features of . . . the "standard run" scenario, which results in collapse of the global system midway through the 21st century' (Turner, 2008, p. 1). This finding was reinforced in Turner's subsequent analysis of the data extending over 40 years (Turner, 2012).

Herman Daly is Georgescu-Roegen's most famous student and it is to his contributions to steady-state economics that we now turn. Professor Daly began writing about the steady-state in the 1960s (Daly, 1968) and has continued to this day. In 1996 he wrote, 'For over twenty-five years the concept of a steady-state economy has been at the center of my thinking and writing' (Daly, 1996, p. 3). His book *Steady-state Economics* (Daly, 1977) still stands as the single most comprehensive treatment of the subject, one made more relevant with the passage of time. The subtitle of the book summarizes Professor Daly's rationale for examining steady-state economics, *The Economics of Biophysical Equilibrium and Moral Growth*.

In his 1977 text Professor Daly defined a steady-state economy (SSE) as:

> *an economy with constant stocks of people and artefacts, maintained at some desired, sufficient levels by low rates of maintenance 'throughput'* that is, by the lowest feasible flows of matter and energy from the first stage of production (depletion of low-entropy materials from the environment) to the last stage of consumption (pollution of the environment with high-entropy wastes and exotic materials). It should be continually remembered that the SSE is a *physical* concept. If something is non-physical, then perhaps it can grow forever. (Daly, 1977, p. 17, emphasis in original)

More recently and more succinctly, Professor Daly says, 'following Mill we might define a SSE as an economy with constant population and constant stock of capital, maintained by a low rate of throughput that is within the regenerative and assimilative capacities of the ecosystem' (Daly, 2008, p. 3).

These two definitions focus on keeping constant the stocks of people and artefacts with low rates of throughput that respect the limited capacity of the environment to generate resources and assimilate wastes. Counting people is relatively easy. We do it on a regular basis through the census and so we know what is happening to the number of people though not necessarily to their mass as average body weight changes. For example, the average weight of adults in the USA increased more than 24 pounds between 1960 and 2002 (Ogden et al., 2004).

Counting artefacts is an altogether different matter. Statistical agencies do not keep systematic and complete inventories of artefacts and to the extent they do, they usually aggregate them in monetary units using market prices rather than in physical units. A constant stock of artefacts in value terms is at odds with Professor Daly's insistence that SSE is a physical concept. Yet, what does it mean to keep the stock of artefacts constant in physical terms? To simply add them up by weight or volume is not very meaningful since it fails to allow for qualitative improvements in the stock and changes in its material composition.

Of course Professor Daly realizes this and offers an alternative, more operational, definition of a steady-state economy that focuses on flows rather than stocks: 'we might define the SSE in terms of a constant flow of throughput at a sustainable (low) level, with population and capital stock free to adjust to whatever size can be maintained by the constant through-put that begins with depletion and ends with pollution' (Daly, 2008, p. 3).

While it is easier to obtain more comprehensive information on the physical magnitude of flows to and from an economy and the environ-ment, the problem remains of determining whether physical inflows and outflows are rising, falling or remaining constant unless we abstract completely from changes in their composition. To do so overlooks the dramatically different environmental impacts of flows of materials and energy of equal magnitude and again is unsatisfactory. But without a suit-able aggregation procedure, empirical implementation of a definition of a steady-state economy based on flows remains problematic.

One of the many ways in which Professor Daly has advanced the analy-sis of steady-state economics is the distinction he makes between growth and development. He defines growth as a 'quantitative increase in size, or an increase in throughput', and throughput as 'the flow of raw materials and energy from the global ecosystem's sources of low entropy ... through the economy, and back to the global ecosystem's sinks for high-entropy wastes' (Daly and Farley, 2011, pp. 486, 493). Professor Daly contrasts growth that 'must end' with qualitative development that can continue indefinitely because it is 'the improvement in the quality of goods and ser-vices, as defined by their ability to increase human well-being, defined by a given throughput' (Daly and Farley, 2011, p. 483).

On the surface this definition of development and the assumption that it can continue essentially without limit is at odds with his former teacher Georgescu-Roegen's critique of the steady-state economy that it is ultimately doomed to fail. In all likelihood, this difference in views stems more from a difference in time horizon than it does about the nature of the biophysical world and the dependence of economies on it. In the exceedingly long term, when the sun expires and likely much before that, human economies anywhere in the solar system are bound to fail, so in that sense Georgescu-Roegen is correct. But with a time horizon of say, a few hundred years or a millennium or two, then arguably Professor Daly's perspective is sound and more relevant.

A more pressing concern than the very, very long run is the lack of a metric for measuring growth as defined by Professor Daly. He eschews the use of changes in gross domestic product (GDP) or gross national product (GNP) for measuring economic growth because they conflate quantitative and qualitative change. 'Note that an SSE [steady-state economy] is not defined in terms of gross national product. It is not to be thought as "zero growth in GNP"' (Daly, 1996, p. 32). But Professor Daly does not provide an alternative metric for a steady-state economy unless by implication he means simply the aggregate tonnage of throughput, which runs into the serious problem of aggregating flows of very different qualities noted earlier. In the absence of such a metric some analysts, this author included, have chosen for pragmatic reasons to address questions about alternatives to a reliance on endless economic growth, using the conventional measure of growth: changes in real GDP and real GDP per person for which ample statistics exist (Victor, 2008).

Another useful analytical distinction emphasized by Professor Daly, based on Georgescu-Roegen's work, is between stock-flow resources and fund-service resources. Stock-flow resources are 'materially trans-formed into what they produce ... they can be used at virtually any rate desired ... ; their productivity is measured by the number of physical units of the product into which they are transformed; can be stock-piled; are used up, rather than worn out' (Daly and Farley, 2011, p. 492). Fund-service resources are 'not materially transformed into what they produce ... can only be used at a given rate, and their productivity is measured as output per unit of time; cannot be stockpiled; and are worn out, rather than used up' (Daly and Farley, 2011, p. 485).

Human-made machine tools are funds that provide services. They wear out but material from them does not end up in the goods they produce. Raw materials and semi-finished products are stock-flow resources that do get used up and are incorporated in final goods. What nature provides to the economy can also be categorized as stock-flow and fund-service resources. But unlike human artefacts, which are typically one or the other, nature's support for human economies, sometimes referred to as natural capital or green infrastructure, can be fund-service and stock-flow resources simultaneously. Examples include forests that as a fund provide services such as habitat and soil stabilization, and as a stock provide a flow of timber. This distinction between stock-flow and fund-service resources can be helpful in understanding the excessive pressures that humans place on the environment. Material flows, such as timber, usually command a higher market price than the immaterial services from the same resource, for which there may be no market price despite their value. This market failure results in the market value of the resource as a stock exceeding its market value as a fund leading to depletion rather than conservation. In a steady-state economy, indeed even in a growing one, attention should be paid to maintaining stocks and funds separately and in combination.

In addition to expounding on the meaning of a steady-state economy, Professor Daly has built a strong case for moving in that direction with developed economies taking the lead. He appreciates the need for operational principles if we are to make the transition to a steady-state economy in a careful and minimally disruptive way. To this end he has proposed a set of principles for sustainable development (understood here as a steady-state economy):

1. Renewable resources: harvest rates should equal regeneration rates (sustained yield).
2. Waste emission rates should equal the natural assimilative capacities of the ecosystems into which the waste are emitted.
3. Maintain natural and man-made capital intact at the optimal level. (Principles 1 and 2 accomplish this for natural capital.)
4. Investment in the exploitation of a non-renewable resource should be paired with a compensating investment in a renewable substitute.
5. Emphasize technologies that increase resource productivity (development), the amount of value extracted per unit of resource, rather than technologies for increasing the resource throughput itself (growth).
6. Limit the total scale of resource throughput to ensure that the scale of the economy (population times per capita resource use) is within the carrying capacity of the region, avoiding capital consumption (summarized from Daly, 1990, pp. 2–3).

These six principles are inter-related and mutually supportive. For example, principles 1 and 2 are required to accomplish principle 3. They are also not the only such set to have been proposed. Douglas Booth turned 'Daly's original formulation of a steady-state . . . on its head' (Booth, 1998, p. 143) by emphasizing the control of emissions rather than throughput '. . . and the result will be a sustainable throughput of energy'. Booth offered the following principles (Booth called them 'components') for a steady-state US economy:

1. A reduction in carbon dioxide (CO_2) emissions by 90 per cent of forecasted levels over the next century and emissions stability thereafter.

2.   The preservation of all remaining undisturbed habitats and ecosys-
     tems on the national forests and the conversion of previously exploited
     national forest lands to natural habitat.
3.   Reduction of non-point pollution to levels sufficient to preserve and
     restore habitat for native aquatic life.
4.   Reduction and elimination of pesticides harmful to human beings,
     species and ecosystems (Booth, 1998, p. 143).

Booth's principles complement Professor Daly's rather than replace them.
Throughput needs to be controlled at the input and output end of the
economy. While material and energy resource inputs to an economy are
related to the material and energy waste outputs, they present distinct
problems and challenges. Concentrating on one end or the other will not
suffice. Also, Booth's inclusion of habitat preservation and restoration is
essential for protecting other species whose livelihood is under constant
and increasing pressure from expanding human population and economies.
    One of the shortcomings of many of these principles is that they are dif-
ficult to operationalize without more clarity about measurement. Perhaps
it is because of this that Professor Daly entitled the widely referenced paper
in which his six principles appear as 'Towards some operational principles
of sustainable development' (Daly, 1990). Given the ambiguities that can
arise from using only physical magnitudes and the lack of comprehensive data, an alternative approach is to work with real GDP and examine
what might be accomplished if its constancy is used as the definition of a
steady-state economy. Providing energy and material intensities (measured
as physical amounts per dollar of GDP) stabilize or decline when GDP is
constant, then a steady-state economy defined in terms of GDP will coincide with constant or declining material and energy throughput so that all
agendas are satisfied.
    In the remainder of this chapter we will continue to discuss steady-state
economics using real GDP and GDP per person and use two different
models for simulating a steady-state economy. The first, simpler model
is based fairly explicitly on Professor Daly's writings and is a model of
the US economy. The second is a more detailed model of the Canadian
economy used in this chapter to examine a transition to a steady-state.

12.3   SIMULATING A STEADY-STATE ECONOMY

It is quite possible to map out the structure of a simulation model of a
steady-state economy as defined by Professor Daly, one in which the stocks
of people and artefacts are maintained at desired, sufficient levels by low

Gross Domestic Product

Population & Labour Force

Replacement Cost

Market Shares

Energy Use

Energy Prices

Weighted Price of Energy

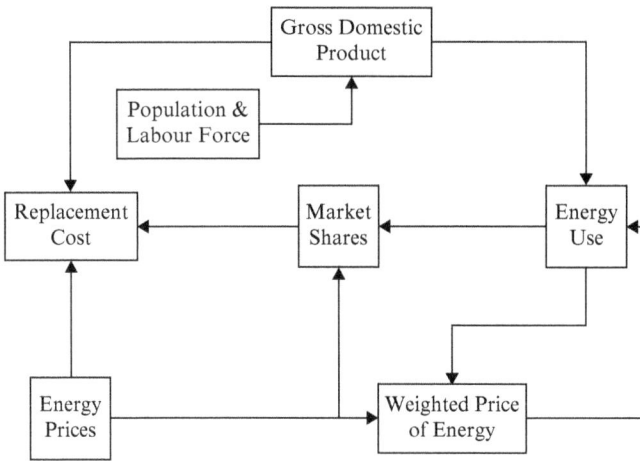

Figure 12.1   High-level structure of a steady-state economy model

rates of throughput and which satisfies all of the principles stated above. It is a much more challenging task to do so in a way that can be fitted to the available data for reasons given earlier about the lack of physical data and suitable metrics as well as because statistical agencies, especially in North America, do not collect comprehensive data on the relevant stocks, flows, funds and services.

Figure 12.1 shows the high-level structure of a model of a steady-state economy that embodies some of the aspects highlighted by Professor Daly and other contributors but uses constant real GDP and constant population to define a steady-state rather than relying entirely on non-monetary measures. This model is highly aggregated and intended only to illustrate some ideas about a steady-state economy, with a focus on energy. It has been built using system dynamics software (Stella), to facilitate exploration of alternative assumptions for generating different scenarios. For a touch of realism, the model has been calibrated using data for the USA.

In developed economies, energy use has increased more slowly than GDP for quite some time. This relationship is captured in the model with an income elasticity of demand for energy less than 1.[2] A default value of 0.55 is used (Gately and Huntington, 2002) but this can be varied in the simulations. A higher value for this elasticity can be used to reflect increasing energy conservation efforts.

The total amount of energy used is also influenced by the price of energy. Here, this is modelled in two steps. First, total energy use is related to the weighted price of energy. The weighted price is calculated from the prices and quantities of the four categories of primary energy.[3] A default value of the price elasticity of demand for energy of −0.5 (US Energy Information Administration, 2008) is used but, as with the income elasticity of energy demand, it can be changed to simulate increasing levels of energy conservation.

In the second step, total energy use is divided among four categories of primary energy according to their individual prices.[4] The four categories of primary energy in the model are: fossil fuels used for electricity generation; fossil fuels in all other uses; nuclear power; renewable energy used for electricity generation. After calculating total energy use, the market share obtained by each of the four sources of primary energy is calculated using an equation that allocates market shares according to the relative costs of the competing energy sources (Rivers and Jaccard, 2005). The changes in energy costs are set exogenously. The sensitivity of the market shares to the relative costs can be varied using a scale of 0 (no sensitivity) to 5 (high sensitivity). A default value of 2.1 was selected because it generates market shares very close to those prevailing in the base year for the model, 2013. The simplifying assumption is made that each of the four sources of primary energy could ultimately provide all of the energy used in the USA.

In the model, the rate of growth of GDP is set exogenously as is the rate of change in productivity (output per employed worker). When combined with the labour force these three variables determine the rate of unemployment (Victor, 2008, pp. 156–8). The rate of growth in population and the labour force, which are assumed to be the same, are set exogenously.

The final component of the model as shown in Figure 12.1 is replacement cost. This refers to an estimate of the cost of replacing non-renewable sources of energy (fossil fuels and nuclear) with renewable substitutes. Two options are provided in the model: (1) replacement by a combination of all renewable energy sources and (2) replacement only by solar, wind and biomass (used for generating electricity). This is similar to the approach taken in Daly and Cobb (1994, pp. 484–7) in their development of the Index of Sustainable Welfare. In this instance, replacement cost as a per cent of GDP can be interpreted as an indicator of how close the US economy is to sustainability, at least with respect to energy.

The model can be used to examine a wide range of scenarios for the USA. Just four are discussed here. 2013 is the base year and the time horizon for the simulations is 50 years. The scenarios are:

Scenario 1 – Base case: The rates of growth in GDP, population and labour force, and labour productivity continue at rates typical of the past two decades, average annual hours per employed worker is held constant and the costs of energy from non-renewable sources rise at 1 per cent per year and remain constant for the renewable sources.

Scenario 2 – Steady-state, constant prices of renewable energy sources: The rates of growth of GDP, population and labour force are set to zero to give a steady-state. The rate of growth of labour productivity is maintained at the same level as in the business as usual scenario. The average annual hours worked per employed worker decline at the same rate as productivity increases. (Such a decline in time spent at work begins to capture an important aspect of development as defined by Professor Daly, that is, a qualitative, beneficial change in people's lives.) The same assumptions are made about energy costs as in the business-as-usual scenario.

Scenario 3 – Steady-state, declining prices of renewable energy sources: This is the same as scenario 2 except that the cost of energy from all renewable energy sources declines at 0.5 per cent per year to reflect gains from technological improvements and economies of scale as market share increases.

Scenario 4 – Steady-state phase-in: This scenario is a combination of scenarios 1 and 2. Values for the rates of growth in GDP, population and the labour force start as in scenario 1 and decline steadily over 50 years to zero as in scenario 2. The average annual hours worked per employed person declines, but less than in scenario 2 to achieve the same rate of unemployment. By the end of 50 years the economy is in a steady-state with respect to GDP, population and the labour force.

The assumptions for the first three scenarios are summarized in Table 12.1 and the simulation results are shown in Figures 12.2–12.7. Figure 12.2 shows indexed values for GDP, energy use and population for the base case (2013 = 100). US GDP increases by 250 per cent over 50 years at an assumed annual growth rate of 2.5 per cent. Energy use increases by 50 per cent over the same period, dampened as compared with GDP growth by the income and price elasticities that are built into the model. The rate of unemployment declines from 7.4 per cent to 6.7 per cent.

Figure 12.3 shows the percentage share of primary energy provided by each of the four categories of primary energy in the base case and scenario 2. (Cost assumptions are the same in both scenarios so the estimated market shares are the same although the quantities of energy used are markedly different.) Fossil fuels not used for electric power generation decline from 73 per cent in 2013 to 66 per cent over 50 years in the base case. Fossil fuels used to generate electricity fall from 9 per cent to 3 per cent, nuclear remains roughly unchanged at 8–9 per cent and renewable sources of electricity

Table 12.1   Summary of assumptions

		1. Base case	2. Steady-state constant prices of renewables	3. Steady-state declining prices of renewables
Rate of growth of GDP	Per cent	2.5	0	0
Rate of growth of productivity	Per cent	1.5	1.5	1.5
Rate of growth of population and labour force	Per cent	1.0	0	0
Rate of growth in average annual hours worked	Per cent	0	−1.5	−1.5
Sensitivity of technology diffusion to prices	0–20	2.1	2.1	2.1
Annual change in cost of fossil fuels (non-power generation)	Per cent	1	1	1
Annual change in cost of fossil fuel power generation	Per cent	1	1	1
Annual change in cost of nuclear power generation	Per cent	0	0	−0.5
Annual change in cost of renewable energy	Per cent	0	0	0

increase from 9 per cent to 23 per cent. These changes in market share are driven by the relative costs of the various sources of energy.

Figure 12.4 shows the first steady-state scenario in which GDP and population remain unchanged from 2013 onwards, while energy use and unemployment decline. Figure 12.5 shows the shares of the primary energy sources for this steady-state scenario. Notably, renewable energy sources account for 23 per cent of total energy supply after 50 years. In scenario 3 (not shown) with a declining cost of renewable energy, the share of these renewable energy sources account for 33 per cent of primary energy after 50 years, mostly at the expense of non-electric fossil fuel.

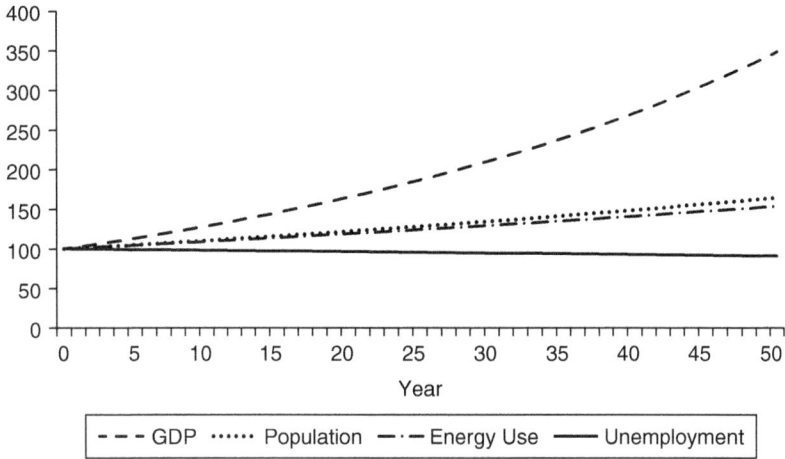

Figure 12.2   Scenario 1: base case GDP, population, energy use, unemployment (2013 = 100)

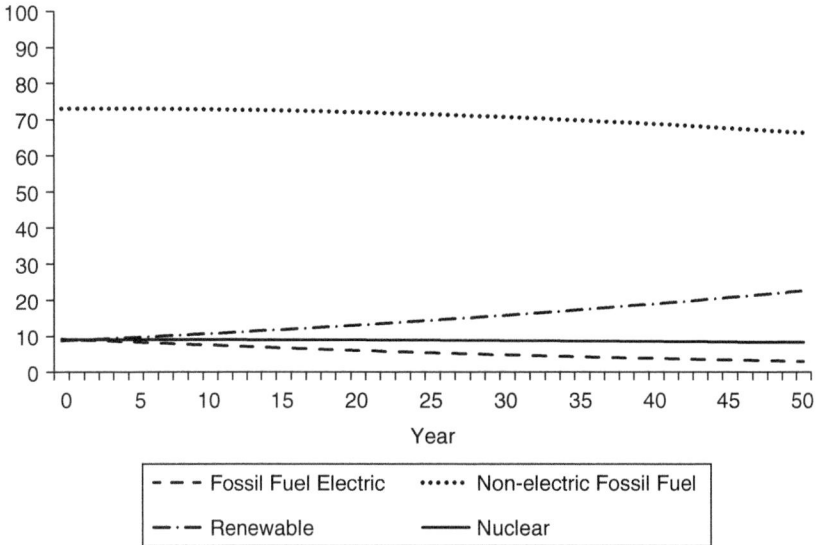

Figure 12.3   Scenarios 1 base case and 2 steady-state with constant costs of renewables shares of primary energy sources (%)

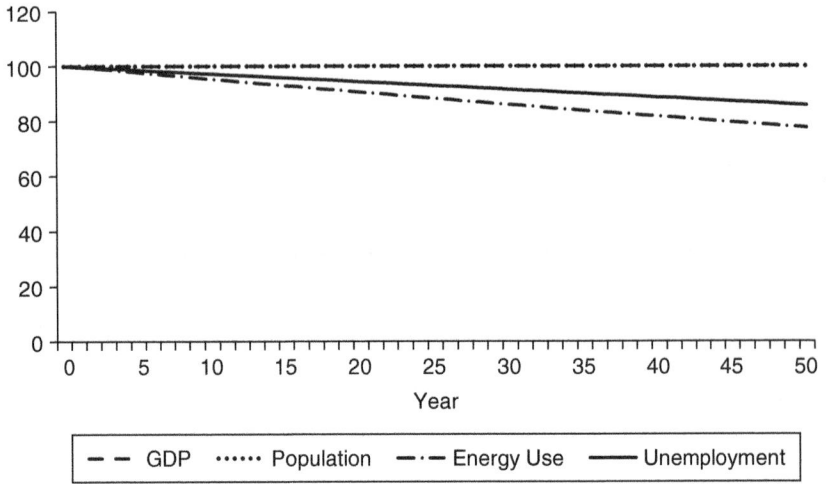

*Figure 12.4   Scenario 2 steady-state with constant costs of renewables
GDP, energy consumption, population (2013 = 100)*

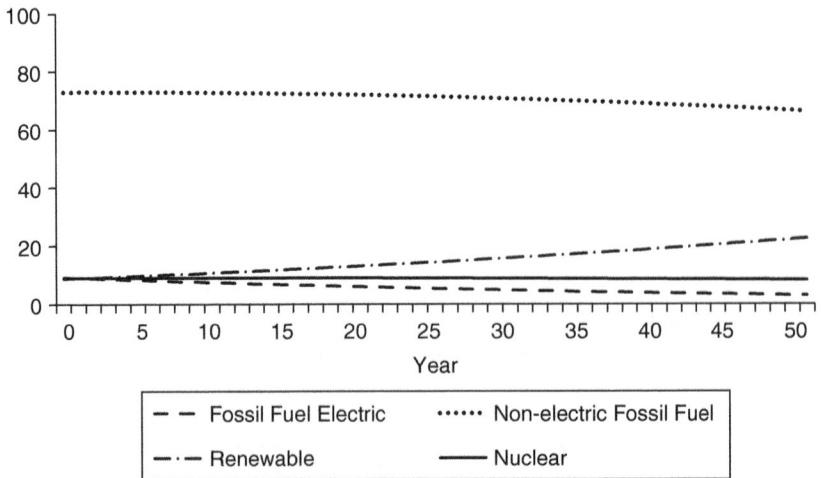

*Figure 12.5   Scenario 2 steady-state with constant costs of renewables
shares of primary energy sources (%)*

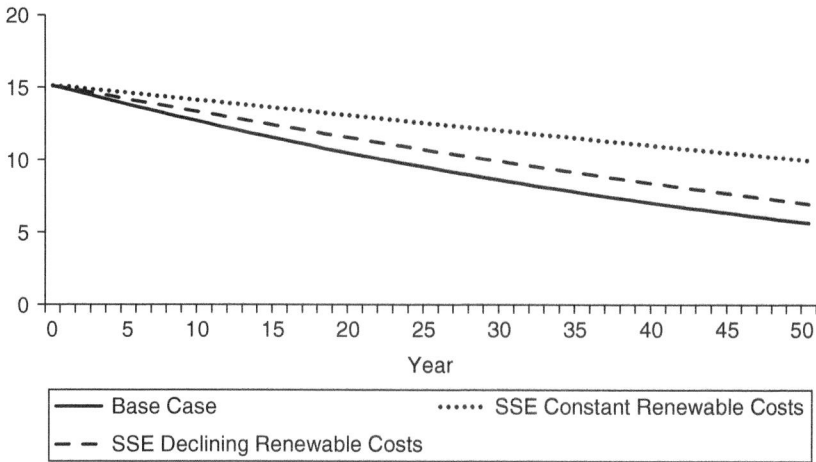

Figure 12.6   Scenarios 1 base case, 2 steady-state with constant costs of renewables, 3 declining costs of renewables replacement costs as a per cent of GDP

Figure 12.6 shows replacement costs as a per cent of GDP for each of the three scenarios. This measure is intended to indicate how close an economy is to sustainability with respect to energy. It is interesting that in Figure 12.6 replacement costs as a per cent of GDP is lower for the base case than for either of the steady-state scenarios suggesting that the base case is closer to sustainability than the steady-state scenarios. The reason for this is due to the increase in the denominator (that is, GDP) over time rather than to a reduction in the numerator (that is, replacement costs). Indeed, in the base case the cost of replacing non-renewable energy with renewable energy rises from $2.2 trillion per year in 2013 to $2.8 trillion per year 50 years later. In the first steady-state scenario the replacement cost falls to $1.4 trillion per year and in the second to $1.0 trillion per year. This result suggests that replacement costs as a per cent of GDP may be limited as an indicator of how near or far an economy is from sustainability with respect to energy. Furthermore, replacement costs as defined here are the gross costs of substituting renewable for non-renewable energy, rather than the net costs, which would account for the avoided costs from the reduced use of non-renewable energy. Also no allowance is made in the model for additional transmission and distribution costs associated with these scenarios or for the possible need for back-up generating capacity to cope with the intermittency of renewable sources.

Nevertheless, the scenarios do show that energy prices can be very important in determining the role that non-renewable and renewable sources of energy have played and will play in determining their use. Equally telling are the very different implications for energy requirements of continuous growth in GDP and population versus, where energy use rises considerably, a steady-state where it declines. The different environmental implications of these energy use scenarios could be very significant.

Energy prices have never simply been set by the market without considerable government intervention through a vast array of subsidies, taxes, direct investment, purchases and regulation. Much of the impact of these interventions has been on prices, directly via gasoline taxes, for example, and indirectly through measures such as more or less stringent regulatory limits. The same will be true in the future so while we can get an insight into the potential impact of costs and prices on the replacement of non-renewable energy with renewable energy, it will be as much a matter of public policy and international politics as geology, biology and engineering as to what these costs and prices will be.

Of course, the economy of the US is not likely to switch suddenly to a steady-state defined either in terms used in the model (stable GDP and population) or using a purely physical definition as proposed by Professor Daly. What is more realistic is that it will converge to a steady-state over a period of decades. Scenario 4 in which reductions in the rate of growth of GDP, population and the average annual hours worked per employed person are phased in throws some light on such a transition. This scenario is shown in Figure 12.7.

Figure 12.7 shows economic growth slowing down until it is not growing at all after 50 years, and similarly for population. Energy use and unemployment both decline over the 50-year simulation period. The market shares of the primary sources are the same as in scenarios 1 and 2 (Figure 12.3) because they are driven by the same set of cost assumptions. Replacement cost of $1.4 trillion in year 50 is half the amount in the base case and a smaller percentage (5.3 per cent compared to 5.8 per cent) of GDP. By this measure, scenario 4 is closer to sustainability with respect to energy than any of the other scenarios.

12.4   MANAGING WITHOUT GROWTH[5]

The scenarios described in the previous section were derived from a model in which the rates of economic and population growth were assumed and the implications for unemployment, energy use, sources and replacement costs were simulated based on assumptions about the costs of energy and the average annual hours worked. This section describes a rather different

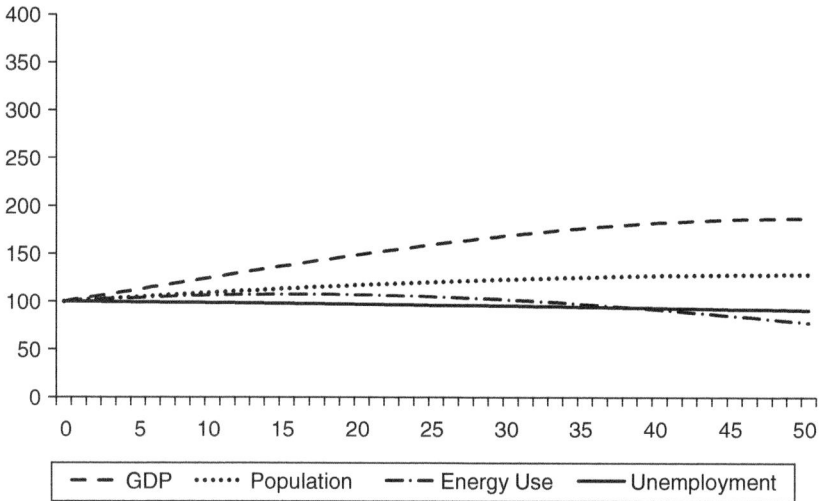

Figure 12.7 Scenario 4 steady-state phase in GDP, energy consumption, population (2013 = 100)

modelling approach that covers a broader range of social and environmental dimensions including poverty, the government's fiscal position, employment, investment and greenhouse gas emissions, within a macroeconomic steady-state setting.

LowGrow is an interactive computerized model of the Canadian economy designed to explore different assumptions, objectives and policy measures related to slowing the rate of economic growth. Figure 12.8 shows the high-level structure of LowGrow. At the top, aggregate demand (GDP) is determined in the conventional way as the sum of consumption expenditure (C), investment expenditure (I), government expenditure (G) and the difference between exports (X) and imports (I.) There are separate equations for each of these components in the model, estimated with Canadian data from 1981 to 2005. Production in the economy is estimated by a Cobb-Douglas production function in which output (GDP) is a function of employed labour (L) and employed capital (K). The time variable (t) represents changes in productivity from improvements in technology, labour skills and organization. The production function is shown at the bottom of Figure 12.8. It estimates the labour (L) and employed capital (K) required to produce the GDP (aggregate demand) allowing for changes in productivity over time.[6]

There is a second important link between aggregate demand and the production function shown in Figure 12.8 by the arrow connecting

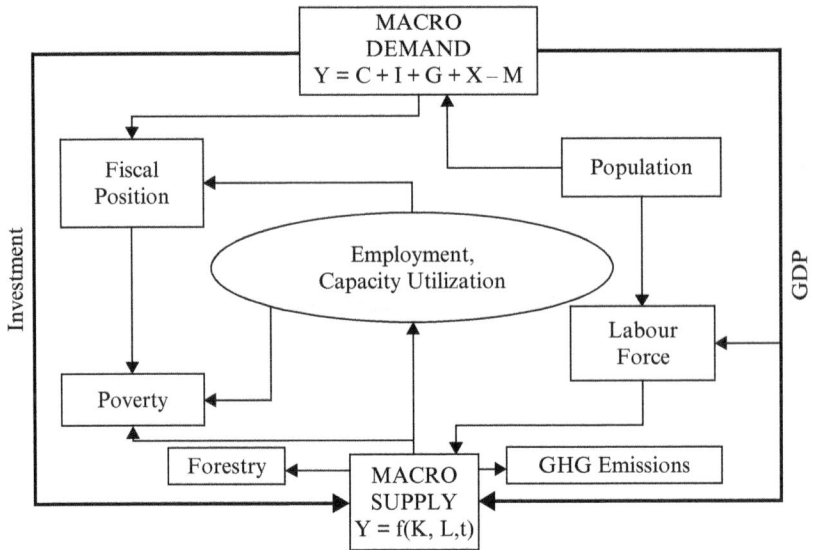

Notes: Y = GDP; C = consumption; I = investment; G = government; X = exports; M = imports; K = capital; L = labour; t = time.

Figure 12.8   The high-level structure of LowGrow

aggregate demand and the production function. Investment expenditures (net of depreciation), which are part of aggregate demand, add to the stock of capital in the economy. Also over time, capital and labour become more productive. It follows that without an increase in GDP these increases in capital and productivity reduce the requirements for labour. Unless an alternative approach is adopted, growth in GDP is needed to prevent unemployment increasing as the productive capacity of the economy expands.

LowGrow includes population growth, which is exogenous, and growth in the labour force, which is estimated as a function of GDP and population. Population is also one of the variables that determines the consumption expenditures in the economy.

There is no monetary sector in LowGrow. For simplicity it is assumed that the Bank of Canada, Canada's central bank, regulates the money supply to keep inflation at or near the target level of 2 per cent per year. LowGrow includes an exogenously set rate of interest. A higher cost of borrowing discourages investment, which reduces aggregate demand. It also raises the cost to government of servicing its debt. LowGrow warns of inflationary pressures when the rate of unemployment falls below 4 per cent but the price level is not included as a variable in the model.

While LowGrow lacks these features, it includes others that are particularly relevant for exploring low or no growth scenarios. LowGrow includes emissions of carbon dioxide and other greenhouse gases, a carbon tax, a forestry sub-model, provision for redistributing incomes and HPI-2, the United Nation's (UN) Human Poverty Index for selected Organisation for Economic Co-operation and Development (OECD) countries (United Nations Development Programme, 2006). LowGrow allows additional funds to be spent on health care and on programmes to reduce adult illiteracy (both included in HPI-2) and estimates their impacts on longevity and adult literacy with equations obtained from the literature.

Implications of changes in the level of government expenditures can be simulated in LowGrow through a variety of fiscal policies including a balanced budget and an annual percentage change that can vary over time. LowGrow keeps track of the overall fiscal position of all governments combined as measured by the ratio of the combined debt of all levels of government to GDP.

In LowGrow, as in the economy that it represents, economic growth is driven by net investment, which adds to productive assets, growth in the labour force, growth in productivity, growth in the trade balance (that is, the difference between exports and imports), growth in government expenditures and growth in population. Low and no growth scenarios can be examined by reducing the rates of increase in each and any combination of these factors. In an economy that is dependent on economic growth, a sudden dislocation in any and all of these growth drivers can be extremely disruptive as witnessed in the global recession that began in 2008. But as Professor Daly reminds us, 'a failed growth economy and a steady-state economy are not the same thing; they are the very alternatives we face' (Daly, 2008; O'Neill, 2008). LowGrow can show how catastrophic a cessation of growth could be if all of the contributors to growth were to fail suddenly and simultaneously (Victor, 2008, pp. 178–80). It can also show that a more measured convergence to a steady-state might be achieved if approached systematically over a number of years.

One example of a steady-state scenario for the Canadian economy is shown in Figure 12.9, which displays the time path of five key variables all indexed to a value of 100 in 2005: GDP per capita; the rate of unemployment; greenhouse gas (GHG) emissions; poverty; and the debt to GDP ratio. In this scenario a variety of measures are phased in over a ten-year period starting in 2010. The rate of growth in GDP per capita begins to slow down and falls to zero by around 2030. Since population growth is declining to zero at about the same time, GDP (not shown) also ceases to

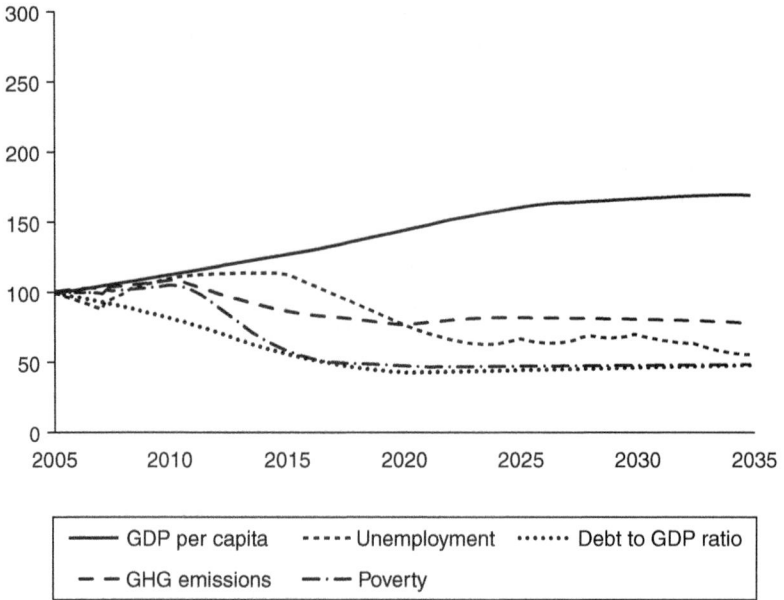

Figure 12.9   Towards a steady-state economy

grow. As Figure 12.9 shows, this decline in the rate of economic growth is accompanied by a reduction in the rate of unemployment to 4 per cent by 2035 (commonly regarded as full-employment in Canada), a substantial reduction in the level of poverty as measured by the UN's Human Poverty Index, a 25 per cent reduction in greenhouse gas emissions and a decline, then stabilization of the ratio of government debt to GDP.

Each of these outcomes can be traced to one or a few specific changes although they also result from the interactions and feedbacks contained in the structure of LowGrow. The reduction in the growth in GDP per capita results from reduced net investment, a slower rate of increase in productivity, stabilization of government expenditure and balanced international trade. Increases in consumption expenditure slow as a result of the lower rate of economic growth brought about by these other changes. A decline in the rate of growth of population coincides with the decline in GDP per capita so that growth in GDP is also reduced, eventually to zero, in this steady-state scenario.

The rate of unemployment is reduced by a 15 per cent reduction in the average number of hours worked by Canadians by 2035, effectively sharing out a stabilized level of labour among a larger number of employees. Even then the average time spent working by Canadians would be higher than levels already reached in 2007 in some European countries (OECD, 2008).

The reduction in poverty shown in Figure 12.9 comes from a lower rate of unemployment and a redistribution of income to bring all Canadians up to the 'low income cut-off' (Zhang, 2010) widely used as the unofficial measure of economic poverty in Canada. Poverty is also reduced in this scenario through an expansion of adult literacy programmes and health care that address components of the UN's Human Poverty Index.

The decline and stabilization of the ratio of government debt to GDP starts from the fiscal regime existing in Canada in 2005, the base year for the simulation. Between 2005 and 2009 this regime changed for several reasons. In particular, the federal government reduced the General Sales Tax from 7 per cent to 5 per cent substantially reducing the federal budget surpluses that this level of government had been running for several years. In late 2008, when the global recession took hold in Canada, revenues for all three levels of government declined and expenditures increased so that the decline in the debt to GDP ratio shown at the start of the scenario in Figure 12.9, before the various measures in the simulation that start in 2010 take effect, did not materialize. This outcome is a useful reminder that LowGrow is useful for illuminating possibilities for the longer term rather than for simulating short-term changes in the economy.

The reduction in greenhouse gas emissions shown in Figure 12.9 comes from a combination of the ongoing decline in greenhouse gas intensity, assumed to continue at the same rate as the rate of increase in overall productivity (which is reduced in this scenario but remains positive) and the introduction of a revenue-neutral carbon tax on energy related GHG emissions. A cap and trade system that resulted in a similar price on these emissions to the carbon tax would have a similar effect.

Beyond 2035 further adjustments would be required to some of the growth drivers to maintain a stable GDP per capita so that the scenario shown in Figure 12.9 is a quasi steady-state. Increases in productivity could continue without increasing GDP if the gains are enjoyed as reduced time spent in paid employment rather than as increased output.

This brief account of a possible transition to a steady-state economy answers some questions (that is, it is feasible to have full employment, much reduced poverty and greenhouse gas emissions, and maintain fiscal balance without relying on economic growth) and raises others. For example, is the top-down, heavy hand of government required or is it just as important, indeed essential, that a steady-state comes about in response to changes initiated at the grassroots? Will a steady-state economy engender more rigid, controlling political and social institutions or will people have more freedom to choose how they spend their time as individuals, families and communities? In a steady-state economy will it become more difficult to achieve an equitable distribution of income and wealth or easier because other measures of success will have supplanted material living standards? Will paid employment and the private ownership of capital remain the principal means by which income is distributed or will new arrangements be required, and if so, how will they affect incentives to work, save and invest? Is it feasible for a single country to strive for a steady-state economy if the rest of the world pursues growth as usual? Will it help or hinder developing countries to achieve their development objectives if rich countries pursue a steady-state for their economies? What will a steady-state economy mean for the rate of profit and the rate of interest; will it be necessary to limit the outflow of capital as it pursues higher profits elsewhere? What are the resource use and waste generation levels required to sustain the economy at the steady-state level of GDP per capita in 2035, which is projected to be over 50 per cent higher in 2035 than in 2005? Are these levels compatible with the biophysical limits that are a major reason for contemplating a steady-state future? Is this kind of scenario compatible with capitalism? Will new and different types of business organizations be required?

On this penultimate question Robert Solow, one of the architects of the modern theory of economic growth, is reported as saying: 'There is no reason at all why capitalism could not survive without slow or even [with] no growth' (Stoll, 2008, p.94). Booth is more circumspect when he says that 'for a steady-state macroeconomy to function effectively, the requirements at a macroeconomic level are an incomes policy, an expanded government sector, and a reduction in the workweek, and the central need at a microeconomic level may be new organization forms that embody principles of economic democracy . . .' (Booth, 1998, p.155).

With respect to the larger rationale for a steady-state economy, Solow showed sympathy for concerns not usually heard from mainstream economists when he observed that 'it is possible that the US and Europe will find that . . . either continued growth will be too destructive to the environment and they are too dependent on scarce natural resources, or that they would rather use increasing productivity in the form of leisure' (Stoll, 2008, p.94). The case for a steady-state economy could not have been stated more succinctly.

12.5   CONCLUSION

It is more than 160 years since John Stuart Mill wrote favourably about the steady-state economy and over 30 years since Herman Daly wrote the book, so to speak, on the subject. In the meantime economic growth has proceeded apace, and for the past half-century or so has been the over-arching economic policy objective of countries and their governments around the world. With the emergence of 'sustainable development' in the 1980s as a possible alternative paradigm, the primacy of economic growth has been called into question and in some circles more atten-tion has begun to be paid to the environmental and social dimensions of development. New measures of progress have been proposed such as the Index of Sustainable Development (Daly and Cobb, 1994, pp. 443–507), the Genuine Progress Indicator (Talberth et al., 2007), Genuine Wealth (Hamilton, 2006) and the Human Development Index (United Nations Development Programme, 2006). These take a broader view of progress than just GDP and GDP per capita. Likewise, measures such as the ecological footprint (Wackernagel and Rees, 1996), the Living Planet Index (Hails et al., 2006) and HANPP (Haberl et al., 2007) provide quan-titative estimates of the environmental burden placed on the planet by people and our economies.

To a greater or lesser extent, the rationale for these alternative indicators stems from concerns similar to those expressed by the many contributors to steady-state economics, some of whose ideas have been discussed in this chapter. Yet it would be premature to say that the option of a steady-state economy has made it on to the public or political agenda in a significant way. The OECD, for example, remains committed to economic growth even as it writes about sustainable development and struggles to recon-cile the demands of growing economies with the biophysical limits of the planet (Strange and Bayley, 2009). In contrast, the UK's Sustainable Development Commission questioned the viability of economic growth over the long term and raised for serious consideration the possibility of seeking prosperity without growth (Jackson, 2009). Going even further, the governments of Bolivia, Cuba, Dominica, Honduras, Nicaragua and Venezuela declared in 2009 that 'the global economic, climate change, food and energy crises are products of the decadence of capitalism that threatens to put an end to the existence of life and the planet. To avoid this outcome it is necessary to develop an alternative model to that of the capitalist system' (ALBA, 2009).

In developed countries outside officialdom, there is a dialogue espe-cially in France about 'degrowth' or *décroissance* (Latouche, 2007), a lively website discussing steady-state economics run by the Centre for Advancement of the Steady-State Economy in the United States (CASSE, 2009) and numerous energy, environment and other groups increasingly making the links between their more specific concerns and the character and conduct of the economy.

In the words of Herman Daly, 'The closer the economy approaches the scale of the whole Earth the more it will have to conform to the physical behaviour mode of the Earth. That behaviour mode is a steady-state – a system that permits qualitative development but not aggregate quantitative growth' (Daly, 2008, p. 1). Whether we will make a careful and thoughtful transition to the steady-state remains to be seen but at least through the work of Professor Daly and all those he has inspired, we are better able to understand the options and choices ahead.

NOTES

1. See also Victor (1980).
2. Income elasticity of the demand for energy can be measured as the percentage change in energy divided by the percentage change in GDP.
3. To be more precise, the costs of producing each category of primary energy are used in the model rather than market prices to avoid the complexity that would be needed to account for differences in taxation, distribution costs in different parts of the country and the variety of energy customers and uses. Levelized costs for electricity generation for 2013 come from www.renewable-energysources.com (accessed 12 February 2015), adapted from US Energy Information Administration (2014). Costs for fossil fuels are from US Energy Information Administration (2013).
4. Since market prices reflect these costs, though not perfectly, changes in the costs influence changes in overall energy use and in its distribution among alternative energy sources.
5. This section of the chapter is adapted from chapter 10 of Victor (2008) where more details of LowGrow and more scenarios can be found. Chapter 11 provides a discussion of policies for managing without growth.
6. The Cobb-Douglas production function does not represent the throughput and substitution possibilities of the economy between manufactured and natural capital. Its role in LowGrow is only to estimate the relation between inputs of labour and capital required to generate output as measured by GDP.

REFERENCES

ALBA (2009), *Document of the Bolivarian Alternative for the Peoples of Our Americas (ALBA) Countries for the Fifth Summit of the Americas*, Cumaná.
Booth, D.E. (1998), *The Environmental Consequences of Growth: Steady-state Economics as an Alternative to Ecological Decline*, London and New York: Routledge.
Boulding, K.E. (1966), 'Economics of the coming Spaceship Earth', in H. Jarrett (ed.), *Environmental Quality in a Growing Economy: Essays from the Sixth RFF Forum*, Baltimore, MD: Johns Hopkins University Press, pp. 3–14.
Boulding, K.E. (1973), 'The shadow of the stationary state', in M. Olson and H.H. Landsberg (eds), *The No-growth Society*, New York: W.W. Norton & Co., pp. 89–101.
Burkett, P. (2004), 'Marx's reproduction schemes and the environment', *Ecological Economics*, **49**, 457–67.

CASSE (2009), Center for the Advancement of the Steady-State Economy, http://steadystate.org (accessed 1 February 2015).

Daly, H.E. (1968), 'On economics as a life science', *Journal of Political Economy*, **76**, 392–406.

Daly, H.E. (1977), *Steady-state Economics: The Economics of Biophysical Equilibrium and Moral Growth*, San Francisco, CA: W.H. Freeman.

Daly, H.E. (1990), 'Toward some operational principles of sustainable development', *Ecological Economics*, **2**, 1–6.

Daly, H.E. (1996), *Beyond Growth: The Economics of Sustainable Development*, Boston, MA: Beacon Press.

Daly, H.E. (2008), *A Steady-state Economy*, UK Sustainable Development Commission, available at http://www.sd-commission.org.uk/publications.php?id=775 (accessed 26 December 2014).

Daly, H.E. and J.B. Cobb Jr (1994), *For the Common Good: Redirecting the Economy Toward Community, the Environment, and a Sustainable Future*, Boston, MA: Beacon Press.

Daly, H.E. and J.C. Farley (2011), *Ecological Economics: Principles and Applications*, 2nd edn, Washington, DC: Island Press.

Gately, D. and H.G. Huntington (2002), 'The asymmetric effects of changes in price and income on energy and oil demand', *Oil Price and Policy*, **23**, 19–56.

Georgescu-Roegen, N. (1971), *The Entropy Law and the Economic Process*, Cambridge, MA: Harvard University Press.

Georgescu-Roegen, N. (1980), 'Selections from "Energy and Economic Myths"', in H.E. Daly (ed.), *Economics, Ecology, Ethics: Essays Toward a Steady-state Economy*, San Francisco, CA: W.H. Freeman and Co., pp. 61–81.

Haberl, H., K. Erb and F. Krausmann (2007), 'Human appropriation of net primary production (HANPP)', in E. Neumeyer (ed.), *Internet Encyclopedia of Ecological Economics*, International Society for Ecological Economics, pp. 1–15.

Hails, C., J. Loh and S. Goldfinger (2006), *Living Planet Report 2006*, Gland, Switerland: World Wildlife Fund.

Hamilton, K. (2006), *Where is the Wealth of Nations? Measuring Capital for the 21st Century*, Washington, DC: World Bank.

Hubbert, M.K. (1956), 'Nuclear energy and the fossil fuels', Publication No. 95, Shell Development Corporation, Houston, TX, available at http://www.hubbertpeak.com/Hubbert/1956/1956.pdf (accessed 26 December 2014).

Hubbert, M.K. (1974), 'M. King Hubbert on the nature of growth', National Energy Conservation Policy Act of 1974, Hearings before the Subcommittee on the Environment of the Committee on Interior and Insular Affairs House of Representatives, 6 June.

Jackson, T. (2009), *Prosperity Without Growth? The Transition to a Sustainable Economy*, London: Sustainable Development Commission.

Keynes, J.M. (1930), *Essays in Persuasion*, reprinted in 1963, New York: W.W. Norton & Co.

Keynes, J.M. (1935), *The General Theory of Employment Interest and Money*, New York: Harcourt-Brace.

Latouche, S. (2007), 'De-growth: an electoral stake?', *The International Journal of Inclusive Democracy*, **3** (1), available at http://www.inclusivedemocracy.org/journal/vol3/vol3_no1_Latouche_degrowth.htm (accessed December 2015).

Meadows D.H., D.L. Meadows, J. Randers and W. Behrens III (1972), *The Limits to Growth: A Report for the Club of Rome*, London: Earth Island.

Mill, J.S. (1848), *Principles of Political Economy: With Some of their Applications to Social Philosophy*, reprinted in 1970, London: John W. Parker.

OECD (2008), 'Average annual hours actually worked per worker', Vol. 2008, Release 01, OECD Factbook 2008, Paris.

Ogden, C.L., C.D. Fryar, M.D. Carroll and K.M. Flegal (2004), 'Mean body weight, height, and body mass index, United States 1960–2002'. Advance data from *Vital and Health Statistics* No. 347, 27 October, National Center for Health Statistics, Hyattsville, Maryland, pp. 1–20.

O'Neill, D.W. (2008), 'Steady state economies and recession: the same or different? Preliminary results of an empirical analysis', in *Proceedings of the Green Economics Institute Conference 2008*, Oxford: Green Economics Institute, pp. 116–22.

Rivers, N. and M. Jaccard (2005), 'Combining top-down and bottom-up approaches to energy-economy modeling using discrete choice methods', *The Energy Journal*, **26** (1), 83–106.

Soddy, F. (1926), *Wealth, Virtual Wealth and Debt: The Solution of the Economic Paradox*, London: Allen & Unwin.

Stoll, S. (2008), 'Fear of fallowing: the specter of a no-growth world', *Harper's Magazine*, March, 88–94.

Strange, T. and A. Bayley (2009), *Sustainable Development: Linking Economy, Society, Environment*, Paris: OECD.

Talberth, J., C. Cobb and N. Slattery (2007), 'The Genuine Progress Indicator 2006. A tool for sustainable development', Redefining Progress, available at http://rprogress.org/publications/2007/GPI%202006.pdf (accessed 26 December 2014).

Turner, G.M. (2008), 'A comparison of the limits to growth with 30 years of reality', *Global Environmental Change*, **18** (3), 397–411.

Turner, G.M. (2012), 'Have we reached the limits to growth?', *Chemistry in Australia*, October, 24–7.

United Nations Development Programme (2006), *Human Development Report 2006*, New York.

US Energy Information Administration (2008), *Renewable Energy Trends in Consumption and Electricity*, 2006 edn, available at http://www.eia.gov/totalenergy/data/annual/ (accessed December 2015).

US Energy Information Administration (2013), *Annual Energy Outlook 2014 Early Release*, December, available at http://www.eia.gov/totalenergy/data/annual/ (accessed December 2015).

US Energy Information Administration (2014), *Annual Energy Outlook 2014 with Projections to 2040*, April, available at http://www.eia.gov/totalenergy/data/annual/ (accessed December 2015).

US Energy Information Administration (2015), *Monthly Energy Review*, January, available at http://www.eia.gov/totalenergy/data/annual/ (accessed December 2015).

Victor, P.A. (1980), 'Economics and the challenge of environmental issues', in H.E. Daly (ed.), *Economics, Ecology, Ethics. Essays Toward a Steady-State Economy*, San Francisco: W.H. Freeman and Company, chapter 13.

Victor, P.A. (2008), *Managing Without Growth. Slower by Design, Not Disaster*, Cheltenham, UK and Northampton, MA, USA: Edward Elgar Publishing.

Victor, P.A. (2010), 'Ecological economics and economic growth', *Annals of the New York Academy of Sciences*, **1185**, 237–45.

Wackernagel, M. and W.E. Rees (1996), *Our Ecological Footprint: Reducing Human Impact on the Earth*, Gabriola Island, BC and Philadelphia, PA: New Society Publishers.

Zhang, X., (2010), 'Low income measurement in Canada: what do different lines and indexes tell us?', Statistics Canada Research Paper 75F0002M-No.3, available at http://www.statcan.gc.ca/pub/75f0002m/75f0002m2010003-eng.pdf (accessed 26 December 2014).

13. Socially sustainable economic degrowth

Joan Martinez-Alier

13.1 INTRODUCTION

Looking back to 2007, we see that the Intergovernmental Panel on Climate Change (IPCC) scenarios never contemplated (self-imposed censorship, perhaps) a decline in the rich countries' gross domestic product (GDP) of 5 per cent and then a long period of non-growth as might perhaps be the case. For the Organisation for Economic Co-operation and Development (OECD) countries as a whole, seven years after the crisis, the public debt has increased but the economy has scarcely recovered from the downturn of 2008–09. This was not in the economists' script. For 20 years, the orthodox slogan had been sustainable development (United Nations World Commission on Environment and Development, 1987), meaning economic growth that was environmentally sustainable. We know, however, that economic growth was not environmentally sustainable. The discussion on *décroissance* or degrowth that Nicholas Georgescu-Roegen started 40 years ago should now be a topic for discussion in the rich countries because *la décroissance est arrivée*. Now is the moment to substitute GDP by social and environmental indicators at the macro-level and to trace progress towards a socio-ecological transition by the behaviour of such indicators.

The economic crisis of 2008–09 afforded an opportunity to put the economy of the rich countries on a different trajectory as regards material and energy flows. Before 2008, world carbon dioxide emissions were growing by 3 per cent per year. Carbon dioxide emissions in many rich countries peaked in 2007. Now would be the time for a permanent socio-ecological transition to lower levels of energy and materials use, including also a decrease in the human appropriation of net primary production (HANPP). The crisis might also give an opportunity for a restructuring of social institutions. In 2008–09 two landmark studies inspired by Daly's *Steady-state Economics* (Daly, 1991) appeared on these lines: Tim Jackson's (2009) *Prosperity Without Growth* and Peter Victor's (2008)

Managing Without Growth. The objective in rich countries should be to live well without the imperative of economic growth.

Moreover, we are on the path for a reduction in world population once it hopefully peaks around 2050 at between 8.5 and 9 billion, thereby reducing pressure on resources and sinks in the second half of the twenty-first century.

Georgescu-Roegen's explicit sponsorship of the concept of *décroissance* (degrowth) in 1979 (Grinevald and Rens, 1979 [1995]), Herman Daly's views on the steady state since the early 1970s, Serge Latouche's success in France and Italy in the last ten years insisting on economic degrowth (Latouche, 2006) and the contributions to an ecological macroeconomics without growth by Peter Victor (2008) and Tim Jackson (2009) have prepared the terrain. Now is the time in rich countries for socially sustainable economic degrowth reinforced by an alliance with the environmental justice movemements and the 'environmentalism of the poor' and the indigenous in the global South (Martinez-Alier, 2012). In my view, ecological economists have not paid enough attention to environmental justice movements within the present generation. The growing environmental justice movements were in a way foreseen by K.W. Kapp's view of 'externalities' not as market failures but as 'cost-shifting successes'. Cost-shifting not only to future generations and to other species but also to poor people in our own generation leads sometimes to complaints and conflicts.

13.2   THE ECONOMY HAS THREE LEVELS

Frederick Soddy's *Cartesian Economics* was published in 1922, and *Wealth, Virtual Wealth and Debt* in 1926. He had a Nobel Prize in Chemistry and was a professor at Oxford as explained in my book *Ecological Economics* (Martinez-Alier, 1987). Soddy's teachings of the 1920s became easy to understand for ecological economists who had read Georgescu-Roegen's *The Entropy Law and the Economic Process* (1971). Soddy's main point was simple and applies today. It is easy for the financial system to increase the debts (private or public), and to mistake this expansion of credit for the creation of real wealth. However, in the industrial system, growth of production and growth of consumption imply growth in the extraction and final destruction of fossil fuels. Energy is dissipated, cannot be recycled. Real wealth would instead be the current flow of energy from the sun. Economic accounting is false because it mistakes depletion of resources and the increase of entropy for wealth creation.

The obligation to pay debts at compound interest could be fulfilled by squeezing the debtors for a while. Other means of paying the debt are either inflation (debasement of the value of money) or economic growth – which is falsely measured because it is based on undervalued exhaustible resources and unvalued pollution. Economic accounting does not properly count environmental damages and the exhaustibility of resources. This was Soddy's doctrine. He was certainly a precursor of ecological economics (as noticed by Daly, 1980; Martinez-Alier, 1987).

In other words, the economy has three levels. At the top there is the financial level that can grow by loans made to the private sector or to the state, sometimes without any assurance of repayment as in the present crisis. The financial system borrows against the future, on the expectation that indefinite economic growth will give the means to repay the interests and the debts. The financial system creates 'virtual' wealth. Banks give credit far beyond what they have got as deposits, and this drives or pulls economic growth at least for a while. Then there is what the economists describe as the real economy, the so-called productive economy. As reported in *The Economist* (8 April 2009), Hakan Samuelsson, Chairman of the German truck-making firm MAN, made this distinction very clearly when he said: 'Creating value through financial leverage will be harder in future, so we can get back to our real job which is creating industrial value through technology, innovation, and efficient manufacturing.'

When the economist's real economy grows, it indeed allows to pay back some or all the debt, when it does not grow enough, debts are defaulted. The mountain of debt had grown in 2008 much beyond what the increases in GDP could pay back. The situation was financially not sustainable. But the GDP itself was not ecologically sustainable. Down below, in the basement and foundations of the economic building, underneath the economists' real economy, there is the third level: the ecological economists' *real-real* economy, the flows of energy and materials (carried by trucks and ships). Their growth depends partly on economic factors (types of markets, prices) and in part on physical limits. At present, there are not only resource limits but also conspicuous sink limits. Climate change is caused mainly by of the excessive burning of fossil fuels.

Returning again to 'debt-fuelled growth' would not only be financially dangerous. It is indeed difficult for the time being, as banks are still loaded with 'toxic assets' and the public debt has increased in many countries. The phrase itself ('debt-fuelled growth') is misleading. Growth is not 'fuelled' by debt and by money, it is prosaically fuelled by coal, oil and gas. The fossil fuels are not produced by the economy, they were geologically produced a long time ago.

The economic crisis of 2008–09 brought John Maynard Keynes back to the main stage. In Keynesian language, we can say that economies had unused productive capacity, there was a gap between effective demand and full-capacity utilization of labour and industrial equipment. Unemployment was increasing, and the appropriate remedy was to increase public expenditure, 'deficit spending' as it is called. Public spending is good because it would indirecly lead to buying cars, and paying off mortgages and even buying new houses, getting such industries out of the doldrums. Governments were under pressure not only to increase spending for public investments or consumption but to refinance private debts to banks that would not be paid ('toxic assets'), converting to some extent such private debts into public debts.

Keynes wanted to get out of the crisis of 1929. The pre-Keynesian prescription of waiting for the market to reach equilibrium, waiting therefore for increasing unemployment to depress wages so much that employers would want to hire workers again, was a recipe for disaster. To make this point clear, Keynes famously said that he did not care what happened in the long run once the economy would recover from the crisis. In the 1950s economists such as Roy Harrod and Evsey Domar converted Keynesianism into a doctrine of long-term growth. Provided there was enough private or public expenditure in consumption and investment to keep effective demand close to potential supply at full capacity utilization, the economy would not fall into crisis. Meanwhile, the investment would have increased potential supply, so that new expenditure would be required in the next round in order for the economy not to fall into a crisis, in a virtuous path of continuous growth. Such economic models were metaphysical in the sense that they did not consider exhaustible resources or pollution.

Keynesianism was triumphant in the 1960s, the era of very cheap oil. Later, both short-run and long-run Keynesianisms were left aside. Neoliberal thought was resurrected. The neoliberals, like Hayek, thought that markets knew much more than the state. But one unanswered objection to neoliberalism raised by environmentalists was that the market did not value future, intergenerational scarcities (as Otto Neurath had already pointed out in Vienna in the 1920s against Von Mises and Hayek in the socialist calculation debate, see Martinez-Alier, 1987).

Since the crisis of 2008–09, neoliberalism has been suffering from ill health. Some bankers asked for the state to take over their banks. Keynes came back to some extent, reincarnated in Stiglitz and Krugman. As ecological economists we must ask, was this a short-run Keynes to get out of the worst aspects of the crisis or also a long-run Keynes to get into a path of continuous economic growth?

Those who proposed a short-run Green Keynesianism or a Green New Deal as a temporary measure were close to ecological economics. If public investment must grow, as indeed it must to contain the rise in unemployment, it is better to channel it to the welfare of the citizens and to 'green' energy production, than into motorways and airports. However, Green Keynesianism should not become a doctrine of continous economic growth. Until now, growth has come with the use of energy from coal, oil and natural gas. In Green Keynesianism it seemed desirable to increase public investment in energy conservation, photovoltaic installations, urban public transport, housing rehabilitation, organic agriculture. But it did not seem desirable to persevere in the faith of economic growth. In rich countries a slight economic decline was already taking place and it could easily be socially sustainable. We were not in the 1930s – in Europe we have economies with incomes per capita of over 25 000 euros. Going back 10 per cent (with a corresponding decrease in energy and material flows) could be managed if institutions of redistribution were in place. Thus, we could enter into a socio-ecological transition. There is already an agreement in Europe for the carbon dioxide emissions to be cut by 20 per cent compared to 1990. In fact, emissions and GDP have been decreasing faster than required to reach this target. The Keynesians therefore pushed for greater government expenditure in 2008–09, sometimes green-coloured, not caring much about the increase in the debt, the weight of which could be mitigated in due course by inflation. Meanwhile, the financial sector and in general the financial creditors (the 'Debtocracy', as it is known in Greece), which includes pensioners, in the European Union (EU) supported 'German' anti-Keynesian policies of austerity to the Keynesians' dismay.

Ecological economists are neither for increasing the debts (because we do not believe in 'debt-fuelled growth') nor for socially suicidal austerity policies and increases in unemployment. We have a third position. We are for 'financial prudence' (as Jackson, 2009 put it) and a steady-state economy (after a period of some degrowth in rich countries) that is socially and environmentally sustainable.

The feminist movement made clear many decades ago that GDP does not value what is not in the market, like unpaid domestic work and voluntary work. A society rich in 'relational goods and services' would have a lower GDP than an (impossible) society where personal relations would be exclusively mediated by the market. The sustainable degrowth movement insists on the non-chrematistic value of local, reciprocal services. Moreover, economists (or rather, social psychologists) now agree that above a certain threshold GDP growth does not lead necessarily to greater happiness. This research updates the literature on the so-called Easterlin Paradox. Therefore, GDP should no longer have the dominant position in politics that it now has, to the detriment of environmental and social considerations.

However, degrowth might lead to social problems that we must confront before it is socially accepted. If labour productivity (for example, number of cars that a worker produces per year) grows by 2 per cent annually, but the economy is not doing the same, this will lead to increased unemployment. The answer must be twofold. Increases in productivity are not well measured. If there is replacement of human energy by machines, does the price of energy take into account the depletion of resources and climate change? We know that it is not so. Furthermore, we should separate the right to receive remuneration from the fact of being employed. This separation already exists in many cases (children and young people, pensioners, persons receiving unemployment benefits), but it should be extended further. We have to redefine the meaning of 'job', taking into account the unpaid domestic services and the voluntary sector and we must introduce or expand the coverage of a universal Basic Income or Citizen Income.[1]

Another objection is raised. Who will pay for the mountain of debts, mortgages and other private and public debt if the economy does not grow? The answer must be that no one will pay. We cannot force the economy to grow at the rate at which debts accumulate. The financial system must have rules different from today.[2] In the United States and Europe what is new is not, therefore, Keynesianism, not even Green Keynesianism. What is new is a growing social movement for sustainable degrowth. The crisis opens up opportunities for new institutions and social habits.

13.3   THE PRICE OF OIL

The teaching of economics in universities is still based on an image of the economy as a merry-go-round between consumers and producers. They encounter each other in markets for consumer goods or in markets for the services of production factors (like selling labour time for a wage). Prices are formed, quantities are exchanged. This is Chrematistics. Macroeconomic accounts (GDP) aggregate the quantities multiplied by the prices. The economy may be described, however, in a different way, as a system of transformation of (exhaustible) energy and materials (including water) into useful products and services, and finally into waste. This is ecological economics (from Boulding, 1966; Daly, 1968; Georgescu-Roegen, 1966, 1971; Kneese and Ayres, 1969).

The critique of conventional economic accounting often emphasizes the forgotten current values of environmental services from ecosystems. The environmental services from coral reefs, mangroves, tropical rainforest may be given a notional money value per hectare per year, and then the lost hectares are translated into virtual economic losses. This approach might be good in order to impress the public with the importance of environmental losses, although it tends to leave aside non-economic values like human livelihoods, indigenous territorial rights, the 'rights of nature'. In any case, it is certainly insufficient in order to grasp the relations between economy and environment because our economy depends not only on current photosynthesis but on the photosynthesis of millions of years ago for our main energy sources. It depends on ancient biochemical cycles for other mineral resources that we squander without replacement. In the case of oil, the extraction peak in the Hubbert curve has perhaps been reached. In 2013 we were taking over 90 million barrels per day (mbd) – in terms of calories, the world average was equivalent to 20 000 kilocalories (kcal) per person per day (ten times the food energy intake), and in the United States it was equivalent to 100 000 kcal per person per day. In exosomatic energy terms, oil is then far more important than biomass.

The EU, Japan, the United States and some parts of China and India are large net importers of energy and materials. The United States, having reached internal peak-oil in the 1970s, imported nearly half the oil it consumed before it increased the extraction of oil and gas with fracking technology. The European Union and Japan continue to be net importers of energy. These imports of energy and materials into rich countries must by necessity be relatively cheap for their social metabolism to work properly. As Hornborg (1998) put it, 'market prices are the means by which world system centres extract exergy (i.e. available energy) from the peripheries', aided some times by military power. The attempt to make Iraq produce an extra 2 or 3 mbd failed for some years after 2003, as Alan Greenspan noted sadly in his memoirs. The Organization of the Petroleum Exporting Countries (OPEC) after the drop in the price of oil in 1998, and helped by efforts of Hugo Chavez from Venezuela and the economic boom in China and India, had successfully managed the restriction of supply. The price of oil peaked in 2008, went down at the start of the crisis, remained stable until 2013 and has come down afterwards because of new 'non-conventional' supplies of oil and gas and the slowdown of the world economy.

During the building boom in the United States, houses were sold to people who were unable to pay the mortgages, or houses were built (as in the large acreage of new empty houses in Spain) on the hope that creditworthy buyers would appear. Real median salaries in the United States did not increase much in the last years but credit to consumers had indeed grown. Income distribution had become more unequal. Household savings were at a minimum when the crisis started. The bankers apparently thought that economic growth would continue and would increase the value of the houses that were mortgaged. They 'packaged' the mortgages and sold them to other banks, which sold or tried to sell them to innocent investors. The housing boom ended in 2008. The private building industry has nearly stopped in some countries.

Part nationalization of some banks in the EU and the United States avoided sudden widespread bank failure, at the cost of raising the public deficit. Deficit spending in a situation of lack of aggregate demand is a Keynesian prescription with which one might agree – it should go to solve the most pressing social problems and to environmental investments, and not to military spending (to secure oil?) or to the car and motorway industries. In any case, the financial free-for-all was not the only cause of the crisis, which was triggered by high oil prices due not only to the OPEC oligopoly but also to the approaching peak oil. In fact, economic theory does not say that an exhaustible resource should be sold at the marginal cost of extraction. One could argue that oil at the 2008 peak of US$140 a barrel is still cheap from the point of view of its fair intergenerational allocation and the externalities it produces.

The present economic crisis is not only a financial crisis, and it was not caused only by a supply of new houses in the United States that exceeded the demand that could be financed sustainably. It was also caused by high oil prices. The stock exchange started to drop in January 2008 but until July 2008 the price of oil kept increasing. As the crisis deepened, the price of oil went down but it recovered in real terms. There is here an automatic 'de-stabilizer' for the economy. It is difficult to find new oil, as we go down the Hubbert curve. Moreover, a low price of oil implies a declining supply in a few years because of declining investment in the fields with higher marginal costs. On top of this, OPEC tried to reduce oil extraction during the crisis to keep the price up. The boom in shale gas fracking has compensated to some extent the difficulty in getting cheap oil. It is yet to be seen for how long it will last, and what the local environmental liabilities will be.

13.4 ECONOMIC DEGROWTH AND CARBON DIOXIDE EMISSIONS

The economic crisis meant a welcome change to the totally unsustainable increase of carbon dioxide emissions. The Kyoto objective of 1997 was generous with the rich countries because it gave them property rights on the carbon sinks and the atmosphere in exchange for the promise of a reduction by 2012 of 5 per cent of their emissions relative to 1990. This modest Kyoto objective was fulfilled by most signatories. One could easily foresee by October 2008 that the carbon trade would collapse unless lower caps were adopted. Air travel, housing starts, car sales decreased in the second half of 2008 in many European countries and the United States. Motorists in the United States were buying 9 per cent less gasoline in early

October 2008 than in early October 2007, so that the declines in emissions during the crisis were not a surprise.

However, the apostles of growth are not willing to use the current crisis to shift the economy to a different technological and consumption pattern. On the contrary, they find reasons to think car sales would remain strong because while the United States have nearly one car for every person of driving age, China has less than three cars for every 100 people and India fewer still. 'Once people have a roof over their heads, meat on the table and a good job, the next thing they want is a set of wheels' pontificated *The Economist* (13 November 2008), announcing that in the next 40 years the world's fleet of cars is expected to increase from around 700 million today to nearly 3 billion.

The economy of India and also that of China (propelled by internal demand) might well continue to grow at rates of not less than 4 or 5 per cent in coming years. The car industry will grow faster than the economy and will be an engine of economic growth together with the building industry. However, a world of 3 billion cars would require a much increased expenditure of energy. How will the real economy impact on the *real-real* economy? How will the cars be fuelled?

There is a historic trend towards increasing energy costs of obtaining energy (a lower energy return on investment (EROI). Brazil's discovery in 2006 of 30 000 million barrels of oil (one year of world consumption) thousands of metres under the sea might become a bottomless sink for energy and money. Coming down from the peak of the Hubbert curve will be politically and environmentally difficult. Conflicts arise all the time in the Niger Delta and in the Amazonia of Peru and Ecuador. Supplies have increased from non-conventional sources but conflicts have also increased. Appeal to some energy sources such as agro-fuels and nuclear energy will compound the difficulties. Wind and photovoltaic energy are fortunately increasing. They will help to compensate for the dwindling supplies of oil over the next few decades. Coal supplies are increasing (they already grew seven times in the twentieth century) but coal is noxious locally, and also globally because of carbon dioxide emissions.

13.5 WHEN WILL CARBON DIOXIDE EMISSIONS PEAK?

Global carbon dioxide emissions declined briefly in 2009 as a result of the economic crisis, offering a unique global chance to stabilize emissions. In 2010, however, absolute emissions achieved record levels, returning to the prior trend more rapidly than in previous financial crises.

Carbon dioxide concentrations in the atmosphere are at the time of writing (March 2014) hovering at a record level of 401 parts per million (ppm) according to the measurements at the Mauna Loa observatory in Hawaii. This means an increase of 33 per cent above the level of 300 ppm that Svante Arrhenius used in his articles of 1896, and his textbook of 1903 when he pointed out that burning coal would increase the concentration of carbon dioxide in the atmosphere and would increase temperatures. Between 1970 and 2000, the concentration had increased by 1.5 ppm per year, and from 2001 through 2007 annual growth in concentration reached 2.1 ppm. In early 2008 the world was still travelling at all speed towards 450 ppm to be reached in about 30 years. The great increase in the prices of oil, gas and other commodities until July 2008, and the economic crisis in the second half of 2008 and in 2009, stopped economic growth and briefly changed the trend in carbon dioxide emissions. Countries still mired in recession continue to have lower emissions than before and others, like Germany, seem to be on a path of real change in the energy mix, permanently decreasing the share of fossil fuels. From the point of view of climate change, the economic crisis should certainly be welcome.

The IPCC argues in its reports that emissions should go down by 80 per cent (and not by the paltry 2 or 3 per cent achieved in 2009). The objective of 80 per cent reduction is far from today's reality, and also from the post-Kyoto commitments in Paris of 2015.

Spain had been the worst offender among the European countries that did not comply with the Kyoto targets under the European 'bubble', followed by Italy and Denmark. This made the Spanish case interesting although her emissions per capita were 'only' double the world average. In 2007, Spanish emissions still grew over 2 per cent in comparison to 2006, reaching an increase of 52.6 per cent compared to 1990, the base year for the Kyoto Protocol. Inside Europe, Spain was allowed to have an increase of 15 per cent in 2012 and she had increased already 52.6 per cent. The government said in 2008 that it would buy permits from Eastern Europe and also use the Kyoto flexibility mechanisms.

In Spain, the 2007 emissions peak seemed likely to be definitive. This is after all an economy with a high level of income per capita that is now declining somewhat while unemployment increases but where the car and electricity markets cannot easily grow as in China and India. There is after the crisis a large unused electricity production capacity. Wind and solar energy had increased while industrial production declined nearly 20 per cent in December 2008 compared to one year earlier. Cement production had gone down to an estimated 11 million tons per year in 2013 from a previous peak of 50 million tons that was propelled by a building boom that produced a large excess of unsold houses and flats, and very large financial debts.

Lack of demand for their products led several industries to sell their carbon emission permits at the end of 2008. The crisis produced in Spain as elsewhere in Europe an abundance of permits and a decline in the price of carbon dioxide allowances. A low price is a disincentive for the introduction of technical changes that would avoid carbon emissions. The EU should have rapidly decreased the allocation of permits. Notice that the present amount of permits is excessive because it was repeatedly based on economic projections that did not include an economic crisis. Economic degrowth could not be imagined by the usually well-informed and competent European bureaucracy. It must be emphasized that the market for carbon dioxide allowances is an artificial market. The supply depends on the political will to restrict emissions, not down to the necessary level (for example, 80 per cent reduction), but what is seen as politically and economically bearable in a mindset that assumes continuous economic growth even in the richest countries. From 2014, Spain is again slowly increasing emissions.

13.6 THE FAILURES OF THE FRAMEWORK CONVENTION ON CLIMATE CHANGE

The GDP of the world decreased over 2 per cent in 2009, while economic degrowth in the United States, the EU and Japan was even larger than this. Fossil fuel use and emissions from the developed nations decreased by even more. This was really high in comparison with the objectives that were admitted politically up to then. However, because of a problem of mental censorship, neither the IPCC nor Nicholas Stern's report had contemplated a scenario of slight economic degrowth in the world economy followed by a period of non-growth in the EU and the United States. This is the scenario that would have converted the carbon dioxide emissions peak of 2007 into a unique historical event.

Increased carbon dioxide emissions from China and India continued, more or less in line with economic growth in India (of about 5 per cent), and a little lower than economic growth in China. India's emissions are per capita much below the world average (India has over 15 per cent of the world population and about 4 per cent of emissions). China's emissions are per capita much closer to the world average. As a country, it is now the largest emitter. Since 2009, increased emissions in India, China and other countries whose economies never ceased growing during the crisis exceeded the decrease in the United States, EU, other European countries and Japan, and emissions broke new records in 2010. The 2007 emissions peak has so far turned out to be an isolated event.

These results can be attributed in part to the failure of the Conferences of the Parties (COPs) of the Framework Convention on Climate Change to take advantage of these emissions reductions, beginning in Copenhagen in December 2009, where there was no real acknolwedgement of the positive effects of the crisis. A slight economic degrowth and a socio-ecological transition towards a steady state in the rich economies was not accepted as a plausible and beneficial scenario. Raw material exporting countries did not change their tune to ask for exporting less and at higher prices, by introducing natural capital depletion taxes, and taxes that compensate for negative local externalities. None of the COPs favoured the idea that OPEC briefly considered in 2007, introducing the Daly-Correa tax on oil exports to help finance the world energy transition. The Yasuni ITT initiative born in Ecuador was a promising idea ('leave oil in the soil' in areas of particularly valuable biodiversity and where human rights are threatened) but it did not make progress although it is still politically alive. As a result, carbon emissions are again increasing with the economic recovery.

13.7   TOXIC ASSETS AND POISONOUS LIABILITIES

The assets that take the form of claims to debts that will remain unpaid have been given the funny name of 'toxic assets'. In the balance sheet of banks, the value of such assets will have to be downsized or written off. On the liability side of the balance sheet, our accounting conventions do not include damages to the environment. An enormous 'carbon debt' is owed to future generations, and to the poor people of the world who have produced little greenhouse gases. Large environmental liabilities are also due by private firms. Chevron-Texaco was fined $19 billion for environmental damages by Ecuadorean courts in 2011 and 2012. Then in 2013, on a second appeal, the Supreme Court of Ecuador halved the fine to $9.5 billion (because 'punitive damages' were not foreseen in Ecuadorian law). In 2014 a US court barred enforcement of the fine in the United States. It is still an open question whether Chevron-Texaco will ever pay for its environmental liabilities in Ecuador. The Rio Tinto company has left behind very large liabilities since 1888 in Andalusia where it got its name, also in Bougainville, in Namibia, in West Papua together with Freeport McMoran, debts to poor or indigenous peoples. Shell has very large liabilities in the Niger Delta. Don't worry. These poisonous debts are in the history books but not in the accounting books.

Look at the current case of Vedanta bauxite mining in the Niyamgiri hills in Orissa. The decline in the price of aluminium if the economic crisis recurs and deepens might save the Niyamgiri hills. The price dropped more than half in the last months of 2008, and bauxite also became cheaper. However, this decline was not permanent. We may still ask: how many tons of bauxite is a tribe or a species on the edge of extinction worth? And how can you express such values in terms that a minister of finance can understand? Against the economic logic of euros and dollars, the peasant and tribal languages of valuation go unheeded. These include the language of territorial rights against external exploitation, the International Labour Organization (ILO) Convention 169 that guarantees prior consent for projects on indigenous land, or in India the protection of the adivasi by the Constitution and by court decisions. Appeal could be made also to ecological and aesthetic values. The Niyamgiri hills are sacred to the Dongria Kondh. We could ask them: How much for your God? How much for the services provided by your God?

13.8   FROM THE SOUTH: THE ENVIRONMENTALISM OF THE POOR

One may readily agree that conventional economic accounting is certainly misleading. The experience that Pavan Sukhdev (with Haripriya Gundimeda and Pushpam Kumar) gained in India trying to give economic values to non-timber products from forests, and to other environmental services (such as carbon uptake, water and soil retention), has been an inspiration for The Economics of Ecosystems and Biodiversity (TEEB) process sponsored by the United Nations Environment Programme (UNEP). As the TEEB team states, a monetary representation of the services provided by clean water, access to wood and pastures and medicinal plants does not really measure the essential dependence of poor people on such resources and services.

While public policies may be improved by giving money values to environmental resources and services that are undervalued or not valued at all in conventional economic accounting, there are nevertheless other considerations. First, do not forget our uncertain knowledge about the working of ecosystems, and about the future impacts of new technologies. Second, do not exclude non-monetary values from decision-making processes. Don't practice the fetishism of fictitious commodities.

In National Income Accounting, one could introduce valuations of ecosystem and biodiversity losses either in satellite accounts (physical and monetary) or in adjusted GDP accounts ('Green Accounts'). The economic valuation of losses might be low compared to the economic gains of projects that destroy biodiversity. However, which groups of people suffer most by such losses? In their project 'Green Accounting for India', Sukhdev, Gundimeda and Kumar found that the most significant direct beneficiaries of forest biodiversity and ecosystem services are the poor, and the predominant impact of a loss or denial of these inputs is on the well-being of the poor. The poverty of the beneficiaries makes these losses more acute as a proportion of their 'livelihood incomes' than is the case for the people of India at large. Hence, the notion of 'the GDP of the Poor': for instance, when water in the local river or aquifer is polluted because of mining, they cannot afford to buy water in plastic bottles. (TEEB Interim Report, 2008). Therefore, when poor people see that their chances of livelihood are threatened because of mining projects, dams, tree plantations or large industrial areas, they complain not because they are professional environmentalists but because they need the services of the environment for their immediate survival. This is the 'environmentalism of the poor'. There are thousands of such environmental conflicts around the world, with many victims. We are collecting many of them in a project called EJOLT (Environmental Justice Organizations, Liabilities and Trade), and have produced an Atlas of Environmental Justice available online in 2014 (www.ejatlas.org).

In *Down to Earth* (15 August 2008), Sunita Narain gave current examples from India where economic growth remains robust, driven by internal consumption, cheap oil imports and domestic coal extraction, and public expenditure:

> In Sikkim, bowing to local protests, the government has cancelled 11 hydroelectric projects. In Arunachal Pradesh, dam projects are being cleared at breakneck speed and resistance is growing. In Uttarakhand last month, two projects on the Ganga were put on hold and there is growing concern about the rest. In Himachal Pradesh, dams are so controversial that elections were won where candidates said they would not allow these to be built. Many other projects, from thermal power stations to 'greenfield' mining, are being resisted. The South Korean giant Posco's iron ore mine, steel plant and port are under fire. The prime minister has promised the South Korean premier the project will go ahead by August. But local people are not listening. They don't want to lose their land and livelihood and do not believe in promises of compensation. In Maharashtra, mango growers are up in arms against the proposed thermal power station in Ratnagiri. In every nook and corner of the country where land is acquired, or water sourced, for industry, people are fighting even to death. There are wounds. There is violence. There is also desperation. . . They had seen their neighbours displaced, promised jobs and money that never came. They knew they were poor. But they also knew modern development would make them poorer. It was the same in prosperous Goa, where I found village after village fighting against the powerful mining lobby . . . . (Narain, 2008)

These movements combine livelihood, social, economic and environmental issues, with emphasis on issues of extraction and pollution. They set their 'moral economy' in opposition to the logic of extraction of oil, minerals, wood or agro-fuels at the 'commodity frontiers', defending biodiversity and their own livelihood. In many instances they draw on a sense of local identity (indigenous rights and values such as the sacredness of the land) but they also connect easily with the politics of the left. However, the traditional left in Southern countries still tends to see environmentalism as a luxury of the rich.

13.9 FROM THE SOUTH: A REFUSAL TO PROVIDE CHEAP COMMODITIES?

The question is not whether economic value can be determined only in existing markets, inasmuch as economists have developed methods for the monetary valuation of environmental goods and services or of negative externalities outside the market. Rather, the question is whether all evaluations in a given conflict (on extraction of copper and gold in Peru or bauxite in Orissa, on a hydro-electric dam in the northeast of India, on the destruction of a mangrove in Bangladesh, Honduras or Brazil to the benefit of shrimp exports, on the determination of the suitable level of carbon dioxide emissions by the EU) must be reduced to a single dimension. Such an exclusion of values should be rejected favouring instead the acceptance of a plurality of incommensurable values.

With the economic crisis, will there now be an end to the boom in exports of energy and materials, thus diminishing pressures at the commodity frontiers? Grandiose plans for more and more exports from Latin America were pushed particularly by President Lula of Brazil, and continue with Dilma Rousseff, his successor. More roads, pipelines, harbours and *hidrovias*, more exports from Latin America of oil, gas, coal, copper, iron ore, soybeans, cellulose, biodiesel and ethanol, this has been the credo of Presidents Lula and Rousseff. In October 2008, and in total opposition to the views of Via Campesina and the Movimento dos trabalhadores rurais Sem Terra (MST or landless farm workers movement) in Brazil, Lula was still pushing for generally opening the world markets to agricultural exports. He went to India asking for the liberalization of agricultural imports and exports in the Doha round. True, the export boom gave Lula money for social purposes and increased his popularity, facilitating Rousseff's election. Petrobras was not less dangerous to the environment and to the indigenous peoples of Latin America than Repsol or Oxy. The Brazilian leaders' obsession with primary exports made them do nothing about deforestation of Amazonia and drove Environment Minister Marina Silva to resign in 2008. This strategy has been scarcely affected by the crash of 2008–09. The continued insistence on the virtues of ethanol for export is misguided. Agro-fuels have a low EROI (especially taking into account the vegetation that already existed before agro-fuels occupy the land), they increase the HANPP to the detriment of the biomass need of other species and they imply large unpaid-for 'virtual' water exports.

In fact, the crisis should have been an incentive to focus on internal development, and not to sell the environment so cheaply. Too many other values (social, environmental) have been sacrificed to commodity exports. In this respect, at the November 2007 OPEC summit meeting in Vienna when Ecuador came back to this organization, OPEC approved in principle a resolution in support of the Yasuni-ITT proposal (to leave oil in the ground in a territory with uncontacted indigenous people and of great biodiversity value), and it also voiced interest in the so-called Daly-Correa eco-tax. The tax was proposed by President Correa at that OPEC meeting and it is based on the concept by Herman Daly in a speech to OPEC in 2001 (Daly, 2007). OPEC countries have dismissed the existence of the enhanced greenhouse effect. This eco-tax would show their concern for climate change. An OPEC imposed carbon tax at the oil wellhead instead of attempted regulation of emissions from the tailpipe (by carbon taxes or cap-and-trade) would be fairer to exporting countries and perhaps more effective in reducing global carbon dioxide emissions. This eco-tax would make acceptance of climate change easier for oil exporting countries (and also, if imitated, for gas and coal exporting countries). The principle is export less at a higher price. Money generated from the tax would go towards financing an energy transition away from fossil fuels, towards helping poor people around the world, and towards helping countries like Ecuador and Nigeria to keep oil (or gas or coal) in the ground when located under fragile and culturally sensitive ecosystems. (Martinez-Alier and Temper, 2007).

The economic crisis brought down the prices of various commodities including oil, in response to diminished demand, but many have since recovered. Nonetheless, even these higher prices remain cheap. In fact, the world economy depends on such cheap prices for the transference of energy and materials from peripheries to industrial cores. However, a refusal from the South to provide cheap commodities to the industrial economy, imposing natural capital depletion taxes and export quotas, would help the North (including some parts of China) in its necessary long-term path towards an economy that uses less materials and energy.

13.10   BOTTOM-UP NEO-MALTHUSIANISM

The socio-ecological transition towards lower levels of use of energy and materials will be helped if the world demographic transition is completed and, even more, if the population after reaching a peak at 9 billion inhabitants then goes down to 5000 million, as some projections indicate (Lutz et al., 2001). Remember that the world population increased four fold in the twentieth century from 1500 million to 6000 million. Environmental awareness might influence birth-rates (as in the European neo-Malthusianism of 1900 and in China since 1980).

The importance of population growth in the increase of social metabolism is obvious. Paul Ehrlich's equation I = PAT could be applied historically, with an adequate indicator for T (technology).

There were many debates around 1900 on 'how many people could the earth feed' focusing only on the needs of the human species. The neo-Malthusians of the late nineteenth and early twentieth centuries were political radicals and feminists. There was a large difference between the original Malthusianism of T.R. Malthus and the neo-Malthusianism of 1900. Scholarly historical work on neo-Malthusianism has clearly documented the radical, feminist movement in favour of limiting births in Europe and the United States around 1900. In France this movement took the name of *la grève des ventres* (wombs on strike). In south India, the 'self-respect' movement launched by E.V. Ramasamy (called Periyar, a Tamil thinker and political activist, 1879–1973) took a similar line. In Brazil the feminist neo-Malthusian anarchist Maria Lacerda de Moura wrote: 'Love one another more and do not multiply so much.' This intellectual and social history allows me to present the following definitions.

Malthusianism: Population undergoes exponential growth unless checked by war and pestilence, or by chastity and late marriages. Food grows less than proportionately to the labour input, because of decreasing returns. Hence, subsistence crises.

Neo-Malthusianism of 1900: Human populations could regulate their own growth through contraception. Women's freedom was required for this, and desirable for its own sake. Poverty was explained by social inequality. 'Conscious procreation' was needed to prevent low wages and pressure on natural resources. This was a successful bottom-up movement in Europe and America against states (which wanted more soldiers) and churches (Masjuan, 2000; Ronsin, 1980).

Neo-Malthusianism after 1970: A doctrine and practice sponsored by international organizations and some governments. Population growth is seen as a main cause of poverty and environmental degradation. Therefore, states must introduce contraceptive methods, even without women's prior consent.

Anti-Malthusianism: The view that assumes that human population growth is no major threat to the natural environment, and that it is even conducive to economic growth as Esther Boserup and other economists have argued.

13.11   SUSTAINABLE DEGROWTH

A transition to sustainability requires new thinking on demography and on the socio-ecological transition. Marina Fischer-Kowalski and Helmut Haberl of the IFF in Vienna, influenced by the work of environmental historian Rolf Peter Sieferle and by ecological anthropologists, ecological economists and industrial ecologists, recently edited a book entitled *Socioecological Transitions and Global Change* (Fischer-Kowalski and Haberl, 2007). From hunter-gatherer societies to agricultural societies to industrial societies, the authors of this book uncover quantifiable patterns of use of energy and materials, population densities, land use and working time. They try also to distinguish possible from impossible futures. For instance, is it plausible to think of a world of 8 billion people with an energy expenditure of 300 Gigajoules (GJ) and a use of materials of 16 tons per capita per year? Are we, on the contrary, on the verge of a socio-ecological transition that will reduce energy and material use in the rich economies even if this implies economic degrowth?

The transition needs a reform of social institutions (to deal with unemployment), and also a reform of financial institutions to stop the financial level of the economy from growing without reference to the underlying physical realities. The imaginative selling of derivatives (financial 'products'), and the existence of unregulated offshore banking, have taken a knock in public opinion. Sensible proposals are made by moderate political forces to turn banking into a nationalized public service. Beyond this, the crisis provides an opportunity for thinking about the *real-real* economy. Taxes at origin on the extraction of resources to finance an environmentally sustainable society should be introduced. There is the need to reduce energy consumption and the use of materials by rich people. Frivolous calls in OECD countries for population growth in order to increase employment that will help pay for old age pensions are not at all convincing from an economic perspective since there is so much unemployment, and they are wrong from an ecological point of view. This is an opportunity for starting a socio-ecological transition.

In some countries, not only the absolute amount of materials but also material intensity (tons of materials/GDP) has increasingly indicating more pressures on the environment. Convergence to a European average of

16 tons per person per year (only materials, water not counted here) would multiply material flows in the world by three, with the present population. Economies can be characterized by such material flows. We may analyse patterns of external trade. While some South American countries export five times as many tons as they import, the EU imports four times as many tons as it exports. We can understand characteristic patterns of social conflicts, for instance, mining and oil extraction conflicts, or resistance against tree plantations for paper pulp or agro-fuels, or the international conflict caused by unequal access to the carbon dioxide sinks (oceans) or the temporary 'reservoir' (atmosphere). Convergence towards 300 GJ per capita per year would mean to multiply by five the present energy in the world economy. If gas and especially coal are used, this would also multiply by four or five the carbon dioxide produced. The HANPP is also increasing in many countries – human appropriation of net primary production of biomass. Population growth, soil sealing, meat eating, paper production and agro-fuels increase the HANPP. The higher the HANPP, the less biomass available for other species.

At first sight, Southern countries have something to lose and little to gain from degrowth in the North because of fewer opportunities for commodity and manufactured exports, and less availability of credits and donations. But the movements for environmental justice and the 'environmentalism of the poor' of the South are the main allies of the sustainable degrowth (or steady-state economy) movement of the North. The movements for environmental justice fight against disproportionate pollution (at local and global levels, including claims for repayment of the 'carbon debt'), they fight against waste exports from North to South (for example, the *Clemenceau* and so many other ships to be dismantled on the beaches of Alang in Gujarat, or electronic waste), they fight against biopiracy, and also against *Raubwirtschaft*, that is, ecologically unequal exchange, and the destruction of nature and human livelihoods at the 'commodity frontiers'. They also fight against the socio-environmental liabilities of transnational corporations.

The world conservation movement should criticize conventional economic accounting and push for the introduction of an economic language that reflects better our relations with nature, while not forgetting, however, the legitimacy of other languages: territorial rights, environmental and social justice, livelihood, sacredness. This is needed for the alliance between the conservation movement and the environmentalism of the poor, as proposed in the International Union for the Conservation of Nature (IUCN) booklet, *Transition to Sustainability* (Adams and Jeanrenaud, 2008). This alliance is difficult because, to judge from the visibility of sponsorship at the World Conservation Congresses, the world conservation movement has sold its soul to companies like Shell and Rio Tinto. John Muir would have been horrified.

The 'environmentalism of the poor' combines livelihood, social, economic and environmental issues, with emphasis on issues of extraction and pollution. In many instances these movements draw on a sense of local identity (indigenous rights and values such as the sacredness of the land). Such movements explicitly oppose annexation of land, forests, mineral resources and water by governments or business corporations.

There could be a confluence among conservationists concerned with the loss of biodiversity, the many people concerned with climate change who push for solar energy, the socialists and trade unionists who want more economic justice in the world, urban squatters who preach 'autonomy', agro-ecologists, neo-rurals and the large peasant movements (as represented by Via Campesina), the pessimists (or realists) on the risks and uncertainties of technical change (post-normal science) and the 'environmentalism of the poor' demanding the preservation of the environment for livelihood. The international environmental justice movements have as their objective an economy that sustainably fulfils the food, health, education and housing needs for everybody, providing as much *joie de vivre* as possible. They know that in decision-making processes, economics becomes a tool of power. This is the case when applying cost-benefit analysis to individual projects, and also at the level of the macroeconomy where increases in GDP trump other dimensions. The question is, who has the power to simplify complexity and impose a particular language of valuation? The environmental justice movements know in their bones and in their brains that conventional economic accounting is false, that it forgets the physical and biological aspects of the economy, the value of unpaid domestic and voluntary work, and it does not really measure the welfare and happiness of the population. What is needed is an Aristotelian *buen vivir* guided by oikonomia rather than chrematistics.

NOTES

1. Lawn (Chapter 8 in this volume) proposes job guarantees as a solution to unemployment, while Victor (Chapter 12 in this volume) proposes shorter work-weeks.
2. See Cobb, Chapter 11 in this volume for a discussion of some alternative financial systems.

REFERENCES

Adams, W. And S. Jeanrenaud (2008), *Transition to Sustainability: Towards a Humane and Diverse World*, Gland, Switzerland: IUCN.
Boulding, K. (1966), 'The economics of the coming Spaceship Earth', in H. Jarrett (ed.), *Environmental Quality in a Growing Economy*, Baltimore, MD: Johns Hopkins Press, pp. 3–14.
Daly, H. (1968), 'On economics as a life science', *Journal of Political Economy*, **76** (3), May–June, 392–406.
Daly, H. (1980), 'The economic thought of Frederick Soddy', *History of Political Economy*, **12** (4), 469–88.
Daly, H. (1991), *Steady-state Economics: Second Edition with New Essays*, Washington, DC: Island Press.
Daly, H. (2007), *Ecological Economics and Sustainable Development: Selected Essays*, Cheltenham, UK and Northampton, MA, USA: Edward Elgar Publishing.
Fischer-Kowalski, M. and H. Haberl (eds) (2007), *Socioecological Transitions and Global Change: Trajectories of Social Metabolism and Land Use*, Cheltenham, UK and Northampton, MA, USA: Edward Elgar Publishing.
Georgescu-Roegen, N. (1966), *Analytical Economics*, Cambridge, MA: Harvard University Press.
Georgescu-Roegen, N. (1971), *The Entropy Law and the Economic Process*, Cambridge, MA: Harvard University Press.
Grinevald, J. and I. Rens (eds) (1979), *La Décroissance: Entropie, écologie, économie*, reprinted in 1995, Paris: Sang de la Terre (a selection of writings by N. Georgescu-Roegen).
Hornborg, A. (1998), 'Towards an ecological theory of unequal exchange: articulating world system theory and ecological economics', *Ecological Economics*, **25** (1), April, 127–36.
Jackson, T. (2009), *Prosperity Without Growth: Economics for a Finite Planet*, London: Earthscan.
Kneese A. and R.U. Ayres (1969), 'Production, consumption and externalities', *American Economic Review*, **59**, 282–97.
Latouche, S. (2006), *Le Pari de la Décroissance*, Paris: Fayard.
Lutz, W., W.C. Sanderson and S. Scherbov (2001), *The End of World Population Growth in the 21st Century. New Challenges for Human Capital Formation and Sustainable Development*, London: Earthscan.
Martinez-Alier, J. (1987), *Ecological Economics: Energy, Environment and Society*, Oxford: Blackwell.
Martinez-Alier, J. (2012), 'Environmental justice and economic degrowth: an alliance between two movements', *Capitalism Nature Socialism*, **23** (1), 51–73.
Martinez-Alier, J. and L. Temper (2007), 'Oil and climate change: voices from the South', *Ecological and Political Weekly*, 15 December.
Masjuan, E. (2000), *La ecología humana en el anarquismo ibérico*, Barcelona: Icaria.
Narain, S. (2008), 'Learn to walk lightly', *Down to Earth*, 15 August.
Ronsin, F. (1980), *La grève des ventres; propagande malthusienne et baisse de la natalité en France, XIXe–XXe siècles*, Paris: Aubier.
Soddy, F. (1922), *Cartesian Economics: The Bearing of Physical Sciences upon State Stewardship*, London: Hendersons.

Soddy, F. (1926), *Wealth, Virtual Wealth and Debt*, 2nd edn in 1993, London: Allen & Unwin.

TEEB (The Economics of Ecosystems and Biodiversity) Interim Report (2008), http:/ ec.europa.eu/environment/nature/biodiversity/economics/pdf/teeb_report. pdf (accessed December 2015).

The Economist (2008), 'Saving Detroit. Politicians, business and the unions all want a bail-out of Ford and General Motors. That would be a mistake', 13 November.

The Economist (2009), 'Flight of the locusts. Will the retreat of activist investors give industrial bosses more leeway to manage?', 8 April.

United Nations World Commission on Environment and Development (1987), *Our Common Future (Brundtland Report)*, Oxford: Oxford University Press.

Victor, P. (2008), *Managing Without Growth: Slower by Design, Not by Disaster*, Cheltenham, UK and Northampton, MA, USA: Edward Elgar Publishing.

14. Politics for a steady-state economy

Brian Czech

After an exhilarating 15 years in the field, working with elk, bighorn sheep, bears, mountain lions and many more of the 'charismatic megafauna,' I wanted to make a lasting contribution to wildlife conservation at a national level. So I went from the San Carlos Apache Reservation, where I was serving as the Recreation and Wildlife Department Director, to the University of Arizona for a PhD in renewable natural resources studies. I minored in political science so I could work my way into public policy. My dissertation was a policy analysis of the Endangered Species Act (ESA), and I used an approach called 'policy design theory' (Schneider and Ingram, 1997).

Policy design theory requires the analyst to account for the context within which a policy functions (or doesn't). I analyzed numerous angles of the context, but I always felt the most direct and relevant angle was the causes of species endangerment. After all, if it weren't for those causes, we wouldn't need an ESA. Conversely, the ESA was all about preventing or rectifying the causes. Tabulating the causes was a laborious (and often depressing) task; the resulting database included all 877 species listed as threatened or endangered at the time, with 18 columns representing distinct causes of endangerment. Although the causes were distinctive enough for categorization, the 'average' species was imperiled by approximately four such causes, and all the causes seemed intertwined (Czech et al., 2000).

After populating this database night after night for many long nights, followed by a bit of reflection on policy design theory, it suddenly struck me that the causes of species endangerment could aptly be described as a Who's Who of the American economy! This, I felt, was an important finding. In a way, it seemed like a no-brainer, but it was important because the *policy* context of ESA was one in which a primary, perennial and bipartisan goal of the American public and polity was economic growth. So here we had two stated goals of the United States – economic growth and species conservation – that seemed to be fundamentally at odds. Meanwhile the primacy of economic growth as a policy goal was especially clear in the 1990s. During the 1992 presidential campaign, when asked to identify the most important policy issue, candidate Bill Clinton responded, 'It's the economy, stupid!' Once elected, he and his Cabinet were fond of exclaiming, 'There is no conflict between growing the economy and protecting the environment!'

After reporting on the causes of endangerment in *Science* (Czech and Krausman, 1997) I started broaching this topic – the conflict between economic growth and wildlife conservation – in classes, conferences of professional natural resources societies and papers (for example, Czech, 2000a; Czech et al., 2000). The responses astounded me. From one side would come, 'No Czech, you're wrong, there is no conflict between economic growth and wildlife conservation,' as if they were all members of the President's Cabinet. Oddly enough, the other camp would submit, 'Of course there's a conflict between economic growth and wildlife conservation! But we're wildlife biologists. We don't do economic policy.' The cumulative response was to the effect, 'Go away!'

So I went away, to the library. I was less concerned about the fatalists in the second camp than the argumentative folks in the first camp who disagreed with my assessment. Did they know something I didn't? It didn't seem like they'd even studied the topic, but they were outspoken about it, so I had to investigate further to assure them and myself that I knew what I was talking about. Using keywords and phrases such as 'economic growth,' 'wildlife conservation' and numerous others, I eventually stumbled upon the ecological economics literature, which wasn't nearly as prominent then as it is now. I also noticed that with the phrase 'economic growth,' I kept seeing the name 'Daly.'

The ecological economics literature, especially Daly's work on the steady-state economy (for example, Daly, 1973, 1991; Daly and Cobb, 1994; Daly and Townsend, 1993), gave me the sense that I was suddenly onto the most potent policy implications ever written for wildlife conservation! It basically had 'the' answer: the steady-state economy in which wildlife and biodiversity in general could be conserved indefinitely. It would take me a little longer to realize that the implications of Daly's work went far, far beyond wildlife conservation.

When I 'discovered' ecological economics and Daly's work, I hadn't yet completed my dissertation on the ESA. That was a good thing, for I still had time to conclude by interpreting the ESA as an implicit prescription for a steady-state economy, albeit one with numerous species lined up on a ledge in the one-way canyon of extinction (Czech and Krausman, 2001). But the conclusion of my dissertation was only the beginning of an immersion in ecological economics, and I continued to find the steady-state economy the most distinguishing feature in ecological economics and the most important concept for ecological and economic sustainability (Czech, 2009, 2013).

14.1   TESTING THE WATERS OF STEADY-STATE POLITICS

Empowered and emboldened by ecological economics and the concept of the steady-state economy, I went back to the wildlife profession to set the record straight on economic growth and wildlife conservation. I discovered that some of the older members, especially, of The Wildlife Society (TWS) were more-or-less familiar with Daly's work. I was puzzled why they weren't espousing it for the rest of the members (more on that later). I proposed that TWS adopt a position on economic growth, a position that would identify the steady-state economy as an alternative to economic growth and an alternative that was consistent with wildlife conservation (Czech, 2000a). I said that a TWS position could help refute the fallacious political rhetoric that 'there is no conflict between growing the economy and protecting the environment,' which by then I'd learned was not just Clintonian but bipartisan.

To my knowledge, this was the first attempt to get a professional natural resource society to venture into the policy terrain of economic growth. It was also a rude awakening. It turned out that the two earlier camps I'd encountered in the wildlife profession weren't about to break ranks and rally around the proposed position, anointing me a new buddy for whom to buy beers. Instead, it seemed like they circled the wagons and fired arrows at the proposal – lots of arrows! To describe all the sordid details of what it took to get TWS to adopt a position on economic growth is beyond the scope of this chapter (or maybe anything in print). Suffice it to say that it took much more than the six years of debates, symposia, papers, committees, working groups and other conventional professional society communications that go on the record. Lectures, visits, emails, listservs, phone calls, pleasantries, arguments, negotiations, exhortations, pleas . . . the ratio of unpublished written and spoken words to words published in the literature seemed an exorbitant price for someone seeking to establish an academic publication record. It turned out to be well worth it, but let this be a warning to any young (or old) man or woman who would advocate a steady-state economy: be prepared for a lot of silly, and some not-so-silly, even slanderous accusations. According to some, you're probably already a communist, an elitist, a pessimist, or a combination of these and sundry pariah traits.

As I've learned over the years, a lot of people just don't want to hear about limits to growth, the conflict between economic growth and environmental protection or the steady-state economy. People are uncomfortable with conflict in general and many won't deal with what they label 'pessimistic' analyses of economic growth, no matter how realistic the analyses are. Still others, with a strategy of sorts, think that dwelling on such 'negative' prospects doesn't keep them in the pleasant majority where politics are easier and grant money flows. Let's brace ourselves for the fact that this is the same type of convenient escapism that led Prime Minister Chamberlain and the rest of Europe to stand by idly, presumably practicing their positive thinking, while the Nazis rolled into Poland.

While some might initially think this analogy gratuitous, on closer inspection it could hardly be more relevant, and we ought to think about it deeply. One of the underlying pressures that empowered the Nazis was the German need for the land, space and natural capital they called *lebensraum*. All the Nobel Prize-winning economists in the rarefied world of the ivory tower couldn't have convinced the Nazis that unlimited economic growth could be administered within the confines of the German state! In the real world, economic growth requires more land, and those with overly aggressive aspirations for growth will take the land from others. That's not a negative or positive vision; that's just reality.

We can only wish that the steady-state economy, or at least progress toward establishing steady states, had become a source of civilized national pride long before the wars in Europe took on their industrial, globalized, genocidal nature. Surely then the international financial institutions borne out of World War II would have taken a different course. The World Bank (or whatever it would have been called), for example, may have focused more on ecological sustainability and international economic justice than global economic growth. Unfortunately, the World Bank wouldn't have a Herman Daly until 1988, and by then, crisis wasted, the World Bank wasn't ready to listen.

14.2 'WHATEVER HAPPENED TO DALY'S STUFF?'

Numerous times I've heard people inquire, as I would paraphrase the collective inquiry, 'Whatever happened to Daly's stuff?' The articles and books are published, pulsing with policy implications, yet we see precious few implications circulating into the policy arena. Early on, I was asking the same question; for example, during my experience with TWS. Now, after 15 years of advocating the steady-state economy, I've developed enough understanding of what happened to Daly's stuff to write about it. The basic categories to explain what happened include: (1) political economy, in particular the effects of 'Big Money'; (2) lack of transdisci-plinary experience in academia and the polity; (3) non-newsy nature of steady-state economics; and (4) egos and competition for leadership in academia and politics. These categories are presented in estimated order of importance, but it is also important to understand that these categories tend to be mutually reinforcing.

14.2.1 Political Economy and Sustainability

Ecological economics and especially its macroeconomic arm, steady-state economics, won't be championed by Big Money anytime soon, which makes it more difficult to get it into the New York houses, broadcast media, big-screen documentaries and the policy arena itself. By 'Big Money' I mean the most prominent and powerful growth interests such as the World Bank, Wall Street, corporations and the Federal Reserve system (Beder, 2002). First, Big Money is unlikely to encounter a Daly publica-tion. Second, if it does, it is more likely to ignore or suppress it than to study or circulate it. That is not to say there aren't individuals within Big Money who have studied Daly's work and agree with it. Of course there are. But here we are talking about political economy; the systemic func-tioning of the integrated political and economic system, replete with trends and probabilities (Czech et al., 2003). For every Daly thesis that might be circulated by a corporate shareholder, how many antitheses are circulated by a corporate board or corporate think tank? Or by a university's eco-nomics department whose research is corporately funded?

Compare Daly with the late business professor Julian Simon, who argued that perpetual population growth is not only possible but desir-able because it results in perpetually more brains to compensate for the problems of growth, and then some. He called this salesmanship a 'grand theory.' Various forms of 'enterprise institute' lined up to praise such an 'optimistic view' and 'positive vision,' to get more of Simon's books on the shelves and to construct a sort of pro-growth folk hero who had proved all those negative tree-huggers wrong.

Simon's salesmanship lives on with the new poster child of the enterprise institutes, the self-proclaimed 'skeptical environmentalist' Bjorn Lomborg. Meanwhile, the aspiring Dalyists are kept down by lack of support. That experience may come as a discouraging surprise to the Dalyists, because most of them come out of an academic background and are accustomed to publications rising to the top based on peer review and scientific merit. But this brings us to the topic of transdisciplinary experience.

14.2.2 Lack of Transdisciplinary Experience in Academia and the Polity

Ecological economics arose partly as a response to the fact that economists didn't know enough about ecology, and ecologists didn't know enough about economics. That much is still true in conventional economics and ecological circles. The ecological economics community stands out as a refreshing exception (although there are non-refreshing non-exceptions mingling therein). The mutual ignorance between economics and ecology is especially problematic for addressing limits to growth, or the 'scale' issue as it's known in ecological economics, thanks to Daly.

In my experience, the more vexing ignorance is among ecologists, who often do not know so much as the meaning of economic growth. It's easy to argue that there is no conflict between economic growth and environmental protection, Big Money smiling down on you and your program, when you invent your own meaning of economic growth. Of course this problem is exacerbated by the fact that the phrase 'economic growth' is often used in multiple ways among economists themselves. But this isn't much of an excuse. 'Cat' is used in many ways, but that seldom derails a meaningful discussion about *Felis catus*. If terms may have more than one meaning, they simply have to be clarified when necessary. That is why Daly's long-standing effort to distinguish between economic growth and economic development is so important for policy purposes. But again, not many ecologists are yet familiar with Daly, for all of the reasons described here. And there are other problems within the ecological sciences community when it comes to engaging macroeconomic policy, including an understandable propensity to eschew social and political affairs (Czech, 2002).

This is not to say that the ecological ignorance of neoclassical economists is *far* less vexing than the economic ignorance of ecologists. Perhaps in a technical sense it is even more vexing, because as Daly pointed out early on, the economist begins with a different pre-analytic vision, and that vision was derived without paying heed to some basic natural science. Most importantly, and most prominently revealed in ecological economics, is the ignoring of the first two laws of thermodynamics. A good grasp of those two laws, greatly aided no doubt by some real-world experience with materials and mechanical devices, is essential for 'getting' limits to growth. Conversely, without citing these laws, the ecologist cannot authoritatively refute an economist's (or any freewheeling technological optimist's) argument that we can have perpetual economic growth through technological progress (Czech, 2008).

Economists are even less likely familiarized with principles of ecology. That is why they also don't realize that ecologists *are* economists; namely, economists of nature, dealing with production and consumption, competition, allocation of resources and many of the same phenomena that 'regular' economists deal with. (Ecologists don't realize that either.) Ecologists just happen to practice their economics with any or all species, and of course their jargon is distinct. Perhaps the only thing that is truly, fundamentally distinctive about the human economy is the monetary sector. Ironically, monetary economics would benefit most of all from the basics of ecology, most notably trophic theory, which so clearly demonstrates that real money originates from agricultural and extractive surplus and is therefore a real reflection of throughput (Czech, 2000b, 2013).

The point here is not to sling mud left and right, but to help readers understand that ecological economics is not amenable to conveying with sound bites or word-of-mouth. Ecological economics is not the proverbial rocket science, but it is a distinct combining of the social and natural sciences that many scholars have not been inclined to undertake. One can't go to a conference of the American Economic Association and get an open forum back on the track to reality by citing Daly's application of the entropy law to productive efficiency. It is quite possible in such a venue to be totally correct and concurrently castigated as a kook. Economists and ecologists alike will need to digest for themselves at least the basics of ecological economics, and for such basics I still recommend 36 pages: 'Introduction to *Essays Toward a Steady-State Economy*' (Daly, 1993, pp. 11–47).

Unfortunately, many ecological economists with a solid background in Daly's work will still fall short of steady-state political productivity. Ecological economics is transdisciplinary in nature, but thus far the ecological economics community has produced very little political science, much less action. Bringing a Dalyist movement into public policy will require a much more sophisticated understanding of concepts pertaining to the framing of rhetoric, the development of political power and the political characteristics of the macroeconomic policy arena. It will also require much more fortitude to 'tell it like it is' in the face of political pressure, on the campus and in the polity per se.

14.2.3   Non-newsy Nature of Steady-state Economics

It would greatly help to increase the political viability of the steady-state economy if the news media were actively investigating and reporting on it. Unfortunately, the steady-state economy isn't the type of thing that grabs the media. It's not a person, place or event. Ecological economists aren't elected officials, movie stars or raving lunatics gunning down innocents, and seldom make the news.

Sometimes a world-changing idea will make the news, but it's because the idea will result in an observable, dramatic event or otherwise have an observable dramatic effect. When it comes to moving from the goal and process of economic growth to the goal and process of a steady-state economy, perhaps nothing could be less observable or dramatic. This is not the kind of transition that will inspire (thank goodness) a bloody revolution. Of course it will make very big news if the steady-state economy is ever signed into law as a policy goal, for example, as an amendment to the Full Employment Act (Czech, 2013), but there are a great many incremental policy developments toward a steady-state economy that, unfortunately, will not make the news and will not, therefore, help to empower *further* movement toward a steady state (Dietz and O'Neill, 2013).

For example, consider the adjusting of the federal funds rate by the Fed. This invariably makes the news. It features a high-profile person (Fed chairman) announcing a decision that results in an observable and often dramatic event (bedlam at the New York Stock Exchange). Let us assume that the Fed has been planning to lower the rate to stimulate economic growth. The question for the news is how much the rate will be lowered. If the decision comes down to the chairman, who happened to finally read Daly's *Beyond Growth* in response to another financial meltdown, it is conceivable that the chairman, with new and unsettling thoughts of uneconomic growth, would lower the rate an eighth of a percentage point less than he or she would have. This would be a compromise and, in a sense, could even be classified as an incremental movement toward steady-state monetary policy because it amounts to a slightly less pro-growth adjustment. Yet this part won't make the news. No one will even know about it unless the chairman makes a point of acknowledging it publicly. Once again, forthrightness and fortitude are required, in this case for making the steady-state economy newsworthy and connecting it explicitly with monetary policy.

The newsworthiness of steady-state economics may be changing though. At the time of writing, the steady-state economy seems to be appearing in opinion columns, editorials and letters to editors more frequently than ever (for example, Dietz, 2013; Hamilton, 2013; Revkin, 2013; Ura et al., 2013). No doubt this is partly due to the financial crisis of 2008, one of those moments in history when people far and wide were looking for alternatives to conventional economic thinking – a 'teachable moment.' But the uptick of steady-state journalism shouldn't be exaggerated. Ecological economics and the steady-state economy remain virtual unknowns in the world of politics and policy, and that is unlikely to change unless the media covers it prominently and for a protracted period.

This brings us back to the previous two subsections on Big Money and transdisciplinarity. Mainstream media are controlled to a significant extent by Big Money, and journalists and reporters suffer from the same lack of transdisciplinary expertise as economists and ecologists. Journalism and newscasting on the steady-state economy is not out of the question, but it will take charismatic people, creatively crafted events and maybe some dumb luck to attract the mainstream media.

14.2.4   Egos and Competition for Leadership in Academia and Politics

There aren't many academics in politics, but there are plenty of politicians in academia. As with elected officials, many of the figures in academia are attracted to the limelight or driven there by ego. Many a student and incidental campus visitor has commented on the arrogance effused by well-known scholars. This isn't the place for analyzing or speculating on the psychology of scholarship, but it is a phenomenon that plays a role in hampering the political advancement of the steady-state economy.

Scholars rise to a place of prominence for different reasons than politicians per se. Politicians can become quite renowned simply for pleasing or appeasing enough constituents. Scholars usually become prominent because they have done something intellectually original, or at least something they have been able to package in an original manner. The latter is an important distinction with direct relevance to steady-state politics. Scholars are jockeying for positions as leaders in sustainability science. A scholar may fully realize that a sustainable economy *is* a steady-state economy. The problem is that the phrase 'steady-state economy' has already been 'taken' in the academe. When the phrase is uttered, it invariably invokes the name of Herman Daly. Therefore, developing a research or community service program around the steady-state economy, at least by that name, will make it more difficult to carve out a unique niche in the upper echelons of sustainability science. The result is a constant repackaging and rebranding process in which precious little original contribution is made. I wrote about this with regard to the part fad, part original 1990s movement toward 'ecosystem management,' which provided elbow space and grant-writing opportunities for numerous academics (Czech, 1995).

Unfortunately, in real-time politics, where decisions are made that directly affect or create public policy, name recognition is a key variable. This means that the continual coining of new phrases in academia has the effect of disempowering the common subject matter – economic sustainability in this case – in the polity. It's a real tragedy of the campus commons.

14.3   A FOUNDATION FOR A STEADY-STATE POLITICAL PLATFORM

Due to its transdisciplinary and non-newsy nature, the steady-state economy is unlikely to inspire a grassroots political movement. Certain grassroots movements (for example, away from conspicuous consumption) will be *conducive* to the establishment of a steady-state economy, but for the steady state to be established as an economic policy goal, focused political activity by a dedicated cadre of Dalyists is required. Where do we start?

First, we need to consider where we are coming from. Most Dalyists are, or are going to be, relatively highly educated, transdisciplinary students and scholars, which means a logical starting place for advancing the steady-state economy is the scientific or scholarly professional community. It's where we are and where we know people. We may not have been born with a silver spoon in our collective political mouth, with a leg up on Capitol Hill, but we are in a key position nevertheless for purposes of political and economic reform. That's because we can provide leverage for individuals and organizations that are 'players' in the development of public opinion and public policy.

Let us consider the professional society position statement as a means by which to advance the steady-state economy. These positions are crucial to advancing the steady-state economy and keeping it supported once it reaches critical mass in political affairs. Professional society position statements are not the *only* means or an absolutely essential condition for the establishment of a steady-state economy. Miraculous alternatives toward any objective are theoretically possible. However, I would argue that the professional society position statement constitutes the optimum approach for Dalyists, at this point in history, when we consider not only our starting point but the nature of the subject, the opposition, and the economic policy arena. An adequate collection of these position statements will comprise a firm foundation for organizations and politicians to stand upon as they seek to educate the public on the perils of growth and as they propose macroeconomic policy reforms (Czech, 2007).

After 15 years of advancing such positions in professional natural resources societies, and even given the modest results, I am more convinced than ever that not only the positions themselves but the position-taking efforts are key to establishing steady-state economies. To start with, these efforts have helped Dalyists to identify one another and capitalize on our complementary strengths. For example, TWS's Working Group for the Steady State Economy, by virtue of its name, assembles TWS members who can safely surmise that they are indeed among members who are interested in advancing the steady-state economy. The Working Group provides an official voice to other TWS interests and leadership, helping to spread awareness of the steady-state economy as the macroeconomic condition necessary for wildlife conservation. Its mere existence, with strength in numbers, helps to empower individuals and units in other professional natural resources societies to form groups with similar traits and effects; for example, the Working Group for Ecological Economics and Sustainability Science in the Society for Conservation Biology.

An overlooked benefit of these position-taking efforts is the political experience gained by the participants. A professional natural resources society, and for that matter any similarly sized society or group, is like a crucible in which many of the same types of issues, concerns and personalities are squished together and forced to react. Taken together, these efforts among the various professional societies constitute an experiment of sorts, an uncontrolled experiment with elements of 'adaptive management.' Participants learn about the technical issues of the steady-state economy, the political issues, the personal concerns of career-minded members, the comparative effectiveness of rhetorical style in different types of venues (for example, the symposium versus the committee meeting versus the open forum), and the uses and abuses of political power that affect collective decision-making. In this crucible, political leadership is forged for advancing the steady-state economy in 'real' polities ranging from municipalities to international unions. A few people involved in these professional society efforts are already advancing a steady-state economy as a policy goal in city, state and national political offices, using their campaigns to educate voters about the steady-state economy.

And that is only the fringe benefit of professional society position-taking! The prize is the position itself, or rather the positions. Thus far, positions have been taken by the US Society for Ecological Economics (2003), The Wildlife Society (2004), Society for Conservation Biology's North America Section (2004), American Society of Mammalogists (2007) and British Columbia Field Ornithologists (2007). Semi-professional organizations have also adopted positions, including the Federation of British Columbia Naturalists ('BC Nature') (2008). These positions mean something; they are no mere slips of paper. For example, as a conservation biologist in the national office of the US Fish and Wildlife Service, toward the end of the second Clinton administration, I proposed that we (Fish and Wildlife Service) develop a campaign to educate the public on the trade-off between economic growth and wildlife conservation. The relevant assistant director (the one between me and the director) brought me to his office and stated, in a nutshell, 'Brian, you get us a position on economic growth by The Wildlife Society and some of the other societies, and then we'll talk about it.' Political appointees striving to do the right thing need cover, or a foundation to stand upon, if they are going to support an initiative that could make waves for the politician who does the appointing. It is also worth noting that this particular appointee modified his own speeches to avoid the win-win growth-conservation rhetoric and help educate the public about the trade-off.

I could list dozens, and with a better memory probably hundreds, of experiences in which the presence or absence of a professional society position statement on economic growth made a difference in the decision or decision-making process of a leader in a capacity to direct significant resources toward advancing the steady-state economy. Frankly, it would be inane to think such positions *wouldn't* make a political difference! Another way of looking at the utility of the professional society position statement is to consider nascent attempts at steady statism in the absence of such positions. For example, toward the end of the environmental movement in the United States, after *Limits to Growth* was published (and Daly's *Steady-state Economics*), a few environmental organizations took up the topics of population growth and economic growth. Friends of the Earth, for example, began raising awareness about limits to growth, and even received some coverage in *U.S. News and World Report* as a result. But they were quickly washed away in the tide of political economy, discredited as nothing but 'Friends of the Earth.' Now if they had been able to base their educational campaign upon a stack of dry, scientific, professional positions that clarified beyond a doubt the fundamental conflict between economic growth and environmental protection, the campaign would have been far more durable and effective. This should be a matter of common sense, but in conversations with me, Brent Blackwelder (then President of Friends of the Earth) verified that, indeed, professional society position statements would have been – and would be – of great help.

Yet naysayers will claim such positions are useless, and perhaps to them they will be. A vehicle is only as useful as the operator. I'll take my cue from Herman Daly himself, who once told me that these professional society position statements, few as there were (and still are, at the time of this writing), were the most encouraging development he had seen in the advancement of the steady-state economy.

14.4   OTHER MEANS AND MOVEMENTS

Plenty of political efforts and movements have shown that the steady-state economy is a potentially viable policy goal. For anyone doubting this observation, I recommend using Google news alerts to monitor the phrase 'steady-state economy' for a while. You'll see letters to editors around the world urging politicians and governments to move toward the steady-state economy. Book authors have a renewed or new interest in limits to growth and the steady-state economy. Politicians pop up here and there advocating the steady-state economy. This is a trend that while certainly accelerating since 2008, is certainly not guaranteed a long continuance or a high plateau. What is needed is an expanding group of Dalyists: people with enough knowledge of ecological economics, fortitude and savvy to function effectively in the polity.

The foundation of professional society position statements needs to be laid thicker and firmer. More such professional societies should take such positions, and the positions need to be stronger than some of the existing positions (see, for example, Gates et al., 2006). But the professional society position-taking needn't delay all other prospective efforts. It is time for the less academic non-governmental organizations known as 'the NGO community' to get to work for the steady state, beginning with the conservation and environmental NGOs. There is already enough of a platform of scientifically derived, professional society technical papers and position statements for them to stand upon. They should be developing educational campaigns to refute the fallacious political rhetoric that 'there is no conflict between growing the economy and protecting the environment,' and they should not shy away from the phrase 'steady-state economy' to identify the sustainable economic policy.

Any individual or organization contemplating steady-state advocacy will be empowered not only by Daly's original work and the professional society position statements but also by the growing list of signatories to the position on economic growth taken by the Center for the Advancement of the Steady State Economy (CASSE). By March 2014, this position had been signed by over 11 000 individuals and endorsed by more than 200 organizations concerned with a wide range of issues including the environment, social justice and public health. Even a mutual fund had endorsed the CASSE position. At this point, no one has to feel like they are sticking their neck out by advocating a steady-state economy. With Daly as a key board member and advisor, CASSE is developing unprecedented political support for the steady-state economy, and the CASSE position on economic growth (Box 14.1) may be taken and tailored to produce positions with more focus on particular aspects of social welfare. For example, the North America Section of the Society for Conservation Biology took a position on economic growth that is virtually identical to the CASSE position, except for including additional references to biodiversity conservation.

When enough positions and educational campaigns have been developed, the time will have come to advance the steady-state economy into

BOX 14.1 CENTER FOR THE ADVANCEMENT OF THE STEADY-STATE ECONOMY POSITION ON ECONOMIC GROWTH

Whereas:

1. Economic growth, as defined in standard economics textbooks, is an increase in the production and consumption of goods and services, and;
2. Economic growth occurs when there is an increase in the multiplied product of population and per capita consumption, and;
3. The global economy grows as an integrated whole consisting of agricultural, extractive, manufacturing, and services sectors that require physical inputs and produce wastes, and;
4. Economic growth is often and generally indicated by increasing real gross domestic product (GDP) or real gross national product (GNP), and;
5. Economic growth has been a primary, perennial goal of many societies and most governments, and;
6. Based upon established principles of physics and ecology, there is a limit to economic growth, and;
7. There is increasing evidence that global economic growth is having negative effects on long-term ecological and economic welfare . . .

Therefore, CASSE takes the position that:

1. There is a fundamental conflict between economic growth and environmental protection (for example, biodiversity conservation, clean air and water, atmospheric stability), and;
2. There is a fundamental conflict between economic growth and the ecological services underpinning the human economy (for example, pollination, decomposition, climate regulation), and;
3. Technological progress has had many positive and negative ecological and economic effects and may not be depended on to reconcile the conflict between economic growth and long-term ecological and economic welfare, and;
4. Economic growth, as gauged by increasing GDP, is an increasingly dangerous and anachronistic goal, especially in wealthy nations with widespread affluence, and;
5. A steady-state economy (that is, an economy with a relatively stable, mildly fluctuating product of population and per capita consumption) is a viable alternative to a growing economy and has become a more appropriate goal in large, wealthy economies, and;
6. The long-run sustainability of a steady-state economy requires its establishment at a size small enough to avoid the breaching of reduced ecological and economic capacity during expected or unexpected supply shocks such as droughts and energy shortages, and;
7. A steady-state economy does not preclude economic development, a dynamic, qualitative process in which different technologies may be employed and the relative prominence of economic sectors may evolve, and;

> 8. Upon establishing a steady-state economy, it would be advisable for wealthy nations to assist other nations in moving from the goal of economic growth to the goal of a steady-state economy, beginning with those nations currently enjoying high levels of per capita consumption, and;
> 9. For many nations with widespread poverty, increasing per capita consumption (or, alternatively, more equitable distributions of wealth) remains an appropriate goal.

mainstream political and policy-making venues. In fact, for smaller polities, enough leverage already exists for serious dialog on the steady-state economy as a policy goal. For example, a commission in Bloomington, Indiana has tailored the CASSE position on economic growth to advance the steady-state economy within the Bloomington polity and to the broader American polity (Bloomington Environmental Commission, 2008). The commission is now working with the city council, seeking adoption of the position by the city at large.

As the signatures and endorsements of the CASSE position grow, larger polities and policy-making units will be approachable. The obvious entities will include city councils, county commissions, and state and national legislatures, executives and even judiciaries. For example, the 2007 US Supreme Court ruling in the case of *Kelo v. New London*, which should be infamous among ecological economists and especially Dalyists, may be used as precedent to rule in favor of municipalities using economic growth and development as a reason to exercise eminent domain over long-standing, low-footprint homeowners. Steady staters should be ready to issue a heavily footnoted amicus brief, noting that economic growth is not a 'public purpose' (the phrase used in *Kelo* to describe increasing economic activity) when growth has actually become uneconomic. Such a brief may not win the day in court, but it will surely produce an educable moment, and perhaps a sustained one.

Political parties are other venues for advancing the steady-state economy. The Green Party of the United States installed a plank on the steady-state economy in its 2004 platform. Several other Green Parties around the world have explicitly supported the steady-state economy, including at least the Green Party of England and Wales, the Green Party of Ireland and, to a less explicit degree, the Green Party of the Netherlands. Provincial governments in Ontario and British Columbia have also adopted the steady-state economy in their platforms.

Political movements mustn't necessarily explicate the steady-state economy as a policy goal to have the effect of advancing the steady state. For example, the movement for *la Décroissance*, emanating from France to other parts of Europe, has followers and observers wondering what comes after an episode of 'degrowth,' for in the long run degrowth is no more sustainable than growth. Clearly they, too, will 'discover' the steady-state economy as the sustainable alternative, much like those of us who discovered it as an answer to biodiversity conservation and environmental protection in general. In fact, the Declaration of the Conference on Economic Degrowth for Ecological Sustainability and Social Equity (Paris, 2008) included the establishment of a steady-state economy as the long-term goal. At least two other economic movements, toward the 'sufficiency economy' in Thailand and the pursuit of gross national happiness in Bhutan, are conducive to raising awareness of the steady-state economy as an explicit and desirable economic policy goal. The same may be said for the 'transition towns' arising in the UK and other parts of Europe. In the United States, Community Solutions and other NGOs are assisting local communities to adapt to peak oil and build self-sufficient, stabilized economies. Community Solutions has also endorsed the CASSE position on economic growth.

14.5   THE BIGGEST IS YET TO COME

In ecological economics, where limits to growth are acknowledged, the measure of success is qualitative development, not quantitative growth. However, when it comes to politics, a lot of qualitative results boil down to quantities, as in quantities of voters, initiatives, candidates, parties and policy proposals. We need big numbers for the steady-state economy: big numbers of ecological economists, Dalyists and steady staters in general, initiating big numbers of campaigns in big numbers of organizations.

Only after the numbers are sufficient will we have a legitimate chance to have an effect in venues such as national legislatures and presidential transition teams. We can talk to the US Department of Commerce, the Council of Economic Advisors, and even the Fed, but they are unlikely to be impressed until we have hundreds of thousands of individuals and thousands of organizations on record as supporting the establishment of a steady-state economy. It is certainly not too early, however, to engage communities far and wide in working toward local steady-state economies with stabilized populations and ecological footprints.

Perhaps in a future book, authors will be waxing joyously on ubiquitous political movements and mainstream parties that have adopted the steady-state economy. Perhaps, some years after that, the steady-state economy will be a commonly adopted public policy goal and a standard of good citizenship in international diplomacy. This is a vision of the future sufficient to proceed with. We already know plenty about what needs to be done to get there. May there be plenty of Dalyists to do it!

BIBLIOGRAPHY

Beder, S. (2002), *Global Spin: The Corporate Assault on Environmentalism*, revised edn, White River Junction, VT: Chelsea Green.

Bloomington Environmental Commission (2008), *Position of the City of Bloomington Environmental Commission on Economic Growth in the United States*, available at http://bloomington.in.gov/media/media/application/pdf/3465.pdf (accessed 7 January 2016).

Czech, B. (1995), 'Ecosystem management is no paradigm shift: let's try conservation', *Journal of Forestry*, **93** (12), 17–23.

Czech, B. (2000a), 'Economic growth as the limiting factor for wildlife conservation', *Wildlife Society Bulletin*, **28** (1), 4–14.

Czech, B. (2000b), *Shoveling Fuel for a Runaway Train: Errant Economists, Shameful Spenders, and a Plan to Stop Them All*, Berkeley, CA: University of California Press.

Czech, B. (2002), 'The imperative of macroeconomics for ecologists', *Bioscience*, **52** (11), 964–6.

Czech, B. (2007), 'The foundation of a new conservation movement: professional society positions on economic growth', *Bioscience*, **57** (1), 6–7.

Czech, B. (2008), 'Prospects for reconciling the conflict between economic growth and biodiversity conservation with technological progress', *Conservation Biology*, **22** (6), 1389–98.

Czech, B. (2009), 'Ecological economics', in *Encyclopedia of Life Support Systems*, developed under the Auspices of UNESCO, Oxford: EOLSS Publishers, available at http://www.eolss.net (accessed 7 January 2016).

Czech, B. (2013), *Supply Shock: Economic Growth at the Crossroads and the Steady State Solution*, Gabriola Island, BC: New Society Publishers, p. 367.

Czech, B. and P.R. Krausman (1997), 'Distribution and causation of species endangerment in the United States', *Science*, **277**, 1116–17.

Czech, B. and P.R. Krausman (2001), *The Endangered Species Act: History, Conservation Biology, and Public Policy*, Baltimore, MD: Johns Hopkins University Press, p. 212.

Czech, B., P.R. Krausman and P.K. Devers (2000), 'Economic associations among causes of species endangerment in the United States', *Bioscience*, **50**, 593–601.

Czech, B., E. Allen, D. Batker et al. (2003), 'The iron triangle: why The Wildlife Society needs to take a position on economic growth', *Wildlife Society Bulletin*, **31** (2), 574–7.

Daly, H.E. (ed.) (1973), *Toward a Steady-state Economy*, San Francisco, CA: W.H. Freeman.

Daly, H.E. (1977), *Steady-state Economics*, San Francisco, CA: W.H. Freeman.

Daly, H.E. (1991), *Steady State Economics: 2nd Edition with New Essays*, Washington, DC: Island Press.

Daly, H.E. (1993), 'Introduction to *Essays Toward a Steady State Economy*', in H.E. Daly and K. Townsend, *Valuing the Earth: Economics, Ecology, Ethics*, Cambridge, MA: MIT Press, pp. 11–47.

Daly, H.E. (1997), *Beyond Growth: The Economics of Sustainable Development*, Boston, MA: Beacon Press, p. 264.

Daly, H.E. and J.B. Cobb, Jr (1994), *For the Common Good: Redirecting the Economy Toward Community, the Environment, and a Sustainable Future*, Boston, MA: Beacon Press, p. 534.

Daly, H.E. and J. Farley (2003), *Ecological Economics: Principles and Applications*, Washington, DC: Island Press.

Daly, H.E. and K. Townsend (eds) (1993), *Valuing the Earth: Economics, Ecology, Ethics*, Cambridge, MA: MIT Press.

Dietz, R. (2013), 'Call for economic overhaul', *USA Today*, 18 August, available at http://www.usatoday.com/story/opinion/2013/08/18/economy-hpi-gdp-column/2669337/ (accessed 7 Janaury 2016).

Dietz, R. and D. O'Neill (2013), *Enough is Enough: Building a Sustainable Economy in a World of Finite Resources*, San Francisco, CA: Berrett-Koehler.

Gates, J.E., N.K. Dawe, J.D. Erickson et al. (2006), 'Perspectives on The Wildlife Society's economic growth policy statement and the development process', *Wildlife Society Bulletin*, **34** (2), 507–11.

Hamilton, C. (2013), 'Geoengineering: our last hope, or a false promise?', *New York Times*, 26 May, available at http://www.nytimes.com/2013/05/27/opinion/geoengineering-our-last-hope-or-a-false-promise.html?pagewanted=all (accessed 7 January 2016).

Meadows, D.H. and Club of Rome (1972), *The Limits to Growth: A Report for the Club of Rome's Project on the Predicament of Mankind*, New York: Universe Books, p. 205.

Revkin, A. (2013), 'Scientists propose a new architecture for sustainable development', *New York Times*, 21 March.

Schneider, A.L. and H. Ingram (1997), *Policy Design for Democracy*, Lawrence, KS: University Press of Kansas.

Ura, K., W. Ryerson, D. Furchgott-Roth and A. Nigam (2013), 'When "growth" is not a good goal', *New York Times*, 16 January, available at http://www.nytimes.com/roomfordebate/2013/01/16/when-growth-is-not-a-good-goal (accessed 7 January 2016).

PART VI

Conclusions

15. The unfinished journey of ecological economics: toward an ethic of ecological citizenship

Peter G. Brown

'Use' as our primary relationship with the planet must be abandoned . . .
Intimacy with . . . its wonder and the full depth of its meaning is what enables
an integral human relationship with the planet to function. It is the only
possibility for humans to attain their true flourishing while honoring the
other modes of earthly being. The fulfillment of the Earth community is to
be caught up in the grandeur of existence itself and in admiration of those
mysterious powers whence all this has emerged.

Berry (2000, p. xi)

15.1 INTRODUCTION

The fundamental insight of ecological economics is to insist that the human
economy must be seen as embedded in the Earth's biophysical systems. An
essential property of those systems is that they are open to energy from
the sun, but closed to matter – that for all practical purposes nothing
ever leaves or arrives on the Earth. This perspective dates from the work
of economists Kenneth Boulding in the 1960s and Nicholas Georgescu-
Roegen in the 1970s and has been developed in the work of Herman Daly
whose life and work we celebrate here. Further advances have been secured
by Robert Costanza and many others educated in physics, biology and
ecology.[1] This profound paradigm shift is still relatively new. It is deter-
minedly unrecognized by mainstream economists who simply do not know
what to do about a finite world. Indeed, in many contexts, mainstream
economics has been able to mount a counterattack under the rubric of
'environmental economics' – a phrasing that may seem to be synonymous
with ecological economics.[2] The epistemic shift propounded by ecological
economics is founded in our understanding of the relationship between
the human economy and its host planet. It is of fundamental importance
in securing the future of life's long sojourn on Earth. To those who have

pioneered this field, all Earth-bound living beings now, and in the future, owe a debt of gratitude.

Yet, the paradigm is incomplete in important ways, and thus the task of reaching a new worldview remains to be completed. There are two main limitations of the current theory that I discuss here – but the larger task ahead is to formulate the foundations of an ecological political economy. First, ecological economists insist that the economy be seen as embedded in the biosphere, but retain, for the most part, the valuing system of the economic paradigm they seek to overturn. At this time the field contains a variety of points of view about its ethical foundations. In the main these are very similar to the neoclassical point of view they seek to escape, but there are those who wish to emphasize respect for nature. This lack of consensus makes it difficult for ecological economists to escape from other assumptions of that worldview they seek to overturn. Second, this also has the effect of retarding the development of new terms of discourse – the vocabulary we have to discuss ideas like money, cost, efficiency and the like. These two factors account, in part, for the 'tar baby effect'[3] that afflicts this discipline at the stage of its maturation: it remains attached to the thing it is trying to escape. It will get free and 'into the briar patch' – to continue the metaphor – only when it develops an embedded ethics, and terms of discourse derived from that ethical system. By an 'embedded ethics' I mean an ethics that is fully informed and shaped by, but not reduced to, the findings of contemporary science. Since ecological economics has insisted on seeing the economy in the context of thermodynamics it is especially germane to trace some of the implications of these laws for ethics. This, of course, only begins the vast task of constructing a scientifically informed ethics – a task well beyond the scope of this chapter, but essential for ena-bling a human presence on a flourishing Earth.

Accordingly, in this brief chapter my aim is fourfold. First, it is to show how the journey of ecological economics remains unfinished; second, to suggest some of the characteristics of an embedded ethics; and third, to describe some of the effects of this repositioning on the ways we discuss what is at stake. Lastly, I briefly discuss the idea of an ecological political economy as an essential element in completing the journey.

15.2   THE UNFINISHED JOURNEY FROM ONE WORLDVIEW TO ANOTHER

For the last 150 years Western culture has been in the throes of a great dispute about the nature of the world and our place in it. On the one hand, there is the Thomistic-Enlightenment Synthesis (TES), which includes

Deism and Newtonian mechanics. On the other hand, there is the Scientific Evolutionary Paradigm (SEP) emphasizing thermodynamics, evolution and emergence; beginning in the early part of the nineteenth century with the fields of geology and thermodynamics. Darwin's *On the Origin of Species* published in 1859 (Darwin, 1859) is, of course, a center-piece of this worldview.

15.2.1   A God and Human-centered Worldview

The TES synthesis was masterfully constructed in the thirteenth century of Thomas Aquinas out of the Old and New Testaments, and the works of Aristotle rediscovered in the West after being kept and studied by Muslim scholars. Essential elements of this amalgamated paradigm are at least three fold. First, there is the idea of Creator God who gives form to an initial chaos and who subsequently stands largely apart from it, but at the same time is nevertheless able to intervene in history, at least in most versions of this worldview. God is thus both immanent and transcend-ent. Second, another crucial element is the idea of human superiority – humanity is seen as created in the image of God and standing above and apart from nature. In the Old Testament narrative nature itself is degraded from its perfect state due to the fall of man. Third, there are thus funda-mental dualisms built into this narrative from the beginning: God apart from both humanity and nature; and mankind apart from the rest of nature. These separations are less prominent in certain strands of Judeo-Christian theology than others. Aquinas also harvests a dualistic feature from Aristotle who emphasized that man was the uniquely rational animal.

The scientific revolution undertaken by Copernicus (1473–1543), Galileo (1564–1642), Kepler (1571–1630) and Newton (1642–1727) kept much of the basic underlying structures of this paradigm, but undertook to explain the world in material terms with God relegated to the role of initiator of the process. In this conception God is often referred to as a clock-maker – who starts the universe on its way, but does not inter-vene thereafter, and could not, given the lawful nature of the universe described by scientists like Isaac Newton. In this era, a major purpose of scientific discovery was understood to be the power over and control of nature; as contrasted to Aristotle's goal of understanding. And a core method of science within this understanding is analytical: the aim is to conceptually, and where possible literally, break things down into parts to better understand them. Its epistemological atomism thus precedes scien-tific atomism of the nineteenth century. It is within this conceptual womb that contemporary economics was nurtured and given birth in the work of Adam Smith, particularly in *The Wealth of Nations* published in 1776

(Smith, 1776). Smith took over the Deist assumptions of the paradigm and argued that economics was the study of the lawful behavior pre-ordained by the clockwork God. To attempt to interfere with the natural operations of the market was to interfere with God's plan – and hence could not avoid making things worse.

Now what is truly astonishing in the whole matter is that neoclassical economics of the twentieth and twenty-first centuries has not rejected or even examined its eighteenth-century assumptions. As Robert Nadeau has pointed out, 'the creators of neo-classical economics disguised the scientific and metaphysical foundations of Smith's natural laws of economics under a guise of mathematical formalism borrowed wholesale from the equations of a badly conceived and soon to be outmoded mid-nineteenth century physical theory' (Nadeau, 2006, p.100). The scientific study of evolution, quantum physics, complexity theory, ecology and its relation to far from equilibrium thermodynamics were and are simply ignored, or given marginal attention at the very best. Economists have forgotten their roots and ignored or misunderstood scientific developments of the nineteenth and twentieth centuries and so have not questioned this dimension of their basic theories.

15.2.2   An Evolution-centered Worldview

While it grew out of the TES the evolutionary paradigm (SEP) takes strong exception to two of its dimensions: (1) the view that the world was created at a particular time in a final form and (2) the dualisms that set humanity (and God) apart from nature. With regard to the first, the current consensus within this view is that the current universe began some 13.8 billion years ago in what is called the 'big bang.' (What, if anything, existed before then is unknown.) Since the beginning of the current universe there has been a long process of evolution characterized by emergent entities and processes (Chaisson, 2006). An emergent entity or system has characteristics where the whole has properties beyond those of the parts that make it up. A molecule of water has physical and chemical properties that the hydrogen or oxygen atoms that make it up do not possess, nor even suggest might occur. Living beings like butterflies have properties that neither the atoms nor the molecules that make them up have. The upshot is that the whole may be surprisingly different than its parts suggest.

Second, the idea of emergence helps to explain the phenomena that the idea of dualism tries to characterize. At the same time it helps to reframe the issue in more informative terms. Butterflies are different than the molecules that make them up – but they are not completely different. Humans have a much more complex form of consciousness than butterflies – so we are different, but not wholly different. Human consciousness is not a special creation of the universe, but rather, though emergent from it, nevertheless embedded in it. Our evolutionary heritage is inscribed in our flesh, bone, brain and mind. We are not only in the world, but of the world (Lakoff and Johnson, 1999).

In the first half of the twentieth century it was unclear how the fundamental theory of biology – evolution – was compatible with the second law of thermodynamics – a fundamental descriptor of the universe. This law holds that all things tend toward simplicity, chaos or lack of complex structure; while the theory of evolution is an account of life's growing diversification and complexity. At least two ideas from thermodynamics are essential to reconciling these two apparently diverse perspectives. The first is to distinguish between isolated, closed and open energy systems. Isolated systems exchange neither energy nor matter, closed systems receive energy but not matter, and open systems receive both. The universe is isolated, and as a whole is characterized by increases in entropy overall.

But within the universe there are systems closed to matter, but which receive energy from the outside. The Earth is one of these. Living things, like human beings and snakes, are open to both matter and energy since they, to use Schrodinger's famous phrase, 'suck orderliness' from their surroundings. People take in new energy and matter in the form of things such as sandwiches and milkshakes. They allow us to maintain our bodies in what is called 'a far from equilibrium condition' characterized by body temperatures of around 37 degrees centigrade, which is generally higher than the background temperature of the ambient environment. The idea of using external energy to create complexity explains macroscopically how far from equilibrium conditions can be maintained. But how are sandwiches and milkshakes possible? In answering this question the role of plants is crucial.

Photosynthesizing organisms, for instance, green plants, take in certain highly selected wavelengths of light. Plants use light in several ways. Some of the light is absorbed into the plant and surrounding air and degrades to heat. The heat evaporates water from the leaves and helps to draw more water up from the ground through the roots and stems of the tree to the leaves. However, certain wavelengths of light are used by the photosynthetic apparatus in the leaves of the plant, to break one oxygen atom from water so that the remainder can interact with carbon dioxide from the atmosphere. Through a process that is complex in itself, the water and carbon dioxide combine to form simple sugars retained by the plant, and oxygen is released into the atmosphere. While the energy stored in the new sugar molecule is less than the photic and heat energy that went into its making, the sugar molecule can be utilized and stored in many ways, and forms the basic energy source for much of the rest of metabolism on Earth. Some forms of the stored energy are so stable that they can become fossilized and stored below ground as coal, oil and natural gas, for millions of years. By using this transient light energy a more stable energy is created that can easily be said to retard the sometimes slow, sometimes fast, process of increasing disorder. The whole of biology depends on slowing the tumble toward disorder. The energy stored is always less than the energy input, but the transformation has permitted the abundant flourishing of life on Earth and the development of all its marvelous complexity at scales from sub-cellular organelles to the functioning of the ecosphere. The slowing of disorder through the capture of energy by the process of photosynthesis and its subsequent storage and utilization by complex life systems is one part of the very definition of life.[4]

But how are far from equilibrium conditions possible to begin with? Why isn't everything like everything else? Why do complex systems like you and me exist? The universe is characterized by profound differences in temperature – and in accordance with the second law of thermodynamics it is 'trying' to reach thermal equilibrium. It seeks ways to be as cool as it can be (Schneider and Sagan, 2005). To do this it needs mechanisms to reduce temperature gradients – to get rid of heat. Here the idea of 'dissipative structures' plays a key role, an idea coined by Prigogine (Schneider and Sagan, 2005, p. 81). When we boil water on a stove, as the water reaches the boiling point little bubbles form. As it passes the boiling point, these bubbles become larger as it reaches what we call a rolling boil. These bubbles are dissipative structures – ways to get cool. Macro equalizing processes on Earth are wind and ocean currents – attempts to cool, respectively. the air and ocean water, which are hotter at the equator than at the poles because of the angle at which the sun's rays strike the Earth. Another earthly heat dissipater is life itself. Life on Earth, including plant life, takes in high grade energy from photosynthesis and degrades it, resulting in a net cooling. Complex ecosystems are efficient heat dissipaters, which, if left unperturbed, do the 'best they can under the circumstances' to degrade the exogenous radiant energy they receive from the sun (Schneider and Kay, 1995). Both cosmic and biological evolution are macro dissipative processes. However, complex ecosystems retard the dissipation of some energy by storing it in complex carbon compounds for longer or shorter durations, though overall they accelerate energy dissipation.

As noted above, mainstream economics remains isolated not only from the implications of thermodynamics, but also from the idea of evolution, complex systems theory and the science of ecology to name just a few. It is a conceptual framework with no systematic integration of biological and physical processes that govern the planet and is thus at odds with the science of the last 200 plus years. With the vast expansion of the human population and even far vaster expansion of economic output, the world's macroeconomic system endeavors to rule the world without even trying to understand it. The sciences may offer interesting analogies or metaphors for thinking about economic processes, but this is not the point I am making here. I am arguing that the economic system and finance must be understood as a fully integrated part of the Earth's biophysical systems. Until we ground macroeconomics and finance in science and an Earth-respecting ethics we can only expect increasing carnage and mayhem.

15.2.3 The Location of Our Knowledge Systems

One way to characterize what we think we know about the world is to look at how universities have organized it. This is typically done in departments and faculties – a way of dividing up our understanding of the world that will likely prove to be a major factor in our undoing. Imagine that we took a pair of scissors and cut out the names of these units, magnetized them and put them in a jar. Then we placed two relatively powerful magnets on a table – one standing for the TES paradigm, the other for SEP. If we then shake all the magnetized slips of paper out of the jar many of the bits will be drawn to the SEP – generally the sciences with other fields such as psychology falling – at least provisionally – somewhere in the middle, though edging toward SEP as it becomes more and more informed and shaped by neuroscience. But some of the slips will head straight for, and be stuck hard to, or remain in the field of, the TES magnet. These are the bits with the names neoclassical economics, finance, ethics, much of philosophy and theology, law and politics on them to name just a few.

Looked at in this way, ecological economics is an attempt to get from one paradigm to the other – to escape from the magnetic field of TES and fall into the field of the SEP. This is the main feature of the paradigm shift from a vision of the economy in standard economics textbooks as a closed, circular flow to one that is embedded in the Earth's biophysical systems, and accordingly subject to the laws of and the limitations imposed by thermodynamics and other laws as played out on this lively planet. This is a beginning of the crucial journey, but it is not its end. Ecological economics is suspended in between – pulled toward SEP by its embrace of thermodynamics and the idea of an economics embedded in the Earth, and pulled toward TES by an ethics (and theology, politics and often philosophy) that belongs to the TES.

15.3   THE ETHICS OF ECOLOGICAL ECONOMICS

In this section I will (1) show that the current ethics used by most eco-logical economists is firmly rooted in the TES paradigm that they seek to escape; (2) discuss a different point of departure found in the work of Aldo Leopold; and (3) illustrate some of the implications of an embedded ethics for how we think about the human place in Earth's systems and in the universe.

15.3.1   The Tar Baby Problem

Ecological economics is bonded to what it is trying to escape from. In *Ecological Economics: Principles and Applications* Herman Daly and Josh Farley state: 'Although we shrink from trying to define the ultimate end, . . . we suggest a working definition of the penultimate end for the ecological economy: the maintenance of ecological life support systems far from the edge of collapse . . . and healthy, satisfied human populations free to work together in the pursuit and clarification of a still vague ultimate end – for a long, long time' (Daly and Farley, 2003, p. 57). The principle of penultimate value continues to be use of the world in support of (sustain-able) consumption, and key terms like 'natural capital' and 'ecosystem services' reveal that many of its premises are still derived from the TES framework. This language signals that ecological economics remains com-mitted to dualism, anthropocentrism and a kind of materialism that views the world as a collection of objects to be used for human satisfaction.

Yet, the dualism is eroding. Josh Farley points out that 'one could hold that humans are one of many species, with no special rights to the low entropy generated by ecosystems. This view explicitly recognizes that humans are a part of nature, and as natural systems unravel, human sur-vival is compromised. It can easily acknowledge that we do not understand ecosystems adequately to state authoritatively that any individual element is expendable, and therefore even for anthropocentric reasons must act as if life were sacred.'[5] From this point of view, 'ecosystem services' is simply a name we use to point out our interdependence; but it still hovers close to the idea that the world is property. To Farley, the phrase 'ecosys-tem services' refers to specific physical characteristics rather than values. Ecosystem services are fund-fluxes in nature. On this view the ecosystem fund is not transformed into what it produces, services are produced at a fixed rate over time, cannot be stockpiled and so on. Some fund ser-vices can be non-rival, in which case their value in terms of human use is maximized at a price of zero. They fall completely outside the transaction dimension of the market model, though it is still important to allocate resources toward their conservation and restoration. This is in distinct contrast to ecosystem goods, which are stock-flow (funds) in nature and always rival. The idea of ecosystem services is discussed in Daly and Farley (2003, pp. 103–10). But fortunately they do not take the next step of trying to assign prices to these 'services.' Nevertheless, their vocabulary on this topic is largely within the neoclassical framework.

In terms of completing its journey from one worldview to another a highly regrettable development has been the current frenzy to assign dollar values to these 'ecosystem services,' a term and way of thinking made popular and legitimated by Costanza et al. (1997).[6] The point of view enshrined in this article still lives in the disenchanted world of the Enlightenment that sees humans as distanced from the world, or better within a fantastical enchantment with the alleged vast power of humans to subordinate the world for our benefit. This is a step back toward environmental economics – a branch of neoclassical economics that tries to analyze the economy–nature relationship primarily through the ideas of 'externalities' and 'public goods.' Tragically, this framework also underpinned much of the work of the Millennium Ecosystem Assessment – an empirical tour de force in terms of understanding the current and evolving, and deteriorating, state of the Earth's life-support systems. But it is also a metaphysical and theological disaster in terms of relying, without apparent recognition, on the premises of the TES worldview. (And these questionable but unstated assumptions are independent of the methodological conundrums that often plague these estimates such as 'willingness to pay,' 'existence value,' or to the fact that market valuation's 'one dollar, one vote' assigns much more weight to the values of the rich than to anyone else.) Ironically, some of the world's best ecologists embraced a way of thinking that imperils the very thing to which they have devoted their life studies, and about which many, if not most of them, care about deeply. By embracing 'ecosystem services' many ecological economists cannot get free of the tar baby concepts from the mainstream.

There are reasons why this way of practicing ecological economics puts the world ecological systems at grave and irreversible risk. For this reason they could undercut Daly and Farley's goal of maintaining ecological life-support systems. The root problem is that, as in a French restaurant, we may want nature services à la carte – perhaps we don't want the whole meal. Rather than order the whole menu – table d'hôte – let's just have the soup and desert. Here are four ways our 'ordering' could help dismember natural structures. First, the value of services will depend in large part on the price assigned to it by the market. So we value bees for their pollination services of a coffee plantation and we value the copse where the bees have their hives for giving the bees a place to live. But when world coffee prices plummet and the coffee trees are cut down, then the 'services' of the copses lose their value.

Second, technical innovation may render nature's services less valuable or even irrelevant. It may be 'cheaper' in dollar terms to build a water filtration plant, thus replacing the 'services' of a forest that is protecting a reservoir than to forego the profits from clearing the forest for timber and replacing it with houses and shopping malls. Third, we can improve on what nature has to offer. For example, in the rush for biofuels we plant fast-growth eucalyptus trees by cutting down the 'inefficient' old growth forest that is in the way. Or, as done in Lake Victoria, we improve nature by introducing the commercially more attractive Nile perch that extirpated a vast number of smaller native fish species. Fourth, nature not only offers gifts, she is also full of menaces – poisonous snakes, deadly viruses like AIDS, trees with rotten tops that kill us when we try to cut them – what foresters call 'widow makers.' The ecosystem services approach suggests that in adding up nature's services we should subtract all the bad things and see where the net value is. And once we have determined what and where bad things are, we get rid of them – if there is a net benefit to some humans, to do so (McCauley, 2006). We may value what a forest does in terms of water filtration and erosion control, but feel menaced by the fact that the woods are also homes to coyotes who control the deer population but also feed on small household pets. And it is this control that keeps the woods diverse and adaptive to begin with since too many deer often retard regrowth and diversity.

In summary, the idea of 'ecosystem services' flies in the face of what is perhaps the core insight of ecology – that everything is connected. The world is not severable into parts in the way this idea suggests. Put another way, ecosystem services in the neoclassical framework are not valued for the myriad, interconnected interactions that the ecosystem provides for itself so it remains in – or striving toward – a stable state far away from equilibrium. Nature – left to her own devices – is already thermodynamically efficient. Yet, in the name of economic efficiency we dismember nature's older and wiser efficiency without having any agreed on standard to judge what we should and should not do. The reason that ecological economics will fail if it does not complete its journey is that it is an economics of humans and not of the human-planet interdependent interface. The best thing that can be said about the idea of ecosystem services is that it is an interim step on the journey toward recognizing the depth of human/ nature interdependence. But it is a very dangerous move for it extends the reach of what it is trying to escape.

15.3.2   Finding a Footing

Why has ecological economics failed to develop an ethics consistent with its own best intentions? Part of the answer is to be found in the disciplinary background of the people who have been its pioneers. They come from the biological and physical sciences or from economics itself. In addition, there have not been many attempts to build a bridge between the relatively new field of environmental ethics and ecological economics.

But there is also great public and professional resistance to the necessary rethinking. A fundamental issue of our era is the relationship between ethics and evolution. Yet, it is one that is seldom addressed head on[7] and is often thought to be too incendiary to tackle. It is hard to know where we should be going without recognizing where we have come from. Along with Albert Schweitzer, who wrote on ethics in the second, third and fourth decades of the twentieth century, Aldo Leopold was one of the leading figures in the first half of the twentieth century to try to systematically address this question (Leopold, 1949).[8] Both rejected the mainstream utilitarian and Kantian traditions of their upbringing; Leopold setting aside Gifford Pinchot's human-centered utilitarianism; and Schweitzer the German traditions that tried to rest ethics on the idea of the rational person (Schweitzer, 1949). Since they wrote, much happened, particularly regarding Leopold's beliefs, to ratify and extend his thinking.

I propose using Leopold as the principal reference point for an adequate environmental ethic. For many years he was an employee of the US Forest Service, and was the founder of the field of wildlife management – a way of managing 'wild' populations principally for human benefit, such as hunting. Toward the end of his career he was a professor at the University of Wisconsin. While there, he bought and began the restoration of, a run-down farm. It was that farm that inspired what is most likely the most influential work in the English language concerning the human relationship to the rest of nature in the twentieth century: *A Sand County Almanac*, published shortly after Leopold's death in 1948 (Leopold, 1949). In that work he wrote:

> Conservation is getting nowhere because it is incompatible with our Abrahamic concept of the land. We abuse land because we regard it as a commodity belonging to us. When we see land as a community to which we belong, we may begin to use it with love and respect. There is no other way for land to survive the impact of mechanized man, nor for us to reap from it the esthetic harvest it is capable, under science, of contributing to culture . . . That land is a community is the basic concept of ecology, but that land is to be loved and respected is an extension of ethics. That land yields a cultural harvest is a fact long known, but latterly often forgotten. These essays attempt to weld these three concepts. (Leopold, 1949, pp. viii–ix)

For Leopold the fundamental principle of ethics is summarized as follows: 'A thing is right when it tends to preserve the integrity, stability, and beauty of the biotic community. It is wrong when it tends otherwise'

(Leopold, 1949, p. 224). In reading the often lyrical account of Leopold's time on his farm one senses his deep respect for 'the land,' and that he laments in a most profound sense that he lives in a society that has lost touch with the fundamental reciprocity that must govern the human-Earth relationship.

Leopold's work helps illuminate an age-old question: how do we go about justifying one ethic while rejecting another? What processes of reflection will allow us to assent to one view, and will fail to affirm another? A way to begin answering this question is: we should accept those ethical views that most accord with our other considered and well-grounded beliefs. This can be broken down into four parts following Daniels (1979): (1) what is the ethical principle or disposition in question? (2) how does it accord with other concepts such as our theoretical views about the nature of the universe, persons, society, evolution, God, the state, the family and the like? (3) how does it accord with our moral intuitions about fairness, duty, liberty and so on? and (4) are all these ideas taken together feasible? Can we do what they suggest? Taken together, these four steps should be used reflexively – so that our beliefs reach an equilibrium where all elements are in accord. In this way it incorporates and adjusts our intuitions, but does not assign them more weight than the other elements. This is how it escapes the trap of intuitionism where each person simply insists that his or hers are authoritative.

In a mature, or rather maturing person, this is not a one-time event, but rather an open-ended process of adjustment, insight and self-expansion. The connection between ethics and science is both integral and extensive, particularly in reference to numbers 2 and 4. In a healthy, adaptive society, this discourse is also a public process by which society reflects on its own values. In this process, science can and should play a key role, for it influences our views about matters such as the nature of the universe, the divine, the characteristics of the person, the earth. It also helps us understand what can and cannot be done; what resources there are and how long they are likely to last, what medical interventions are likely to work, how to design an airplane and ways to run our farms and economies.

Understanding how our beliefs can be justified also helps us understand how they are undermined and sometimes collapse. The unraveling of the TES narrative has been a lengthy process stretching over centuries. In the nineteenth and twentieth centuries we have seen the reconstruction of another, especially since the 1940s. It is changing the story from created to creative – the thermodynamic account of how creation happens. It undermines the idea of human dominion, and the two dualisms that separate the self from 'the environment' and the sacred from nature. For ecological economics to be part of the worldview toward which it wishes to travel, a standard of respect for nature must inform both its theories and practices.

Since Leopold wrote, many scientific developments have helped put his scientific and ethical insights into larger contexts by connecting them to chemistry and physics; thus providing them with important, but not conclusive, support. Of course, science is not the sole determinant of our ethical beliefs, but it is not irrelevant either. The significance of the developments in physics, chemistry, and molecular and evolutionary biology since the 1940s, when Leopold wrote, is that they 'fill in' much of the background needed to support, understand and operationalize Leopold's 'land ethic.' A wonderful, and to me beautiful, coherence appears on the horizon, in which our moral, scientific, political and theological views, like a geodesic (Buckminster) Fuller dome, support and strengthen each other. The ethical and policy implications of these discoveries are fundamental but nearly wholly unexplored. Therefore, we must begin afresh. A few ideas follow.

15.3.3 Toward a Value System for Ecological Economics

A new beginning will be based on understanding what we can about the origins and evolution of the cosmos, the place of the Earth in this epic, life's emergence on Earth, the biophysical functioning of the planet, and human origins, capacities and institutions. Any contemporary ethic would be incomplete without including an ethic of atonement and reconciliation for the enthusiastic carnage our 'civilization' has wrought on the natural world. Ideas of penance and the like, of course, have deep roots in the Judeo-Christian and many other religious traditions and fit well into a Leopoldian framework.

Ironically, ecological economics itself calls attention to a place to begin reconstructing our understanding of ourselves and our place in the world, though for reasons we have discussed it makes little or no use of this perspective in rethinking its value premises or many of its key ideas. The basic insight that for all practical purposes Earth is a system of systems closed to matter and open to energy has profound implications for ethics (Daly, 1996, pp. 27–30). As a way to begin, let's look at the implications of these two points – closed to matter and open to energy – in turn from the perspective of Leopold's ethic.

15.3.4 What Goes Around Stays Around

15.3.4.1 Closed to matter
Judged by mass and frequency hardly anything arrives here – small amounts of cosmic dust and an occasional meteor, and very little ever leaves – a rocket now and again. According to the first law of thermodynamics – the

conservation of energy and matter – this means that whatever is done here stays here in one form or another. There is no such thing as production as orthodox economics would have us understand this idea, only transformation (Faber et al., 1996, p. 218). If we had an economics connected to the idea of the planet closed to matter, climate change would not be seen as an inconvenient truth (Gore, 2006), but as a necessary and fully foreseeable consequence of a carbon-based economy. Destabilized climate is just one example of our failure to integrate economics with how the Earth works. The vast dead zones in coastal waters, fish loaded with mercury, flame retardants in the flesh of living beings, PCBs (polychlorinated biphenyls) in the breast milk of women living in the Arctic are the predictable consequences of the systems *we* have designed and promulgated globally as the 'best' way to live.

We must recognize at least three sources of these dangers to understand what we are doing. One is the societal concentration in the ecosphere of elements found in the lithosphere typically in very dilute concentrations – such as lead we use in our batteries. Another is the dispersion of such heavy metals and other toxic natural elements that persist in the ecosphere even after their primary use is terminated – such as lead in batteries; or from the release of elements as a side-effect – such as in the burning of coal containing mercury. Third, the processes of chemical engineering that lie at the foundations of industrial society also often constitute assaults on the Earth's living systems and the plants, and human and other animals that make them up. This results from introducing compounds to which life has little or no opportunity to adapt. These same three phenomena threaten human rights around the globe due to the toxic effects of these elements and compounds on human health (Pimentel et al., 2000).

From both a Leopoldian and human rights point of view we should favor those chemical and physical transformations that are respectful of ecosystems, and avoid those that impede their functioning and resilience. Building society around ideas like 'green chemistry' and certain understandings of industrial ecology are mandatory from the point of view of an ethics of respect and reciprocity. These ideas have to include, at a minimum, careful imagination of potential side-effects, exhaustive testing and observation over appropriately long terms, continued alertness to unexpected side-effects and a willingness to say 'no' to proposed chemicals. All approvals should be tentative, preserving the option to stop production, distribution and use should this be required. An adequate value system for ecological economics has to build in from respect for Earth's life support systems, not out from human desires and satisfactions. Ecological economics must seek to be embedded in a conceptual revolution that constructs an ecological political economy.

It is essential to distinguish between the 'operating ethics' of an economy – what actually motivates peoples' behavior – and the overall goals toward which the economy strives. For example, Keynesian economics is an attempt to design an economy that achieves social stability by dampening the business cycle, but relies on stimulating people's propensity to consume to reach this goal during economic downturns. Tragically, contemporary macroeconomics has partially lost sight of Keynes's counter-cyclical goals and now seeks growth in consumption all the time. An adequate ethic for ecological economics would build on Keynes's ideas by taking social and ecological stability, or better a resilience respectful of a flourishing Earth, as its goal and design its institutions accordingly.

Keynesian economics could not be thought through without ideas like the 'liquidity trap' and 'aggregate demand.' Similarly, ecological economics needs to build a vocabulary that begins where it does – with the fundamental processes that govern Earth's life-support systems. Ideas like 'public goods' and 'externalities' will likely be retained in such a system but they will not be the key conceptual points of intersection between the economy and Earth's systems. Rather, like a smaller 'Russian doll' in a set, they will be part of a nested system that begins with the characteristics of the Earth's ecosystems. A step toward designing such a system will require a rethinking of our vocabulary – a preliminary step in this direction is taken in Section 15.4 below. Once we have a new and more functional vocabulary we will need to design new institutions and policies, as Keynes did in the development of macroeconomics.

15.3.4.2 Open to energy

Open to energy is also critical in understanding and enhancing life's prospects. On Earth there is substantial negative entropy – the capacity to enhance complexity due to free energy from the sun. The sun also powers Earth's ability to process the waste generated by human activity and all other life forms. Put in its simplest form, almost all of Earth's complex life is made possible by the success of photosynthesis in temporarily slowing the conversion of light energy to heat. The current levels of the human population and consumption are simply taking the natural world apart faster, and increasingly far faster, than sunlight and photosynthesis can put it back together again. Humans now appropriate a substantial percentage of the Earth's life support budget (Haberl et al., 2008; Vitousek et al., 1986). From a Leopoldian perspective this trend is a, likely *the*, paramount injustice – the confiscation of more and more of the Earth's life-support budget. This is why we must reconceptualize what it means to budget, and bring the whole ecosphere and its flourishing into consideration.

Understanding, metering and carefully regulating (by reference to physical quantities, not prices alone – which are means to alter behavior) the Earth's 'complexity-support budget' (that is, photosynthesis and all that it supports) is more fundamental and vastly more intricate and meaningful than doing the same things for the money supply. The ecosphere budget is the fount of wealth on which all other wealth depends. An ethic that sees humans as members of the natural community rather than its masters is led in the direction of compassionate retreat from the global project of human domination of Earth (Brown and Schmidt, 2010, p. 278). As Thomas Berry has stated, 'our own special role, which we will hand on to our children, is that of managing the arduous transition from the terminal Cenozoic to the emerging Ecozoic, the period when humans will be present to the planet as participating members of the comprehensive Earth community' (Berry, 2000, pp. 7–8).

Any satisfactory value system for ecological economics will have to come to terms with issues of fairness in the use of Earth's life-support budget, and the fact that by any account the human population is already much too large. These equity issues pertain to shares among living persons, between generations of people and between people of all generations and other species. In the Western tradition, issues of fairness are thought of primarily, even exclusively, as matters between persons. Here again a reinvention of our vocabulary is essential to think through these issues. Current macroeconomics has a vocabulary for thinking about the money supply in support of growth, such as M1 and M2. Ecological economics urgently needs to develop a vocabulary that systematically connects economic management to a fair and flourishing Earth.

But we can go beyond these initial insights stimulated by understanding the Earth as both a closed and open system. Overall, there should be an isomorphism between ethics and a holistic science of nature. This is only the very simple point that responsible community membership requires knowing the characteristics of the community in which you are a member; for instance, being Amish requires knowing the rules and expectations of the community. We need an ethics that reflects the evolutionary paradigm with regard to the characteristics of the complex system in which we live. As Robert Costanza has noted, some of these characteristics include at a minimum: (a) path dependence; (b) recognition of multiple equilibria – there is no one best way; (c) optima are seldom achieved and are always unstable. Costanza argues that 'path dependence, multiple equilibria and sub-optimal efficiency [must] be the rule rather than the exception in economic and ecological systems' (Costanza et al., 1993, p. 550).

Here are some of the ways ethics and complex systems theory relate to each other. Path dependence suggests that any ethical framework will have to take into account how the present situation came to be; for example, history matters. What makes sense for the forest of the future is heavily influenced by the soil conditions laid down by the forest of the past. What we can and should do will be substantially influenced by antecedent conditions. Historical trajectories produce complex interdependent systems at scales from the sub-cellular to the ecosphere. The capitalist system that dominates in the Anglophile countries has rewarded and hence reinforced behaviors that have contributed to the rapid decline in life's prospects. Yet, this is a fact with which we must work at this point as we try to set a new, more responsible course. The idea of multiple equilibria suggests that there is no one best state of affairs toward which to aspire; but multiple ways of flourishing that are themselves path dependent. It is akin to the idea of tolerance in political liberalism, which suggests that there are multiple ways of understanding and living 'the good life.' But, also akin to political liberalism, there are boundary conditions such as an 'equal liberty for all' – as John Rawls put it (Rawls, 1999). We should seek individual and ecosystem flourishing that supports and enhances the flourishing of others. The erosion from a clear cut on my property can impede the flourishing of my neighbor's woodlot. But this is an inter-human example; we must now purposefully extend the principle of care for the flourishing of others to all of nature with all its interdependent participants, including humans. The concept of rare and fragile optima should help us understand that any optimization project, such as gross national product (GNP) maximization, will bring ruin in a world of complex interdependent systems. Lastly, lock-in should help us recognize that the road not taken is often the road that cannot be retaken. If we take a wrong turn in traffic we can usually retrace our steps and come out where we intended. But this is typically not the case in complex biophysical systems. Once the top predator from an ecosystem is eliminated, the system will head off in a new direction even if that predator is restored. The massive soil erosion following tropical storms in the Philippines strips the land of its fertility, and the resulting silt destroys the inshore fishery in ways that are not restorable in historic time.

15.4   RETHINKING HOW WE THINK

If ecological economics is to complete or at least approach the shore toward which it so boldly set sail in the second half of the twentieth century it will require new terms of discourse that reconsider and reposition ideas like 'ecosystem services' and 'natural capital.' In an embedded ethic, some common economic terms take on new meaning that reflects how the economy relates to the biosphere. This is what I call a 'whole earth economy' (Brown and Garver, 2009). Here are some of the core ideas.

15.4.1 Wealth

Wealth, which we now tend to think of in terms of money and what it can buy, takes on a fundamental new sense. Wealth in a whole earth economy is not monetary wealth. Low entropy stocks are wealth; and flows are income. Photosynthesis is a flow while biomass and stored carbon are stocks created from that flow. Fundamentally, fairness is the share of photosynthesis rightly available to each species (or individual), a share of the Earth's life and what supports it and keeps it going. Thus, for humans as community members in Leopold's sense, wealth can only be conceived and held as a trust.

15.4.2 Budgets

Normally, a budget refers to a flow of money – it is a record and often a projection of income and expenses. In a whole earth economy, the primary income is sunlight. Spending is a matter of using up life and other matter and energy. It's important to remember that the Earth's capacity to support life, in part made possible by life itself, is limited but not fixed. We need to develop indicators for measuring the health of the Earth and its living systems. Photosynthesis is the primary agent of transformation in support of life, and the primary limiting factors on it are: (1) the ability to capture sunlight that is used to create the food that plants and animals (for example, humans) consume, and to absorb or process the wastes we throw back into the environment and (2) toxins, which, if allowed to build up in the ecosystem, will affect the ability of plants to survive and perform photosynthesis; and/or the destruction of the land that allows plants and animals to live. Over the course of life's earthly evolution, some 3.8 billion years, the budget of complexity-creating capacity has, for the most part, been in surplus. That means that life has been able to create more apples, more wildebeests or more sardines than are needed for a species to survive; the surplus is available for feeding other life forms and for evolutionary change. There are substantial deficits from time to time, however, such as the mass extinctions we humans are now causing.

15.4.3 Absolute Advantage

Absolute advantage in a whole earth economy is a country's or region's ability to transform and consume material and energy with the lowest draw on the Earth's capacity to create and maintain complexity (the complexity budget). That would mean that a country that produces goods to sell on the global market at the lowest cost to life's budgets, not the lowest cost in terms of money, would become the one with lowest absolute cost. Countries could pursue comparative advantage, producing for trade the goods with the lowest draw relative to other goods they produce. For example, Brazil might be able to produce both aluminum and timber with a lower draw on Earth's reproductive capacity than Canada, but if it can produce timber with a much lower draw and aluminum with only a slightly lower draw, then by trading timber for aluminum, the total draw could be reduced.

15.4.4   Cost

In a whole earth economy, the cost of something is how much of the integrity, resilience and beauty of Earth's life-support systems must be exchanged to get it. The idea of costs and prices reflects the full cost to life, as grossly measured by the use of Net Photosynthetic Productivity (NPP), or other such measures of Earth's life-support capacities. The gross measure must be further refined to reflect enormous geographic variation in NPP and the robustness or fragility of ecosystems in specific places.

15.4.5   The Relativity of 'Opportunity Cost'

From the neoclassical point of view if we do not cut a forest that we own there are opportunity costs in foregone income and consumption. But from the point of view of ecological citizenship this can be a benefit because the citizen looks at the effect on life's abundance. In complete contrast to the neoclassical viewpoint, to cut the forest is to forego something, not to gain it. The meaning of opportunity cost is relative to the conception of the self who is making the choice. The self can be understood narrowly in terms of interests, or broadly in terms of identification with the widening community or ecosystem, up to and including the commonwealth of all life. And the universe itself.

15.4.6   (Re)Distribution

Claims on shares of Earth's budget(s) in a whole earth economy are not limited to persons, but can be made by and on behalf of life generally. Distributive justice in terms of distributing stocks and flows (wealth and income) concerns shares of the capacity to build, sustain and enhance the entire commonwealth of life. Fair distribution in our time is often a question of limiting people's or species' ability to take for themselves more of Earth's complexity and assimilation capacity than they deserve.

15.4.7   Money

In a whole earth economy, money, and its many surrogates like credit, is a socially sanctioned right to intervene, now or in the future, in the Earth's life-support complexity budget – in essence, a license to exert an influence on the local or global ecology. It may count as a cost because it uses up complexity or produces wastes and toxins. It may count as investment by acting to maintain or build up the complexity producing capacity of the ecosystem. Inequalities in income and wealth give people different power over the Earth's complexity.

15.4.8   Production/Transformation

Production and transformation normally describe processes of manufacturing or growing something that is useful. In a whole earth economy, there is no actual production of matter, only transformation. All transformations are net entropic – which means that they convert useful energy to dissipated heat and increase the disorder, or loss of complexity. The concept of 'goods' is a partial illusion. All consumption causes a net increase in entropy and decrease in usefulness to humans, though some high entropy wastes may still be rich resources for other parts of the ecosystem.

15.4.9   Resources

What we know as natural resources all have a role in natural systems that human use alters. For example, logging a tree removes habitat and changes ecosystem function; mining metals or tar sands uses up energy and contaminates the environment with substances previously held safely at some depth beneath the Earth's surface. Humanity is a product of evolution and cosmological processes but not their goal, and hence does not have any special privilege with respect to any aspect of the natural system, living or non-living. The Earth and all life on it should be looked at as the commonwealth of life – as the result of biological and cosmic evolution.

15.4.10   Waste

From the point of view of a whole earth economy, industrial processes have to be analyzed with a view to their effects on the whole commonwealth of life. Every time something is made there is a waste stream, and the energy used in the process always declines in its ability to do work. Thus, industrial processes and waste must be reconceptualized because there is no production as normally understood; only transformation. The key to applying this principle is to think of costs in terms of elimination of self-organizational capacity or the interference with recovery – as with toxins that impede life's resilience. The final waste is heat at too low an energy level to do any more work, to maintain self-organizational capacity.

15.5   SOME STEPS TOWARD AN ECOLOGICAL POLITICAL ECONOMY

To bring these ideas of an ethic for ecological economics and its terms of discourse into a broader context we must begin the construction of an ecological political economy. In my view there are six questions that are essential to answer in furthering the journey begun by Herman Daly and the other pioneers of the twentieth century. Beginning with a scientific understanding of the world we need to rethink:

1. Who we are.
2. What we know about what we know, and what we do not know.
3. What we should do.
4. What we should measure.
5. An economics for the Anthropocene; and a politics informed by an Earth systems point of view.
6. The place of religion and spirituality in light of our answers to these questions.

Though many will fear that the SEP is a threat to religion this need not be so. What this perspective tells us is that we are in the presence of, and also are a part of, a vast evolving, learning system (of which consciousness is one manifestation) that is far older and more powerful than we are. It has a scale, a beauty and a glory that cannot be fully grasped. Wisdom is to be found in respect and reverence for all that is. And achieving a state of self-transcendence, however temporary, allows us to return to a question nearly forgotten in our frantic and tragic age: what is civilization for? Here is my tentative answer: civilization is for the cultivation and elevation of the mind and spirit of the human animal who lives respectfully on the Earth with reverence for life and the sources of its being. 'Citizenship' should be understood as the dimension of human self-conception that takes the long view. Ecological citizenship is to recognize our role as co-celebrants in the evolution of life and the world in an entropic universe.

To me, this is the challenge and gift that my dear friend Herman has set before me and us.

NOTES

1. I have worked on the ethical dimension of such a shift in some of my earlier works (Brown, 2007; Brown and Garver, 2009), and I am indebted to my colleagues and co-authors for many of the ideas herein.
2. I am indebted to Brendan Mackey for reminding me of this point.
3. The *Brer Rabbit Story* is a tale of a rabbit who gets stuck to a scarecrow made of tar and covered with straw. When Brer Fox captures the trapped rabbit, the rabbit begs the fox not to throw him into the 'briar patch' where he would be safe. Finally, not understanding the ruse, the fox frees the rabbit by throwing him into the briars.
4. I am indebted to Paul Heltne for assistance in drafting this paragraph.
5. Personal correspondence.
6. A thorough discussion of the case for 'ecosystem services' is contained in Ruhl et al. (2007). It documents how, in the United States, law, policy and social norms all fail to protect natural systems. Regrettably, the overall framework of this book remains neoclassical.
7. Wilson (1975) is an exception to this, though it is unfortunately very reductionist.
8. Parts of my discussion of Leopold draw on Brown (2009).

REFERENCES

Berry, T. (2000), *The Great Work: Our Way into the Future*, New York: Three Rivers Press.

Brown, P.G. (2007), *The Commonwealth of Life: Economics for a Flourishing Earth*, London: Black Rose Books.

Brown, P.G. (2009), 'God shed his grace on thee', in S. Kellert and J.G. Speth (eds), *Toward a New Consciousness*, New Haven, CT: Yale School of Forestry and Environmental Studies, pp. 86–109.

Brown, P.G. and G. Garver (2009), *Right Relationship: Building a Whole Earth Economy*, San Francisco, CA: Berrett-Koelher.

Brown, P.G. and J.J. Schmidt (2010), 'An ethic of compassionate retreat', *Water Ethics: Foundational Readings for Students and Professionals*, Washington, DC: Island Press, pp. 265–83.

Chaisson, E. (2006), *Epic of Evolution: Seven Ages of the Cosmos*, New York: Columbia University Press.

Costanza, R., L. Wainger, C. Folke and K.-G. Mäler (1993), 'Modeling complex ecological economic systems', *BioScience*, **43**, 545–55.

Costanza, R., R. d'Arge, R. de Groot et al. (1997), 'The value of the world's ecosystem services and natural capital', *Nature*, **387**, 253–60.

Daly, H.E. (1996), *Beyond Growth*, Boston, MA: Beacon Press.

Daly, H.E. and J. Farley (2003), *Ecological Economics: Principles and Applications*, Washington, DC: Island Press.

Daniels, N. (1979), 'Wide reflective equilibrium and theory acceptance in ethics', *Journal of Philosophy*, **76** (5), 256–82.

Darwin, C. (1859), *On the Origin of Species by Means of Natural Selection*, London: John Murray.

Faber, M., M. Reiner and J. Proops (1996), *Ecological Economics: Concepts and Methods*, Cheltenham, UK and Brookfield, VT, USA: Edward Elgar Publishing.

Gore, A., Jr (2006), *An Inconvenient Truth: Planetary Emergency of Global Warming and What We Can Do About It*, New York: Rodale Books.

Haberl, H., K. Erb and F. Krausmann (2008), 'Global human appropriation of net primary production (HANPP)', in C.J. Cleveland (ed.), *Encyclopedia of Earth*, Washington, DC: Environmental Information Coalition, National Council for Science and the Environment, available at http://www.eoearth.org/view/article/51cbede37896bb431f694846/ (accessed 07 March 2016).

Lakoff, G. and M. Johnson (1999), *Philosophy in the Flesh: The Embodied Mind and its Challenge to Western Thought*, New York: Basic Books.

Leopold, A. (1949), *A Sand County Almanac*, New York: Oxford University Press.

McCauley, D.J. (2006), 'Selling out on nature', *Nature*, **443** (7107), 27–8.

Nadeau, R. (2006), *The Environmental Endgame: Mainstream Economics, Ecological Disaster, and Human Survival*, New Brunswick, NJ: Rutgers University Press.

Pimentel, D., L. Westra and R.F. Noss (2000), *Ecological Integrity: Integrating Environment, Conservation, and Health*, Washington, DC: Island Press.

Rawls, J. (1999), *A Theory of Justice*, Cambridge, MA: Harvard University Press.

Ruhl, J.B., S.E. Kraft and C.L. Lant (eds) (2007), *The Law and Policy of System Services*, Washington, DC: Island Press.

Schneider, E.D. and J.J. Kay (1995), 'Order from disorder: the thermodynamics of complex biology', in M.P. Murphy and L.A.J. O'Neill (eds), *What is Life? The Next Fifty Years: Speculations on the Future of Biology*, Cambridge: Cambridge University Press, pp. 161–74.

Schneider, E.D. and D. Sagan (2005), *Into the Cool: Energy Flow, Thermodynamics, and Life*, Chicago, IL: University of Chicago Press.

Schweitzer, A. (1949), *Philosophy of Civilization*, New York: MacMillan.

Smith, A. (1776), *An Inquiry into the Nature and Causes of the Wealth of Nations*, London: W. Strahan and T. Cadell.

Vitousek, P.M., P.R. Ehrlich, A.H. Ehrlich and P.A. Matson (1986), 'Human appropriation of the products of photosynthesis', *BioScience*, **36** (6), 368–73.

Wilson, E.O. (1975), *Sociobiology: The New Synthesis*, Cambridge, MA: Harvard University Press.

Index

green chemistry 336
green infrastructure *see* natural capital
Green Keynesianism 77, 283–4
Green New Deal 283
Green Parties 316
Green Revolution 221, 236
green tariffs 176–7, 180
    see also environmental standards
green taxes *see* eco-taxes
greenhouse gas emissions 7–8, 18, 29,
    34, 42, 60, 142, 146, 224, 269–73,
    291
    see also carbon dioxide emissions
Greenspan, Alan 286
gross domestic product (GDP) 12–13,
    18, 23–4, 26–7, 37–8, 42–3, 51,
    56–7, 79, 92, 120, 136, 144, 148,
    169–70, 172–5, 180, 185, 197–9,
    209–10, 218, 226, 241, 258, 260,
    262–76, 280, 282, 284–5, 290,
    292–3, 297, 299, 315
    see also economic growth
gross national product (GNP) 121,
    252, 258, 315, 339
group cohesiveness 115–17, 127
    see also cooperative behavior
group-think 150
Gull, F. 108–9
Gundimeda, Haripriya 292–3

Habert, Helmut 297
Hall, Charles 52
Hannon, Bruce 48, 52
happiness 10, 43, 56, 87, 92, 121, 151,
    153, 198, 284, 299, 317
    see also well-being
Happy Planet Index 198
Hardin, Garrett 214, 227
Harris, Jonathan 14–15, 79
Harrison, F. 228
Harrod, Roy 283
Hayek, Friedrich 186
Heal, Geoffrey 86
health 121, 211, 314, 336
health care 78, 121, 271, 273, 299
heat waves 71
hedonic adaptation hypothesis 92
hedonism 87, 93, 102
Heidegger, Martin 149, 159
Heineken Prize 58–9, 106

Heltne, Paul 344
Henderson, Hazel 112
Herendeen, Robert 48, 60
Hicks, John 26, 43, 106, 137, 184–6,
    188–9, 197–201
    later thoughts on income 193–4
    and the steady-state economy 190,
        194–6
    on valuation 196–7
    Value and Capital 189–94
    on welfare 197–8
    see also Hicksian income
Hicksian income 137, 184–5, 187–90,
    195, 198–9
    later thoughts on 193–4
    in *Value and Capital* 190–92
    from wasting assets 192–3
Hirsch, F. 92, 179
Hodgson, G.M. 94
Holland, A. 87–8
Holocene 4–5
homeostasis 124–5
Honduras 275, 294
Hornborg, A. 286
Hotelling, H. 71
Hubbert, M. King 251–2, 254
Hueting, Roefie 22, 31, 43, 52
human appropriation of net primary
    production (HANPP) 275, 295,
    298
Human Development Index 198, 275
Human Poverty Index 271–3
human rights 173, 336
Hume, David 87, 223
hunter-gatherers 27, 88, 92, 94, 297
hydroelectricity 293–4
hyperbolic discounting 123

illth 24, 38, 42
immigration 174–5
Import-Export (IMPEX) system 177
income 5, 7, 10, 16, 26, 28, 33–6, 42–3,
    79, 136, 138, 166, 169–71, 177,
    179, 197–8, 210–13, 215, 219, 226,
    228, 254, 273–4, 341
    wages
        definition of 185–8
        Hicksian income 137, 184–5,
            187–90, 192–5
        maximum 167, 179, 216